Melvin L. Greenhut,
Texas A & M University

This book not only provides an excellent survey of the literature in this field of study, but also makes significant theoretical contributions. In particular, the author adds the dimension of economic space to standard-classical assumptions in microeconomics in order to determine its impact on microeconomic theory.

Professor Greenhut proposes that when communication and transport costs over distances are notable, physical space becomes economic space. Economic space then is shown to imply the prevalence of oligopoly over the space; and oligopoly, in turn, is shown to imply behavioral uncertainty. A microeconomic theory predicated on the dimensions of *time and space* thus must resolve the twin dilemmas of including behavioral uncertainty as a basic component of the theory of the firm and deriving a determinate solution for a competitive (unorganized) oligopoly over the space. These problems are treated jointly in two steps.

First, the author formulates a theory of the spatial firm under competitive conditions which is the transform of the basic classical model of pure competition. Pursuant to this transform, he resolves the welfare questions of minimizing costs under budget constraints and maximizing consumer satisfactions notwithstanding the existence of negatively sloping average revenue curves.

Economic space connotes, however, a problem extra to classical welfare matters. As with classical theory, any variant of the classical formulation *in effect* would assume as a datum that the representative firm has discovered (and utilizes) the best long-run average cost curve. But when economic space is assumed, the question arises whether firms and cities are located properly. If they are not, the long-run average cost curves would not be the best possible in the economy. As part of the same problem, the most efficient sizes and shapes of market areas—under alternative cost and demand conditions— must be determined since, if the distances or shapes of the firms' (and the cities') trading areas are economically nonoptimal, the cost curve levels cannot be the best possible. An illusion of efficiency and maximizing of consumer satisfactions would then exist. Accordingly, a major portion of this book is concerned with the questions whether firms and cities are located properly in a free enterprise system, and whether their trading areas are of most efficient size and shape.

A THEORY OF THE FIRM
IN ECONOMIC SPACE

A THEORY OF THE FIRM IN ECONOMIC SPACE

Melvin L. Greenhut
TEXAS A & M UNIVERSITY

New York

APPLETON-CENTURY-CROFTS
EDUCATIONAL DIVISION
MEREDITH CORPORATION

PRINTED IN THE UNITED STATES OF AMERICA
390-38520-4

Preface

THIS BOOK IS AN EXTENSION OF THOUGHTS published previously by this author. At the same time, however, the present book actually goes far beyond any of my earlier writing(s) on the subject. Contained herein is not only the determinate equilibrium properties of a space economy, as viewed from the classical welfare standards, but also a formulation of the spatial "market area" equilibrium properties.

Readers will note that three chapters in the book deal with the intra-and inter-*urban* landscape to supplement the general evaluation of microeconomic relations over the entire (regional) landscape. They will further find herein a more precise formulation of the basic theory that this writer recorded in *Microeconomics and the Space Economy*. At least 75 percent of the contents of the present book is completely new. Nevertheless, I should like to make acknowledgements to publishers of earlier writings for permission to re-use some materials.

I acknowledge, accordingly, a debt of thanks to the editors and directors of the Scott, Foresman Co., publishers of *Microeconomics and the Space Economy*, for excerpts included. Also, the University of North Carolina Press has kindly permitted re-use of some materials originally contained in my book, *Plant Location in Theory and in Practice*. The editors of the *Southern Economic Journal*, the *Manchester School*, the *Review of Economics and Statistics*, *Kyklos*, and the *Journal of Regional Science* have also kindly permitted re-use of some selected materials. Specific acknowledgements to other publishers for permission to re-use materials of other economists are given in the text.

I would like to take this opportunity to thank my secretaries Mrs. Sandi Ledesma, Mrs. Ruth Williams, Miss Barbara Hejl, Mrs. Judy Mikel, and Mrs. Margaret Hase for their long hours of work on this book. Other secretaries have helped over the years in the preparation or typing of this manuscript and are hereby thanked collectively. Many students, in particular Helmut Merklein, Bill Newcomb, Gerald Sprott, Michael Proctor, Hiroshi Ohta, Dale Smith, John Greenhut, and Catherine Bowlus have provided thoughts, comments, critiques, and other forms of help which warrant acknowledgement. Here too, many others must be thanked collectively.

Recent colleagues, chiefly Eirik Furubotn, Al Chalk, John Allen, Steve Pejovich, and Charles Ferguson, have patiently reviewed materials and provided ideas which helped me greatly in the writing of this book. Other readers, such as Dave Maxwell and Frank Mossman, have labored over the manuscript and helped me so much that the word "thanks" strikes me as being a great understatement and I trust they will accept my use of this word in that spirit. They provided me with an average of 12 detailed pages of comments and suggestions.

I must acknowledge specifically my appreciation to Walter Isard, Trout Rader, and John Moroney for their comments, suggestions, and help with respect to specific subjects. And there are many others, such as Bill Ross, Dick Leftwich, and Ben Stevens, who have read prior materials, or closely related materials, to my great advantage. I can only hope that all the other friendly reviewers I have been fortunate enough to be able to call upon will accept a collective vote of thanks.

Finally, I would like to express my gratitude to a friend who provided me with many ideas on a particular subject in oral and note form for my use but whose humility led to a request for anonymity rather than the specific personal references I would have preferred to make in this book. To my wife and family go my final thanks for their love and understanding.

M.L.G.

Contents

PART II PRICES AND RESOURCE ALLOCATION

PART III SPATIAL DISTRIBUTION

PART IV GENERAL EQUILIBRIUM, WELFARE, AND SOCIAL POLICY

A THEORY OF THE FIRM
IN ECONOMIC SPACE

Part I

IMPACTS OF ECONOMIC SPACE
ON MICROECONOMIC THEORY

Introduction

THE PROPONENTS OF PURE COMPETITION THEORY use some concepts, such as utility; they accept certain laws, such as diminishing returns; and they develop these into demand and production functions which they treat as fundamental parts of their science. Next, they implicitly add to the framework some unrealistic assumptions, such as the location of buyers and sellers at a given point. They postulate products or services which are homogeneous (at least in the eyes of the buyer), perfectly flexible prices, and capital and labor resources which are fully mobile in the long run. Often they assume perfect knowledge. They conceive typical business units of atomistic size, and generously refer to the number of sellers as infinite. These assumptions are valid from the standpoint of positive economics, even though within a twentieth-century, free-enterprise economy many are rather tortuously removed from reality. Do they explain; do they furnish hypotheses which work; do they yield an advanced science of economics; in short, what do we gain from the theory they provide?

This book agrees with the widespread claim that pure competition theory offers vital descriptive and explanatory insights. It accepts the contention that for selected problems this framework of thought predicts reasonably well. It regards the theory as a basic part of positive economics, notwithstanding its use by many as a benchmark for describing systems that ought to be rather than what are. However, because the fundamental properties of the theory are quite unrealistic, we assert and shall seek to establish the existence of fundamental advantages in other systems of thought.

Take the concept of large firms or spatially separated firms. Assume next the creation of a well-developed framework of thought along these lines. What would be (or might be) its points of difference with pure competition?

For one thing, the model would contain primitive (undefined) concepts, such as possibly "the industry." The model would be likely to utilize and hence include a vast body of accepted doctrine, such as a production function based on diminishing returns, the law of demand, and the like. Also it would employ assumptions, some of which may be *more* realistic than those in pure competition theory. We might find that a distance between people and

3

institutions is permitted in the model. Moreover, advanced technology and comparatively small total demand may be postulated, with a less than infinite elasticity of demand prevailing for the product of a firm. These assumptions serve to distinguish our present-day set of differentiated and alternative products from the small group of standardized products that one might well have found a few decades ago. The aforementioned comparatively small demand might, in fact, be specified to reflect the poverty of a group of people (indeed, an underdeveloped nation could be our subject area of interest). Or the comparatively small demand might be said to reflect the spatial restrictions to markets that relate to the cost of shipment, the need for quick delivery (perishability), and the like. Manifestly, the theory derived from this set of assumptions might well differ from pure competition theory in many respects.

In this book we shall treat pure competition theory as a body of early thought which has helped to shed light on economic relations and readily serves as a departure point for other theories which better answer the problems of different periods in the history of man. Manifestly, as the chemist and physicist long ago realized, scientific advances require willingness to place the old theories in a proper perspective, to challenge them, and, in fact, to discard the simple and narrow answers wherever possible. The underlying purpose of this book is to move toward such a new theory in economics. We strive here to add the dimension of distances (i.e., economic space) between people and their institutions, and believe that we shall thereby achieve a more general microeconomics.

In moving toward our objective, the reader will find that the inclusion of economic space requires recognition and acceptance of uncertainty as a basic property of the system. We also will find that economic space, uncertainty, and oligopoly go hand-in-hand. We shall attempt to resolve the theoretical chaos expected of this kind of world so that deterministic solutions will be identified and proven. We aim to map the concepts and theory of pure competition onto what we shall call an unorganized oligopoly market. Alternative foci for use by theorists and empiricists will thus emerge to allow selection of the most usable and far reaching theory according to the different objectives of the researcher.

The theory of pure competition may shed more light on a given problem than our theory of unorganized oligopoly. But, most significantly, our system of oligopoly will be seen to be underscored by a body of rules and relations comparable to those intrinsic to pure competition. Thus, the efficiency and viability of free enterprise economy, viewed spatially through oligopoly theory or nonspatially through classical theory, will underscore our final conclusions. We suggest that the oligopoly theory of the firm in economic space, as discussed in this book, is the more general theory of the two; by stripping our theory of selected assumptions (e.g. economic space and uncertainty), and working backward the theory of pure competition reappears.

I. PLAN OF THE BOOK

We shall not, at this point, give a summary of methodology, plan of study, etc. Rather, we shall point out in various chapters the subjects to be considered in the immediately following chapters, as well as the conclusions to be derived at such points. The reader will be advised from time to time that he may omit several pages of reading in a particular chapter without losing his overall perspective. This recommendation to omit selected pages should be understood to apply chiefly to a first reading, and especially to readers who are not particularly interested in historical reviews of the literature or selected proofs which may be rather lengthy and detailed. Of course, only the reader can decide whether he wants initially to follow the shorter path through the book that will be charted for him at the appropriate places, or prefers the more complete probing into selected topics or models that a second reading, we believe, should include.

II. LOCATION ECONOMICS, REGIONAL SCIENCE, AND THE SPACE ECONOMY

It would be useful for us to note in this introductory chapter the relation between our theory of the firm in economic space and the well-established fields of location economics and regional science. In particular, which is the offshoot of which, and what is included in each?

Location economics has long formed what this writer would call a "tangential" part of microeconomics. From von Thünen on up to the near-present, this field of speculation has centered attention on the problems and forces governing the location of plants and industries. Most of the literature on the subject has centered its attention on the input side of the problem and in particular the principle of factor substitution. Some attempts have been made in recent years to determine the output relations of the firm in economic space, especially the type of market area over which it sells and the interdependence of firms over the landscape. Empirical extensions of economic location theory have, however, typically failed to follow the same "recent" route. The depth of the problem of measuring locational interdependence and distinguishing output from input substitutions had led most empiricists in the field to surveys following the lines of Alfred Weber's theory.

Regional science, in this writer's opinion, was originally an extension of location economics, and, as such, primarily conceived by Walter Isard. But it should be noted that according to Isard, all aspects of the economic landscape were to be studied, not just the location of firms. Regional science thereby included in its design a many-faceted analysis. Coefficients of localization and dispersion, *à la* P. Sargent Florence, became proper inclusions. Even money and income flows from region to region appeared relevant for study and analysis by regional scientists. In fact, the delineation of a region by factor analysis and other methods was soon brought into play. It was but a small analytical step to gravity and potential models which seek to explain the attractive force of one production center—in terms of goods and services sold—to people located a distance away, and in turn to the classical problem of trade between nations. In corresponding manner, regional scientists moved readily from mathematical programming and from the open input–output matrix to interregional programming and to interregional input–output dependencies. If separate designation of regional science is desirable at all from the standpoint of the economist, it might be based on the facts that regional scientists have in practice (a) stressed their methodology, and (b) sought to apply their models almost at the very moment of their formulation. That regional science is here to stay—as far as the economic geographer and the "planners" of the world, especially those living in eastern Europe are concerned—is readily indicated by the membership of the Regional Science Association and the contributions to its Journal. From our standpoint, we could classify regional science as a body of methods designed to explain the theoretical *short-run* structural relations between people and institutions distributed over a space, with emphasis given to altering existing relations so as to guide the region to a better path.

Our theory of the firm in economic space is derived from both location economics and regional science. It assumes from the former the problem of the size and shape of the market area of the firm, and the locational interdependence and spatial equilibria of firms. From the latter, it adopts the pragmatic question: Does the derived model shed light on microeconomic regional interdependencies and is it applicable in practice? Perhaps more than anything else, the conception of the space economy herein formulated is concerned with the problem: What happens to classical microeconomic theory when distances between firms and people are postulated? Do welfare criteria hold? Are the wants of consumers maximized in the free enterprise system distributed over an economic space? Are firms efficient from the standpoints of location and technology? And can the resulting theory be used by those who seek to apply microeconomic theory to nonspatial problems—such as the theory of consumer behavior—or to spatial problems—such as the identification, characterization, and forecasting of the position of an industrial complex as part of the regional economy? It is hoped that the present book will help bridge some of the gap that stands between the regional scientist and the theoretical economist, and in the process enable each to probe still deeper into his area of emphasis and specialization.

2

The Economic Man and Uncertainty

THE CONCEPT OF THE ECONOMIC MAN and his quest for maximum profits loses its traditional meaning when uncertainty is treated as a basic property of economic theory. We shall examine in detail in this chapter how the concept of economic man is modified by the assumption of uncertainty. In turn, the relation between uncertainty, oligopoly, and economic space will be considered in Chapter 3. Thus, we shall be able to demonstrate later why uncertainty is important to economic theory and how it is intrinsic to oligopolistic markets and to economic space. Moreover, we shall eventually examine other impacts of uncertainty on different aspects of economic theory, such as on final equilibrium conditions, on product and factor prices, and on social-economic policy. For the present, however, let us turn to the basic inquiry of this chapter, namely the impact of uncertainty on the concept of economic man and his quest for maximum profits.

I. UNCERTAINTY AND MAXIMUM PROFITS

Hurwicz, Luce-Raiffa, Savage, Wald, and others have recently pointed out the differences in decision-making under conditions of certainty, risk, and uncertainty. For a long time, writings on pure competition economics centered on conditions of certainty, though they were extended years ago to include the state of risk. But what about uncertainty? Better yet, what about that uncertainty which would account for long-run profits? Is maximum profit theory applicable to markets in which uncertainty and long-run profits exist? We shall contend that it is, first by accepting a simple transformation that combines risk and uncertainty, and then by formulating a general theory of maximum profits which, by its very nature, will cover the states of certainty, risk, and uncertainty.

Risk and Uncertainty: A Distinction Based on Probabilities

Our initial task, to distinguish risk from uncertainty, is the most elementary and hence the easiest to fulfill. We need only remember the well-established rule that risk differs from uncertainty because statistical probabilities are assignable to every possible return under risk but not to the alternative returns indicated by uncertainty. It follows in the literature that when uncertainty prevails, the decision-maker must select some criterion which, in effect, enables him to apply "his own" probabilities, distinct from the statistical probabilities applied to risk with which all observers will agree. The decision-maker under uncertainty is able to resolve his problem on the basis of some personally preferred criterion, such as regret, optimism, or rationality. Under the last criterion, for example, also called the Laplace criterion, each unknown (uncertainty) is considered equally likely to happen; accordingly, the probabilities are equal, and the value of the alternative strategies take the form of the sum of $1/n$ times each of the payoffs estimated for each strategy. It is significant that as soon as the criterion is selected, such as the equal probability solution, the payoff matrix will appear the same as that under risk. It follows further from the above that the general theory of maximum profit which we shall formulate is stated in terms of probabilities, and that it includes the statistical probability relevant to decision-making under risk as well as the nonobjective probability (which often appears in the form of some personal criterion) that is applied to resolve uncertainty.

Risk and Uncertainty: Other Preliminaries

Whenever there are only a few sellers in the market because either technology or economic space restricts their number, entrepreneurs tend to develop a belief that each seller is important. In turn, a "watchful waiting" business policy arises under which sellers conjecture about the policy and reactions of their rivals. It is small wonder that decision-making in this kind of market is complex. The prevalence of risk causes a range of probable profit or loss values to arise, while the element of uncertainty—attributable in part to stochastic events and in part to unpredictable business behavior patterns —yields alternative (i.e., two or more) *ranges* of profit or loss given a particular risk. Company officials are therefore faced with a double-edged problem: (1) determining the maximum value under existing conditions of risk; and (2) selecting the best set under existing uncertainties.

A Classical Risk Matrix

A very simple matrix will serve our introductory needs most effectively. Consider one location and one commodity, and assume only two alternative processes of manufacture, A and B. Production carries a well designated risk because the raw materials used tend to vary slightly in quality. Process A yields the highest profit if raw materials are subject to a 1 percent flaw factor, but if a 2 or 3 percent (the maximum possible) flaw factor holds, Process B is best. Table 2–1 records the assumed data. Which process should be selected?

TABLE 2–1: PROFIT RETURNS UNDER RISK

(In thousands of dollars)

	1% Flaw Factor	2% Flaw Factor	3% Flaw Factor
Process A	70	20	5
Process B	50	35	20

To help solve the problem, a set of probabilities is needed. For example, if the probabilities are 50 percent that the raw materials used will have a 1 percent flaw factor and 40 and 10 percent, respectively, for the 2 percent and 3 percent flaw factors, the values of the alternative strategies (Process A and Process B) will be:

$$\text{Strategy A} = 70 \ (1/2) + 20 \ (2/5) + 5 \ (1/10) = 43.5$$
$$\text{Strategy B} = 50 \ (1/2) + 35 \ (2/5) + 20 \ (1/10) = 41$$

Manifestly, Strategy A (i.e. Process A) offers the maximum mean value. If the probabilities of raw material flaws change to 30-50-20 percent, the alternative process (i.e., Process B) would offer the greater mean profits.

Means and Variances. The activity or risk in question may be of the type that when things go well, they go very well, but when things go badly, they are very bad. The quantitative reflection of this kind of risk ranges from very high positive values to very large negative values. The statistical mean may prove to be positive, but, in any case, the variance will be large if the probabilities assignable to the more extreme values are significant. Clearly, different activities may offer different risks so that we might assign to one activity a smaller set of numerical values (both positive and negative) and hence a smaller range of values compared to the other set; in effect, the smaller set could be wholly contained within the other—or, of course, there could be overlapping of extreme values.

The concept of maximum profit under risk does not point to the greatest possible return but rather to the most favorable expected return when evaluated with regard to the variance of returns around the mean. It is a *range of values* instead of a fixed value which distinguishes risk from certainty. Under risk, the possible losses from an activity are considered, and the foolish or pure "let us do it or die" policy is laid to rest as exceptional. But what about the near gamble, or to be even more specific, what about the all-inclusive set which has a large mean associated with a large variance in contrast with a smaller mean coterminous with a much smaller variance?[1] Which is the maximum?

[1] For another form in which this question appeared, see W. J. Baumol, "Discussion," *American Economic Review, Papers and Proceedings*, XLIII (1953), 415–416. And in this connection, note that the analysis system proposed here might treat smaller variance as increased utility and larger variance as reduced utility.

Economic Positions of Individuals Differ. An individual's position in life helps to explain what his maximum will be. Thus, the individual who has large reserves (either in the form of cash or in the guise of smaller responsibility) is likely to seek a greater mean, even if subject to a larger variance, than the person who has a small reserve. While it may be that some of the precision is lost when risk replaces certainty, the concept of maximum profit applies to either case and remains formally valid. No problems arise with the introduction of risk, because the economic man will seek to equate marginal revenue with marginal cost in order to realize his selected return.

Comparable results occur even though decision-makers differ in their desire to assure themselves of future returns (near or distant). The quest for some security in the future simply modifies the present outlook. And this is all it does! It limits and defines in its own way the maximum that each decision-maker seeks to attain just as differences exist among men in their mapping from dollar values to utilities. The selection process and the viability of the economy will be seen to remain otherwise unaffected.

To account for the distinction between dollars and utilities, recall our Table 2–1, and notice that when the individual's position in life (e.g., his financial resources, personality, etc.) causes him to select a given program, he may or may not be complying perfectly with the dollar mean value derived from the table. If he is not, it does not signify nonprofit-maximizing behavior; rather, it signifies only that "his utility for dollars cannot be measured by the dollar amounts."[1] In effect, he redesignates the dollar values shown in the matrix to account for, say, his inability to stay in business if he earns a low profit or suffers a large loss; or, the redesignation may reflect the extra utility he derives from an extremely large profit. This type of revaluing of dollars in deference to utilities is interwoven with the economic position of the decision-maker; it remains, accordingly, within our purview of the economic man and will be distinguished later on from noneconomic revaluations. Under an economic redesignation, if one is made, the adjusted mean value (which defers to the variance of returns) can be determined. The rational decision-maker will select the highest adjusted mean value to attain his ends.[2]

---

[1] D. W. Miller and M. K. Starr, *Executive Decisions and Operations Research* (Englewood Cliffs, N.J.: Prentice-Hall, Inc. 1960), p. 84.

[2] Actually two alternative solutions immediately come to mind for situations in which the utility for dollars is, in effect, not identical to the dollar amounts. One entails an arbitrary change in payoff values by the decision-maker in compliance with the utility he ascribes to the dollar amounts and, since it is rather simple in form, it is used in the text. The other, while more involved, comes closer to the underlying techniques used in decision-making theory and, accordingly, would be described in detail in studies specializing in this side of operations research. We shall set forth in this note a risk situation to illustrate the general form of this second technique, and indicate how it corresponds to the system used in the text. In the process, we will relate this example to uncertainty.

Consider the two payoffs in the matrix:

The Uncertainty Matrix

Uncertainty appears in the picture of Table 2–1 when we remember that the mean values for Process A and Process B hold only under a given situation, for example at a given location. If we consider the feasibility of alternative situations, such as alternative locations in different market areas, it is logical to assume that the forthcoming (or existing) competition may differ. It may be possible to predict the degree of competition in each market area on the basis of accepted probabilities. If this is so, the decision-making process would still be that of selecting an outcome under conditions of risk. But, as suggested by Table 2–2, a matrix may not involve objective probabilities, for in the market areas belonging to locations 1 and 2, there may be different firms, different historical backgrounds, different situations. We find only two mean or "likely" payoffs in Table 2–2, each being applicable to a given location under a specified price system; significantly, uncertainty prevails as there are no objective probabilities attributable to the alternative price systems of 2-2.

DECISION-MAKING UNDER RISK
Profit Returns (in thousands of dollars)

	40% *Probability*	60% *Probability*	*Mean Payoff*
Activity 1	80	40	56
Activity 2	120	20	60

All other things being equal, Activity 2 should be selected because it proffers the higher mean payoff. But suppose we ask the decision-maker what probabilities would make him indifferent to a lottery offering a 120 return *or* a 20 return compared to a guaranteed return of 56. If he considers the return of 20 so appallingly low that he insists on, say a 48–52 percent chance for the 120 return compared to the 20 return or, in fact, any probability ratio greater than 40/60 percent, he would have to select Activity 1. In contrast, if the subjective probabilities the decision-maker chooses are in smaller ratio than 40/60 percent, he would prefer Activity 2. If the subjective and objective ratios based on this mean of 56 are the same, the decision-maker would be indifferent to the alternative activities.

When the subjective probability ratio desired by a decision-maker exceeds the actual probability ratio, a redesignation of matrix values is required in order to make mean dollar values comply sufficiently with utility preferences. For advantages relating to applied research and internal consistency, the values selected for redesignation could readily be those which can be downgraded; that is to say, the figure 20 might, for example, be changed to 10, or, in another payoff matrix, a next to the highest value (e.g., 80) might be redesignated to 75. Such change recognizes that a decision-maker may attribute a comparatively greater utility to the highest return. By revaluing the return 20 to, say 10, the mean utility payoff under Activity 2 becomes 54 in the table above.

Any payoff revaluation which resolves a risk situation where the values of one set are contained within those of another is similar to the objective indeterminateness found under uncertainty. In states of uncertainty, the decision-maker cannot be sure of any mean payoff and may therefore select a position which assures him of only a minimum acceptable return which is higher than the lowest "likely" return proffered by another position. He may select this even though each of several higher alternative "likely" returns in the rejected position exceeds its counterpart in the chosen position. (We shall illustrate, and later define, "likely" returns in the text. Also, we shall later distinguish between what we will claim is the impersonal quality of revaluation of money values under risk and the personal nature of decision-making under uncertainty.)

TABLE 2–2: EXPECTED PROFIT RETURNS UNDER UNCERTAINTY FOR A FIRM

	Price Following With Price Set by A	Price Following With Price Set by B	Competition in Price
Location 1	60	45	25
Location 2	90	40	35

Profit maximization under uncertainty involves the subjective creation of probabilities. How individuals may assign their own probabilities to each case is actually of no vital concern to us. We must just remember that probabilities are applied on the basis of some criterion: optimism, regret, rationality, or others. For those who have not read the developing literature in operations research on decision-making under uncertainty, we shall illustrate the selection process by reference to possibly the simplest criterion of all, the so-called criterion of pessimism. This criterion holds that if the individual always expects the worst, he will look for and select the maximum of his minimum "likely" payoffs, i.e. *the maximin*. In Table 2–2, this would be Location 2, value 35.[1]

Regardless of the particular criterion used, the individual is actually engaged in a decision-making process which, in matrix *form*, ultimately becomes identical to that of decision-making under risk. Although the market type stressed in this book is blanketed by uncertainty, a full understanding of maximum profit under risk is basic to a theory of the firm in economic space and must be emphasized.

II. SPECIAL DETAILS OF THE THEORY

We have suggested that different enterprisers with different reserves will have different incentives, fears, and drives. Accordingly, an action that offers, among possible outcomes, a high mean with a large variance may possess greater appeal for one person than an action that offers a somewhat smaller mean with such a small variance that all of its values fall within the range of values of the alternative action. The ends sought by two different enterprisers may be the same but the means or actions they select may differ because their

---

[1] The maximin under uncertainty should not be confused with the maximin of game theory, for, by the very meaning of uncertainty, the utility of a payoff to, and the reaction of, any rival is not known. Hence, even if we are considering a two-person situation, the game involved under uncertainty would in general not be a constant sum. What on the surface appears to be a maximin-minimax solution is then, in fact, simply a maximin solution by "a" decision-maker who has already accepted his rival's reactions (e.g., his rival's spatial price policies) under alternative uncertainty states as unknowns. If collusion is ruled out, what the rival will do "depends upon his surmises about his opponent's choice of strategy, and, as a matter of general theory, there are no compelling reasons in favor of any one particular surmise." R. Dorfman, P. A. Samuelson, and R. M. Solow, *Linear Programming and Economic Analysis* (New York: McGraw-Hill Book Co., 1958), p. 443.

expectations over time or the ends attainable by each are different.[1] Probabilities may be applied to original data or else to data changed to reflect the special fears, drives, etc., of the decision-maker. When is the choice not economic?

Nonmaximum Profit-Seeking Behavior

We include in the category of nonmaximum profit-seeking activity: (1) the case of a "hell-bent" gamble and (2) the case where the risk is unnecessarily minimized by avoiding some nearly impossible very low return in favor of the security of some equally unlikely higher minimum return offered by another position. In effect, the decision in such cases is governed by psychic satisfactions which revalue the mean and deviations around the mean, thereby stressing the impact of some unlikely extreme.[2]

Quantifying Our Concept of the Maximum Profit

We may ask, of course, how a distinction can be drawn between a "go for broke" gamble and a quest for maximum profit. Conversely, we may ask how a maximum-profit activity involving some obvious business conservatism—for example because cash reserves are low—can be distinguished from a psychic income obsession appearing in the form of an uneconomic drive for security. Our distinctions admittedly must be fuzzy. Perhaps the best approach available is the juridical type which would speak in terms of a reasonable or average man. If so, we may even sharpen this approach by quantifying the idea of reasonableness. We could use the possible return(s) lying outside the second or third standard deviation from the mean and say that it is not considered by reasonable economic men. Thus, whoever selects an activity because of a revaluation of dollar values based on the "defined" *unlikely* return is not an economic man.

A Mathematical Development

Suppose that there are r kinds of risks and that the ith risk has s risk states; we designate this situation as s_i, where $i = 1, \ldots, r$. Then the number of all possible combinations of risk states, say, S, will be given as follows:

$$(1^*) \quad S = \prod_{i=1}^{r} s_i$$

For an illustration, suppose there are three kinds of risks determining the payoffs in a given business venture, e.g. (1) precipitation, (2) temperature, and (3) machine breakdown. Suppose further that risk (1) has two states, e.g.

[1] The reason that attainable ends tend to differ among people is frequently related to the difference in their present resources or responsibilities.

[2] Elsewhere this quest has been called "purely personal considerations." Unfortunately, whether it determines an action by itself or is an inseparable part of some definite pecuniary reward has often been ignored.

rain or shine, risk (2) has three states, e.g. high, medium, or low temperature, and risk (3) has four states, e.g. one day to four days breakdown. Then $r = 3$, $s_1 = 2$, $s_2 = 3$, and $s_3 = 4$. The number of all possible combinations of risk states S will be $s_1 \times s_2 \times s_3$ or $2 \times 3 \times 4 = 24$.

Now, each and every possible combination of risk states can be so arranged to form the risk payoff vector A

(2*) $A = [A_1 \ldots A_S]$

We may next conceive of m kinds of uncertainties with the jth uncertainty having y_j uncertainty states. Then the number of all possible combinations of uncertainty states, say, Y, will accordingly be given as follows:

(3*) $Y = \prod_{j=1}^{m} y_j$

Now, it must be understood that each different compound uncertainty state gives rise to a corresponding different payoff vector A. However, to simplify our exposition for a while, let us consider in relation to the risk payoff vector defined above only one particular uncertainty combination, say, the $\hat{n}$th combination where we circumflex the n to stress the fact that it is one combination among all possible *compound* uncertainty states. Then our risk payoff vector A under the $\hat{n}$th compound uncertainty state might be redesignated as follows:

(2*) $A_{\hat{n}} = [A_1 \ldots A_S]/\hat{n}$

Consider then a vector of probabilities associated with the $A_{\hat{n}}$ payoff vector which we define as

(4*) $W = [W_1 \ldots W_S]$

It is requisite that the particular probability subset W_k associated with the kth compound risk state (e.g. the probability of rainy weather occurring together with low temperature and four days of machine breakdowns) correspond to the payoff A_k ($k = 1, \ldots, S$). Otherwise, we would be applying a subset of probabilities to the expected payoffs of a different risk subset. Let it be noted here that because the risk probabilities should be independent of uncertainty, we do not subscript W in (4*) by $\hat{n}$, as the particular uncertainty combination which may happen to prevail is irrelevant to the risk probabilities that characterize the activity in question.[1] W, therefore, represents the entire set of compound probabilities. The summation $\sum_{k=1}^{S} W_k$ is, needless to say, equal to unity.

The expected value of the payoffs $[E(A_{\hat{n}})]$ is given as

(5*) $E(A_{\hat{n}}) = A_{\hat{n}}W'$

---

[1] Though we propose that risk probabilities are independent of the uncertainty state that prevails, our theory actually does not require statistical independence of risk. That is to say, the fundamental probability theorem $P[A_2/A_1] = P[A_1, A_2]/P(A_1)$ may be applied. Then, rather than multiply the probabilities $P(A_1)\,P(A_2)$ in formulating the W matrix, as we would if the events were independent, we would derive W by $P(A_1)P[A_2/A_1])$ where $P[A_2/A_1] \neq P(A_2)$. Only the actual W_k values would be different; all other aspects of our formulation remain unchanged.

Any particular permutation of the elements of A and hence W may be assumed; for example, A_1 may correspond to the case where all risks are in their individually most favorable state (i.e. A_1 is the best payoff possible), A_2 then corresponds to the second best payoff possible, and so on until A_S is reached, the worst possible payoff.

An alternative permutation offers some advantages. Remembering that the ith risk has s_i risk states, each state of the ith risk can be combined with S/s_i elements. The sum of the probability elements in any sub vector of W thus represents the cumulative compound probability of the ith risk being in all of its s_i states along with a particular combination of risk states for all of the other risks. The sum of every s_{ith} element of the original vector represents, accordingly, the cumulative compound probability of the ith risk in a particular state with all the other risks assuming all possible compound states. This particular permutation enables us to recast the interdependent structure of risks and uncertainty in the revealing form of a set of matrices.

Let risk $i = 1$ have p states and assume all other risks $(r-1)$ occur in z combination states. These other risks in concert with risk 1 yield the z by $p = S$ payoff matrix A (mapped from the payoff vector A) under the uncertainty $\hat{n}$.

$$(1) \quad \mathbf{A}_{\hat{n}} = \begin{bmatrix} \mathbf{A}_{11}\mathbf{A}_{12} & \ldots & \mathbf{A}_{1p} \\ \cdot & \cdot & \\ \cdot & \cdot & \cdot \\ \cdot & \cdot & \\ \mathbf{A}_{z1}\mathbf{A}_{z2} & \ldots & \mathbf{A}_{zp} \end{bmatrix} \hat{n}$$

The $\mathbf{W}$ matrix is therefore—

$$(2) \quad \mathbf{W} = \begin{bmatrix} \mathbf{W}_{11}\mathbf{W}_{12} & \ldots & \mathbf{W}_{1p} \\ \cdot & \cdot & \\ \cdot & \cdot & \cdot \\ \cdot & \cdot & \\ \mathbf{W}_{z1}\mathbf{W}_{z2} & \ldots & \mathbf{W}_{zp} \end{bmatrix}$$

Its transpose is—

$$(3) \quad \mathbf{W}' = \begin{bmatrix} \mathbf{W}_{11} & \ldots & \mathbf{W}_{z1} \\ \mathbf{W}_{12} & & \mathbf{W}_{z2} \\ \cdot & & \cdot \\ \cdot & & \cdot \\ \cdot & & \cdot \\ \mathbf{W}_{1p} & \ldots & \mathbf{W}_{zp} \end{bmatrix}$$

Multiplying (1) by (3) yields the weighted values

$$(4) \quad \mathbf{X}_{\hat{n}} = [\mathbf{X}_{gh}]\,(\delta gh) = \begin{bmatrix} \mathbf{X}_{11} & & & \\ & \mathbf{X}_{22} & & 0 \\ & & \cdot & \\ & 0 & & \cdot \\ & & & \cdot \\ & & & \mathbf{X}_{zz} \end{bmatrix} \quad \text{where } [\mathbf{X}_{gh}] = \mathbf{A}_{\hat{n}}\mathbf{W}',$$

and $g, h = 1, \ldots, z$ and δ is the Kronecker delta defined as unity when

$g = h$ and zero when $g \neq h$. The matrix in (4) of dimension zz thus is nonzero in diagonal values only.

We may accordingly write (5*) in any of the forms

$$(5) \quad E(A_{\hat{n}}) = A_{\hat{n}}W' = Tr\, \mathbf{X}_{\hat{n}} = \bar{\mathbf{X}}_{\hat{n}}$$

Rents and the Risk Index: A Digression. In classical economic theory, rents have been viewed as the difference between the price paid to a factor and the minimum price necessary to elicit a supply of the factor; the latter can be called the transfer price. In the case of differential skills of management, the rent paid to the more skilled manager or entrepreneur is equal to the entire product he produces (his actual value or price) compared with that which the *marginal* manager or entrepreneur would obtain. In a corresponding manner, an inter-industry payment obtains in the case of risk. However, though the *inter*-industry rent is distinguishable from an *intra*-industry payment such as the payment attributable to different skills, a basic similarity prevails. As with skills, the rents of those engaged in more risky ventures are in the limit (i.e., in the long-run equilibrium) equal to the differences in payments obtainable under the subject venture and the *marginal* riskless venture. This thought brings us to the idea of risk index.

We specify, in conformance with classical economic theory, that an index of risk is derivable as the difference between the payoff the entrepreneur expects to receive and the lowest likely payoff he may receive. More generally, we are able to include alternative uncertainty conditions by stipulating that the risk index relates to the difference between that which the subject entrepreneur expects to earn and the minimum he "might" earn *under the best uncertainty combination.* So if (4) above pertains to the best state of uncertainty (that is, we let $\hat{n}$ be the best combination of uncertainty possibilities), the difference between $E(A_{\hat{n}})$ and the related lowest A_k value which carries a statistically likely probability serves as the *basis for deriving an index of risk* for the firm. We simply divide the difference in question by the firm's total investment.[1] To see this relation most clearly, let us identify and go beyond certain constraints implicitly included in our previous developments.

---

[1] While this is not the place to demonstrate the operational qualities of our risk-uncertainty formulation, nor perhaps even really the place to mention operational possibilities, a brief comment might be helpful. In this key, we should observe that the difference between the expected A under a designated uncertainty state (e.g., under the best combination of uncertainties if more than one uncertainty prevails) might be compared with the lowest A_k value under that uncertainty state, provided the related W_k is statistically likely. The $E(A)$ and the appropriate lowest A_k may be weighted by various techniques which would yield a dollar measure (i.e., a difference in expected and lowest likely returns) of the risk accepted in the given venture. An estimate of uncertainty based on the lowest likely values under the best and worst uncertainties may, in turn, be conceived. Profit variances under conditions of economic expansion and over the whole cycle may be used in practice to approximate the risk and uncertainty measures suggested above.

Different Uncertainties. The trace of X in (4) applies to only one state of nature, one project, one investment, one location, one uncertainty, etc. That is to say, in establishing the matrices (1)–(3), we not only assumed a given uncertainty combination, but took as data the location, the size of the investment, the process selected for production, *etc.* of the firm. If we continue to assume as we did implicitly above that the best production technique is to be applied regardless of where the activity is located, and if, further, we assume that our payoffs are in terms of the optimal rate on investment alternatives, we may introduce as a major variable the location of the firm, *ceteris paribus.* In other words, suppose we conceive of a *t*th location, where $t = a, b, \ldots, f$, and let us assume that the optimal investment and process has been selected at each of these locations under all conceivable risks and uncertainties. These alternative locations are shown in (6) by columns. In turn, let our rows now designate *all* of the alternative *uncertainty combinations* that are possible, with each element in (6) therefore denoting the expected value of the payoffs under all risk possibilities given an uncertainty combination at a particular location. Matrix **U** in (6) therefore generalizes our model still further by enabling us to conceive of an *n*th combination of uncertainty ($n = 1, \ldots, Y$) in addition to the risk combinations, with each uncertainty combination applying to each alternative location being considered by the firm.

$$(6) \quad \mathbf{U} = \begin{bmatrix} \bar{\mathbf{X}}_{1a} & \bar{\mathbf{X}}_{1b} & \cdots & \bar{\mathbf{X}}_{1f} \\ \cdot & \cdot & & \cdot \\ \cdot & \cdot & & \cdot \\ \cdot & \cdot & & \cdot \\ \bar{\mathbf{X}}_{Ya} & \bar{\mathbf{X}}_{Yb} & \cdots & \bar{\mathbf{X}}_{Yf} \end{bmatrix}$$

Subjective probabilities now must enter so that the responsible manager or entrepreneur can resolve the decision problems. Bernouilli's principle of insufficient reason may be applied which, in effect, would cause us to multiply each element in each row by $1/y$. Or, on a priori grounds, the decision-maker may prefer instead to apply different probabilities to the different rows. The **U** matrix of (6) then becomes Matrix **Û** in (7)

$$(7) \quad \hat{\mathbf{U}} = \begin{bmatrix} \hat{\mathbf{X}}_{1a} & \hat{\mathbf{X}}_{1b} & \cdots & \hat{\mathbf{X}}_{1f} \\ \cdot & \cdot & & \cdot \\ \cdot & \cdot & & \cdot \\ \cdot & \cdot & & \cdot \\ \hat{\mathbf{X}}_{Ya} & \hat{\mathbf{X}}_{Yb} & \cdots & \hat{\mathbf{X}}_{Yf} \end{bmatrix}$$

How the decision-maker ultimately selects the optimal value(s) and hence location will be discussed briefly later in this chapter, and in greater detail in Chapter 12. For the present, two vital relations must be examined:

Distinction between Budgetary and Personal Forces

When an entrepreneur is short of cash, or for other reasons tends to adopt an extremely short-run profit-maximizing target, we may expect him to weight downward the conjectured, possible returns that lie on the lower end of his expectation scale. Let us say the disutility of small income values (or negative income returns) may be expected to be greater *ceteris paribus* the tighter is the budget position of the decision-maker. In terms of risk alone, the redesignation of matrix values may be such that an investment which to others proffers a high mean may suggest a low mean to this person (our subject decision-maker) and hence be rejected. The horizon of the profit seeker (one- or two-year optimum *vis-à-vis* an optimum running over a long period) enters the risk matrix by producing a redesignation of dollar values into utilities (or utils).

Uncertainty ties up with the decision-making process in a slightly different way, for uncertainty molds and is reflected in the personality and general characteristics of the decision-maker himself. Some men like to gamble, some are conservative, some will apply a maximax criterion, or a pessimistic approach in reaching their final decision. (See the Glossary of terms at end of this chapter.) Simply put, decision-making under uncertainty may reflect individual quirks and personality traits alone, disregarding financial differences. Thus, the particular focus of the decision-maker leads him under conditions of uncertainty into selecting, say, location "f" because the highest of all highest returns under any and all uncertainties is obtainable there whereas another decision-maker selects location "d" because the lowest mean return proffered there is at least greater (and hence more satisfactory to him) than the lowest expected return at any other location.

In general, we propose that budgetary factors such as existing financial statement ratios may cause a redesignation of the income values that are projected for management; in this way, decision-making under risk is influenced by the economic status of the individual. In contrast, we propose that nonbudgetary-oriented personal characteristics induce the manager or entrepreneur to select his preferred criterion in resolving a decision-making problem under uncertainty. We would suggest as a matter of personal preference that the difference in value between the lowest *likely* return under the best uncertainty state and the lowest *likely* return under the worst uncertainty state, given the decision-maker's investment selection, would serve as the basis for an index measure of uncertainty. (Again, see note 1, p. 16 for a brief discussion of this concept and the computing of a risk-uncertainty index.) However, significant alone to our theory is the idea that for successful decision-making under risk, a long-run rent is obtained, whereas successful decision-making under uncertainty yields a long-run profit.

Maximum Profit under Risk and Uncertainty

Our concept of maximum profit is more liberal than that which many economists maintain. It includes, among other things, the effect on a firm's behavior of such items as the firm's financial resources (including its past and present asset policy), the owner's willingness to take chances, his desire for some security, and his expectations for the future.

Maximization under conditions of uncertainty is basic to our concept. Maximization over time, not maximization at a given moment, is also fundamental. Our concept retains original economic terminology, reflects traditional economic meaning, and is readily usable in empirical work because it is tied to risk and uncertainty rather than to perfect knowledge.

Our general theory of maximum profits is available for us to use in complex as well as simple market models. Significantly, it permits differences in individual goals and in resources and daring. On the other hand, it does not permit or include the gambling instinct or those extreme cases where ultraconservatism dominates the business activity. It is fully general, for it may be used in basic theory, such as pure competition, and in applied economics as well.

One last comment about our maximum profit concept should be mentioned at this point. As opposed to classical economics where a sum certain or mean profit return could be specified by all and sundry so that rational men everywhere would make the same decision, our concept centers on differences. Especially when uncertainty is brought into focus, personality and character variations are central parts of the decision-making matrix. It is therefore natural to ask whether chaos rather than order must prevail in the system. And this book, therefore, endeavors to determine whether uncertainty and its related concept modifications are as specifiable in final impact as the simpler, more convenient, classical assumptions of certainty, or even risk. Let us finally note here that, although at this point we are emphasizing the claim that entrepreneurs differ substantially from one another in the presence of uncertainty, we shall ultimately demonstrate the existence of an order to such system; in fact, we shall propose that a special common character arises among the firms of a given industry which reflects a logical pattern.

III. SUMMARY

The idea that economic units may, "with full economic rationality," select different outcomes and allocations because of the different criteria they happen to apply in reaching a decision is well established in the literature, for example in the theory of consumer choice. In that theory, we find allocations of scarce means among competing ends being predicated on individual differences; in fact, it can be shown that it is an inherent part of the theory that some consumers maximax in selecting a product, some maximin and so forth.[1] Thinking of the businessman in this way appears, at first blush however, to

[1] See M. L. Greenhut, *Microeconomics and the Space Economy* (Chicago: Scott Foresman, 1963), Chapter 2.

violate a fundamental tenet of classical theory, namely the concept of the economic man who seemingly behaves like all other economic men. And we have said earlier that decision-making under uncertainty does involve different selections of criteria by decision-makers. We shall see, however, that it is not essential to economic theory to assume behavioral consistency of businessmen and that, in fact, varying actions and reactions do not lead to inexplicable confusion. In fact an orderly pattern prevails in the system via rational behavioral differences among businessmen. Such demonstration as that of Professor Becker, which shows that irrationality does not require the discarding of maximum profit assumptions, thus serves, in turn, only as an alternative extension (and is therefore not a required part) of the theory to be developed herein.[1]

Appendix to Chapter 2
Glossary of Selected Decision Theory Terms

In this glossary only selected terms of decision theory used in this book are defined. It, therefore, does not claim to give all decision theory terms; and it does not strive for precision. Its purpose is simply to provide an easy reference source for readers who are not familiar with decision theory and who have neither the time nor desire to read original sources or otherwise study in detail the derivation and meaning of the decision-making terms used in this book.

CRITERIA UNDER UNCERTAINTY

Under uncertainty, the decision-maker is forced to rely on some subjective criterion because he is unable to use objective probabilities. Among the subjective criteria which have attained general acceptance are the so-called rationality criterion, the maximin-minimax criterion, and the criteria of pessimism, optimism, and regret. Since we have already discussed rationality and pessimism, only a few brief words about these criteria are necessary. Similarly, we shall define fairly briefly the other criteria referred to above.

1. *Rationality.* The rationality criterion is popularly known as the Bayes or Laplace criterion; it relates also to the Bernouillian principle of insufficient reason. Simply put, because anything is likely to happen under uncertainty, each uncertain event is equally likely to occur. Accordingly, the payoff under rationality may be designated mathematically as $(1/n)$(Payoff 1 + Payoff 2 + . . . + Payoff n). No respective different probabilities are admitted.

2. *Maximin-Minimax.* Particularly in game theory, where two units are competing (as individuals or as rival coalitions) or where a definite number of alternatives within a fixed total payoff are possible, the best of the worst possible alternatives for one competitor will correspond to the lowest return the other

---

[1] G. S. Becker, "Irrational Behavior and Economic Theory," *Journal of Political Economy*, LXX (February, '62), pp. 1–13.

competitor may permit his rival to have. In effect, the lowest return permitted a rival establishes, by subtraction from the total available in the market, the greatest return the decision-maker may guarantee for himself. In game theory, the maximum of the minimum amounts is referred to as the *maximin*, and the minimum share thus left to the competitor establishes the rival's maximum and is called the *minimax*.

It is basic to the described alternative that a fixed (or finite) total is to be shared by the competitors. The fixity of the sum leads us to refer to the situation in question as a *constant-sum game*. If the total payoffs are variable, the payoff which in a constant-sum game would be the maximin need not equal the minimax. By forming a coalition, each player would gain.

3. *Pessimism*. Pessimism as a criterion is actually similar to the maximin of game theory—it is the maximin that would obtain in a nonconstant-sum game. Pessimism involves the making of a decision in complete disregard of the actions and reactions of any rival or set of rivals. In other words, the decision-maker decides it is hopeless to predict the action of his rival(s) and, accordingly, selects the best payoff from the worst set of alternatives he is able to visualize. To be sure, he may consequently undersell his position, and similarly his rival(s) may fail to reap or magnify the remaining return(s). What is important to the decision-maker, however, is that he has guaranteed for himself an acceptable minimum.

4. *Optimism*. The optimistic criterion involves a maximizing. Here, the decision-maker selects from the best set of payoffs the payoff return that will give him the highest value.

In some decision theory, a more moderate approach may be followed and accepted as optimism. A coefficient of optimism is worked out which involves finding the probability that would make the best and worst payoffs of one set equal to the payoffs of other sets. The set requiring the lowest probability for the highest (i.e., most favorable) alternative value establishes "a" coefficient of optimism, and the decision-maker is then able to resolve his dilemma by comparing his subjective expectations with the relevant coefficient. Of course, if he likes the odds, he will select the action requiring the lowest probability of occurrence to assure the desired return.

There are other coefficients of optimism besides the one mentioned here. These alternative coefficients are all described in the literature. For our purposes, however, we will simply think of the criterion of optimism as more or less equal to a maximax choice and will not concern ourselves with working out any of the coefficients.

5. *Regret*. The last criterion we will mention involves the computation of lost opportunities. For example, if a decision-maker selects some combination of AT & T stocks, G.E. bonds, and other investments, he presumably forgoes an alternative combination. By estimating the value of all opportunities forgone, an index of regret may be formed. Moreover, by estimating the losses suffered under all "likely" alternatives, a payoff may be evolved which shows the respective dissatisfaction under each alternative. Thus we try to minimize these dissatisfactions, and we refer to this as decision-making under the criterion of regret.

3

The Relation between Oligopoly, Uncertainty, and Space

WE SHALL HYPOTHESIZE THE FOLLOWING SET OF RELATIONS: People and institutions are scattered over a landscape in which the friction of distance carries a significant cost. In a particular market area, the member firms of any one industry usually are few, distributed as they are over the space. Partly because there is a relatively small number of plants and firms in a given market area, and for reasons to be derived analytically in Chapter 6, we further propose that the firms act oligopolistically towards each other. The watchful-waiting policy which develops between the oligopolists reflects personalized relations between firms, and these are of uncertain order. Indeed, the term uncertainty in this book generally will relate to the behavioral uncertainty of oligopolists, as the objectively unpredictable actions and reactions of these businessmen add a dimension to theory which must be evaluated and stressed in any analysis of the firm in economic space.

We shall propose in the present chapter that the uncertainty of oligopolistic behavior elicits a unique conception of the firm's average revenue (AR) curve; specifically, it applies to the firm's AR function a parametric variable [later symbolized in equation (1) as c] which prompts the firm to make comparatively few changes in its prices over time. To the risk-uncertainty matrix of Chapter 2, where we found that decision-makers have varying backgrounds, responsibilities, time horizons, personalities, and instincts, we shall notice here that a reflection of these differences is shown in the contrasting ways each firm views its AR curve. The value c will be posited as a conjectured parameter which becomes increasingly important besides changing over time. What one firm sees another does not, what one firm accepts another rejects, where one firm maximizes another minimizes, ad infinitum. The first section of this chapter sets forth this picture of differences by focusing attention on the oligopolistic firm's conception of its AR curve.

In section two we begin to justify more formally the claim that uncertainty is intrinsic to a space economy. In particular, selected aspects of the relation between uncertainty, oligopoly, and economic space are developed. But most importantly, this section of the chapter moves from the short-run specification of individual differences to our basic view of the long run which proposes intra-industry homogeneity and stable equilibrium. The comparative statics picture drawn in this chapter therefore points to both the short-run variations in practices that were indicated in Chapter 2 and the long-run stability that will be proven to prevail in Parts 2 and 3 of the book. The present chapter, in other words, is still introductory in nature, as it demonstrates more by assertion than by formal analysis those underlying *forces* in a space economy which relate to short-run differences and long-run identities.

I. A SHORT-RUN VIEW OF OLIGOPOLY: SOME GENERAL OBSERVATIONS

One vital factor influencing the intensity of competition that prevails in a market is the number of firms in the industry. Other important factors are the spatial relations between firms and the standardization of the industry's products. These forces quite often blend into the market type in which each seller believes he should watch his own actions because he is being watched by others. When this situation exists, the complex market or, as it is more popularly called, the duopoly-oligopoly market, prevails. For simplicity, we shall usually refer in this book to the complex market as just the oligopoly market.

The condition of watchful-waiting which stems from the ability to identify one's most important rivals is intrinsic to the oligopoly market while being extraneous to the simple market types (i.e., the pure or monopolistically competitive or the simple monopolistic market). This watchful-waiting or interdependence between firms is influenced significantly by the homogeneity—heterogeneity of products. But interdependence on account of some similarity of products is not sufficient alone to satisfy the requirements of the complex market. The number of firms and their spatial relations must enable any one firm to limit noticeably the potential market of another. Then the consequence could be a market in the form of an oligopoly tied together over economic space in a chainlike way.

The complex market may develop on a regional scale, or it may involve a few firms trading throughout the nation. Whatever its precise make-up, there must be a noticeable identification of rivals, such that any buyer who shifts from one seller to another is influenced by the action of rival sellers as well as the action of the subject oligopolist himself. Unlike the pure and monopolistically competitive markets, the firm is not so small among so many as to be able to set up (or accept) its policy without reference to the practices of specific competitors.

Buyer Attachments

A unique pattern is formed when many buyers strongly prefer a particular firm's product. The greater the attachment, the less is the inroad of a price cut by any one firm on the sales of another; and, if attachments are strong enough, there is little, if any, likelihood of forcing an identical response from rivals. In fact, the market form may be pure monopoly rather than oligopoly. When attachments are weak, however, a price cut by one tends to induce an identical price response from rivals. In tautological fashion, we propose that a price cut which could have led to a large increase in individual sales if ignored by all rivals will result in an imperceptible gain in sales if it is not ignored. The price policy of the complex market firm is governed largely by the expected price reactions of its rivals. In contrast, product prices in the simple market are set either in substantial disregard of the prices of other identifiable sellers or else by forces which appear to lie wholly outside the control of any one seller.

An Average Revenue Conception

Consider an industry which has one member firm (firm r) located at a distance from a production center where f homogeneous firms are located. For the present, we assume transport and other costs are zero but conceive of a regional bias in terms of proximity of sellers to buyers such that at least a spatial (and perhaps also a product) differentiation prevails. The average revenue (AR) function of the firm r may be of the form

$$(1^*) \quad p_r = a_0 - b_0 q_r - c_0 \sum_{s=1}^{f} q_s$$

where q_r is the quantity produced of the r_{th} firm, q_s represents the quantity produced by one of the f_{th} other firms in the market, b_0 is a positive number whose magnitude depends upon the extent of the spatial (and product) differentiation in the industry, and c_0 is a much smaller positive number whose magnitude is similarly influenced. Because a linkage of few firms underscores oligopoly, $s = 1, \ldots, f$ runs to a comparatively small number. The aggregate demand for the products of the f other firms is of similar form

$$(2^*) \quad p_f = a_1 - b_1 q_r - c_1 \sum_{s=1}^{f} q_s$$

where p_f is used to stand for the price of any of the f firms, b_1 is a very small positive number, and c_1 is a slightly larger positive number whose value helps establish the proportion of total demand allocable to the f firms at a particular moment in time. We specify $a_1 > a_0 > b_0 > c_1 > c_0 > b_1 > 0$ by approximately the same absolute amounts.

It is manifest that multiplying (1^*) by q_r yields total revenue which when differentiated with respect to q_r and set equal to zero establishes the reaction function of r (i.e. q_r in terms of Σq_s). Proceeding similarly with respect to (2^*) establishes the reaction function of the f firms. The intersection point of the reaction functions yields the equilibrium solution, with the competitive profit maximizing p_r, p_f, q_r and Σq_s derived accordingly.

Suppose firm r considers increasing its price while assuming that p_f will be unchanged at the production center. Substituting that value of p_f into (2*) yields Σq_s in terms of q_r. Further substitution into (1*) designates r's price as a function of q_r alone and hence q_r as a function of p_r. The AR curve above the market price designated by the intersection point of the reaction functions is predicated on p_f being continued at its profit-maximizing value.

Suppose firm r considers a lowering of its price but assumes the f firms will seek to maintain their market shares. By elementary derivation we would find

$$(3^*) \quad p_r = a_0 - \left[\left(\frac{c_0}{c_1}\right)a_1 - \left(\frac{c_0}{c_1}\right)p_f\right] - \left[b_0 - \left(\frac{c_0}{c_1}\right)b_1\right]q_r.$$

In effect, the oligopolist drops off the AR curve that relates to the profit-maximizing price of the f firms and moves to a lower curve which reflects the lower price of the f firms. Attaching all new p_r, q_r points to the original curve establishes a new, rather steeply sloped AR section below the profit-maximizing price of r.

Equations (1*) and (2*) establish a kinked AR schedule under the assumption that other prices are unchanged with respect to a price increase by a given seller and are lowered pursuant to a price decrease by that seller. As noted above, c_0 is a technically (i.e. objectively) determined coefficient, which implies that (1*) is a market formed function for firm r. In any meaningful kinked AR curve (which incidentally we shall later accept as explanatory only in the early stages of an industry's development), there exists in contrast to (1*) an imagined function in which the parameter c_0 is a conjectured one. Let us denote it as

$$(1) \quad p_r = a - bq_r - c \sum_{s=1}^{f} q_s$$

where c is now a positive variable whose values are conjectured for every possible p_r, and depend on the degree to which r believes it would price itself out of the market at higher prices or cause a price war with lower prices. The magnitude of c is great with respect to either an increase or decrease in p_r. It is clear that if a larger value of c is inserted in (3*) in place of c_0, the AR schedule shifts downward and is flatter above the equilibrium price and steeper below the equilibrium price than the kinked curve based on market (not imagined) data. Actual q_r at any new price differs from conjectured q_r to the extent that r's conjecture is in error. Suppose buyer attachments are expected to be strong over a small range of p_r (e.g., with p_f unchanged Σq_s will change only slightly, as given by the market reaction function). Then, the c value over this range of prices will be much smaller than that conjectured for other changes of price (i.e. for still higher or lower prices). Because the c value over this range of prices is conjectural and subjective, albeit we know it is a positive number of substantially smaller magnitude than the c values that are applicable to much greater or lower prices, we shall assume in our references to this particular c that it approximates unity. Significantly, a three-section AR curve arises under the different c's including $c \to$ unity; but we must reserve our discussion of this three-sectioned AR curve to later chapters.

Facility in applications later on in the book is obtained by rewriting (2*) as

$$(2) \quad p_f = a' - b'q_r - c' \sum_{s=1}^{f} q_s.$$

It is, therefore, our thesis that the oligopolist's kinked AR curve reflects his imagination or, let us say, his expectation of his rival's behavior pattern and the consumer's reaction to changes in price by one seller or many or all sellers.[1] Significantly the AR functions (1) and (2) point to the interdependence between firms in a space economy. The different b and c values reflect the spatial differentiation that exists. Significantly, the intersection of the reaction functions establishes the Cournot solution and the conjectures as to effects of price change yield the kinked AR curve. A Stackelberg leader-follower or his disequilibrium solution also may be obtained from (1) and (2); e.g. substitute r's reaction function in (2) or the f firm's reaction function in (1), or assume that in fact neither will accept the follower's role. Indeed (1) and (2) are applicable to the monopolistically competitive market by assuming each $q_s = q_r$, under which assumption (1) reappears as a $-[b-(n-1)c]q_r$; thus the steeply sloped market equilibrium curve of the monopolistically competitive industry appears against which the individual firm's AR conception may be viewed. Under the theory to be set forth herein, the Cournot and the kinked AR conceptions will later on be stressed. For the present, it suffices that the interdependent spatial system of firms combined with the uncertainty of an oligopolist leads to imagined AR conceptions such that any of the AR possibilities of Figure 3–1 may apply, including again the short-run possibility of a *sharp* kink.

The AR curve of the complex market type in Figure 3–1 is based primarily on unsupported hypotheses. A slight variation in the assumed conditions— for example, in regard to the price reaction of rivals—could cause a drastic change in the conjectured value of c. It is in order, therefore, to stress the expression "probably relevant assumptions," because this emphasizes the

---

[1] Once price is established following the imagined demand curve, there is a tendency to adhere to the selected price. Of course, the imagined curve may be incorrect; that is, the oligopolist may have anticipated a certain quantity of sales at the selected price, but greater or lesser sales actually take place. In time, the oligopolist will realize his error, and the imagined curve will move to the right or left, as the case may be, while any kinked portion, if depicted, will stay at or near the original price. The imagined curve will then coincide in time with the actual curve at the prevailing price. Below this price, the curve may be more steeply sloped than the basic curve. This would occur if price wars were expected. Indeed, the steepness of the slope would be exaggerated if consumers tend to hold back their purchases in the hope that the price of rivals may be lowered still more. Similarly, what happens to the curve above this price also depends on the policies of rivals and consumer reactions.

state of diverse possibilities. The fact is that the unorganized oligopolistic market involves many forms—indeed, more forms than we can hope or have need to discuss here. But among all complex market types, there is a similarity in outcome: competition is fostered in product differentiation and in sales promotion rather than in price.

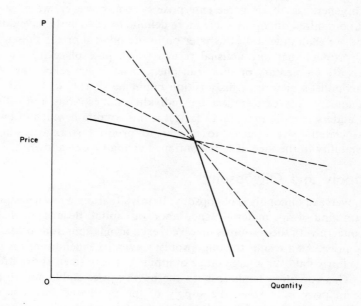

Figure 3–1: The Oligopolist's AR Curve

Special Considerations. The conclusions obtained from oligopoly theory are numerous, limited only by the several "possibly relevant assumptions" which may be formed. Increases in demand may lead to higher prices, to the same price, or even, in fact, to lower prices.[1] The different conceptions of the value of c in equation 1, reflecting as they do the different personalities and backgrounds of the decision-makers, cause the existing price patterns to take diverse forms. In any case, an element of conservatism tends to permeate the market which generally limits the intensity of price competition. This con-

[1] See M. L. Greenhut, *Microeconomics and the Space Economy* (Chicago: Scott Foreman, 1963) Chapter 5, where, for example, the last situation of lower prices in the face of increasing demand is shown to occur when the AR curve is shifted to the right and upward and is more elastic than the original AR curve at the given price. This unusual situation arises when the original curve (or the applicable arc of the curve) is of constant or increasing elasticity. It may also occur, of course, when the whole demand curve changes in shape, such as when a range of downward pricing is established which does not lead to any change in the price of rivals.

servatism finds expression in the pricing as well as in other decisions of the firm. Thus a maximiner with two alternative price policies at his disposal, one of which appears to offer very high profits or significant losses while the other promises smaller profits or smaller losses, would tend to select the latter. But whether or not a maximax, maximin, or another policy controls, it should be clear that changes in demand *could* cause anticlassical results.[1]

To generalize about a free enterprise system, however, we must impart to an unorganized oligopoly some more definite form than we have done thus far, and we shall indeed do this later on in the book. For the present, let us simply propose that any unusual results which take place in oligopolistic markets are momentary or short-run phenomena which reflect the fact that the oligopolist's picture of his position might be sharply out of focus with reality and, in any case, reflect the individual conceptions and differences which underscore the market. In fact, it is this condition which often causes his associated price policies to appear to produce strange results (e.g., price stability in the face of long-continued changing demand).

Oligopoly and Oligopsony

The converse of oligopoly is oligopsony. In this situation, a few firms purchase a certain kind of raw material, land, labor, or capital. Because of their common concern with the resources involved, each firm is conscious of the other's buying price. As a result, the oligopsonist's average expenditure for units of input is fairly flat over a large range of inputs but very steep above prevailing prices. This condition tends to keep the buying price stable and to allow a change in price only when the supply of the purchased factor is sharply changed. As in oligopoly, the analytical possibilities of oligopsony are myriad, but examination of this subject is best left to theory courses concerned with distribution economics. Our interest in this book is chiefly on the selling side of economic activity.

Hypercompetitive Oligopoly and Chain Oligopoly

Economists speak of many kinds of unorganized oligopoly. We will briefly discuss two of these types here: hypercompetitive oligopoly and chain oligopoly.[2]

Hypercompetitive Oligopoly. Hypercompetitive (or cutthroat) oligopoly prevails in trades where the custom of making an offer, a counteroffer, a new

[1] Recall that we use the term *maximin* to cover an uncertainty decision governed by comparisons of worst possible positions. In turn, we use the term *maximax* to refer to an uncertainty decision governed by the desire to maximize highest returns even though at the same time there is the possibility of suffering very bad returns if rivals act unfavorably.

[2] See F. Machlup, *The Economics of Sellers' Competition* (Baltimore: The Johns Hopkins Press, 1952), p. 504. Also see E. H. Chamberlin, *The Theory of Monopolistic Competition*, 5th ed. (Cambridge: Harvard University Press, 1946), p. 103.

offer, a further counteroffer, and so on has developed. Typified by the retail furniture trade, this oligopoly develops when each seller is not only conscious of competition with others but believes that a customer who walks out of his store will actually gain the buying advantage he seeks from the store across the street. The essence of this form of oligopoly is the belief that one's actions are watched and that the watcher will outdo the watched if given a chance. Gaudy advertising signs, bargain prices in windows, a cigar for good prospects, the friendly pat on the back—all combine with a fast line of sales talk in poorly lighted and stuffy rooms to set the stage for a high sensitivity of price in response to any buyer resistance. The market tends to be demoralized by secret transactions, bargain sales, gimmicks, and rumors. It degenerates at times into incompatible relations where the policy turns into a "get the rival" rather than a "get the customers." The variable c in equation (1) assumes—in practice—very large positive values with respect to a price decrease. A few victims barreling into bankruptcy is often enough to cause this market to return to its basic puffed-up price.

Chain Oligopoly. Although a market having many firms is generally called purely or monopolistically competitive, the dispersion of these firms over densely populated but scattered areas alters the effective number of firms competing for a given set of buyers. Rivalry between only a few identifiable competitors who watch each other's actions tends to arise; in the process, a chain oligopoly is formed. A may be linked to B and C, B may be linked to A and D; C could be linked to A and E; while D is linked to B and F, with diverse other permutations and combinations prevailing over the space. In such markets, price oscillations spread in wavelike form from one center to others.[1] Of course, if a large number of new firms enter the market and spatial costs are basically unimportant, the oligopolistic chain would prove to be weak and competitive impacts significant. As we have already noted and shall explain in full in Chapter 5, the sharply kinked AR curve becomes more continuous as a mid-section is formed over which the subject firm prices independently of others. The value of c, we stipulate, approaches unity over this section of the AR curve. Indeed, the conversion of a chain oligopoly into a competitive oligopoly with some range of price freedom open to each firm is the ultimate theory of our book. For the moment, however, let us only suggest that in some cases the industry might shift back and forth from a simple chain to a nearly monopolistically competitive market, to one marked by hypercompetition, back to a simple more stable chain, and so on, as entry and exit occur. Space may permit alternative degrees of competition; but at the same time it limits the number of market forms that typically could prevail.

[1] A. Lösch, *Die räumliche Ordnung de Wirtschaft* (Jena: Gustav Fisher, 1944), Chapter 20.

Organized Oligopoly

When firms follow each other's price leads, the AR curve for any one seller is steeply tilted. A decrease in price will, then, fail to elicit a large increase in sales. Under cartelized pricing, the real AR curve for any one firm becomes a compressed reflection of the total demand curve; accordingly equation (1) is technically unnecessary and (2) alone applies, with c' in (2) assuming different values depending upon whether s stands for some or all the firms in the industry. The market shares of the firms tend to remain constant, *ceteris paribus*, under organized oligopoly; $\sum_{s=1}^{f} q_s = Kq_r$ where K is a constant greater than unity. We may visualize this and the unorganized oligopoly situation in Figure 3–2, where the IDID curve stands for the industry demand curve, the DDp curve denotes the individual firm's demand curve under organized cartel pricing (or price leadership), and the dd_1 curve depicts the demand for the individual firm's product under independent pricing.[1]

Inherent to any independently formed demand curve is the assumption that all other things are equal. Because this assumption enables us to think of a set price policy by rival firms with no great inroads by any firm on another, we are able to define the dd_1 curve in Figure 3–2. More generally, as we have seen, the value of c in the unorganized oligopolist's AR curve determines the conjectured form of the curve. Parenthetically, if a seller expects rival firms to retaliate to any lowering of his price below P in Figure 3–2, the portion of the dd_1 curve lying below P is shifted to the left. The quantity likely to be sold by the firm, at any given price, will be less under this condition than it would be under independent pricing. If changes in price over different values elicit alternative price-cutting reactions, the results may best be illustrated by a series of broken AR curves such as were shown in Figure 3–1.

We may summarize by illustration. Assume with reference to Figure 3–2 that a seller has been charging price X and that his rivals have generally held to price Y. Assume further that he reduces his price from X to X_1 and that this drop in price causes the other firms to reduce their price from Y to Y_1. In

---

[1] The elasticity at any given price on the DDp curve is the same as on the IDID curve in Figure 3–2. If the IDID curve, completely unchanged in shape, were moved to the left, the elasticity at any particular price would be increased. Although formal geometrical development is more conclusive, a simple heuristic explanation of this point should suffice to explain the matter. In the following remarks, we shall be considering two identically sloped, linear demand curves:
Elasticity is the measure of the relative increment of quantity caused by a relative decrement of price, and vice versa $(\Delta x/x)/(\Delta y/y)$. On a curve closest to the vertical axis, the relative abscissa change as compared to a given relative ordinate change must be greater than on the curve to the right. Absolute measurements are the same because the slopes are the same. Price changes are identical, absolutely and relatively; quantity changes are equal absolutely but not relatively. The relative change in quantity is greater on the curve closest to the vertical axis. At any comparable price, therefore, the elasticity is greater on the linear curve displaced to the left.

such a situation, the quantity sold by the initial price changer cannot be determined just by looking down the demand schedule (dd₁) from price X to price X_1. This is so because price X_1 and its related quantity, as obtained from the demand schedule (dd₁) are relevant only when the price charged by rivals is Y. A new frame of reference is clearly required, which will indicate that the lower portion of the industry DDp curve is the true function for the firm subject to downward retaliatory pricing.[1] If price following extends to upward changes as well, then the entire DDp curve is relevant as organized oligopoly exists.

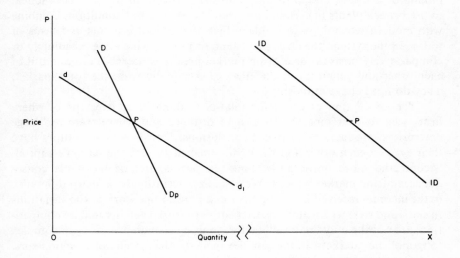

Figure 3–2: Industry and Individual Demands

The possibility of organized oligopoly also *suggests* that under a cartel or price-leadership pattern the price for the industry might be fixed at or near the point of maximum industry profits, from which any departure tends to require the stimulus of a definite change in economic data.[2] This tendency toward stability makes the pricing of organized oligopoly similar to that reflected in the kinky demand curve situation. Yet a great difference prevails between organized oligopoly and unorganized oligopoly and this difference will be seen to be critical to the effectiveness of the system in economic space.

[1] If price following is only to a price cut, unorganized oligopoly exists and a broken curve will be formed (e.g., dDp, Figure 3–2, with a break at P, the existing price).

[2] The point of maximum industry profits is found at the point of unitary elasticity when zero costs and a negatively sloping, straight-line demand are assumed.

II. OLIGOPOLY, UNCERTAINTY, AND SPACE

Consider a space economy over which resources, people, and economic units are dispersed in some unspecified order. Because of spatial limitations, uneven distribution of resources, and the tendency of some people to agglomerate, a series of markets and market areas develop, each linked to others in varying combinations.

Oligopoly and Space

In any given economy there tends to exist a sharply limited number of sites at any production center, substantial transport costs over distance, the chain linking of markets, and an overall industrial pattern in which it is practical to use branch plants in certain industries. These physical conditions combine with modern technology to yield, in fact, the large-size plants and firms of today. In the system, the large plants and firms (speaking either absolutely or comparatively in so far as a given market area is concerned) are mindful of each other and cognizant of the effect of their policies on the total market. They do not behave atomistically.

The conception of economic relations taking place over space, where firms seek to overcome the friction of distance and where there are large enterprises, produces nonclassical conclusions. First of all competitors have their eyes on each other and their ears directed toward the nation's capital. Second and more importantly, long-run profits become inevitable consequences of the market pattern. We visualize, accordingly, a sharp difference in the incomes received by oligopolists and pure competitors, as the variations in skills and risk, which alone restrict entrepreneurial activity in pure competition, are not the only "natural" factors limiting economic activity in complex (oligopolistic) markets. In the complex markets, the scarcity of entrepreneurs, and of entrepreneurial activity, is attributed to some combination of *three natural forces*: (1) the limited number of people who have the required skills, or let us say abilities, (2) risk, and (3) uncertainty. That resources and abilities may exist and yet not move into the market because of uncertainty is the vital cornerstone of our space economics. It follows that each firm in the market tends to have a chance of profits, both in the present and the long run.

In classical economics, all firms are considered to have similar costs. That is to say, classical economics assumes a state of natural scarcity among the factors of production, and holds that this condition brings about differential rents attributable to the differences in the skills and risks of doing business. A space oligopoly market theory accepts this concept, but then goes one step further. It asserts that, over and above costs, firms are entitled to a long-run return in the form of profits; and that such return, which measures the uncertainty conditions in the market, is fundamentally necessary to the market. The answer to the question why we must include uncertainty as a basic force in a space oligopoly market, but not in a purely competitive market, demands

our immediate attention. First, however, as a brief aside, we might note that
—apart from product similarities—the concept of an oligopolistic industry
could require the identically same risk set plus uncertainty set among the
firms being classified, though later in the book we shall accept the same uncertainty set without reference to risk as the prerequisite condition for our
identification of the firms comprising an industry.

Uncertainty and Oligopoly

When economic units are atomistic, market price is the resultant of an
extremely large number of independent decisions. No firm or group of firms is
important enough in the classical model to have discernible influence, and,
hence, control over price. In space economics, however, firms may be large in
size, absolutely or comparatively, in any market area. Such firms are capable
of influencing and controlling price. The market pattern which emerges
differs, as a consequence, from the traditional one.

In complex markets, the act of a representative firm does not generate a
fixed determinable response on the part of each and every competitor,
chiefly because a firm's behavior is not limited to accepting the established
market price and equating the market-determined average revenue with
marginal cost. Instead, market reactions and policies are unknown, and sometimes capricious. Except in the case of collusion, firms may predict specific
policies of rivals only under a fortunate mixture of guess and luck. Alternative
pricing systems, among other special characteristics and unique phenomena,
are intrinsic to complex markets and at best predicted only roughly for any
time and place.

When objective probabilities are applicable to the possible alternative
states which confront a decision-maker, the condition of risk is defined to
hold; when, however, these probabilities cannot be assigned, because history
is an inadequate guide to future practices, the condition of uncertainty is
defined to hold.[1] Over any considerable period of time, such as a decade,
certain pricing alternatives may have been used by large-size competitors.
When, however, history cannot be expected to serve as an adequate guide to
the particular price system that might prevail in the market at a given time,
the several price patterns of oligopolists appear as different states of the given
uncertainty condition.[2]

[1] For statements on risk and uncertainty similar in definition to ours, see Frank
Knight, *Risk, Uncertainty and Profit* (Boston: Houghton Mifflin, 1921); also see J. R. Hicks,
"The Theory of Uncertainty and Profit," *Economica*, Vol. II (1931), pp. 170–9 and A. G.
Hart, "Risk, Uncertainty, and Unprofitability of Compounding Probabilities," in O. Lange,
F. McIntyre, and T. O. Yntema ed., *Studies in Mathematical Economics and Econometrics*
(Chicago: The University of Chicago Press, 1942); pp. 110–18. Consider also the operations
research practice of regarding risk as an objectively measurable phenomenon and uncertainty
as an objective unknown. (See notes 1 and 2, p. 34.)

[2] Hart, *op. cit.* Uncertainty proper cannot be insured against. Knowledge under
uncertainty is quite imperfect.

It is critically important for us to observe here that in the purely competitive economy of classical theory, business units were conceived to be subject in the long run only to objectively measurable and predictable alternatives. As a result, they experienced only skill and risk differentials. In complex markets, however, the number and size of firms are such, and the kind of competition they practice so different, that the impersonal market forces of classical theory are joined and/or altered by personalized relations which are objectively unpredictable.[1] Because of this, these forces can be distinguished from those usually considered in economic theory.[2]

Atomistic Firms May Be Subject to Risk. As a working postulate, then, we propose that the atomistic firms of long-run pure competition theory are subject only to risk. Let us say a risk pattern prevails among industries which distinguishes one from another. It may be that one industry is influenced more strongly by weather conditions than another. Therefore, it has risks related to the "probable" adversities of mother nature. Obviously, the importance of weather, or more generally of any other probabilistically determined business component, differs from industry to industry. Decision-making in these cases involves choice between the alternative payoffs statistically evaluated. If, then, the risks of a given activity are great, the market must provide large enough payoffs. If the market returns are excessive, new firms will enter and normal returns will result. If market returns are inadequate, old firms will leave the industry and normal returns will ensue. A fair-return competitive equilibrium tends to arise in time.

Oligopolists and Returns for Risk and Uncertainty. Under pure competition, the economy guarantees long-run differences in net returns *within any given industry* on the single basis of rent differentials attributable to differences in skills.[3] As between industries, long-run differentials relate only to risk. The rents for skill and risk are, in classical economics, costs of production. In the long run, the purely competitive system guarantees that all costs of surviving firms will be covered.

[1] Knight, Hicks, Hart and others. And see D. Miller and M. Starr, *Executive Decisions and Operations Research* (Englewood Cliffs: Prentice Hall, 1960), pp. 79–98.

[2] And see C. W. Churchman, *Prediction and Optimal Decision* (Englewood Cliffs: Prentice Hall, 1961), p. 170, where he observes that under "uncertainty" the past is unknown and, hence, we have two choices: (1) turn our backs on the situation, or (2) attempt to do something about it. In effect, the attempt involves converting subjective values into a similar "form" as the objective probabilities one finds under risk. Earlier F. Ramsey, "Truth and Probability," in *The Foundation of Mathematics and Other Logical Essays*, (London: Kegan Paul, 1931), had contended that subjective probabilities could always be assigned. But Knight, A. Wald *Statistical Decision Functions* (New York: John Wiley and Sons, 1950), and others did not accept this idea fully.

[3] A. Marshall, *Principles of Economics*, 8th Edition (London: Macmillan, 1938), pp. 613–14 . . . in trades where the work of management consists chiefly in superintendence, the earnings of management follow closely the amount of work done.

A space economy, as noted, adds uncertainty to risk and skills. This inclusion is clearly necessary when it is recalled that the uncertainty intrinsic (and special) to a space economy is that which is due to competition from identifiable rivals. By the very nature of the relations involved, these rivals are not atomistic. They are, in fact, significant in size, at least in their own market areas, limited in extent as these tend to be by transport cost, availability of sites, and other geographical features.[1] These rivals produce similar or at least competitive products. Most important, the type of competition we visualize is not predictable; there are no objective probabilities available to the decision-maker to help him in selecting among his alternatives.[2]

Uncertainty is at its highest where the inroads of competitors are likely to be substantial, where the market frequently degenerates into a "dog eat dog" affair, and where the spatial market pattern is such that, from one market area to another, the particular regional economy in which a would-be efficient firm must operate might at any moment become chaotic.[3] Between industries, then, firms are entitled to returns commensurate with whatever risk and uncertainty patterns may be found to exist. Of course, the risk a firm runs could be great while its uncertainty might be small, or *vice versa*. In any case, the practice of organizing production factors under uncertainty is already a constrained-complex matter; from the standpoint of entrepreneurial *services*, the return for uncertainty may readily be seen to be functional, as will be further stressed in Chapters 5, 9, and 13.

Uncertainty and Pure Competition

It is fair to ask whether or not some uncertainty is present under pure competition, and certainly Knight dealt primarily with a competitive situation in his discussion of uncertainty. In similar vein, it would also be fair to claim that the mercurial tastes of consumers are surely not all measurable in terms of known probability distributions, and yet they play an important role in classical economics. How can we reconcile these observations with our previous discussion?

We suggest that the existence of a chaotic demand for a particular product is chiefly a short-run phenomenon. Companies with a long history are able to forecast their sales fairly well on the basis of anticipated disposable income and other projections. In effect, a sales function becomes discernible.

[1] E. Chamberlin, *The Theory of Monopolistic Competition*, 5th edition (Cambridge: Harvard University Press, 1946) Appendix C, and J. Robinson, *The Economics of Imperfect Competition* (London: Macmillan and Co., 1934), Book III.

[2] F. H. Hahn, "A Note on Profit and Uncertainty," *Economica*, N. S., Vol. XIV, (August, 1947), pp. 211–25, 211 . . . The organizational function includes planning output, setting price policy, and deciding among policies which involve a great deal of uncertainty. If not for these, management could be delegated entirely to a salaried employee.

[3] The economic upheaval suggested here for a given market area is not to be confused with the cycle behavior of the economy which may be predictable.

Moreover the policies and practices of *atomistic competitors*, in response to varying demand, can be forejudged, whereas in complex oligopolistic markets competitive responses remain somewhat unpredictable. Whatever uncertainty may be defined to hold in pure competition must, therefore, have exclusively short-run status and fail to have any roots in what may be styled the unpredictable policies and reactions of firms. They can have roots only in demand and here too the theory ruled uncertainty out. This is, of course, not the same as saying that classical theorists and their followers did not recognize that demand may sometimes practically disappear nor did they rule out the possibility of its reaching hitherto unimagined magnitudes. It is simply that if tastes for a product and/or the policies of firms prove to be extremely variable, the state is either one of risk or uncertainty, depending upon whether or not significant probability values could have been assigned to the state affected by these forces before these forces occurred. In practice, classical economics assumed that these probabilities prevailed and did not deal with behavioral uncertainties. One might also presume that all businessmen evaluated other uncertainties in an identical way.

Space, Oligopoly, and Uncertainty: Chaos or Order

Earlier we questioned whether or not chaos must rule in a system where personality differences enter into the action-reaction process and where decision-makers would thereby tend to weight alternative uncertainties differently. At this point, we can rough out certain properties of our ultimate conclusions as well as provide an answer to that question by reconsidering below our matrix (7) of Chapter 2. However, before we reexamine this matrix, let us note that henceforth the term uncertainty is used in this book in a generic sense—i.e. to include any type of uncertainty which may be conceived to have been part of classical economics *and* the behavioral uncertainty of primary concern to us. Whenever stress is or is not to be placed on behavioral uncertainty, for example, depending on whether we are referring to oligopolistic investments or, say, occupational uncertainty involving the physical survival of the factor (e.g. deep pit coal-mining), the meaning intended will either be apparent or specified.

The Investment Project and Resource Allocation. Whatever the basis for assigning subjective probabilities—and this is not really central to the theory —the decision-maker possesses in (2–7) only the prerequisites for making an investment decision. The solution is not indicated in the matrix unless the decision-maker is following a particular type of decision criterion, e.g., the Bernoulli principle of summing the expected (i.e., mean) payoffs under each uncertainty state in each column and selecting the column that promises the highest expected value.

$$(2\text{-}7) \quad \hat{U} = \begin{bmatrix} \hat{X}_{1a} & \hat{X}_{1b} & \cdots & \hat{X}_{1f} \\ \hat{X}_{2a} & \hat{X}_{2b} & \cdots & \hat{X}_{2f} \\ \cdot & \cdot & & \cdot \\ \cdot & \cdot & & \cdot \\ \cdot & \cdot & & \cdot \\ \hat{X}_{ta} & \hat{X}_{tb} & \cdots & \hat{X}_{tf} \end{bmatrix}$$

Suppose, for example, that two columns, b and f, dominate all others. Let element $\hat{X}_{1f}$ proffer the highest expected return while element $\hat{X}_{tf}$ proffers the lowest expected return. As the alternative, element $\hat{X}_{1b}$ may promise a rather high return but not nearly as high as $\hat{X}_{1f}$; in turn $\hat{X}_{tb}$ points, let us assume, to the lowest expected return in column b although this return is more favorable than $\hat{X}_{tf}$. Suppose further that all other corresponding expected payoffs in b and f are identical. Now, a conservative entrepreneur (for example, one who maximizes the minimum payoff) would tend to select column b, anticipating that under the worst circumstances he would have maximized his minimum return. Of course, an entrepreneur applying a different decision criterion might make a different choice. We shall refer to the range of returns applicable to the actual decision (i.e., the column in $\hat{U}$ actually chosen) as the risk and uncertainty *accepted* by the decision-maker.[1] The economic meaning of selecting a column in $\hat{U}$ simply involves selecting an investment project at a specific location. Clearly there will be only one actual or *ex post* return realized from the project *at a point in time*, namely that return attributable to the combination of risk and uncertainty that actually occurs. In terms of the matrix, only one element in the column chosen will obtain, *ex post*.

It is central to the theory that among surviving firms the *ex post* returns earned over time will tend to conform to the risk and uncertainty pattern accepted in the system. This proposition recognizes that the short-run risk and uncertainty range *accepted* by one firm may well be different from that accepted by another, simply because different firms apply different decision criteria. Those members of an industry who survive the rigors of competition tend, in any case, to face not only a comparable range of risk and uncertainty

---

[1] Given the location (or the investment project, *etc.*), one may identify and then evaluate the measure of risk and uncertainty *accepted* by the entrepreneur as follows: To recall part of our procedure from Chapter 2: first we select the highest return in matrix (7) of Chapter 2 under the chosen column, and further make note of the related uncertainty state. Then we examine the applicable A matrix *for this uncertainty* to ascertain the lowest return. If this lowest return [see the matrix (1) in Chapter 2] has a "significant" probability [see the matrix (2) in Chapter 2], the weighted difference between the expected and lowest likely payoffs serves as the basis for our measure of risk. [There are various ways which could be used in weighting the expected and lowest likely values; we shall not, however, go into this matter here.] Proceeding similarly with respect to the lowest return under the worst uncertainty state, that is, weighting the lowest weighted return under the worst uncertainty and taking the difference between it and the lowest return under the best uncertainty state yields the basis for our measure of uncertainty. And see note 1, p. 16 in Chapter 2 for further details.

through entry and exit, but the *ex post* return they earn over time will conform to the *accepted* risk and uncertainty. This is not equivalent to saying that all firms *within an industry* will realize identical factor returns, for manifestly differential skills within the industry will enable some firms to provide higher rates of return than others. It seems reasonable, however, that *survivors* in an industry will have tended to apply the same decision criteria, and in the long run to have earned returns commensurate with the prevailing differential abilities and the risk-uncertainty range that is accepted.[1]

A Mapping of Returns. It follows that rates of returns would vary from the zero-level under conditions of perfect certainty to very high rates of returns under conditions of risk and uncertainty. Moreover, inter-industry rates of return tend to be continuous, inasmuch as surviving firms in industries subjected to greater risk and uncertainty obtain commensurately higher rates of return. The notion of rates of return varying in direct relation to risk and uncertainty holds true provided that decision-makers prefer lower risk and uncertainty for any given rate of return: that is, so long as they have no positive preference for gambling.[2] Assuming choices are transitive, higher expected returns are required if more risky and uncertain ventures are to be selected.

An Example. The theory of risk and uncertainty and its influence on rates of return may be summarized by considering a case in which the realized returns in industry A are greater than the set indicated by the accepted risk and uncertainty range. In other words, we assume that the firms in industry A can do no wrong. Fortune is on their side, at least in the short run, in the sense that the most propitious uncertainty state exists.

Suppose the given firms happen to be subject to a smaller accepted risk and uncertainty than those in an industry earning lower returns. *Then* it follows that the relative short-run returns to the firms in industry A are even higher than decision-makers conjectured them to be. The invisible hand of competition must, however, come into play, *provided entry is open*. As potential entrants observe the disparity of payoffs *vis-à-vis* the risk and uncertainty accepted, entry will occur, thus lowering the rate of return in the industry in question. We find, accordingly, a tendency for the industry to expand and the proper hierarchy of rents plus profits—based in proportion to risk and uncertainty—to come into being. Alternatively, if this short-run uncertainty state happened to be unduly favorable, it would seem likely that a change in luck would take place in the long run.

Good or bad fortune in the short run tends to have lasting impact on the

---

[1] This contention is in the same spirit as A. A. Alchian's "Uncertainty, Evolution, and Economic Theory," *Journal of Political Economy*, LVIII (1950), pp. 211–221.

[2] This same assumption has been made to analyze choices involving risk by expected utility maximizers. Cf. M. Friedman and L. J. Savage, "The Utility Analysis of Choices Involving Risk," *Journal of Political Economy*, LVI (1948), pp. 279–304.

industry by shaping the character of the firms' managers. Thus, decision-makers within the industry who have poorly conceived matrices of expected returns, or who make the wrong investment because, for example, they were maximiners in an industry where more daring policies succeed, are eventually eliminated. In the long run, the entrepreneurs who survive in an industry are those who have made the "right" decision. Their firms will tend to have the proper set of *ex post* rates of return on capital.

Although this chapter is not the place to discuss in detail the following principle (which stems from the risk-uncertainty matrix and the *ex post* solution just recorded), we suggest that underlying an oligopoly economy, subject as it is to risk *and* uncertainty, is a set of rational economic rewards. This set is comparable to those sets which apply to systems characterized by risk or by "certainty" alone. Indeed, to contend otherwise, owing to the indeterminacy so often characteristic of oligopoly models, is tantamount to accepting particular short-run models that seek to explain short-run oligopolistic behavior as if equivalent to long-run results. More to the point, the acceptance of a kinked demand curve (where c in equation (1) assumes great values) or the acceptance of oligopolistic indeterminacy in the long run requires a denial of the deductive implications of the risk-uncertainty matrix, i.e., a denial that entrepreneurs are able to identify returns commensurate with the risk and uncertainty they have accepted. We maintain instead that the risk-uncertainty matrix provides a framework for viewing a free enterprise economy, and that entrepreneurs are able to identify instances of windfalls (positive or negative) over a period of time. We further maintain, and shall demonstrate in full in Part 2 of the book, that oligopolistic rigidities may well prevail in the short run (i.e., c in (1) will be a large positive number for a while) as firms in one production center simply watch those in another. The combination of entry at near-by *and* at distant sites increases, however, the likelihood of maximining; in turn, this means that the c in (1) approaches unity in value over a range of prices as an acceptance of smaller returns and non-hypercompetitive price reductions characterizes the maturing industry.

III. CONCLUSION AND SUMMARY

The complex pattern of risks and uncertainties that one finds in modern economic society points to a range of prospective returns for business firms formed partly by the existing risk probabilities and partly by conjectured payoffs. By comparing the best expected-accepted return with the lowest statistically relevant return, we envision "a range" bounded by the maximum return an entrepreneur can reasonably *expect* and the lowest return he could logically *fear*. In the process of selecting alternative locations, investments, processes of production, and so on, decision-makers cause slightly different ranges of risk and uncertainty to prevail among industries which might otherwise be identical. The character of industries reflects not only the risk and uncertainty that underline an activity, but the type of entrepreneur who is attracted to the occupation.

In modern society, several uncertainty states [rows in the matrix $\hat{U}$] are confronted, and it is, accordingly, impossible to designate a "normal" return in the *ex ante* sense. By the very meaning of uncertainty, one can never know which particular uncertainty state will occur. On the other hand, risk probability distributions are well-defined. They fail to point, however, to a unique rate of return because they must be considered in conjunction with the full number of alternative uncertain states (and consequent alternative returns) that prevail.

Some industries with a given range of accepted risk and uncertainty will —at any moment—experience much greater rewards than others of equal accepted risk and uncertainty. Over time, we should expect that industries plagued with bad fortune in their uncertainty combination sooner or later gain better fortune. Either this must happen or else the industry is actually subjected to greater hazards, in which event the prevailing low return for relatively large risk and uncertainty will eliminate some members and raise the level of returns allocable to survivors. The underlying true risk and uncertainty range requires that a set of inter-industry returns exists which makes the yield among industries fully commensurate in the long run. The ultimate regulator of the economy is therefore its inherent competition; and this competition will be governed by the returns that take place in the system as they relate to the matrix of risk and uncertainty.

It is, accordingly, significant to note that disparities in returns tend to be eliminated in time if entry and exit of competitive firms are maintained. All industrialists (and investors) who select a given activity subject to a particular risk and uncertainty require a return commensurate with the risk and uncertainty they accept. The rent they receive for risk and the profit they earn for uncertainty must be set on the basis of an onto mapping from the indices of risk and uncertainty that prevail.[1] Otherwise entry and exit results.[2]

[1] This elementary requirement defers to our definitions of risk and uncertainty. Specifically, the indices of risk and uncertainty are based on the difference between expected and lowest likely returns—including losses. In contrast, the rent for risk and the profit for uncertainty will be seen to be based on the difference between the value product formed by the average cost and the quantity sold of a hypothetical firm operating under certainty and the corresponding value product of the firm which earns the amount commensurate to its accepted risk and uncertainty. We shall later in the book specify how this "commensurate" amount is determined. For the present, we require only the understanding that the indices of risk and uncertainty are predicated on the expected and lowest likely returns as defined earlier, and that long-run rents and profits are always based on positive values—e.g. the positive difference between average revenue times the quantity sold and average cost times the quantity sold; hence these returns simply *reflect* the indices in question.

[2] For readers who wish to probe into possible exceptions to our theory it may be desirable to include here a special case which, at first glance, would appear to be a real exception to our claims above. We will, however, actually find that, as in the example cited in the text,

It is finally relevant to note again that for some of the general purposes of this book, we could define an industry as a collection of firms subject to the same index of uncertainty. We might, of course, narrow the definition to require the same risk index as well. And, if our focus centered on applied economics, such as the anti-trust laws, our definition might require (1) a similarity of products (specifying what is meant by this), as well as (2) the same risk index and uncertainty index. Whatever the definition be, a competitive space economy in the long run is overwhelmingly influenced by businessmen who—within any well-defined industry—are homogeneous in motivation, expectation, and requirement.[1]

the open-competitive entry and exit process must leave a hierarchy of returns commensurate with the index of risk and uncertainty.

Consider the possibility of entrepreneurs in a given industry who consistently maximin but, as a consequence, suffer lower returns than they would if they had resolved the decision problem differently. In fact, one may ask, is it not conceivable that the maximin selection might involve a location (or investment) which proffers a lower subset of expected returns (i.e. for the several traces of X) under all uncertainty combinations with the exception of the trace of X applicable to the worst uncertainty combination? And is it not also conceivable that, in addition, the lowest likely return under the worst uncertainty combination might be significantly lower for the maximin strategy than it is for the alternative strategy? It could, then, possibly follow that the risk and uncertainty index would be greater for the maximin strategy than for another strategy. In turn, if we further suppose that the uncertainties are true uncertainties, in the sense that each is as likely to happen as any other, the long-run payoffs would then appear to sum up to a lower total for the larger risk and uncertainty index than that which would hold for decision-makers who decide not to follow the maximin criterion. Two reasons, however, militate against this exception to the claims (and theory) entered in the text:

(1) If the firms are maximiners, and the E(A) under the worst uncertainty combination is greater for the selected strategy than holds for an alternative strategy, while its related lowest possible return is sufficiently lower than that applicable to the alternative strategy, it is scarcely conceivable that the decision-makers would not revalue the lowest return further downward. Such revaluation could cause the E(A) under this uncertainty actually to be lower than that applicable to the other strategy, in which case it would not be the maximin compared to the other.

(2) But even if we assume that no revaluation of particular low payoffs takes place, it follows that if the average returns are lower for a larger accepted risk and uncertainty than for a smaller one, the character of industry will change as new "wiser" decision-makers and firms enter, or some existing decision-makers and firms exit. Whether or not an industry remains in the maximin camp or finds itself in some other category depends on the number and type of people in the economy who have entrepreneurial potential and desire. What really counts is that our theory must work in the long run, for those firms which have consistently accepted a higher risk and uncertainty than did others, and which continue in their particular activity, must receive the higher total return. This consistency is the "time" guaranteed property of competitive entry and exit and of our matrix of risk and uncertainty and its associated theory.

[1] We observed in Chapter 2 that certain risk takers might revalue selected large payoffs under a given strategy such that, compared to alternative strategies, the mean they visualized would be relatively lower in terms of utilities than it would be in terms of dollars. Conservatism of this kind might be expected to be coterminous with a "maximining" nature under conditions of uncertainty. The accepted risk and uncertainty index of the subject decision-

Review of Chapters 1–3 and Preview of Chapters 4 and 5

We have in the last two chapters turned our attention to the problem of determining how uncertainty affects the decisions of the economic man; and we observed that oligopoly is the outgrowth of a watchful-waiting policy between firms distributed over an economic space. Manifestly, conjectures about the actions and reactions of rivals reflect (and arouse) a state of uncertainty. Our next chapter will add to this theme by demonstrating even more forcefully the idea that oligopoly and economic space go hand in hand. However, it does not do this by formally proving the correspondence between oligopoly and economic space; such demonstration—via an analytically advanced model—is reserved for Chapter 6. Rather, Chapter 4 points to this conclusion indirectly by showing why pure and monopolistic competition are actually incompatible with economic space. We thus are left at the end of the chapter with the basic question: "what remains of economic theory if, in a system over which distances prevail and are important, pure competition is a theoretical impossibility?" Chapter 5 will try to answer this question. It outlines our theory of a long-run oligopolistic equilibrium. From this vantage point, we can probe fully in Parts 2 and 3 into the fundamental properties and details of our theory of the firm in economic space.

Appendix to Chapter 3

A Brief Note on Risk and Uncertainty in Theory and in Practice

A few further words about how the risk and uncertainty matrix (7) ties up with abstract economic theory warrant brief inclusion here. In this regard, we stress our anticipation that "in the practice of the short run" no distinction is typically made by entrepreneurs between two sets of risk and uncertainty, where each is possessed of the same total but where different values prevail for the risk and uncertainty components of the two sets. Nevertheless—as noted in the text—in theory we must maintain the (classical) practice of distinguishing rents from profits, and hence risk from uncertainty. The purpose of this appendix is, then, to illustrate our claim that "in practice" errant entrepreneurs did not distinguish readily between, say, a 4%

makers would thereby tend to be rather low in the hierarchy of risk and uncertainty. Though not vital to our theory, we propose that a common perspective prevails within a risk-uncertainty group in revaluing dollar payoffs downward (see paragraph 3 of note 2, p. 10, Chapter 2). Therefore decision-makers reject the strategies which have payoffs for which disparity exists between the different utilities derived and the varying dollar amounts expected. It follows, accordingly, that in the long run we conceive not only of decision-makers who are similar in "make-up" within an industry, but we are able to focus our attention strictly on actual dollar expectations. The concept of conjectured utilities thus serves essentially as a device to explain short-run behavior alone.

risk $+2\%$ uncertainty payoff and a 3% risk $+3\%$ uncertainty, considering instead the two combined, but that long-run survivors will distinguish between the two.

Assume that an industry is faced with two uncertainties and several risks. By the definition proposed in Chapter 2, let risk be measured to equal L and uncertainty to equal M. $L + M$, we assume, equals Q. Suppose another industry is faced with some risks and several uncertainties with the total $L + M$ again adding up to Q. Clearly, if the very best expected return compared to the very lowest likely return in each set involves the same weighted differential, it does not matter that in the one case there might be more alternative in-between values (i.e., states of uncertainty) than in the other, unless we suppose (a) unequal probabilities for in-between states, which supposition rejects the pure meaning of uncertainty and hence would have short-run significance alone, or (b) we contend that the utility for dollars cannot be measured by the dollar amounts for the "in-between values," which contention would do violence to the meaning of "in-between values." Most important is the fact that the constraints on entry are the same in the two situations. This identity is easily seen if we apply our measures of risk and uncertainty to matrix (7).

In contrast to the above, note that if one industry had risk E and uncertainty F, again adding up to Q, where $E \neq L$ and $F \neq M$, the degree of strain (ulcers if you will) to which the entrepreneurs would be subject must be different. We propose, accordingly, that long-run survivors do distinguish between the risk and uncertainty components from industry to industry. (As already indicated in Chapter 3, we shall later suggest that in an oligopolistic industry an essential requirement is that the member firms be subject to the identically same range of uncertainty, though others might prefer to require an identical range for the risk set and the uncertainty set experienced in the business. Most importantly, we shall present in Chapter 5 the basis for the statement that the strain to which entrepreneurs are subject differs if $F \neq M$ and that long-run survivors accordingly must distinguish between these uncertainties.)

4

Impacts of Space on Economic Markets

OUR OBJECTIVE IN THIS CHAPTER IS THREEFOLD. One, we will review the spatial distribution of people and things which underlies each of the traditional simple conceptions of markets in economic theory. Our aim will be to show that extreme kinds of spatial distribution are essential to these market types. Two, as a by-product of the above, we will consider the extent to which the simple market types are compatible with, let us say, an empirically verifiable spatial ordering. This examination will show that the introduction of space requires practically no modification of some traditional market types (the complex markets in particular), some modification of others, and the elimination of the most extensively used traditional type.[1] Finally, we will explore in an introductory fashion the implications of these modifications both for theory and for policy. These implications are particularly significant where normative theory and empirical research are concerned.[2]

I. NONSPATIAL MARKET TYPES

General Category—Buyers and Sellers at Adjacent Points

Perhaps the simplest conception of a market is that in which all sellers are located at one point and all buyers at an adjacent point. Land rent may then be considered a function of differential fertility alone, and transportation costs assumed to be zero.

This general category admits of all the traditional market types in economic theory. In the simple competitive market type (which includes pure or perfect competition and monopolistic competition), the product of each firm competes with the product of firms belonging to an identifiable group *and*

[1] Throughout the text we will observe differences between the simple and complex markets. However, a basic distinction should be emphasized here. By simple market, we mean pure or monopolistic competition or simple monopoly. The complex market types relate, accordingly, to markets in which firms adopt a given policy only after anticipating the likely reaction of rivals to their alternative policies.

[2] Chapter 15 examines in detail the theoretical impact of space on anti-trust policy. References elsewhere in the text point to other writings by the author which examine the impact of space on selected economic policy problems.

the individual seller considers himself to be an unimportant part of the entire market. Sellers in the market are indifferent to buyers, and buyers are indifferent to sellers. The simple market type also includes the pure monopoly firm. We may further speak of the complex market types (such as homogeneous duopoly or oligopoly) when sellers and buyers are located at adjacent points. In sum, when sellers and buyers are at adjacent points, all classical market types are possible.

1. The Perfectly Competitive Market—Short Run. Perfect competition is frequently defined to exist when, to the simple competitive market features of (a) seller independence, (b) an identifiable group of competitive firms, and (c) one's self-evaluation of unimportance, we add such additional-supporting (i.e., reinforcing) characteristics as (d) homogeneity of product and person, (e) perfect knowledge of market data among sellers and buyers, (f) complete flexibility of prices, and (g) mobility of hired factors over time. Many sellers and full access by the buyer to any seller are customarily also added to emphasize the unimportance of the individual seller. Although a case may be made for the existence of pure competition *vis à vis* perfect competition without some of these reinforcing conditions, in this book we will generally treat these two forms of the simple market as if they are identical. As a generalization *in this chapter*, we will more often than not refer to perfect and imperfect competition rather than to pure or monopolistic competition.

One final comment is needed about this market. Economists usually associate free entry and exit with perfect competition; but, this free entry and exit condition is not a short-run requirement. During the short run, the horizontal nature of the average revenue curve (AR), not any upward or downward shift, is alone stressed. We, accordingly, exclude free entry and exit from the short-run specifications of the perfectly competitive market.

2. The Imperfectly Competitive Market—Short Run. Varying the data only slightly, so that differentiation of either the product or the person is assumed, establishes the conceptual basis for the simple imperfectly competitive market, henceforth called the imperfectly competitive market. Perfect knowledge, etc., may remain, if the theorist desires.

3. Unorganized and Organized Homogeneous Oligopoly—Short Run. The unorganized homogeneous oligopolistic market type is also suggested by a slight change of the basic data when buyers and sellers are assumed to be located at adjacent points in space. Here, rather than hypothesize many sellers, we generally assume the existence of only a few sellers. What is most vital, however, is that each seller *must be* mindful of the others. This mindfulness of rivals and the related action-reaction expectations in the market lead to complex relations between the firms rather than simple relations. As a rule we shall think of buyers with limited access to sellers, and of inflexible prices over short periods of time. The unorganized character of the market will be emphasized by the fact that—when applicable—we shall consider each seller to be independent and relatively significant in size.

In the absence of qualifications as to size and independence, the price-leadership market may be expected.[1] Such leader-follower markets belong with cartels, as together they form component parts of the organized, homogeneous oligopoly market.

Free entry and exit may or may not prevail in the short run of a homogeneous oligopoly. Indeed, it is as extra to the meaning of homogeneous oligopoly in the short run as it is to the short run of perfect and imperfect competition. In economic thought, free or restricted entry or exit—in any market—is identifiable essentially as a long-run condition. And it is only in long-run analysis that we must specify the existence or nonexistence of this feature of a market.

4. Unorganized and Organized Heterogeneous Oligopoly—Short Run. If imperfect competition is modified by substituting a few sellers for many sellers, the result (with other minor variations that the reader can readily apply) is the complex market type referred to as heterogeneous oligopoly. This market may, of course, be unorganized, but, if domination exists in the form of price leadership or other agreements, it is organized. Distinctively defined rivals is the main characteristic feature of the oligopoly market, and generally it goes hand and glove with small numbers. As with homogeneous oligopoly, free or restricted entry or exit is a long-run specification.

5. Unorganized and Organized Homogeneous and Heterogeneous Duopoly—Short Run. If the number of sellers in homogeneous or heterogeneous oligopoly is reduced to two, clearly the result is homogeneous or heterogeneous duopoly. No additional description is required.

6. The Long Run. A long-run state can exist for all the above markets. The long-run state is obtained when free entry and free exit conditions prevail, and when ample time has elapsed in which the fixed factor relations that existed in the short run have been altered.

7. Monopoly. One seller in an industry posits the existence of monopoly. The product of the seller is not a substitute for the product of identifiable rivals nor for the products of an identifiable group. Substitution exists only in the broad terms of one expenditure being part of all expenditures. By definition, no entry into the industry arises, nor is it conjectured to arise in the foreseeable future.

8. Other Types. There are several other market classifications which may be made. We may speak of markets characterized by destructive competition, discriminatory competition, fair and unfair competition, international cartel arrangements, and other special situations. Generally speaking,

---

[1] Of course, price-leadership markets may also include several sellers of the same size, but quite often there exists one very large seller and several smaller sellers, one large seller or a few large sellers and many small sellers, and like combinations of unequal sizes of firms. See W. Fellner, *Competition Among the Few: Oligopoly and Similar Market Structures* (New York: Alfred A. Knopf, Inc., 1949), pp. 136–140. Also see C. E. Ferguson, *Microeconomic Theory* (Chicago: Irwin and Co., 1966), pp. 286–296.

these market phenomena are actually subtypes of those outlined above. While their inclusion may be desirable for some particular analytical emphasis, these divisions are not required here.

General Category—Point-Formed Buyers, Scattered Sellers

A more realistic—but largely nonspatial—conception of a market is that in which only the buyers are located at a given point while the sellers are scattered around the consumption center. This category is largely a reflection of the von Thünen system.[1] It differs essentially from the previous general category in that land rent must be considered a function of distance as well as of fertility. Transportation costs which increase with distance become, therefore, a complete substitute for the "distance" land rent at the extensive margin of cultivation. Under this arrangement, the transportation cost and the distance-land rental costs at any seller's location are basic costs of production which must be defrayed in the long run in the same way as fertility land rent, labor cost, and capital cost.

This general category admits of the same nonspatial market conceptions already outlined for the preceding general category. When only the buyers are visualized as being located at a given point, perfect and imperfect competition as well as oligopoly, duopoly, and monopoly may still exist.

The conception of all buyers at the same point in space supports the possibility of a single price prevailing in the market. Net revenues would be the same for any one seller on the unit sales to any buyer, and each seller would be indifferent to each buyer insofar as the buyer's location is concerned. Thus if sellers are numerous, consider themselves individually unimportant, and are homogeneous with respect to product and person (except for location and resulting rent), the market formed when all buyers are at one point may be the perfectly competitive market. A single price would prevail in the market and the seller's average revenue curve would be horizontal. If, on the other hand, sellers are few (or two in number) and each watches the other,[2] homogeneous oligopoly (or duopoly) exists. This market may or may not be organized.

If all buyers are located at a point and there are many sellers, each differentiated as to product or person (in addition to location), imperfect competition exists. If the sellers are few (or two) in number and/or are conscious of each other, there is heterogeneous oligopoly (or duopoly). Obviously, the market may or may not be organized. Indeed, if there is only one seller located at a distance from buyers who are concentrated at a point, monopoly would exist. All of the classical market types are, therefore, possible when buyers are located at a point in economic space.

[1] J. H. von Thünen, *Der Isolierte Staat In Beziehung auf Landwirtschaft und National-ökonomie*, 3rd. Ed. (Berlin Schumacher-Zarchlin, 1875).

[2] F. Machlup, *The Economics of Sellers Competition* (Baltimore, The Johns Hopkins Press, 1952), pp. 100–101.

The conception of a seller(s) located at a distance(s) from a consumption center causes rent to be a partial function of distance; accordingly, space becomes an independent force in economic analysis. This conception changes traditional economic theory only slightly in that any general equilibrium system based on it must include land rent *plus transportation cost* as the function to be minimized. Apart from this technical modification of theory, the impact of the assumption of a seller(s) at a distance from a point-formed buying center is not great. The traditional market types therefore remain effective descriptions of the economy when sellers are scattered but buyers are concentrated.

General Category—Point-Formed Sellers, Scattered Buyers

Another spatial conception which in large part supports traditional economic analysis is that in which all sellers are located at a point while all buyers are scattered around the production center at varying distances from the sellers. In this case, rental payments for land by sellers would be a function of fertility alone, while transportation costs would appear as a determinant of the rental cost to buyers.[1] Because, even under the conditions of zero production costs and of identical demand among buyers, each extension of the sales radius generally elicits a downward change in the profit-maximizing f.o.b. net-mill price of the seller, the equilibrium for this economy is basically of a monopolistic order.[2]

This general type of market structure requires, in a sense, the abandonment of the perfectly competitive market type as a norm. On the other hand,

[1] Except for the case of the seller who absorbs freight costs under a discriminatory delivered-price system, the buyers would directly bear the burden of transport costs based on their distance from the seller. See J. Robinson, *Economics of Imperfect Competition* (London: The Macmillan Co., 1946), p. 89, " . . . the customer must take costs of transport into account."

[2] See M. L. Greenhut, *Plant Location in Theory and in Practice* (Chapel Hill: University of North Carolina Press, 1956), pp. 42–57, where it is shown that the elasticity of total demand varies with an extension of the sales radius. This variation occurs in accordance with the basic kinds of individual demands that exist, even if each individual demand apart from the location of the buyer is identical. Thus the monopolistic seller who is expanding his sales radius finds that spatially separated buyers cause a downward move in f.o.b. mill price—whenever the individual demands are of the decreasing elasticity type. In a rather unusual contrasting case, i.e., when the individual demands are of constant or increasing elasticity, a price increase is indicated by an increase in the sales area. A priori, the general case is the former. The vital point apart from the direction of the change in price is the distinction between changes in monopoly price due to expansion of the firm's trading area and the fixed monopoly price that would continue in the face of expanding demand in non-spatial markets. That is to say, in nonspatial models the monopolist's price will remain the same when his market expands, his marginal costs are constant, and all of his buyers have identical gross demands. In contrast, buyers at greater distances just do not have as strong a net demand for a seller's good as do buyers situated nearby, *ceteris paribus*; thus the spatial monopolist reduces his price in the general case as his market (area) expands.

we may retain without any qualification the remaining market types already described in this chapter.

Perfect competition should be abandoned in the sense that it cannot exist under the designated location assumption in the same way as in the previously discussed general categories. The market becomes somewhat imperfect when buyers are dispersed over space simply because the expansion of the firm's output tends to require a change in price. Thus, we find the same effect as when the monopolistic competitor changes his total market sales; i.e., a variation in price occurs. We may have perfect competition only if we assume that there are many buyers with identical demands who are grouped around the production center at set distances. And even then we would have to imagine that any increase in the firm's output involves the maintenance of the same proportion of sales over the several distances within the market.[1] More important is the following intuitively obvious proposition: when *many* sellers are at a point in space with buyers distributed over the plain, freight costs on the final product must be very insignificant; otherwise branch plants would be established. And if branch plants are set up, sellers are no longer at a point. In particular, the perfectly competitive market just does not materialize when the cost of distance is significant and only sellers are located together at a point in economic space. It is, indeed, only when freight costs on the final product are insignificant that a beginning assumption of all sellers at a point may be conceived to eventuate in perfect competition. But then there is no real cost of distance and accordingly one would be left with a trivial example of economic space.

The imperfectly competitive market could conceivably exist under the spatial distribution of many sellers at a point with buyers distributed over a plain. And, the simple monopoly over space may prevail. What is distinctive about the distribution of point-formed production with buyers scattered over a plain is the condition that, if freight cost on the final product is significant, each extension of the sales radius brings about a noticeably different price for

---

[1] The general monopoly model of a falling price with an expansion of the sales (area of) the firm has, interestingly enough, a parallel under atomistic competition in space. We cite two situations which reflect this condition. Consider the following:

(1) If the delivered price is the same for all buyers, all sellers (even though atomistic) experience a declining net average revenue on their sales to more distant buyers. That is to say, net revenues decline over distance.

(2) If a uniform, f.o.b. mill price exists but the maximum sales radius is fixed, the net average revenue might prove to be constant. However, any expansion of output by one of many homogeneous sellers will tend to have a different effect when the buyers are scattered than will an expansion of output by one competitor when all buyers are located together. The expansion of output through increased sales to certain buyers located "within the existing sales radius" implies a change in the average sales distance; this, in turn, implies a change in price apart from the total quantity produced. Hence, even the price in an industry where the maximum sales radius is fixed is not necessarily invariant to the expanded output of a microscopic firm.

the seller as the elasticity of demand changes.[1] Regardless of the pricing method (f.o.b., equalizing delivered, *etc.*), the profit a seller obtains on sales to any one buyer will thus differ sharply from that which he obtains on his sales to another more distant buyer, *ceteris paribus*. In other words, there is a well-defined limit to sales at a particular price for any one seller when his sales radius is enlarged. A caveat, however, should be given. If transport costs on the final product are significant, the firm will establish branch plants elsewhere unless, of course, all basic resources in the industry are heroically assumed to exist at the point and transport cost on the raw materials governs the location of firms. Given the resource and transport cost constraints, the Chamberlinean market type is conceptually conceivable, albeit not perfect competition. However, the likely development of substitutable goods produced at a distance and/or the limited size of the market area suggest the existence of oligopoly provided that the transport constraint is operative. (We shall formulate these statements analytically in Chapter 13.)

All the market types except perfect competition are therefore conceptually possible under the assumed "spatial" conditions. But, as suggested above, conceivability and likeliness are two different things. If all sellers are at a point and buyers are scattered, we must anticipate that freight costs on raw materials are relatively high while those on the final product are relatively (but not necessarily absolutely) unimportant. In turn, ignoring the possibility of substitutable goods produced elsewhere and the comparatively small size market (area) which can be expected, the limited space available at the raw material center alone *suggests* the likely existence of what, in effect, may be called a classical example of spaceless oligopoly. Of course, this oligopoly differs from the one typically conceived (where all sellers *and* buyers are at a point) in that there prevails a rental-transportation cost to the buyer, as was specified above in our general category description. This aspect of difference, let us note, actually lies outside the industry under examination (the seller's industry). Thus, the effects in the market when sellers are located at a point and their customers are dispersed at varying distances around them sum to an approximation to the market results when both sellers and their customers are located at adjacent points. Our present assumption of a spatial ordering can, in any case, generally be used by theorists concerned with classical equilibria patterns and market analysis.

Summary of the Nonspatial Market Types

Economists traditionally define the market situation from a temporal standpoint alone. The situs of sellers and buyers (or, let us say, the visualization of their space relations) is not taken into account. But even though space is

---

[1] E. H. Chamberlin, "The Product As an Economic Variable," *Quarterly Journal of Economics*, LXVII (1953), p. 11, " . . . the only buyers who are getting exactly what they want are those few located at the identical points with the shop."

ignored, the traditional market types do not exclude this dimension altogether, as some space relationships are compatible with the classical market types and hence may be assumed if desired. Thus, (1) it may be specified that all the buyers are located at one point and all sellers at a proximate point. This conception allows for complete retention of the market types that economists traditionally describe, but it fails to a large extent to describe conditions in the real world. (2) A better alternative is to assume explicitly that all buyers are located at a point while sellers are geographically separated. This conception of spatial relations, as we have noted, modifies traditional economic theory only by making distance-rent a cost factor of production.[1] (3) The assumption of all sellers located at a point with buyers scattered over space also fits traditional theory, more or less. Except for the perfectly competitive market and to a lesser extent the imperfectly competitive market, this last modification readily permits retention of traditional market types.

II. SPATIAL MARKET TYPES

General Category—Even Dispersions of Buyers and Sellers

The simplest complete spatial distribution exists when both sellers and buyers are rather evenly dispersed over the landscape. This arrangement makes rent a partial function of distance and also sets up a monopolistic type of general equilibrium that possesses certain very special properties which we will mention later in this chapter.[2] The subject type of spatial ordering renders many of the traditional market types irrelevant.

1. The Perfectly Competitive Market—Short and Long Run. Perfect competition does not exist under this alignment of sellers and buyers for the simple reason that price is functionally related to distance. Clearly, when sellers and buyers are dispersed, each seller in space is, to some extent, a monopolist, and, hence, not a perfect competitor.

2. The Imperfectly Competitive Market—Short and Long Run. It is conceivable that an imperfectly competitive market pattern may arise from the defined dispersion of sellers and buyers. But a long-run prototype in the form of monopolistic competition would seem to be impossible in the real world because: (1) a spatial monopolistic competition would require homogeneity in the distribution of resources and population. [The reason for this will be explained in detail later in the book. For the moment, *let it suffice* to say that the monopolistically competitive market distributed over an economic space will be seen to require market areas of hexagonal shape scattered evenly over the space. Only under such pattern will discontinuities and locational (inter-

[1] See E. S. Dunn, Jr., *Location of Agricultural Production* (Gainesville: University of Florida Press, 1954), p. 21.

[2] See M. L. Greenhut, "A General Theory of Plant Location," *Metroeconomica*, VII (1955), pp. 59–72.

dependent) uncertainties not arise; in turn, only then could economic profits be eliminated in the long run.[1]] But the spreading of Mother Nature's gifts evenly over a landscape is scarcely to be expected. (2) Even if these prerequisite conditions are met, it is evident that inter-industry differences in the sizes of hexagons must be expected. And, the different sizes of hexagons that arise due to the different transport conditions of the different products will lead to some concentrations of industries, and these would result in different size concentrations of sellers (and buyers). The development of large and small communities, in turn, must convert any prospective hexagonic market into somewhat uneven size areas, and irregularities would bring out uncertainties and open up the possibilities for long-run profits in the system. That spatially separated sellers would be able to identify their closest competitors leads to other uncertainties. Some market area control by firms and interdependence between all will prevail.

The condition of uneven scattering over space promotes uncertainty and thus precludes the monopolistically competitive market type that admits of a long-run zero-profit equilibrium.[2] Instead, we assert that a spatial dispersion of sellers and buyers, apart from uneven resource distribution, produces a chain oligopoly,[3] a hypercompetitive oligopoly,[4] a kinky demand-curve oligopoly,[5]

---

[1] See A. Lösch, *Die räumliche Ordnung der Wirtschaft* (Jena: Gustav Fischer, 1944), or translation, *The Economics of Location*, trans. by W. H. Woglom with the assistance of W. F. Stolper (New Haven: Yale University Press, 1954), in which the hexagonic market area is established as the polygonic arrangement in space that would yield zero long-run profits. Also see E. Mills and R. Lav, "A Model of Market Areas with Free Entry," *Journal of Political Economy*, 1964, pp. 278–288; and for our own detailed analysis of the issues at hand, see *infra* Chapter 13.

[2] See M. L. Greenhut, *Plant Location in Theory and in Practice, op. cit.* pp. 270–272. Also see W. Isard, *Location and Space Economy* (New York: John Wiley and Sons, Inc., 1956), p. 274, footnote 17. This is a critical matter which E. H. Chamberlin missed. For example, see *Towards A More General Theory of Value* (New York: Oxford University Press, 1952), p. 7, where Chamberlin states that location theory supports monopolistic competition. And see D. Dewey, "Imperfect Competition No Bar to Efficient Production," *Journal of Political Economy*, LXVI (1958) pp. 24–33, where the writer argues that spatial competition does not give rise to the so-called equilibrium of monopolistic competition. In the strictest sense, it supports only the oligopoly side of a monopolistically bent economy.

[3] E. H. Chamberlin, *The Theory of Monopolistic Competition*, 5th ed. (Cambridge: Harvard University Press, 1946), p. 103, " . . . any individual seller is in close competition with no more than a few out of a group . . . Retail establishments scattered throughout an urban area are an instance of what might be called a 'chain' linking of markets." And on p. 104, "the general conclusion must be that the considerations relevant to competition between small numbers are much more generally applicable than might at first be supposed." By confining, in effect, his idea of chain linking of markets to retail establishments, Chamberlin limits his approach and his conception of economic relations.

[4] F. Machlup, *op. cit.*, p. 507, "The kind of grouping created 'sectional oligopolies' within an industry of 'many firms' . . . the result is not any restraint in selling effort or in price competition but merely an attempt to keep things secret . . . "

[5] See P. Sweezy, "Demand Under Conditions of Oligopoly," *Journal of Political Economy*, XLVII (1939), pp. 568–573.

and other oligopoly types,[1] either unorganized or organized.[2] Spatial indivisibility becomes an additive force to any existing uncertainty, as well as to other nonspatially related indivisibilities. They deny the existence of both monopolistic competition and perfect competition.[3]

3. Unorganized and Organized Homogeneous and Heterogeneous Oligopoly and Duopoly—Short and Long Run. The oligopolistic and duopolistic market types (homogeneous and heterogeneous) are intrinsic to a world in which sellers and buyers are dispersed. Economic space restricts the number of firms that will prevail at any point in a broadly defined market area, and the spatial cross-interdependence between firms that arises produces some degree of watchful-waiting in place of atomistic type of action.

4. Monopoly. The monopolistic market is admissible in spatial analysis, but is limited chiefly to the early stage of an industry's development. Over a long enough period of time, rivals may be expected to enter most markets, albeit probably at a distance from the original firm. This kind of entry reflects the natural limit to any firm's demand imposed by transport costs. A spatial duopolistic or oligopolistic market type tends to develop for practically all goods, leaving monopoly chiefly as a conceptual point of departure for other market types. The assumption of a pure monopoly is surely less intriguing when space conceptions are introduced than when such realities are abstracted by the economist.[4]

General Category—Buyers and Sellers Distributed Heterogeneously over Space

As we have noted, an even scattering of sellers and buyers is improbable even

[1] See F. Machlup, "The Characteristics and Classifications of Oligopoly," *Kyklos*, V (1952), pp. 145–163.

[2] J. S. Bain, "Pricing Monopoly and Oligopoly," *American Economic Review*, XXIX (1948), pp. 448–464.

[3] See A. Lösch, *op. cit.*, pp. 82–83; translation, p. 120. Also see G. Ackley, "Spatial Competition in a Discontinuous Market," *Quarterly Journal of Economics*, LVI (1942), pp. 212–230. See E. H. Chamberlin, *The Theory of Monopolistic Competition*, *op. cit.* On the general subject of indivisibility and entry, see, in particular, H. Hines, "Effectiveness of Entry by Already Established Firms," *Quarterly Journal of Economics*, LXXI (1957), pp. 132–150, and R. B. Heflebower, "Economics of Size," *Journal of Business* of the University of Chicago, XXIV, (1951), pp. 252–268.

[4] Any distribution of industry policy has the effect of promoting a seller dispersion and, hence, some buyer dispersion. See J. Sykes "Some Results of Distribution of Industry Policy," *The Manchester School*, XXIII (1955), pp. 1–21; particularly pp. 6 and 14. Also see D. C. Hague and P. K. Newman, *Costs in Alternative Locations: The Clothing Industry* (London: Cambridge University Press, 1952), and this writer's review in the *Southern Economic Journal*, XX (1953), pp. 95–96, which suggested that market areas might not always be point-formed, and that an evaluation of alternative locations on the single basis of costs might therefore be insufficient. It is worth mentioning in this regard that in a country the size of the United States, more so than in a nation of smaller geographical extent, the distribution of sellers and buyers is more likely to yield our spatial market effects than the nonspatial relations of traditional theory.

assuming original homogeneity in the distribution of resources and population, since some concentration of sellers and buyers tends to take place in time due to the different trading areas of the products of firms and the advantages of agglomeration.[1] Such a concentration in space becomes even more likely when heterogeneity of resources and population are assumed to be the natural assignment of nature's gifts. The visual pattern of this space economy includes many sellers at one site, some sellers scattered, many buyers at one site, some buyers scattered, or, in general, a system of alternating troughs and peaks in the number of people, firms, and industries located across the surface of the earth.[2] Uncertainty blankets the system. This type of spatial economy makes distance-rent a cost factor of production and transforms the general equilibrium system into one of a monopolistic order while denying the classical zero economic profit stability of the system.

As with perfect competition, imperfect competition is not very likely to exist under such a distribution of buyers and sellers. Agglomerating gains alone, we have seen, would cause a potentially even distribution within an industry to give way to an uneven distribution, and this uneven distribution ties up with a limited number of sellers over an economic space and behavioral uncertainty to form the core of our present spatial model. Significantly, any zero economic profit, monopolistically competitive type of equilibrium rules out behavioral uncertainty and would be a strict happenstance rather than expected situation.

The other specific spatial types follow the same general order that we described for the first spatial model. Because it was shown there that a stable, zero economic profit, monopolistically competitive equilibrium is not deducible, it follows, indirectly, that the earlier discussion was geared largely to the idea that, even if buyers and sellers in a given industry remained rather evenly distributed, this even distribution would be attributable to forces other than those which inevitably would yield zero profits. Thus, the relations between firms follow the same general form here as they did in the previous general category, albeit here it is stated by definition rather than by deduction that there is no tendency toward long-run zero economic profits. The descriptions of spatial market types are, therefore, the same when resources and people are initially distributed heterogeneously as when they are originally dispersed in space in a generally homogeneous pattern. Complex market types characterize the spatial economy.

Summary of the Spatial Market Types

Myriads of space formulations may be conceived. We may imagine buyers and sellers scattered evenly or unevenly, in clusters of increasing or decreasing

---

[1] See footnote 2, p. 52.

[2] For an empirical display of spatial discontinuities in economic activity which nevertheless reflects an underlying ordering, see A. Lösch, *op. cit.*, Part IV.

or alternating concentrations. We may conceive of river or mountain boundaries, linear or areal markets, ocean frontiers, and political boundaries, *ad infinitum*. No matter what the formulation be, the broader outline of the discontinuous spatial model (where buyers and sellers are distributed heterogeneously over space) seems applicable. The market types which tend to arise are of the complex order.

III. SPACE AND ECONOMIC THEORY

Apart from the obvious destruction of zero economic profit general equilibria systems, space conceptions in economic theory have a vital impact on resource allocation and consumer satisfaction. The timeworn conclusions that optimum resource allocation and maximum satisfactions result from pure competition, as well as the claim that less efficient allocation but some different satisfactions result from monopolistic competition, must be completely re-examined. Fundamentally, a long-run theory of oligopoly in action must be developed showing the effect of a complex oligopolistic economy on resource allocation and consumer satisfaction. Until this is accomplished, microeconomics will suffer from limited predictive and explanatory powers; and, because of its relative inapplicability to policy formulation, it will remain essentially descriptive. Any claims that the free enterprise system is economically effective must also suffer from a lack of comprehensive scientific content. For only if the more complex model produces conclusions comparable to those derived from simpler and traditional theory may we continue confidently to apply the simpler theory to any given problem.

A complex market model embodying space conceptions also affects distribution theory. The differential rental income applicable to unique ability, and the monopoly rents due to artificial scarcity must be described along with long-run economic profit, which becomes a vital factor in distribution economics as a result of distances. The economist must not only measure the return to land, labor, and capital (including the transport factor), but must also realize that the subject of profits takes on a completely new twist. Is the return to the spatial oligopolist in the nature of an earned rent or not? At present some economists will probably say no, though we shall adopt the opposite position in this book.

The introduction of the dimension of distance produces such significant impacts on economic theory that mention of other affected subjects must now be made, even though full discussion is impossible. Input–output and trade theory distance effects have been described at some length by Isard;[1] and price discrimination based on locational differentiation is commented on in

---

[1] W. Isard, *op. cit.*, Chapter 9. Also see his "Interregional and Regional Input–Output Analysis: A Model of a Space Economy," *Review of Economics and Statistics*, XXXIII (1951), pp. 318–328.

numerous texts. But the effect of space on competitive pricing and location, though a more general subject, is seldom even mentioned. Surely we will find that the impact on prices of differently located producers and consumers diverges from the theoretical deductions drawn in nonspace economics. Let us recall here a case in point: The aggregation of what otherwise would be identical demand curves in nonspatial economics becomes an aggregation of different demands when consumers are scattered over an area, *ceteris paribus*. Consequently, the sales extent of the market, the impact from distantly located firms, and the price reactions and techniques developed in spatial competition are not fully revealed by nonspatial models.

Simple Theory versus More Realistic-Complex Theory

It is often claimed that economists should choose assumptions which conform as closely as possible to observed reality but should discard assumptions which, even though seemingly realistic, yield results not conforming to reality.[1] On these grounds, many will support traditional competitive theory. However, if the missing parts in the model significantly change the consequences of the theory, and if the more complete model yields results actually conforming more closely to observed reality than does the less complete model, the need for such an inclusive model is obvious.[2] To say the least, space reshapes the preference (decision-making) scheme of businessmen. And when and where it does, the more complete models tend to be needed. The purpose of this book is to determine just how different are the norms yielded by nonspatial and spatial economic theories. Only then may we ascertain the extent to which we are able to avail ourselves of the simpler models.

A Special Example of Interpretative Differences

We shall conclude this chapter with an example of the impact of space on economic theory and policy. Our illustration will be of particular rather than general importance; but, since it is only one of many examples, it suggests the widespread impact of space on economic theory. It will stress the fact that although a general model of a space economy may yield results substantially similar to those suggested by nonspatial theory and that simpler models may be used for certain purposes, yet the more complex framework may be required for other purposes. Our illustration follows.

Traditional theory argues that corporate income taxes do not influence monopoly pricing because they do not affect the prices which produce maximum profits. At one time it was also argued that this would be true for competitive pricing as well, because the marginal firm earns no economic profits at all. The realization that zero economic profits involve positive accounting profits led, however, to a modification of this last conclusion.

---

[1] See F. Machlup, *The Economics of Sellers' Competition, op. cit.*, p. 8.
[2] *Ibid.*, pp. 7–8.

In the long run, capital leaves the competitive (corporate-structured) industry if the income tax causes the returns on equity capital to be less than adequate as compensation for the possibility of loss.

What about a spatial oligopoly which produces long-run *economic* profits? The initial reaction may be that, as in monopoly, an income tax has no price effect in this type of market. However, our consideration of the theory of distribution in a space economy—which is presented in Chapter 9—will indicate that such a conclusion must be re-examined. We derive long-run economic profits there and hold that, unlike the economic profits of a monopolist, they are *earned* in oligopolistic markets formed by economic space. The corporate income tax thus must affect price.

The individual's theoretical conception of the workings of spatial economic system quite obviously will influence his public-policy proposals. To what degree his assumption of space would change his basic perspectives depends on the way the individual would "correct" the discrepancy between classical theoretical economics and empirical reality.[1] To paraphrase Friedman, who paraphrased Mill, we shall assert: A person is not likely to be a good economist if he does not have a firm command of nonspatial economics; equally, he is not likely to add substance to form if he knows nothing else.[2]

Conclusion

There is no denying that the conception of a space economy could be theoretically vital. Certainly, it is evident that the market types deducible from the hypothesis of scattered sellers and buyers *may* yield a different set of deductions from those derived in neoclassical economics. We shall in fact now assert that this is true, though in Chapters 6 through 13 the assertion will be replaced by formal analysis which reveals the homology and the *differences in the frameworks and theories.* It is obvious that a broad philosophic gauge is needed to determine the types of situations and problem areas for which the one system is preferable to the other, and we must, in the end, tackle this problem. But, we are now ready to formulate our model, and, in doing so, we shall probe deeper into the matter of changing concept requirements in economic theory than we have so far been able to do.

IV. SUMMARY

The perfectly and imperfectly competitive markets implicitly require buyers and/or sellers to be located at a point or adjacent points in economic space.

---

[1] F. H. Knight, *Uncertainty, Risk and Profit* (Boston: Houghton Mifflin Company, 1921), recognizes that the deviations of classical economics from real life must be corrected when its conclusions are applied. We shall argue later that in some cases the danger of error via corrections is less under our space economy theory than under traditional spaceless economic theory.

[2] M. Friedman, "Walras and His Economic System," *American Economic Review*, XLV (1955), pp. 900–909, argues well that pure form without substance is not enough.

Unless this is so, the friction of distance becomes significant and uneven-sized market areas must arise. Heterogeneous distributions of people and institutions tend to dot the landscape. In turn, between market areas (or within market areas) costs differ, firms identify and watch specific competitors, and uncertainty spreads. A long-run return for organizing and operating an economic activity under conditions of uncertainty characterizes the system. What this means to classical economic theory and whether it should be considered are vital questions which remain to be answered.

In a sense Chapter 4 has, therefore, reiterated the assertions made in Chapters 2 and 3 that uncertainty and oligopoly go hand-in-hand with economic space. But this relation has been established indirectly by referring to a theory (to be recorded later in the book) which demonstrates the necessity of an uneven distribution of firms and people over any economic landscape. It is because of this unevenness and the consequent agglomerative (deglomerative) economies (diseconomies) that costs vary over the space. It follows in turn that the many sellers (actual and potential) who are distributed over the economic space will evaluate and forecast their rivals' actions with conjectural uncertainty.

Later in this book, specifically in Chapter 6, we shall give a more direct view of the correspondence between uncertainty—oligopoly—and economic space. We shall there establish the subject relationships analytically and directly—without recourse to some other theory which indirectly suggests these relations via resulting spatial indivisibilities. We shall find that the very fact of distance (if significant in cost) requires spatial separation of sellers, and leads each seller to regard any rival with oligopolistic uncertainty.

Our formulation in Chapter 6 of Part II of this book involves the beginning of both our formal inquiry into and our formal analysis of the development and the effectiveness of a spatial economy. However, before moving to this level of inquiry, there remains in Part I the need to indicate broadly what our basic theory will consist of, what its general properties are, and what its fundamental conclusions will be. This task is assigned to Chapter 5, where economic space—uncertainty—and oligopoly are accepted as data so that a sketch may be drawn of the long-run equilibrium which could result in such a world. Though formulated along analytical lines rather than definitional or axiomatic lines, Chapter 5 continues in the generally descriptive pattern of our previous chapters, at least in the sense of analytical incompleteness. This incompleteness relates to the fact that Chapter 5 will assume an economic space in its postulates and then ignore the locational interdependencies that prevail among firms. The whole of Part 3 of the book is required for an analysis of the locational interdependence side of our theory of the firm in economic space.

5

A Sketch of our Theory

THROUGH THE PIONEERING WORKS of Chamberlin and Robinson,[1] Lewis and Lösch,[2] the space economy was viewed as being of monopolistic form. Indeed, partly through these writers and a few others,[3] it has been generally well established in the literature that the condition of economic distances (i.e., economic space) promotes, as it were, an oligopolistic economy. Though we have already suggested and will further develop the basis for this conclusion in the present chapter, we take this proposition as our present departure point. For those readers who disagree with the idea that distances inevitably bring about a state of spatial oligopoly, we should point out that we shall justify this assertion analytically in Chapters 6 and 7. In any event, the theory of oligopolistic equilibrium finally set forth in this book is a general one; it relates to any oligopoly whether spatially justified and conceived or not.

I. FORMATION AND DEVELOPMENT OF THE OLIGOPOLY

Consider a homogeneous distribution of consumers, a homogeneous landscape, a given market area, a new product, and an initial seller of the good.

[1] E. H. Chamberlin, *The Theory of Monopolistic Competition*, 5th ed. (Cambridge Harvard University Press, 1946). J. Robinson, *The Economics of Imperfect Competition* (London: Macmillan and Company, 1934).

[2] W. A. Lewis, "Competition in Retail Trade," *Economica*, XII (1945), pp. 202–234. A. Lösch, *Die räumliche Ordnung der Wirtschaft*, (Jena: Gustav Fischer, 1944).

[3] F. Fetter, "The Economic Law of Market Areas," *Quarterly Journal of Economics*, XXXVII (1924), pp. 520–529. H. Hotelling, "Stability in Competition," *Economic Journal*, XXXIX (1929), pp. 41–57. A. P. Lerner and H. W. Singer, "Some Notes on Duopoly and Spatial Competition," *Journal of Political Economy*, XLV (1937), pp. 445–486. A. F. Smithies, "Optimum Location in Spatial Competition," *Journal of Political Economy*, XLIV (1941), pp. 423–439. F. Machlup, *The Economics of Seller's Competition* (Baltimore: The Johns Hopkins Press, 1952), p. 53. M. L. Greenhut, *Plant Location in Theory and in Practice*, (Chapel Hill: University of North Carolina Press, 1956). W. Isard, *Location and Space Economy*, (New York: John Wiley and Sons, 1956). G. A. Churchill, "Production Technology, Imperfect Competition, and the Theory of Location: A Theoretical Approach," *The Southern Economic Journal*, XXXIII, (1967), pp. 86–101.

Assume that a new competitor or two enters the market at distant points. Then note that as new market areas develop and new firms with new plants begin to dot the economic landscape, a chain linking of their markets develops. If initially the industry is characterizable as a generally homogeneous one, except for plant and firm location, each seller will visualize substantially the same average revenue function. If no cartel type of organization occurs (or is allowed), an unorganized oligopolistic industry results.

Entry and Demand

The entry of unorganized-competitive rivals causes the demand curve viewed by an initial seller to shift to the left. Accordingly, the elasticity of the new curve rises at a given price. But the market is scored by more than just an increase in elasticity due to a decrease in the demand allocable to an original seller. A general flattening out of the average revenue curve also tends to arise, as entry increases the overall homogeneity of the industry and provides a natural advertising (i.e. demand expansion) effect. An increasing total demand over the economic space is therefore coterminous with the leftward-shifting individual AR curve; this curve thus tends to become both flatter and elongated as the differentiation between firms attributable to location (and other matters) decreases at the same time that the number of alternatives open to the consumer increases. Let us say that the control possessed by very distinctive sellers over buyers decreases sharply at the same time as total demand and buyer indifference to products and sellers increase.[1]

Special Impacts of Entry at a Distance

It will be shown in Chapter 6 that a location distant from an existing production point is feasible if and only if (1) any production-cost disadvantage that may hold for the distant site is offset by freight-cost savings over the market

[1] The equations $p_f = a_1 - b_1 q_r - c_1 \sum_{s=1}^{f} q_s$ and $p_r = a_0 - \left[\left(\frac{c_0}{c_1}\right)a_1 - \left(\frac{c_0}{c_1}\right)p_f \right] - \left[b_0 - \left(\frac{c_0}{c_1}\right)b_1 \right] q_r$ were presented as (2*) and (3*) respectively in Chapter 3. If the f firms have zero sales, $p_f = a_1 - b_1 q_r$. Substituting this value of p_f in (3*) leaves p_r as a function of q_r. From 3* we also see that the initial impact of a positive quantity sold by the f firms (i.e. when their price is lower than $p_f = a_1 - b_1 q_r$) is to lower and flatten the effective AR curve of firm r. Moreover, we see that the full set of prices by the f firms which provide these firms with some sales—including the competitive profit-maximizing price for these firms obtained from the intersection of the reaction functions—yields a set of parallel price lines (i.e. alternative AR curves for firm r). These alternative AR curves are flatter in slope than the AR curve applicable to $p_f = a_1 - b_1 q_r$; they fall to lower levels as p_f is lowered. Manifestly any further flattening, and any elongation of r's AR requires a change in taste related to entry, the natural advertising effect resulting from the larger number of alternative sources of supply, the greater homogeneity of firms, etc., as suggested above. It can be shown that the statements presented above, drawn directly from the linear AR function, also apply to concave and convex demand curves.

area surrounding the distant site, and (2) demand over this region is sufficient to warrant establishment of the new firm. We will further demonstrate that under these preconditions the distant firm may compete actively in price for markets extending from its site towards the older production point while monopolizing those in the other direction. A price war could be won by the distant firm so long as any production-cost disadvantage to which the firm may be subject is more than offset by the freight-cost savings it gains on sales to buyers who are located at very great distances from the older production point but close to the distant firm. This requirement leads to the conclusion that oligopolistic relations will become inevitable.[1] In fact, a kinky average revenue function is brought about by the condition of distances between firms and their buyers. It follows from the delivered-cost advantages possessed by distant sellers as regards selected buyers that price cuts (wars) must portend financial difficulties for at least some firms, while price increases could also prove to be damaging. We shall see that the kinked average revenue (AR) curve in a system marked by distances explains spatial pricing, and is not a rationalization to account for the stability of prices recognized to prevail in a world of oligopolies. Indeed, the kinked AR curve explains short-run relations, as we shall better appreciate later on in the book.

Special Impacts of Entry at an Established Center of Production

In the absence of collusion, we shall propose that increased output and lower prices tend to arise—sooner or later—from the location of new firms at already established production points. This is not to say that distant entry, if occurring to any significant extent, will not also cause a breakdown in oligopolistic rigidities. We aim, however, to stress the fact that long-run oligopolistic *competition* is spurred initially by competitive impacts from firms located close to each other and, in turn, spurred later on by competition from firms located at distant market centers. Over short-run periods, we attribute oligopolistic rigidities essentially to the existence of distant firms. Again, we shall develop this theory in full in Chapter 6.

A Three-Section Average Revenue Curve

We propose that a three-section kinked average revenue curve tends to arise in a maturing oligopolistic industry. Its *form* can be briefly reviewed here, albeit the full basis for this conception must be left for later chapters.

One section of the curve—above the prevailing price—is gently sloping; in fact, the elasticity is high along this section of the curve, as the contract, service, name and product advantages which a concern may have are insufficient over the range of prices relevant here to provide it with many sales *if*

[1] And see M. L. Greenhut, *op. cit.*, pp. 65–80.

rivals' prices are low.[1] The third or lowest section of the curve is the steeply sloping (in fact, a highly inelastic) portion of the curve. The setting of prices along this part of the average revenue function would provoke sharp reaction from some rivals and would lead to but small increases in sales.[2] Between the upper and lower portions of the curve, we find the moderately sloping part. This part resembles in appearance the curve that is usually drawn to illustrate the average revenue function of a monopolistic competitor.[3] Over this range of the average revenue (AR) curve, the oligopolist has some effective price freedom. That is to say, adjustments in his price do not cause reaction: upward revisions do not cause substantial loss of sales nor do downward revisions occasion price wars.

Over the middle section of the curve, the oligopolist finds that his buyers generally remain with him while other buyers are at best influenced slightly by a change in his price; as a consequence, other sellers are largely unaffected by the changes in price of the subject seller. Indeed, we might suggest that the subject seller has lost his identity to rivals over this range of prices, being in a sense "infinitesimal" in much the same way as the monopolistic competitor

---

[1] Recall that the demand function of the firm is of the type $p_r = a - bq_r - c \sum_{s=1}^{f} q_s$ where r stands for the representative firm, c is a positive number greater than unity whose value is conjectured and depends on the degree to which r believes it would price itself out of the market at higher prices, and s represents any one of the other f firms in the market. Because we are considering an oligopolistic chain, $s = 1, \ldots, f$ runs to a comparatively small number. The aggregate demand and prices for the f other firms, let us recall, is of similar form, $p_f = a' - b'q_r - c' \sum_{s=1}^{f} q_s$. The values of the parameters are given. In general, substituting the initial prices yields q_r and q_s. If r then raises its price and the other firms maintain their original price, this price can be substituted into the other firm's equation with q_s solved in terms of q_r. In this way, p_r can be stated in terms of q_r alone. Actual q_r would deviate from conjectured q_r to the extent that conjectured c is in error. Significantly, we should realize with regard to the top section of the curve—as conceived by the oligopolist—that its significance lies only in leading the oligopolist towards his short-run price. Once price is fixed, and firm's true sales determined, the imagined AR curve would be realigned so that its apex would be formed at the actually prevailing price and quantity sold.

[2] The price received by r is a partial function of the quantities sold by each of the other firms; to repeat, $p_r = a - bq_r - c \sum_{s=1}^{f} q_s$, where c, as was the case with an increase in the price of r, is again a positive number much greater than unity with respect to a downward change in price. This value for c stems from the conjecture by officials of firm r that a decrease in its price will induce no significant shifting of customers to it. In fact, adverse consumer reactions are expected, either because rivals might undercut or consumers will hold back in their buying in anticipation of further decreases in price. This lowest portion of the curve does not relate to the actual demand for a firm's product that one would find under orderly (and normal) market conditions.

[3] Here the prices and sales of other firms are expected to remain unchanged, so $\sum_{s=1}^{f} q_s = K$, and c can be specified as being equal to unity. Substituting K into r's demand function yields r's price as a function of q_r alone.

of Chamberlinean tangency theory, or "alone" as is the monopolist of classical theory.[1] With increasing entry, especially at established production points, the price-rigidity traceable to the location of new firms at a distance tends to breakdown, and the mid-section of the curve becomes longer and longer, ultimately being instrumental in determining output and prices. The length of the mid-section of the curve is then an increasing function partially of the number and locations of alternative sources of supply.

Uncertainty and the Limits to Entry

With additional new entry, the differentiations due to space, name, and possibly service and product diminish in character and importance causing the representative firm's demand curve to become still more continuous and generally flatter. With greater numbers of firms located at all points in the market and over all areas, it becomes increasingly difficult for buyers to distinguish between them. If it were not for the limits placed on numbers by uncertainties, the market could become a many-seller market in which each firm becomes so small and so much like its rivals that downward changes in price would stimulate large increases in sales for any given firm without causing great inroads on the sales of any particular rival. In this event, the relative size of each firm would approach the atomistic market type, and the inroads on service, product, and spatial distinctions would generate an increasingly homogeneous competition.

But again, the condition of uncertainty acts as a brake. It places natural limits on entry, being influenced by the existence of mountain barriers, waterways, movements of population, sandy-desert areas, limited numbers of grade A, B, and C sites, including even limits to effective police and fire protection and the control of municipalities—and the availability in general of usable sites. Technological indivisibilities in plant and equipment, in advertising, in research, in finance, and in organization control add further uncertainty to the world of personalized relations between the oligopolists; they restrict entry in the process. The intense competition between identifiable rivals is abetted by forces which individuals evaluate and emphasize differently.

The existing uncertainties reach forward and backward into price wars—price truces, advertising wars—advertising truces, branch-plant competition, research competition, *ad infinitum*. The technological efficiency approached by the original member of an industry and by selected later entrants stimulates new research and development of new product lines. The production and sales side of business activity are enlarged; in the process a noticeable advantage is gained by the firm which establishes multiple products and related product mix. All of these changes increase in number for a while, ultimately

[1] Stackelberg disequilibrium and other solutions, we shall see later, are ruled out in our theory.

limiting the opportunities for new ventures in a given market; thus it is that the brand new enterprises tend later on to be replacements rather than additions, as the uncertainty constraint will be seen to limit the number of firms in the market. The Chamberlinean tangency solution, where economic profits disappear, proves to be inconsistent with uncertainty, as the market adjusts itself to a return called *profits*. We shall develop this general theme in the sections that follow. But before we stress the tie-up between uncertainty and profits, we must present in detail our concept of opportunity costs. This examination of opportunity costs will be detailed and, we trust, all inclusive, for the opportunity cost concept is vital to our theory; it underscores the long-run determinate equilibrium which we shall claim prevails in an unorganized oligopolistic economy.

II. OPPORTUNITY COSTS AND THE BEST ALTERNATIVE

Opportunity costs are based partly on what we shall call the "energy utils" expected to be expended by a factor in another employment. And because by the very nature of an oligopolistic economy "any" other employment opportunity might be the best alternative, our concept of opportunity costs, in effect, includes any noncost outlay sum that may happen to apply. That is to say, the best alternative may be in a similar or vastly different opportunity.

The measurement of lost opportunities which shall be advocated here is also predicated in part on what we shall refer to as the "income utils" expected to be received by a factor in the alternative employment. These income utils may be thought of in terms of dollar receipts or abstractly as utils. In turn, energy utils may relate either to kilowatt hours of energy used or to some other measure of wear and tear on the human being or the capital machine; or we may simply regard these energies abstractly as used up utils.

Symmetry exists in that we speak of *expectations* as to energies to be expended and income to be received by a factor in the alternative employment. This stress on expectations might appear to be bringing into the theory intrapersonal utility analysis rather than objective market evaluations, and hence proposing a subjective measure of opportunity costs. Significantly, however, if there are any long-run survivors belonging to the set of owner(s)-manager(s) who erred in their "guesstimates" of alternative energy utils and income utils, they must be members of the subset who ascribed a lower set of relative costs than actually should have been applied. In other words, those whose estimates deviated from objective data but survive in the long run must be owner(s)-manager(s) who are receiving a natural rent; and this rent may be added to opportunity costs in the long-run imputation process. In fact, for our purposes, we will henceforth loosely use the term opportunity costs to include not only the income value of the opportunities forsaken but any natural rent (e.g., rent for special skill or performance) received by the owner(s)-manager(s). We shall do this except when precise meaning of the term is needed and accordingly indicated. Thus, in our theory, objective market data prevail, as our attention is on those who survive in the long run and on how the costs of these survivors are resolved in the market.[1] But enough of these preliminaries. We are ready to set forth the whys and wherefores of our concept of opportunity costs.

Time and Opportunity Costs

Ask yourself the question as to what is (or are) your own "best" alternative opportunity(ies). Conceivably, you might have a reserve status in the military establishment of your country; you could have an editorial opportunity with a publisher, or a government or private industry position alternative, or even a background or opportunity as a steeplejack or basketball player. To select the best alternative requires a comparison which recognizes the indefiniteness of other returns. More specifically, it involves an evaluation of the alternative ratios of income utils expected to be received from an activity *vis-à-vis* the energy utils intended to be expended. Continuing an athletic career when one is subject to a knee or back ailment which might upon reinjury cripple the athlete entails a "potential-shortening" of one's economic activity life—if not one's entire life—that must be considered in measuring opportunity costs. An estimate must be made for every economic factor which compares the total energy utils expendable in different activities to the total income utils received, with each one "guesstimated" over the expected alternative "lifetimes" of the activities. For a factor to expend a much smaller amount of energy utils per day than the factor would be able to (and wants to) expend over that calendar period of time suggests undesirable applications. More fundamentally, it suggests an income receipt over the probable economic activity life of the factor (and post-economic activity life of the human factor) which is much smaller than the likely income exchange expected from an alternative performance in which optimality in energy utils and hence income receipts is possible. If the factor we are considering is, for example, the entrepreneur's capital investment rather than a human services input, we must conceive similarly of the "best return" under uncertainty for the alternative "optimal" size investment.[2]

[1] In the appendix to this chapter, we shall work with a residual sum which we shall call total profits, and allocate this to the owner(s)-manager(s) of the firm for their services and equity investment. However, this practice will be for a special purpose as explained at that point.

[2] Because we are operating under conditions of uncertainty, risks, etc., alternative sets of returns must be conceived, a mean value identified for each state of uncertainty—on the basis of objective probabilities assigned to the diverse risk combinations that prevail— and some criterion applied to select the particular state(s) of uncertainty which dominates the final decision. (Supra Chapter 2). As soon as all relevant decisions are made, the optimal opportunity return conjectured for another employment becomes identifiable.

The Optimal Alternative Involves a Discounting Process. Any determination of what is the optimal opportunity involves a discounting process. Let us consider two alternative performances: alternative one requires a very substantial number of energy util expenditures in a given calendar period of time; accordingly, the planned "working" lifetime of the factor may well be (and we assume is) shortened. Alternative two involves a long economic activity lifetime of small expenditures and receipts per calendar period of time. Now, in each case, not only must future income and energy utils be discounted to present values, but we must apply an additional (special) discount to future income utils to give effect to the relative preferences one may have for a given type of expenditure of energy (i.e. use). The relation $d = f(I, E)$, where I stands for income and E for energy requirements applies. Our forthcoming remarks deal with this special discount d.

Suppose alternative one is preferred over two in so far as concerns the expected mental and/or physical wear and tear on the factor, the rate and years of work required, the uncertainty involved, etc. In effect, a low discount rate would be applied to the revenues expected under alternative one and a high one applied to alternative two, *ceteris paribus*. This low rate for alternative one reflects the decision-maker's *preference* to employ the factor (some capital item or the decision-maker himself) in the indicated way rather than in the activity indicated by alternative two. Alternative one then would yield a greater (discounted) ratio of income utils/energy utils compared to that which would follow the selection of a high rate of discount. If we let $\dot{r}^a$ stand for the revenues allocable to the factor in the alternative employment net of such costs as work-clothing that may be provided for the human factor or depreciation on the capital used in the activity, it follows that when the special discount is applied to those revenues [e.g. $\dot{r}^a/(1+d)$], we would obtain the net revenues (i.e. income) available to the factor ($\dot{r}^a$) in the alternative activity. More generally, we shall let $\dot{r}_j^a$ relate to the conjectured series of income returns, where $j = 1, \ldots, n$, and combine the discount required to bring this series to its present value with the special discount obtaining a composite discount c. In turn, the revenue expectation r^a is derived (i.e. $r^a = \sum_{j=1}^{n} [\dot{r}_j^a/(1 + c)^j]/n$).

It might be the case that a large discount applies to alternative one due to an undesired use of the factor (e.g. higher uncertainty). And if we confine our present and immediately following remarks to the human factor of production alone (though only a slight change of wording would be required for generalization), we could then propose that a large discount might reflect the factor's disaffection with the strain to which he would be subjected; for example, there is the possibility that ulcers (perhaps tied to uncertainty) could be expected to arise more readily to shorten unduly his economic activity lifetime (even his total lifetime as well). Under the possibility of what in effect would be an arbitrary shortening of his economic activity lifetime (and perhaps his entire lifetime), the total income utils expected could be less than otherwise would be possible; significantly, the discounting adjustment takes such possibility into consideration.[1]

The utility map of expectations and the discounting process involve intrapersonal decisions, a condition which defers to the fact that only the factor himself is able to evaluate his likely performance elsewhere as well as to select the activity which will make him most effective (and hence enable his firm to survive). Fortunately, let us recall at this point that our long-run imputation of the owner's (or manager's[2]) opportunity cost includes any applicable natural rents. Through this inclusion we gain equivalence with objective market conditions. It follows that if the amount actually earned by an owner-manager compared to the energy utils actually expended is less than the opportunities foresaken, this owner (or manager) will tend to leave the firm with related loss to the firm. Surviving firms are obviously those which tend to meet their full opportunity costs more amply and often over time than nonsurviving firms; so we say that the long-run picture is focused on those who tend regularly to earn their costs in full. (Incidentally, as suggested in note 2 below, we included the managers of corporations in selected references above since we shall justify treating them in the same way as single proprietors later in the book. For the rest of this section, however, we shall no longer refer to a possible theoretical identity between managers and single proprietors or partners and let the reader think only of the single proprietor or partner if he prefers.)

[1] Income utils expected and energy utils to be expended could be distinguished more sharply than we are proposing above. Thus, uncertainty in income receipts could alone serve as the basis for the special discount applied to expected incomes. Then a separate discount to reflect special physical *and mental* wear and tear would be applied to the energy util component of opportunity costs. To illustrate, if the factor is employed over a longer work-day than desired, not only is a greater amount of physical energy expended but the factor's disaffection with the required workday entails an extra cost. Simply put, the health of the factor could be impaired so that the effective energy cost per unit of time is greater than the physical energy units which appear to have been used up. A special discount which relates to the unpleasantness (or danger) of the employment would then be applied. This special discount relates—let us say—to the "mental" disutility involved in certain activities. (Note— since energy utils are in the denominator of the opportunity cost ratio, the greater the "mental" disutility, the smaller will be the *total discount* for time preference *plus* the "mental" disutility involved in the activity.) But note, we shall not follow this particular format in the present book. Rather, we will simply apply the present value discount to the energy util component of the opportunities cost ratio and, for simplicity, combine the present value discount for income annuities *with the* special discount for uncertainty, mental strain, danger to the factor, etc. *along with the* special discount for uncertainty of income returns. In other words, a composite discount reflecting time preference, uncertainty of income returns, danger to the factor, etc., is applied to the income conjectures of the decision-maker, and only a simple time-preference discount is applied to future energy expenditures.

[2] Though managers of corporations typically receive an explicit salary payment, we shall, except when indicated otherwise, consider the manager's services on the same plane as the services of the single proprietor. We shall ascribe their costs to the firm on the basis

Details of the Discounting Process. We have identified the optimal alternative (for the human factor of production) as that activity which, via the discount process, involves an expected economic activity (and retirement) lifetime of acceptable magnitude(s). Manifestly, the uncertainties of any lifetime must be considered, though because the function is monotonic, its essential effect is to increase (decrease) the discount as the uncertainty increases (decreases). Uncertainty thus has the same impact on the discount rate as has the relative desirability of the energy requirements in the activity per calendar period of time. A factor preferring earlier retirement—even in the presence of a greater daily energy requirement—would apply a lower discount to his expected returns in the subject activity than he would if he did not have such a preference. The relatively greater value of his income expectations under the low discount rate entails a greater opportunity cost for the factor as he evaluates other employments that may be available.

Any identification of the optimal alternative requires, accordingly, the projection of the greatest ratio of discounted income utils expected *vis-à-vis* energy utils to be expended. There are, of course, other alternatives to the best alternative which are not part of the original computation because they would so exhaust the factor—in the sense of requiring excessive energies per unit of time—that, in effect, the factor would burn himself out too quickly. The discount levied against the expected income utils would weigh heavily against such alternative(s) compared to the more preferred activity of smaller energy requirement per calendar period of time. There is, in sum, an extra mental disutility over the physical wear and tear on a factor in an activity requiring too much uncertainty and/or the expenditure of too many energy utils per calendar period of time. (As fully explained in in note 1, p. 67, we could have applied this cost to the energy util component of the opportunity cost ratio; however, for purposes of simplification, we lump this cost together with the uncertainty of income receipts in the form of a special discount applied against the conjectured income stream.)

The Employment Preference Formula. We have thus conceived of a simple discount which relates to time preference; this discount is applicable to expected income utils and to expected energy utils. Over and above whatever preference may hold for a present performance (asset) compared to a future performance (asset), a special discount is identifiable which relates to the "health" energies to be used up and the preferred working lifetimes of the factor. Uncertainty may also apply as an additive or joint force to these energy applications in yielding the applicable special discount. Partly because the classical concept of opportunity costs speaks in terms of the dollars given up as a result of a particular selection, we apply the special discount only to the

of their lost opportunities plus any rent reflecting special skill. Most importantly, any discrepancy between our imputation and explicit payments must be short run.

income utils that are expected. The derived income estimate helps to measure the lost opportunities.

Our concept of alternative economic activity lifetimes must be recognized to include the possibility that in the best alternative the optimally desired energy applications per calendar period may equal s' while in the selected activity the preference may be to expend s utils of energy, where $s \neq s'$. The discount applied to the income for s may, therefore, be the same as that applied to the income under s'. But note, even though s is the transform of s', such that in employment "A" the factor desires to expend s energies while if he is employed in "B" his preferred expenditures are s', he might still prefer s over s'. Then the discount would be lower, not the same, for activity A compared to B, *ceteris paribus*. Finally, s' may be preferred to s, in which case the discount is greater for prospective employment "A" than "B", *ceteris paribus*.

It is significant that the best alternative not only may involve a given expected economic activity lifetime based on s' expenditures per period, but it will also include the possibility of expending more (or less) than s' expenditures per period; of course, any departure from optimality involves a disutility. Symmetry again holds: the trials and tribulations of the *actually selected activity* involve possible departures from its own norm; again any such departure carries a disutility.

It is thus a basic part of our concept that the lifetime to be worked in the chosen activity not only may cover a greater (or smaller) number of years than in the best alternative, but that variation is also possible within each activity. In the language of the theory of the firm, inputs may vary over a wide range. What apparently governs the selection of a job (or activity) is the factor's expectation that he will expend, say, s energy utils per calendar period and his acceptance of this as the acceptable transform from, say, s'. (Clearly, s may also equal s'.) We may conjecture, accordingly, that the total discounted income utils (e.g. w) that are expected for the total s expended over the factor's economic lifetime (i.e., $\sum_{i=1}^{m} w_i \big/ \sum_{i=1}^{m} s_i$) must be equal to or greater than those expected for s'; i.e.

$$(1) \quad \sum_{i=1}^{m} w_i \bigg/ \sum_{i=1}^{m} s_i \geq \sum_{j=1}^{n\,(+)} w'_j \bigg/ \sum_{j=1}^{n} s'_j$$

where m and n stand for the corresponding lengths of the respective economic lifetimes, the $(+)$ mark following n will be explained later, and s_i, s_j are in present values. [Note that $\Sigma w'_j = n\,(r^a)$.] This employment preference formula does not provide the lost opportunity cost per se, as we shall see, but the $\geq$ requirement is the necessary and sufficient condition for selecting the subject activity over the alternative activity.

When equality holds, (1) implies factor indifference to the periods m and n. It implies this since the calculation requires consideration of (a) the different retirement lifetimes expected after periods m and n are complete, (b) the uncertainty applicable to the economic and retirement lifetimes conjectured, and (c) the giving effect to (a) and (b) via the process of discounting the future incomes. In short, the act of discounting, in effect, makes the periods a matter of indifference in the formula.

We may best appreciate this condition by stressing the fact that even the expected retirement lifetimes, say m' and n', are implicitly assumed by the formula to be acceptable to the factor. Thus even if $m = n$, m' may not equal n' since the whole lifetime is not independent of the activity chosen, with $m+m' \geqslant n+n'$ under the assumption that relatively better health is always desired. The discounting process, however, considers naturally any preference for, say, $m+m'$ over $n+n'$ or vice versa. Indeed, though *up to this page in the text* the factor's preference was taken into account in the discounting process, with m assumed to be equal to n, two adjustment patterns are henceforth available. If the one activity (location, energy unit expenditure per period, etc.) is preferred over another, either its discount may be lowered or a greater number of years (i.e. working lifetime) may be designated for it compared to the other.

It is vital to note that if $m > n$, the active working lifetime $j = 1, \ldots, n$ must be supplemented by a period of years $(n+1, \ldots, m)$ over which returns on (extra) savings might be received. The income-energy ratio over m years in the subject employment must, in other words, be compared with the alternative income-energy ratio over the same m years whenever $m > n$. The $n(+)$ in (1) is designed to convey this idea. [Incidentally, it is only where reference is made to the employment preference formula that we must complement n with the plus mark. All other references to n are to be strictly interpreted. Of course, if $m < n$, an $m(+)$ would, in effect, apply.]

The Optimal Alternative Requires Technological Identity with Subjective Preferences. Suppose technological conditions in the chosen activity require t units of inputs in order to produce at optimal efficiency but that t input units entail entrepreneurial inputs greater or less than s. Then, the factor's energy preference does not conform to technological conditions, and it is likely that the factor would actually expend more or less than the s units he prefers to spend. The activity would involve an undesirable application for him, e.g., working 2 (or say 10) hours a day instead of, say, 6 or 7. A disutility (or let us now say extra discount) is ascribable for performances unequal to s. When technological conditions do not conform to the entrepreneur's preferred schedule, the said entrepreneur will tend to be a high cost producer. But this means that the entrepreneur will sooner or later leave the field. Hence we may ignore as entrepreneurial prospects those enterprisers who expect that their optimal performance (i.e., the expenditure of s units per period) will fail to conform to the technological conditions of the trade; the requirement that s coincides with t becomes a precondition for entering (and we shall see remaining) in the subject activity.[1] Simply put, we choose that activity which tends to fit our personality and objectives.[2]

The Governing Ratio

We propose the existence of a selected activity, a best alternative, and we also assert that an optimal average rate of return R_0 per period is identifiable for this alternative. Let R_0 be defined as follows:

$$(2) \quad n(R_0) = \sum_{j=1}^{n} (w'_j/s') \text{ or } R_0 = \frac{1}{n} \sum_{j=1}^{n} (w'_j/s')$$

where s' stands for average s'_j, i.e., $s' = 1/n\Sigma s'_j$. The elements in the right-hand side of (2) are expressed as a rate, for example dollars per k.w. hour or more abstractly as a certain type of utils (income utils) per k.w. hour. R_0 is, accordingly, the optimal alternative rate of return the decision-maker would receive on the average in the alternative employment.

A mapping is possible from this best alternative return to the activity for which the imputation is to be made. However, because the subject activity may involve a different lifetime of optimal production points and periods, besides its own set of nonoptimal expenditures, any mapping process will require (and entail) conception of a transformed rate of return R_t which takes into consideration any existing different economic activity lifetimes involved. This transformed rate R_t, henceforth R for simple reference, in effect is mapped from the rate of return R_0 to the subject activity's optimal cost point. It is definable as:

$$(3) \quad mR = nR_0 \text{ or } R = \frac{1}{m} \left[\sum_{j=1}^{n} (w'_j/s') \right]$$

where the value of m *is conceived in* (3) to depend partly on and to vary the level of uncertainty in the selected activity.

Related to the transform R is an ideal *absolute* return r sought by the input factor in question. This r is assigned as a fixed cost in traditional theory. If the selected activity requires a longer working lifetime in order for

$$\sum_{i=1}^{m} w_i \Big/ \sum_{i=1}^{m} s_i = \sum_{j=1}^{n(+)} w'_j \Big/ \sum_{j=1}^{n} s_j \text{ (i.e., } m > n\text{), the transformed rate } R$$

will be less than R_0, and vice versa. The absolute dollar value r defined as $(R)(s)$ where $s = (1/m)\Sigma s_i$ is assignable on the average to any of the i_{th} periods

---

[1] Our thesis is that a person who desires "x" units of work per period in a given activity has a chance of being successful as an entrepreneur only if the activity requires the same "x" units of effort for optimal results.

[2] The full basis for stressing optimal performance elsewhere and conformance with one's personality and objectives will become clearer when our basic model is presented.

as the amount which must, in general, be defrayed to justify the selection of the subject activity.

The Imputation of Opportunity Costs as a Fixed Cost

If the discounted income utils of the best alternative are allocated to each production period of time to be worked by the factor, a fixed cost per period is obtained. This fixed cost will raise the total cost curve when such is plotted against output. The tangent drawn from the point o,o to this total cost curve is steeper than the corresponding tangent drawn from o,o to the total cost curve that does not include the imputation. Average cost and marginal cost are therefore greater under the imputation at the firm's optimum cost point; and, this optimum cost point takes form at a greater output than otherwise would obtain. (We shall soon see that uncertainty has exactly the same type of impact on investment costs.)

Finally, though we have only occasionally referred to the capital factor of production in developing our concept of opportunity costs, our remarks should be understood to relate to any factor for which implicit costs apply. Thus, as in the case of services, alternative investments (capital use) may be distinguished for which an optimal R_0 is identified. Any mapping to the subject activity for capital involves a transformation to an alternative optimal size input (investment), and an equivalently transformed return R is identifiable. In turn, an absolute level r is applicable to the activity under consideration; this r is the *ideal* return sought for this activity. Our discussion of opportunity costs therefore not only sets the stage for presenting the impact of uncertainty on the firm's input–output level, it also ties up directly with the factor input comparisons we shall draw. In particular, since we shall distinguish the service inputs of the owner(s)-manager(s) from the service inputs on the capital (entrepreneurial) investment, but yet tie the two together in terms of optimal and nonoptimal energy input expenditures, a full derivation of opportunity costs on the basis of a discounted income/energy ratio had to be made. Any analysis confined to uncertainty alone would have been too limiting. It is in light of these main considerations that the entire concept of opportunity costs warranted detailed formulation here before our model could be presented. We are now in position to sketch this model.

III. OUR BASIC MODEL AND THEORY

Financial practices of firms and industries differ, some trading heavily on the equity and some not at all. While these practices alter the risk and uncertainty which underscore any given activity, our concern is with the underlying forces only, not the financial manipulations which may be effected in practice.[1]

[1] The firm's financing practice (i.e. its division between equity and loan capital) is

Indeed, the likelihood that the viable firms of a given industry follow similar financial practices suggests that our focus is not purely an academic abstract one but rather provides a generally close view of a real firm. In any case, when we speak herein of equity capital, we are referring to the total investment required of a firm, as we are indifferent to the question how much of the total actually was borrowed and how much was owner invested.

We will often use the term equity capital investment rather than just capital investment simply to emphasize our interest in the return that is due to the owners of the enterprise for the risk and uncertainty which underlies their investment. Indeed we even tend to obfuscate the risk component, in effect, focusing our attention on the value of the flow of services left over after all classical factors have received their just compensation; in other words, the residual flow attributable to the uncertainty on the (equity) capital investment stands as the focal point of our interest, and model.

It is perhaps worthy of further introductory note that classical theory does not necessarily rule out uncertainty as a component part of the labor input. Indeed, because the owners of the viable firms in an industry would tend to be men of similar character and perspective, we could impute an uncertainty component to the owner(s)-manager(s) services under the guise that such ascription would not violate classical theory too much, if at all. In other words, our model and the diagrams used to present this model will distinguish between the uncertainty ascribable to the owner(s)-manager(s) services and that attributable to the equity investment. But let us explain these thoughts in greater detail.

We add to the explicit costs of the firm the full implicit costs of the entrepreneur's (or manager's) services, as described in section II. All short- or long-run average cost curves drawn in this book, unless specified otherwise, therefore include the service inputs of the owner(s)-manager(s) of the firm. The only significant departure from classical practice might be that part of the rental payment earned for services will be due to uncertainty.[1] However, whether or not we say the owner(s)-manager(s) services are subject to uncertainty will be seen to have no effect on our final theorems. And we shall, in turn, refer to the average cost curve which includes the imputation for services (subject to or not subject to uncertainty) as the *classical* average cost curve.

We shall also ascribe to average costs the opportunity costs of the entre-

irrelevant to us for two reasons: One, the right side of a firm's balance sheet reflects financing techniques, and we would expect that these tend to be homogeneous within properly defined industry groupings. Two, and more importantly, the financing methods change the degree of uncertainty faced by, and hence the actual dollar returns required by, equity investors. But financing techniques thus apply to specific investors and are *non sequitur* to a general theory concerned with oligopolistic returns.

[1] Uncertainty has long been basic to the theory of consumer demand, but has not been a part of the theory of the firm. For example, see J. Henderson and R. Quandt, *Microeconomic Theory* (N.Y., McGraw-Hill, 1958), pp. 34–38, and pp. 49–55.

preneur's equity capital investment. However, here, a sharp distinction between the classical imputation (without uncertainty) and ours (with uncertainty—actually oligopolistic uncertainty) must be drawn. Distinction must, we contend, be made between that part of equity capital subject to risk and that part subject to uncertainty. So we propose that of the total percentage return attributable to equity capital, part relates to the risk portion of the investment and part is allocable to the equity capital for uncertainty. Because the return on equity capital for risk is a rental payment, just as is the return for the owner(s)-manager(s) services, we shall refer to the average cost curve which includes these rents as the classical average cost curve. This practice will be followed, we repeat, even though uncertainty is included as part of the imputation for services. Only the uncertainty applicable to the owner's investment requires special handling since in an oligopoly economy this uncertainty is a behavioral one and the intra-industry action-reaction plans will differ.

Following the above, the classical average cost curve in the diagrams to be found later on in this chapter should be understood to include all opportunity cost sums for services and the risk portion on investments. A glance at Figure 5–3 *infra*, for example, will show both the curves AC and LRAC adjusted as well as to the classical AC and LRAC curves. The former set—as we shall explain later—includes an extra (i.e., ascription) based on the uncertainty component of the equity investment of the entrepreneur. The unadjusted curves are the classical curves. All AC curves thus include the rentals for risk on investment and for services. The adjusted AC curves include the uncertainty requirement r on capital investment. In the process of earning this r on the investment, we shall see that the human factor's opportunity r cost is also earned. But before turning to the proof of this thesis, we may note that in Chapter 9 we shall equate entrepreneurship with the equity capital investment of the owner, treating his services the same as a hired manager's input whose opportunity costs must be covered in full. Also as indicated earlier, we shall establish in Chapter 8 the mid-portion of the oligopolist's three-section AR curve as the relevant portion of this function in the long run. Accordingly, in the following diagrams we shall simplify the problem by setting forth only this portion of the curve, thus leaving the kinked portions of AR exclusively to the reader's mind's eye.

IV. THE OWNER'S INVESTMENT, UNCERTAINTY, AND THE RETURN r: THE THEORY CONTINUED

The return for uncertainty on equity investment may be designated in terms of r (as defined previously) in substantially the same way as we have done for opportunity costs in general. And when this additional r, standing now for the absolute value of the prevailing uncertainty on the given investment, is ascribed as a fixed cost, the average cost curve (AC) is raised accordingly by r/q, where q stands for a given output. The same application will hold for the long-run average cost curve (LRAC). They form respectively the adjusted AC and LRAC curves.

Suppose average costs were least on the classical AC curve at output OL, again see Figure 5–3. Then add r to total costs, but divide the derived total costs by the exact amount of output shown. Because of the greater fixed-cost burden applicable to any size of plant, the resulting adjusted LRAC curve will be more steeply formed than the unadjusted LRAC as one moves from output OL in the direction of smaller values, i.e. towards the vertical scale. In light of this tendency and because of the importance of the increasing returns section of the curve, we shall occasionally refer to the r adjusted LRAC curve as the steeply sloped curve. Most significantly, note that the AC and LRAC adjusted curves include the full r returns demanded by owner(s)-manager(s) for their services and investments on the basis of their optimal opportunities elsewhere (section II, this chapter).

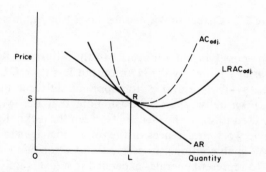

Figure 5–1: The Adjusted Average Cost Curves and Long-Run Equilibrium

Consider Figure 5–1, and let us suppose the AR curve is steeper than drawn and lies above the average cost curves at certain outputs while intersecting the AC curves at R, where output is OL. Profits are thus obtainable at some outputs less than OL and, of course, are zero at OL. Entry, if free, would take place and the newly formed AR curve (that is the one reflecting a larger number of alternative sources of supply) would be flatter and generally more elastic at any given output than the curve originally applicable to the smaller number of sellers.[1] But must the new AR curve be tangent to the

[1] See M. L. Greenhut, *Microeconomics and the Space Economy* (Chicago: Scott, Foresman 1963), Chapter 8, and section I *supra*, this chapter.

AC adjusted curve at R as it is drawn in Figure 5–1? Could not a tangency to the left of R arise, such as we find in Figure 5–2 at S? And if LRAC adjusted includes all lost alternatives as optimally ordered, stable equilibrium would appear to prevail at a tangency point such as S in Figure 5–2. The equilibrium would, accordingly, be of the monopolistic competition kind.

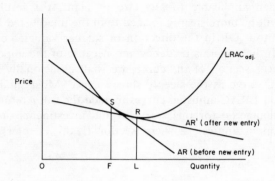

Figure 5–2: Change in AR and the Long-Run Equilibrium

Consider the possibility of a tangency to the adjusted LRAC at S under output OF, or at any point involving an output less than OL. In doing this we shall use the symbols e and e' to represent different utils of energies expended in a *given* activity; in contrast, note that the symbols s and s' were previously used to show the identity between the technological optimum and the subjective work preferences of the owner-manager in *two alternative performances*. We shall continue to reserve s and s' for that context alone, as we use e and e' to represent energies expended in a given activity, the former amount referring to the optimal expenditure and the latter being non-optimal. In other words, e is an alternative expression for s, but e' and s' are unrelated.

Any tangency with respect to an output (such as OF) along the decreasing cost portion of the adjusted curve would be unstable for two reasons: (1) outputs less than OL imply an energy expenditure, again call it e', less than the optimal energy expenditure e at L; thus (2) tangency at a point short of output OL implies a unique offsetting between an inadequate entrepreneurial expenditure (in services and/or capital) and a surplus windfall return. What appears as an equilibrium at S in Figure 5–2 is a position of profits in the sense that the income utils received (which are equal to r) are relatively great compared to the actual energy utils expended.[1] These profits may be appro-

---

[1] Realize that though we shall stress the value related to uncertainty on equity capital, the average cost curves include all the applicable opportunity cost r values.

priated by management as a bonus for managers or paid out as an extra return on the investment. In either case, outsiders are encouraged to enter as a result of the windfall, and insiders want to increase their investment. The impact of entry will be to shift the AR curve in Figure 5–2 leftward and somewhat downward. As a result of the increase in the number of alternative sources and products, the slope of the curve will flatten out and possibly be elongated to a new point of tangency such as at R in Figure 5–2.[1]

More generally, suppose as an initial condition that entry was so great that the AR curve falls below the relevant adjusted AC curves over all outputs. Many enterprisers will, thus, be failing to earn their opportunity costs r and, for example, a very large firm may exit and be replaced by a few very small firms which prove to be a viable part of the market.[2] Then the AR' curve of Figure 5–2 tends to result. But, suppose for the sake of fuller discussion that the altered AR curve continues to fall below the adjusted LRAC. A larger number of smaller firms, with managers possessed of smaller opportunity costs and different preferred energy expenditures (e.g., s, s', . . .), will sooner or later replace the smaller number of larger size firms previously in the market.[3] The result will be to elicit the rather flat (generally more elastic) AR' *type of curve* compared to AR.[4] Of course, the tangency of the flatter curve to the small firm's adjusted LRAC curve occurs at a smaller input-output point than that indicated in Figure 5–2.[5]

Figures 5–1 and 5–2 therefore indicate that production will take place at some point to the right of the Chamberlinean tangency point along the LRAC adjusted curve, but to the left of the optimal cost point on the LRAC adjusted curve. We shall now prove that this means that production takes place at the optimal cost point of the classical LRAC curve.

[1] The general flattening out of the AR curve, including the possibility of the stretching out of the curve, reflects the idea that the desire for a good increases as alternative sources of supply come into being. This thesis will be considered further in Chapter 13. Correspondingly, the reason why any AR curve below the adjusted LRAC curve does not provide a stable solution (i.e., why it cannot involve offsetting conditions between inadequate energy expenditures and relatively great income returns) must be reserved for consideration in the Appendix to Chapter 5 and, in particular, to Chapter 8. For the present, we can only "sketch" selected aspects of our theory.

[2] Later on in the text (Chapter 13), we shall outline in detail a continuity (or divisibility) effect throughout the system, such that both large and small firms tend to dot the economic landscape in a given field of production. For the present, only suggestive references are feasible. (And see note 1, p. 82).

[3] We shall establish the basis for this claim also in Chapter 13. For the present, let it be agreed that the statement above does imply a higher average cost curve for small firms than that initially presumed for large firms.

[4] The reason why we did not propose a still smaller number of large firms but specified as the required outcome of our given conditions the formation of a larger number of small firms is thereby manifest.

[5] We shall see in Chapter 8 that the adjusted costs of all sizes of firms lie on the same level as—to repeat—we can only "sketch" selected aspects of our theory here.

Decreasing Costs on the Adjusted Curve; Optimal Costs on the Classical Curve

It was earlier stated that the uncertainty associated with any economic activity could be regarded as a cost. By regarding uncertainty on the equity investment as a fixed cost, the classical AC curves are adjusted to curves relevant to a space economy. Following well-known principles, the minimum cost point on the AC adjusted curves (short and long run) must obtain at an output greater than that which yields optimum cost on the LRAC curve of classical economics. The result is shown in Figure 5-3.

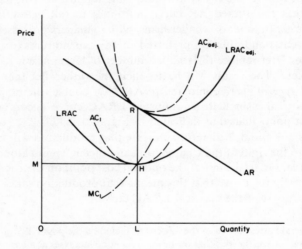

Figure 5–3: Oligopolistic Equilibrium is Classical Equilibrium

Figure 5–3 implies that firms optimize their allocation of scarce resources (land, labor, captial, and owner-manager services) since costs excluding uncertainty on the equity investment are at their lowest level, i.e. LH. In turn, the return for uncertainty on the equity investment (HR) appears as a residual return, and since (HR)(MH) is equal to r, uncertainty is fully compensated for when the hired factors of production are allocated optimally. Stability prevails because the owner-manager is inclined neither to increase nor decrease his inputs, and outsiders are not attracted to enter since no effective windfalls exist. This, then, is our theory. Its generality is further sketched below, though more formal, complete analysis must be reserved to Parts II and III of this book.

Variability of Returns

It was earlier noted that economic lifetimes change from one opportunity to another. The energy utils expended in an activity during a normal period of time may so exceed those in another (partly because of uncertainty) that the expected planned lifetime of the factor is shortened. But shortening or lengthening of lifetimes (planned or actual) is also a partial function of working at input levels greater or less than the optimal level for that activity. That is to say, though a normal optimal workday may be identified for a given activity, the factor's input may proceed regularly over a greater (smaller) number of hours, and the returns commensurate with such energy expenditure would vary accordingly.

Any variation in returns for inadequate or excessive applications of energy utils in a given activity may usually be expected to require nonlinear differences in receipts of income utils. For purposes of simple methodology, however, let us assume in the following discussion that if a factor regularly works overtime (or undertime), the income utils required rise or fall linearly in conformance with the rate R. Pursuant to this "convention", $r' = Re'$, where as before e' refers to the actual energy utils expended, R is the optimal rate of return transformed from the best alternative, and r' serves as the income utils directly related to e'. When we speak, then, of actual energy utils expended or income (energy) utils received, we will be referring to e' and r'; in contrast, when we speak of optimal expenditures and receipts, the values e and r apply. Manifestly, e and r may also obtain in fact.

V. THE GENERALITY OF THE THEORY

By stressing the input side, e' and e, and comparing the absolute value of the difference between these energy applications, the underlying micro-properties of a free enterprise economy are readily derived and the generality of our theory easily seen. We shall continue in this section to restrict our attention to the downward sloping portion of the steeply sloped cost curve, although our basic conclusions will be seen to apply to any input–output level.

Viewed from the Input Side $e' \rightarrow e$ Under Special Conditions

Suppose we assume the existence of substantial indivisibility in the industry. The relevant classical LRAC curve would, accordingly, have steeply inclined slopes in the direction of the optimal cost point. If AR is tangent to the r adjusted LRAC curve at a point far removed from the classical minimum average cost point, the difference $|e'-e|$ would be substantial. This can be shown when the relevant part of the AR curve lies significantly above the classical AC curves; the result is that the income receipt is substantially greater than that called for by e'. Windfalls thus exist and new firms will enter. Moreover because the r return should be understood to provide income r for services as well as equity investment, the owner-manager may feel encouraged to apply still greater inputs. In particular, because of entry in this case, we shall see that the scale of operations will be increased towards the end of decreasing the difference $|e'-e|$, and that the return on inputs declines.

A limit to $|e'-e|$ obtains at the zero value. This zero value would exist at *all* input–outputs if perfect divisibility prevailed throughout the economy.[1] Under such conditions, e assumes all values; i.e. $e = e'$, and an undetermined number of pure competitors would prevail in the market if AC is constant.

Divergence between e' and e requires the state of indivisibility of capital investment and entrepreneurial services. An inexorable tendency, however, permeates indivisible systems towards the end of minimizing the value $|e'-e|$. To appreciate this tendency, let us suppose that AR is tangent to the steeply sloped curve; at this point of tangency the return r is $>r'$. Windfalls therefore obtain and new firms will tend to enter. The added competition leads to a flattening out and elongation of the AR curve at the same time that existing entrepreneurs seek to expand their scale of activity. A new tangency of AR with the r-adjusted LRAC curve ultimately tends to arise in the region close to but short of its minimum cost point. Significantly, the prevalence of the fixed factor (indivisibility) makes the nonidentity between the returns r and r' possible. But before proceeding further, we must discuss systems in which either uncertainty does not exist or is combined with perfect divisibility.

Indivisibility Without Uncertainty. Indivisibility without uncertainty requires only brief discussion as classical theory has long centered attention on this situation. Any market type desired can be assumed, as entrepreneurs in any industry may be conceived to be veritably unlimited in number. Horizontal AR curves could apply and be related to classical curves of average cost. These classical cost curves would include explicit and implicit (opportunity) costs, with risk—if applicable—chiefly changing the level of the curve and the point of tangency with the horizontal AR curve.

Perfect Divisibility With Uncertainty. Uncertainty in the presence of perfect divisibility and constant costs adds little, since $e' = e$ and an undetermined number of atomistic firms dots the landscape. Uncertainty with perfect divisibility simply requires a higher return for extra hazard.

Indivisibility With Uncertainty. It is when indivisibility is combined with uncertainty that not only may e' differ from e and r' from r but the lowest cost points on the adjusted and classical LRAC curves must then occur at different outputs. Uncertainty (and we think here chiefly of behavioral uncertainty) is

---

[1] If perfect divisibility could apply to the best alternative, it would also tend to apply to the activity in question.

a vital constraining force on entrepreneurship as the preference set of uncertainties desired by (and acceptable to) any entrepreneur extends over a very limited range. One's alternatives thus are few rather than practically unlimited, as they would be under conditions of divisibility and/or perfect certainty or objectively probable risk. The greater the uncertainty, the fewer are the number of rivals in the market *ceteris paribus*. Uncertainty is, in effect, a cost which limits the entry of firms to numbers less than that assumed in the theory of pure or monopolistic competition.

We have observed that indivisibility establishes a fixed factor. When combined with uncertainty it yields AR curves of negative slope. Because uncertainty has meaningful impact in our theory only in conjunction with indivisibility, one should properly refer to the uncertainty–indivisibility factor. For terminological simplicity, however, we shall continue the practice followed in general in Chapters 1–4 wherein we referred simply to uncertainty, and only occasionally to indivisibility or to both, depending upon the stress intended.

A Final Formulation

A final formulation of our theory may now be set forth. Note that although throughout this chapter we have treated opportunity cost as a fixed cost, there is nothing in our theory which prevents our considering opportunity costs (and any uncertainty component) as a variable implicit cost. If this is done, the basically same conclusions will emerge. Let us now treat the opportunity cost of the owner(s)-manager(s) services as a variable while continuing to treat equity capital as a fixed input. [We shall present the corresponding (symmetrical) application for equity capital as a variable in the Appendix to Chapter 5 and also in Part II of this book.] Not only the AC curves but the MC curves must be adjusted to include the variable opportunity costs.

When viewed as a variable implicit cost, the expenditure of lesser energies than those optimally conceived for a given activity in an uncertain world would call forth a required income-utils return $r' < r$ at outputs short of the classical optimal cost point. The ascription of the relevant r' over the region in question would lead to a more gently sloping U-shaped curve up to the classical optimal point than would an r fixed-cost ascription. In such range of outputs, AR tangency to an AC curve which included r (not r') costs of services is, therefore, readily seen to be a position of windfall for these services.

Under the given variable imputation of r' for services, we have completely separated the owner(s)-manager(s) service inputs from the uncertainty component of the equity investment. The entrepreneur's capital investment is thus a fixed factor of parametric magnitudes, depending on the character of the industry. It has steep sloping effects over the increasing returns portion of the LRAC curve that lacks this imputation because it comes in an optimal size. Actually it tends to have a range of (more or less) equally desirable alternative expenditure amounts, a range wider in fact than the service input factor might have. That is to say, many investors will be relatively indifferent to investments slightly larger or smaller than that which might be optimal for them whereas the optimal service input (e.g. 8 hours per day) is sharply distinguishable from another input amount (say 9 hours per day). The fundamental problem in treating the opportunity cost on services as a variable and that on the entrepreneur's investment as a fixed cost is that our adjusted AC curves would not contain the r component throughout but would contain something less. It is for this reason that we can go no further with our present dichotomy, but instead will reserve for a later point the variable input picture (that is to say, an r' adjustment to explicit costs) for both owner(s)-manager(s) services and equity capital. We shall do this in order to acquire certain insights which otherwise would remain obscure, even though ultimately we shall express preference for the fixed factor focus. Significantly, when we finally use the fixed factor focus again all service inputs will be regarded as an integral part of classical cost, with uncertainty on the capital investment then being taken as the required oligopolistic adjustment to these costs.

Summary of the Fixed Factor Focus

Let us summarize now the fixed factor results: Recall that the addition to the classical cost curve of the r uncertainty component on the entrepreneur's capital investment causes the minimum cost point of the adjusted LRAC curve to lie at a greater input–output point than that which holds for the unadjusted curve. A negatively sloping AR curve *may*, accordingly, be tangent to the LRAC adjusted curve at an output which involves optimal costs on the unadjusted LRAC curve. In turn, the income return for equity (or capital) investment is revealed as a residual which attains its stable equilibrium value at the point where classical costs are least.[1] If we recognize the identity between r returns for e energy applications and the lost opportunity of the same (transformed) value, the force behind this result is clear. But though we must reserve our detailed proof of this contention as well as the following proposition to later analyses, let it be stressed here that the classical optimal cost point involves not only service inputs of quantity e (which we know, like s, reflects the technological optimum for the service input factor) but *it also involves* the application of e units of capital inputs. (This last proposition, which we shall go into further at a later point, can be reviewed here rather simply—all we need recall is the requirement that technology must conform to the input intentions of the decision-maker, for otherwise the firm would be a high-cost producer and drop out of the market in time.) With e established for

---

[1] Apart from a few statements appearing in this chapter, we shall find later in the book that, in a spatial system, a set of adjusted LRAC curves applies rather than just the single adjusted LRAC curve referred to in this chapter. Our basic conclusions will be seen to be unaffected by this refinement.

the factors that warrant the imputation of opportunity costs, the stability of the equilibrium becomes clear. No forces eliciting factor reallocation prevail. Optimization, we therefore see, occurs in spite of uncertainty, and the competitively rooted free enterprise system which is distributed over a landscape tends to be efficient.

VI. SPECIAL CONSIDERATIONS AND CONCLUSIONS

Let us deal with the three main cases where equilibrium might *appear* to exist at points other than the classical optimum point.[1]

Consider initially the return r for input e', where $e' < e$. Under this condition, a windfall exists and new firms will enter. The AR curve will shift leftward and flatten out somewhat such that input $e' \to$ input e. Equilibrium requires return r for input e.

Suppose return r applies to input e' (but $e' > e$). In this case, some entrepreneurs will exit while others will rationalize their operations: e.g., by altering the size of their firm. In the process, returns greater than r arise. A larger number of firms will, in time, prevail in the market, some of which possess a different (often a greater) optimal e level than had many of the original members of the industry. (These energy levels and hence opportunity costs reflect the individual's s and s' which may, of course, deviate from that of other individuals.) A return r for an input e ultimately must arise.

Perhaps the most difficult stable-like "appearing" equilibrium is one we shall also describe in detail later, but which can be briefly treated here. This is the classic Chamberlinean equilibrium. If an owner-manager receives r' return for e' inputs (with $e' < e$), he would—in one regard—be covering his opportunity costs in full; at the same time, windfalls which would induce entry do not apply. In this case, however, the owner-manager realizes that he wants to invest more than e' energy units. Otherwise, he would be idle to an undesired extent and accordingly have to work over a longer economic lifetime than that which he planned to work in order to satisfy his wants. (In terms of s, he would be working, say, s_0 when he desires s as the alternative to s'.) He would just not be fulfilling the optimum he determined for himself when selecting the given activity instead of the alternative employment. Some enterprisers will expand their effort accordingly while others will exit from the market. The AR curve tends to rise as the result of the exit of some firms, and the inputs of all firms increase in the presence of greater returns. If the system over-reacts so that profits (windfalls) arise, some additional new firms will enter, very likely those of different (smaller) size (and smaller energy expenditure preferences) than the firms which dropped out of the market. Opportunity costs of these new producers thus differ from those of the enterprisers initially in the market. Ultimately, a return commensurate

---

[1] A fourth case—as observed in note 1, p. 77—must be reserved for later discussion.

with input intentions and alternatives must be approached if production of the good is to be at all economic.

Implicit to our theory is the thought that though there are a large number of most efficient men in any economy, there are fewer men of the indicated order actually found in any given industry than could be available to it. But this is equivalent to saying that all industries develop a character such that owner(s)-manager(s) are distributed over the hierarchy of industry types in accordance with the demands each place on these men and the costs of and consumer needs for each good. The best officials available to an industry working at their optimal efficiency mark the long run of a fully employed free enterprise system; however, note again, not all owner(s)-manager(s) in an industry can be classified as the best.

It is further implicit to our theory—especially in light of economic space, alternative market areas, and hence the development of branch plants—that a set of LRAC curves actually prevails in the system, not just the one typically conceived in classical theory. This set includes member curves which are on different levels, albeit in the subset of each member there may be two LRAC's (e.g. one for a single plant firm with alternative plant-size possibilities characterized along the curve, and one for a multiple-plant firm, again with alternative plant-size possibilities for one of its plants characterized along the curve). Each subset level is, of course, determined by the overall size of the firm, itself partially a function of the number of plants conceived to comprise the firm. The full significance of this conception will be examined in Chapter 13.

It might finally be noted here that our theory will be cast in terms of welfare economics, and that the impact of return r, of uncertainty, and of oligopoly on the classical welfare equations will be evaluated. We will find that the already mentioned technological optimum occurs coterminously with fulfilling all welfare criteria in the oligopolistic economy. Of course, our theory is subject to the charge of being static, as is all present-day micro-welfare theory. Even our conception of a set of LRAC curves can be said to be insufficiently dynamic in that it presumes a given technology, and a given point in history where wants of consumers and decisions of businessmen are formed by existing knowledge and forecasts. Our set of LRAC curves can be said to present only *one path* to the long run. We hope ultimately, however, not only to establish the optimality in production described above and the fulfillment of welfare equations as in pure competition economics, but at the same time to indicate that certain dynamic forces are contained within the system and the theory formulated herein.

As a final comment, let us point out that except in Chapter 9, where we follow the practice of this chapter, we shall employ the word entrepreneur in the typical loose sense customarily found in the literature. The entrepreneur will be conceived to be the owners of the firm who supply equity investment and possibly service inputs. In Chapter 9, we shall specify in detail our reasons for separating their service inputs from their equity capital inputs.

VII. PLAN OF PARTS II AND III

In Part II we shall prove the statements made in the initial chapters of this book as well as enlarge the theory presented here in Chapter 5. Specifically, through selected models of spatial competition, we shall verify the claim that economic distances between people and their institutions lead to a state of oligopoly. In turn, uncertainty as to reactions of rivals (in their prices, location, etc.) will be seen to exist.

After this cornerstone is laid, we shall be able to present the equilibrium properties that are part of an unorganized, noncollusive oligopoly. And we shall do this as an extension of the theory recorded in this chapter. Welfare attributes, including inquiry into the extent to which consumer wants are satisfied in the system, will be subsequently examined. And inquiry into the returns for owner services and equity investment—as a functional or residual return—will be tackled.

In Part III of this book, we shall analyze the spatial configurations that arise in a system marked by unorganized oligopoly. We shall compare the results with those that would occur if collusion (or simple monopoly) prevailed. It is one thing, of course, to speak of technological efficiency in the allocation of the classical factors of production. It is another matter to speak of spatial allocation and efficiency where the transportation factor is added to the capital factor of classical theory. So Part III adds on to Part II the basic matter of location and market areas, and, in particular, specifies the market area shapes required in the spatial equilibrium.

Part IV completes this book with a brief mathematical restatement of the welfare economics requirements. It shows how our theory complies with classical theory. A few words about economic policy and economic development will finally be given.

Appendix to Chapter 5

The Instability of the Chamberlinean Tangency: Another View

This appendix presents a rather abstract-artificial view of the theory sketched in the main chapter. As such, it may tend to have a rather restricted appeal to readers, depending ultimately upon their willingness to conceive of businessmen who "do as they do" even though the mathematics underlying their activity seemingly calls for a different act. We include this appendix only for those who wish now to probe further into our theory, and especially for those who are reading the book for a second time. In it, we apply a variable cost treatment for uncertainty with respect to the equity investment of the entrepreneur. In fact, variable cost imputation is made for all inputs of owner(s)-manager(s).

I. A FEW REPEATED WORDS ABOUT OPPORTUNITY COSTS

Let it be recalled that a lowest-cost producer is one whose energy expenditure performance happens to dovetail sufficiently closely to technological conditions to make the activity a feasible and acceptable one to him. Thus the individual's optimal performance should equal the industry's underlying requirements.

We also found that in any unit period of production, the actual input–output relations of services *may* involve energy expenditures $e' \gtreqless e$. However, instead of ascribing increasingly extra costs (i.e., requiring increasingly greater returns r') for service energy applications greater than e, we assumed linearity; similarly we did not *deduct* increasingly smaller costs (or let us say apply decreasingly smaller returns) for energy applications less than e. We assumed linearity for simple methodology.

Among entrepreneurs who have a chance to succeed, we will continue simply to ascribe a linear increase in imputed cost for any service efforts greater than the quantity optimally *planned*, and also deduct linearly for efforts less than e. In the case of the investment, as distinct from entrepreneurial services, the e units of expenditure (i.e., the equity investment) or acceptable alternatives may well occur over a small range of values, e.g., $m \leq e \leq n$, this because alternative capital-investment sums (or small changes in capital use) are often acceptable to a given investor. Thus we conceive of e taking any value between m and n albeit requiring r to be proportionate to the actual expenditure of e.

Uncertainty Ascribed as a Variable Cost

It was noted in Chapter 5 that the cost of uncertainty "could be" ascribed as a variable (or fixed) input. Variable input treatment, though in many respects the more precise, is the more difficult to depict. One tends to have to look at the physical capital (plus other input) side of the investment rather than at the equity (fund) side, and even then the variable input focus is rather difficult to grasp. In any case, part of the capital factor may be damaged by being used over too many units of time within a given time period. The variable input cost (i.e., the income utils required) thus rises linearly (following our previous proposition) with an over-application of the factor. Let us say that the income utils allocable per extra unit of energy util expended in a time period will rise as the factor's economic life is shortened. In the opposite case of being used too little, the economic life of the factor will be lengthened, if changed at all, and the allocable income utils per time period fall accordingly. But though all this seems clear, a problem arises in that any adjustment to marginal costs because of a variable cost treatment of uncertainty would seem to throw the marginal cost-marginal revenue calculus out of line.

II. EQUITY INVESTMENT AND OWNER-MANAGER SERVICES AS A VARIABLE COST: A CONCEPTUAL PROBLEM

In Chapter 5 all entrepreneurial-like inputs were treated as either fixed or variable. To do otherwise would require references to r' opportunity costs, say, for services and r opportunity costs for equity capital at some given input–output point. Statements ré such point, including applicable theorems, would be extremely wordy, and we shall, accordingly, leave such "in-between" interpolation to the reader. *All* entrepreneurial inputs will thus be treated here as variable input "ascriptions" to the classical cost curve. In turn, the difference between the adjusted and the unadjusted curves will provide a functional return which we could call revenues allocable to the entrepreneur's investment and related service inputs. Note, however, that if we are lumping the service and investment inputs together, we may as well describe as profits the total sum allocable to these inputs. Then our semantics will be more pleasing and no loss to theory results just so long as we further realize that profits (as used and designated later on in the diagrams of this appendix) is a more inclusive term than was the case in Chapter 5 where we related it to the equity investment (not service) input alone.

Variable Inputs and Marginal Costs

The average variable and marginal cost curves which include imputed opportunity costs as a variable input are naturally different from the curves which do not include them. However, as we shall later explain, if we assign variable cost treatment only up to the value r, the adjusted curves will merge at input point e (related to r) under the fixed and variable input treatments. Moreover, we shall see that the MC curve which includes imputed opportunity cost as a variable will intersect the variable adjusted AC curve at the same input e.

Now, we have noted that if compensation is due a factor for uncertainty, this uncertainty itself may be added in the form of income utils, just as is done for skill differentials or risk. The basis for including uncertainty either as a fixed or variable input is, therefore, manifest. In the following discussion we shall stress the uncertainty component on the capital investment of the entrepreneur, for this is the vital (new) property of our theory; but let us also observe that our remarks should be broadly understood to apply to any particular component of the investment (e.g. risk) and to entrepreneurship in general.

Opportunity Costs and the Variable r' (Not Fixed r) Uncertainty Adjustment

We generalize as follows: The return for uncertainty required in any given venture *is a partial function* of the investment (i.e., energy expenditure) total. In more detail, think of the best alternative activity. Allocate its income utils to the activity under examination. (As suggested above, this allocation must be adjusted to the different lifetimes of the factor in the two activities, as determined at the input point where classical optimality holds for each activity.) Then the absolute "payoff" r is the one to be mapped onto the subject firm's cost on the basis of the optimum performance in the best alternative venture. Add to it a component value v that is tied directly and linearly to the actual size of the investment (i.e. energy expenditure) which may apply at a given moment to the subject venture. Let v be positive for investments greater than the optimal one in the subject venture and negative for smaller expenditures. In other words, conceive of some value r plus a variable value v; in turn define $r + v$ (where $v \neq 0$) as being equivalent to variable value r', where r' is based on the rule that the more the subject investment exceeds the optimum investment, the larger is the dollar total ordered for the satisfaction of uncertainty, and vice versa. This monotonic function is traceable to the condition that when a greater than optimum output is multiplied by its related average cost, the total investment (e.g., long and short term capital) exceeds the total attributable to an optimum output.[1]

---

[1] How do we know that the investment (energy) expenditure of the firm increases as one moves to the right along any LRAC curve? Or, if you prefer, why is v (i.e., the investment —or energy—expenditure) negative at outputs smaller than the optimal one and positive at

The converse is equally true. Any artificial adjustment to the classical technological cost curve on account of uncertainty must, in other words, be based partially on the extra size (or smaller size) of output compared to the optimum output. We may view the equity investment of the entrepreneur in terms of a capital fund or, when an approximation suffices, in terms of capital equipment.

Opportunity Costs and an Adjustment to MR. We have seen that the average and marginal cost concepts are subjective in the sense of involving omnisciently inspired imputations relating to opportunities foregone. Nevertheless, they are basically objective, for psychic pleasures that have no bearing on energy expenditures and returns are not considered; only long-run concepts are applicable here. We find in general economic theory that the classical average and marginal *revenue* concepts relate to objective market data, or to conjectures about them. The market that is under consideration and the focus the theoretician has adopted is all-important. In the long run, only objective relationships matter and these always prevail.

When uncertainty is ascribed to marginal cost, it would seem, however, that some corresponding "imputationally-based" modification is needed for marginal revenue. Symmetrical treatment would enable us to compare the classical MC and MR values directly, and, as an artificial counterpart, the adjusted MC and MR values. For example, if AR is tangent to the variable adjusted AC curve, we know that the r' income received by the entrepreneur is commensurate with the e' energies expended. But the tangency of AR to adjusted AC does not signify a stable market situation; rather, the firm will either leave the market or increase its size. We may view this larger size requirement from either of two directions:

When AR is tangent to the r' adjusted AC curve, adjusted MC = classical MR; it follows that classical MC < classical MR and the firm will expand its output. (Of course, in the Chamberlinean world of monopolistic competition, as we shall later see, classical MC = classical MR when AR is tangent to AC).

When adjusted MC = classical MR, we alternatively find adjusted MC < adjusted MR, if to classical MR we artificially add the same (or a similar) value to that added on to MC. By comparing the adjusted MC's and MR's, we thus obtain the same conclusion as that obtained when the classical values are compared. Though the adjustment to MR is purely an operational one, we shall use it often in the following pages because, among other reasons, it sheds light on a thesis shortly to

---

larger than optimal outputs? To answer, let us designate I_o as the optimum size plant in its optimal performance (x_o), and let I_n refer to a smaller than optimum output (x_n) produced by the same plant. Then let II_n represent the plant of optimal size for the smaller than optimum output (x_n). Plant size II_n thus appears on the LRAC curve for output (x_n), while I_o, of course, establishes the optimal cost level at output x_o. We know that AC = TC/Q and total cost (TC) for plant operation I_o must either be greater than or at the least equal to what would be the corresponding total cost of the same plant in the production of x_n; this follows because if x_n were less than the optimal output, and the total cost in producing and maintaining it exceeded the total cost in producing and maintaining the optimal output, x_o would be produced with the difference $x_o - x_n$ stored or discarded. In short, $I_n \leqslant I_o$ in total investment, short and long term. But plant size II is more efficient in producing x_n than is I: hence, total cost of II_n is less than I_n. It follows that total cost (investment or energy expenditures) decreases with smaller than optimal size plants. Similarly, if the total cost of producing (i.e. the investment or energy expenditure in producing) $x_t > x_o$ were less than that of producing x_o, plant I_o could not be optimal as we assumed it is. Q.E.D.

be proposed: namely that the Chamberlinean tangency solution is not a stable equilibrium solution *even* in the world of certainty or risk to which the theory of monopolistic competition is assignable. But let us consider at this time another reason for proposing the alternative view to the classical evaluation of MC and MR, i.e. our comparison of adjusted MC with adjusted MR.

The MC adjustment is itself, let us note, a basically artificial adjustment in the sense that the firm's "accountants" or "engineers" would never uncover the MC adjusted value but would only derive the classical MC value. Thus, those who advise the owner(s)-manager(s) whether or not output should be expanded would only consider the classical MC and MR values. What *appears* as a tangency, i.e. AR = variable adjusted AC and hence MR = adjusted MC, represents to them the non-profit-maximizing point where MR > MC. Correspondingly, though the owner(s)-manager(s) of the firm recognize they are earning at the rate R (i.e. $r' = Re'$) when AR = variable adjusted AC, they too recognize the instability of the present case because adjusted MR > adjusted MC. They too will want to expand output and, in time, will exit from the industry (being replaced by smaller firms), or continue on in the presence of changes in AR stemming from the exit and entry of others. We could add to MR the same r'/q value we add to MC. However, to stress the income goal of earning r amount, we shall add to MR the value r/q at any given output rather than r'/q, where q stands for the given output.[1] In other words, under the variable *cost* treatment we ascribe the actual r' ($= r + v$) opportunities to the MC and AC curves at the given output, but only r to MR. (Incidentally, when we speak henceforth of ascribing r to MR at any output, the addition to MR should be understood to involve r/q; in turn, the ascription of r' to costs should be understood to involve the addition of r'/q at the same output q.) Because the adjustment to MR is strictly an operational one alone, we shall not present it graphically. Nevertheless, from the standpoint of entrepreneurial imputations, the following disequilibria become identifiable.

Case I. At outputs greater than the classical optimum, the addition to AC of that dollar amount of uncertainty which might make AR = adjusted AC entails an adjusted MR < an adjusted MC; i.e. the r ascribed to MR is less than the r' ($= r + v$) ascribed to AC and MC. If applying r' to costs makes AR = AC adjusted, an *illusion* of stability but nothing more exists. Significantly, in greater than optimum output cases, the engineering data may diverge from the imputed data; i.e. classical MR could equal classical MC, while AR = AC adjusted. But adjusted MR < adjusted MC. The entrepreneur alone would recognize the instability of the situation.

Case II. At points short of the optimum technological point, any AR = AC adjusted would involve adjusted MR > adjusted MC (and classical MR > classical

[1] Consider also the following: we add r'/q to the AC and MC of a given investment because all costs must be defrayed in the long run if the plant (firm) is to survive. But we add only the uncertainty "cost" (r/q) to MR since the requirement for a viable, truly efficient system does not, *ipso facto*, select the particular firms that survive. By adding r'/q to costs and only r/q to revenues, we have adjusted our MC and MR curves such that all imbalances are emphasized. Significantly, we will see that the condition of unadjusted MR = unadjusted MC *may* indicate that the firm is not utilizing its given plant optimally. In fact, to repeat, the entrepreneur will find some tangency conditions illusory since he would not be using the proper size plant if MR adjusted ≠ MC adjusted.

MC). In the imputation process, we would apply r amount to MR while altering MC by an amount reflective or r plus $v = r'$, with v being negative in this case. In short, r is greater than r'. (To repeat, by applying r not r' to MR we are emphasizing the requirement that the entrepreneur or manager seeks from any activity at least the return he would receive elsewhere in an optimal performance. On the other hand, his costs relate to actual expenditures.)

We are proposing in Case I above that if a firm has been operating with, say, too large a plant, then even though the classical values show MR $=$ MC, and profits happen to equal those required by uncertainty, the entrepreneur will recognize that a disequilibrium condition exists compared with his best alternative. He must rationalize his plant (and firm) size to the optimum scale or leave the industry. If, as in the second case above, a firm has been operating with too small a plant, we should realize that again a disequilibrium condition exists, even though profits appear to equal the amount required by uncertainty.

To best appreciate these conclusions, consider the instances where profits exceed those required by uncertainty. Here, new firms (and plants) would enter, reducing profits, and all entrepreneurs would seek to rationalize their operations to the optimal size. Even when AR is reduced to the point where it exceeds AC by the "right" amount (i.e., AR $=$ variable adjusted AC), the entrepreneur's own imputation process would induce an expansion of energy utils if the plant is smaller than optimal size; manifestly $r' < r$ for such sizes of plants. (Briefly put, the mR transform of nR_0 is not being met.) If this situation is representative of the entire industry, some firms will exit and there will be a rationalization and adjustment of the plants and firm sizes of others. The market eventually will contain only entrepreneurs whose lost opportunities are met in full. A similar sequence results when there are greater than optimal size applications with profits prevailing initially. We shall have much more to say about these situations later on.

Summary of Cases I and II. If at points greater than the classical optimum, AR is $>$ AC by precisely the amount of uncertainty applicable to the activity, then ascribing an r value to MR and an r' value to MC yields adjusted MR $<$ adjusted MC since v in $r' = r + v$ is clearly positive. At input points short of the classical optimum where AR $>$ AC by r' amount, adjusted MR $>$ adjusted MC. Remember, here, the classical MR also $>$ classical MC.

Unorganized oligopoly tends accordingly to produce at the technologically optimal point. Indeed, our formulation establishes two long-run "equilibrium" requirements of the marginal values: not only must (1) classical MR $=$ MC, but as an added condition (2) the last unit of good sold must, in effect, carry an added revenue, r, which relates to the optimal performance and return elsewhere, and which is identically the same as the ascribed cost added to MC. The ascribed cost added to MC in turn reflects (a) the actual investment undertaken, and (b) the optimal rate R derived from the best foregone alternative.[1]

---

[1] It might be recalled here that an optimal R_0 for the alternative investment is identifiable. The mapping to the subject activity then involves a transformation to the alternative optimal size investment for which the equivalently transformed return R is identified. An absolute level r is therefore, applicable to the firm under examination. This r is the *ideal* return sought for the activity in question. It is based—to recall—on the economic lifetime the entrepreneur expects (and intends) to have in the subject activity; and it is subdivided (i.e., allocated) on a unit production period basis. Of course, the facts of economic life may

III. A DIAGRAMMATIC PRESENTATION OF THE THEORY

We may trace the alternative situations that are possible schematically, and in the process review the basic properties of our theory. We shall begin with the short-run situation described in Figure 5A–1, where the variable service inputs are treated in

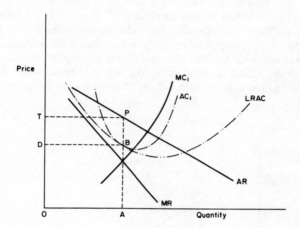

Figure 5A–1: Short-Run Windfalls, Increasing Economies of Scale

the same way as the equity capital inputs. There we impute the return for each as profits, even though in Chapter 5, and again in Chapter 9, we observe that it is only the positive return for uncertainty on the capital investment which is the true profit of the entrepreneur.[1]

Suppose initially that AC_1 and MC_1 include only explicit cost items, and that the profits obtainable (DBPT) are greater than the profit requirements of the owner(s)-manager(s). More specifically, let r_1 stand for the optimum amount of

render any entrepreneur's expectation a far cry from reality as the actual investment inputs are reflected in $r' = r + v \ (v \neq o)$.

Note further that related to r is the absolute return in the best alternative r_o. This r_o may be viewed backwards as the transform from r to R to R_o to r_o. Our critical requirement for engaging in the subject activity is, therefore, that an ideal absolute return r exists which, in the transformed sense, must be $\geq$ to any corresponding r_o. Because of this requirement $(r \geq r_o)$, we are able usually to refer in the text only to the transformed values R or r not to R_o or r_o.

[1] We might further mention here that in developing the concept of opportunity cost in Chapter 5 our references centered on the individual, as, in effect, implicit wages of management were considered. In particular, it warrants emphasis (as we shall stress later on in the book) that our framework of thought is a general one since the imputed wages of management which bring costs of all surviving firms to the same level actually apply to any type of business organization in the long run, e.g. the single proprietorship, partnership, or corporation.

income utils that could be earned by the owner(s)-manager(s) for services in the optimal alternative employment, and let r_2 stand for the optimal alternative return on the investment of equity capital under the same uncertainty; in turn, let $r_1 + r_2 = r$. Next assume that actual profits DBPT are greater than r. New firms then will enter the market. In fact, they would even enter the market if DBPT equalled r since input energies would be less than e at output OA in Figure 5A–1.

Suppose next that profits DBPT are identically equal to $r'_1 + r'_2 = r'$ where $r'_1 < r_1$ and $r'_2 < r_2$; then related energies $e'_1 < e$ and $e'_2 < e_2$. Otherwise put, DBPT $= r' < r$. To some outsiders, the industry might appear to be in equilibrium since DBPT $= r'$, so that all explicit costs are being met *and* the entrepreneurs are receiving full returns r' for their personal efforts and expenditures e'. By ascribing r' to MC_1 and AC_1, and focusing attention only on the adjusted short-run cost curves, Figure 5A–1 reappears as 5A–2. A Chamberlinean tangency position has been reached.

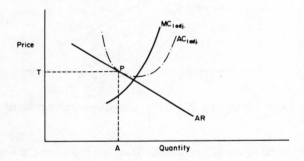

Figure 5A–2: Chamberlinean Tangency (Equilibrium)

The equilibrium shown in Figure 5A–2 is not stable for an oligopolistic industry because classical MR > classical MC. Alternatively viewed, adjusted MC includes only r' while the related adjusted (or artificial) MR requires the addition of r, so adjusted MR much > adjusted MC. Only the classical marginal revenue curve intersects the adjusted marginal cost curve. The residual left for the entrepreneurial function is therefore inadequate. The entrepreneur knows he is investing less in services and capital than he desires to invest in the subject activity, a condition not shown by the tangency position in Figure 5A–2. Significantly—it is the existing firm itself not new firms which leads to the change in its input–output level when a return r' commensurate with $e' < e$ initially prevails.

Consider an opposite type of situation, as represented in Figure 5A–3. Assume initially that actual profits FGHJ are much greater than the requirements r of the entrepreneur. New entry will occur, AR will shift leftward, and conceivably a set of profits will arise which is commensurate with the entrepreneur's actual expenditure of energy and capital.

It is vital to note that any profit return commensurate with relatively large energy expenditures also reflects an unstable situation. To illustrate, suppose FGHJ is identically equal to $r'_1 + r'_2 = r'$, where r' *here relates to* a scale of effort e' reflected in *a larger than optimal size endeavor*. Figure 5A–4 now applies.

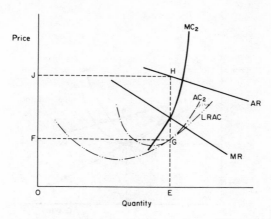

Figure 5A–3: Short-Run Windfalls, Decreasing Economies of Scale

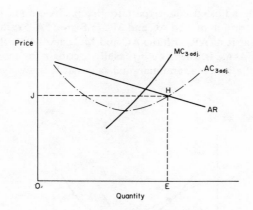

Figure 5A–4: Firm [Plant] Too Large

Unlike Figure 5A–2, Figure 5A–4 depicts the situation where not only would the adjusted MC and MR values be unequal but a *contraction* in the size of the firm is indicated. (Recall to MC we here ascribe r' ($> r$), and to MR we artificially impute r.) Each change towards the optimal size via a rationalizing of the number and size of plants makes profits temporarily greater than those required by entrepreneurs. Outsiders readily identify the windfalls, and with each entry the AR curve shifts leftward, provided competitive (not monopolistic) impacts on supply and price occur. Ultimately, Figure 5A–5 appears, where now MHRS $\equiv r \equiv r_1 + r_2$.

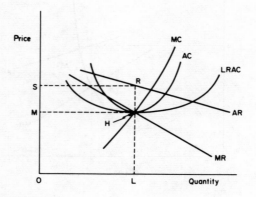

Figure 5A–5: Long-Run Equilibrium and the r' Adjusted Curve

What does the adjusted counterpart to Figure 5A–5 look like? In answer, observe that the ascription of r' to AC and MC in Figure 5A–5 establishes at output OL a convergence at R of AR with the AC and MC curves after they are adjusted. (Thus see Figure 5A–6.) If, then, we artificially ascribe r for the quantity OL to MR, the identity of all average and marginal values at R is revealed.

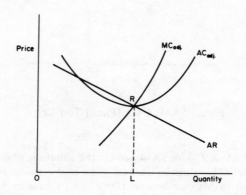

Figure 5A–6: The Illusory r' Adjusted Curve

Figure 5A–6 accordingly depicts the convergence of AR with adjusted AC and MC, and implicitly with adjusted MR. But Figure 5A–6 seemingly indicates the possibility of profits at outputs less than OL, such that an area of indeterminacy would at first glance appear to apply over the range between a Chamberlinean tangency point (as shown in Figure 5A–2) and the alternative zero profit point (as indicated at R in Figure 5A–6). This indeterminism does not hold, however, for the simple reason that what appears to be profits at outputs < OL in Figure 5A–6 represent returns which, in fact, though greater than r', are still less than r. To understand this point more clearly consider the following:

In Figure 5A–6 the AR curve over some points to the left of OL is above the r' energy requirement. Suppose we assume it is so much greater than r' that if we superimposed the r adjusted (i.e. the fixed cost adjusted) AC curve over the AC adjusted curve of Figure 5A–6, its AR curve would be tangent to the r adjusted curve. But then entry and rationalization would eventuate as described in Chapter 5. Suppose instead that the AR of Figure 5A–6 falls between the r adjusted curve and the r' adjusted AC curve actually drawn in Figure 5A–6. Again an unstable situation

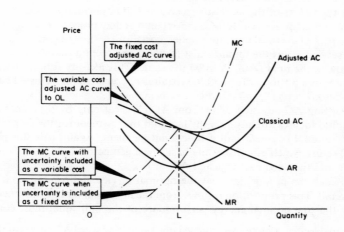

Figure 5A–7: The r and r' Curves together

holds. On the one hand, firms would not be earning the r opportunity costs, though some owner(s)-manager(s) may feel that a return greater than r' for an effort e' justifies the longer economic lifetime over which the factor would be used. At the same time, however, outsiders holding this opinion would consider entry to be desirable. In fact, smaller units with optimal opportunity costs set by r' (not r) because their optimal energy expenditures are e' (not e) would tend to enter and replace some of the firms in the market. Manifestly, what is e' to pre-existing firms would be e to such new firms, and correspondingly what we referred to as r'—in the above sentence—is r' only to the old firms but r to the new.

Our Figure 5A–7, though not an all inclusive representation, summarizes the theory rather fully. In it, we ascribe to costs the variable returns r' for all variable energies $e' < e$; Beyond e, no further variable ascriptions are entered.[1] Hence, the fixed opportunity cost adjusted curve (i.e. the curve adjusted by r returns) merges with the variable adjusted AC curve at the point where the variable opportunity costs r' become equal to the fixed opportunity costs r. We are following this practice in order to simplify the figure and because the vital areas at issue typically run up to the output OL. Moreover, our algebraic references to a variable adjusted AC curve at outputs greater than OL should be clear without the aid of any diagram.

We find in Figure 5A–7 that a tangency to the r adjusted curve at output OL yields the classical "optimal" allocation of resources. Indeed, if the difference between the adjusted and the classical AC curves should include only the uncertainty on the capital investment rather than also the returns r or r' for all service inputs and the risk portion of the equity investment input, several other conclusions will emerge:

(1) At outputs short of OL, any tangency to the r adjusted curve (i.e. the fixed cost adjusted AC curve) provides returns greater than those indicated by e' energy expenditures.

(2) Tangency to the r' adjusted curve (i.e. the variable cost adjusted AC curve) manifests the failure of the factor to receive its full opportunity costs.

(3) Whether or not we follow the recommended procedure as to costs [i.e. impute as part of classical costs all implicit costs for services (including uncertainty on these services) plus the implicit cost for risk] or accept a modified treatment of this approach, the final results will be the same. This identity follows because our equilibrium (or a position of windfalls) requires reference to the adjusted curve, and this includes *all* costs (i.e. *all* required payments).

(4) Letting AC adjusted differ from AC classical only by the uncertainty on equity capital focuses attention on the fact that the payment for the owners' investment is a residual payment, not a functional payment. Again, it is this particular (residual) return which establishes the basis for a geometrical tangency between the AR curve and the fixed cost adjusted AC curve.

(5) Recall the proposition that the optimal service and capital input energies must dovetail. This proposition follows from the argument already advanced where we noted that the optimal energy performance of the individual must conform to

---

[1] If variable ascriptions were continued, the variable adjusted AC curve would be seen to be the mirror of the classical adjusted curve, with the least cost combination on each curve involving the same e expenditure. This relation follows readily from our opportunity cost concept. Thus:

$$(1) \quad c = f(Q) + u, \text{ where } u \text{ stands for uncertainty.}$$

$$(2) \quad u = u(Q)$$
$$= \phi Q, \ \phi = \text{constant}$$

$$\therefore (3) \quad MC = \frac{dc}{dQ} = f_Q + \frac{du}{dQ} = f_Q + \phi$$

$$(4) \quad AC = \frac{c}{Q} = \frac{f(Q)}{Q} + \frac{u}{Q} = \frac{f(Q)}{Q} + \phi$$

The variable adjusted MC and AC curves therefore mirror the unadjusted curves, being greater than the latter by the constant ϕ, which itself is equal to the constant increase of Re' as e' is increased.

the prevailing technology in the industry, because if this were not the case the firm would be a high-cost producer. Supporting output OL is, therefore, energy applications e in services and in capital.

(6) Uncertainty combined with indivisibility limits entry; together they promote the tilt of the AR curves. Uncertainty and indivisibility in capital investment require our evaluation of the adjusted AC curves. And if no collusion is permitted, and if oligopolists are free to enter or leave the market, the economy is viable and efficient.

(7) The returns r for inputs e establish the industry equilibrium.

(8) It follows from all the above that the monopolistic competition tangency solution of Chamberlin restricts its attention to the engineering aspects of economic decision-making and in the process violates the fundamental concept of opportunity costs. This condition may be readily seen first by assuming—for simplicity—a world of certainty rather than one of risk. Indeed, we can also ignore occupational hazards (e.g. uncertainty of survival, health, etc.) to stress the fact that our concern is with other matters. Simply assume entrepreneurial opportunity costs of r or r' amount depending on the fixed or variable approach to opportunity costs that may be taken. Two tangency and one in-between tangency solutions warrant consideration.

(A) Suppose AR is tangent to the r adjusted AC curve. Classical MC = classical MR; there are no adjusted marginal curves. From an engineering standpoint, equilibrium exists. But other would-be participants in the market identify the tangency as a position of profits and will enter the market if free entry exists.

(B) Suppose Chamberlin's tangency is interpreted to apply to the situation where AR is tangent to the r' adjusted AC curve. Classical MC now is less than classical MR and from an engineering standpoint inputs must be increased to a point where total income more closely approaches r returns than is now the case. (Incidentally, this is why the final equilibrium shown in Figure 5A–7 requires an AR curve which is above the r' adjusted AC curve at points before least cost on that curve.) Only at the optimum cost point with an AR curve intersecting the r' adjusted curve would classical MC = classical MR.

(C) Suppose the AR curve falls between the r and r' adjusted AC curves, being tangent to some imaginary curve that falls halfway between the two adjusted AC curves. In other words, we are conceiving of an imaginary AC curve where a variable r' adjustment plus a partial fixed r adjustment has been made. Because the slope of the AR curve would be steeper than the slope on the r' adjusted curve at an energy expenditure less than e, but flatter than the slope on the r adjusted curve at the same energy expenditure, the following relations hold:

Classical MC (derivable from the rate of change along the classical AC curve) is < classical MR (determined as some value falling between the classical MR related to the steeply formed AR curve that is tangent to the r adjusted AC curve and the greater classical MR value which is related to the flatly sloped AR curve that is tangent to the r' adjusted AC curve). From an engineering standpoint, the firm will expand its inputs; meanwhile, other firms will enter the market, and eventually the equilibrium solution of Figure 5A–7 is reached.

It is manifest that Chamberlinean theory had to focus on the AR curve which is tangent to the r adjusted AC curve if the mathematical requirement of MR = MC was to be complied with in the classical sense (i.e. if the engineer's MR, MC calculus was to be complied with). What Chamberlin overlooked was the potential entrant in the market because of the profit which, in effect, exists when firms cover their lost opportunity income in full at smaller expenditures than they otherwise would have to bear. In other words, the actual cost of producing the subject output is revealed by the r' adjusted AC curve at that output, where $r' = Re'$, not the r adjusted AC curve.

We must finally observe with respect to the Chamberlinean world that, in the absence of uncertainty, free entry could signify the replacement of many large firms by a great number of small ones. Our development of costs of a multi-plant firm in Chapter 8 will indicate that though some large firms may be more efficient than small ones in selected industries, after the imputational process all firms are on the same level of costs, *ceteris paribus*. But though our conception of monopolistic competition in equilibrium at the intersection point of AR and AC (= MC) points to efficient operation, it is proposed that a dynamic development of costs would indicate that—through research and related activities—technological developments by larger firms take place which, in effect, are ignored in static comparisons of market equilibria. The entry-restraining effect of uncertainty, combined with the better position of larger firms to survive short-run uncertainties, provide a picture of oligopolistic markets in which the more efficient firms (i.e. before opportunity cost imputations are effected) tend to prevail in the long run. In other words, though we derive efficient operation whether or not uncertainty exists, we propose that uncertainty is part and parcel of spatial economic systems. It follows that the monopolistically competitive market, even in the modified form presented above, fails to provide meaningful insights. It further follows that the essential theoretical impact of uncertainty is to explain market structures in which large firms may be found to coexist with small firms.

(9) A V-shaped AC adjusted curve may be conceived which avoids the stable equilibrium picture of AR intersecting the r' adjusted AC curve at its optimal cost point. Instead, under the conditions of stable equilibrium, tangency occurs at the low point of the V. This V-shaped adjusted AC curve reflects a broken adjusted MC curve which, itself, is formed by variable opportunity cost imputations; these imputations decrease to zero at the classical optimal energy expenditure point becoming positive again beyond that point. Since our basic results are unchanged, we shall relegate the discussion of the V-shaped alternative to the r' adjusted curve to a footnote discussion for readers interested in pursuing further the variable cost imputation process.[1]

[1] Recall, initially, the suggestion entered in Chapter 5 that the value of the lost opportunity is probably best conceived as a fixed cost because it is the measure of the entire set of dollar incomes foregone. However, there is a variable aspect in the use of capital or the application of human capital inputs which, in accounting terms, could be called user depreciation; at the same time, the fixed nature of lost opportunities also has a referential base in the depreciation or obsolescence of a factor which occurs naturally with the passage of time, apart from use. If realism were an end in itself in theory, one would, therefore, have to treat the lost opportunity in a dual role, partly as a fixed cost, partly as a variable. It is because of this possible preference that the variable cost side of lost opportunities warrants recording. And most significantly, a less artificial approach than that which was set forth in the text above *is available* for those who desire to visualize the variable input side of lost opportunities. As with most things (and thoughts) in life, this alternative carries its own cost for it requires our surrendering the conception of a classical bell shaped AC curve. Consider the following:

The lost opportunity income requirements of the factor, in reality, are nonlinear, much

IV. A CONCLUDING REVIEW—THE FIXED AND VARIABLE COST ADJUSTMENTS

We have given two contrasting ways of looking at the equilibrium process of a competitive (i.e. unorganized) oligopolistic economy. One treats all costs that warrant imputation as a fixed cost, and the other as a variable cost. In the latter case, a rather artificial manipulation of marginal costs takes place; so a corresponding adjustment to marginal revenue becomes desirable. The adjustments we have proposed to the marginal values are, of course, basically definitional, but they have the advantage (and logic) of dovetailing precisely (in so far as final results and conclusions are concerned) with the fixed cost adjustment technique for imputed costs. We therefore have alternative ways of viewing the same phenomenon, and the following selected alternative short-run states will illustrate this fact.

Initially Greater than Optimal Output

Suppose the representative firm is producing an output greater than its least cost output and that its price is so much greater than its average cost at that output as to yield an economic profit in excess of the amount an omniscient economist would say is required for the prevailing uncertainty. This situation of windfalls, we know, would promote entry in a competitive system. Therefore, let AR shift to the left such that the difference between AR > AC—at the output where classical MR = MC—falls to the level of being commensurate with uncertainty. What seemingly is an equilibrium state is, however, not a stable state.

greater for initial inputs but eventually zero at the classical-least cost input point. The true r' adjusted AC curve is, therefore, of steeper slope than the r' adjusted AC curve drawn above in the text, but not as steep as the r adjusted AC curve. The related marginal cost must, in turn, generally be above that drawn previously, through merging with classical marginal cost at the classical least cost point. This unity obtains because as the extra unit of input is applied which brings the factor to the classical optimal input-output point, the required additional opportunity cost return for the extra energy application approaches zero. It is, therefore, the case that the true adjusted marginal cost curve is of negative slope over some ranges of output and, in fact, may fall continuously to the point of classical least cost. Thus it is also possible that MR intersects adjusted MC at two points, the last one occurring, if stable equilibrium prevails, where adjusted MC = classical MC since the variable r' value at the classical optimal cost point is zero. A discontinuity, therefore, prevails because at input–output points immediately following the classical least cost input–output point, a new (positive) ascription for lost opportunity income applies to the greater energies being used. Thus the adjusted marginal cost curve is really a broken curve, and the related adjusted average cost curve is not smoothly continuous but actually approximates the shape of a V. As noted above, equilibrium requires tangency of the AR curve at the low point of the V shaped adjusted curve, which point lies directly above the classical least cost point. We might point out that if the MR intersects the MC adjusted curve at an input point short of the optimal cost input point, the AR curve may be expected to lie below or above the adjusted AC curve. Of course, it is possible that a tangency may apply at some point short of the lowest point on the V adjusted curve. The firm, itself, would appear to be in equilibrium, but as was described above in the text for this type of situation, the equilibrium would not be stable. The prevailing rate of return would induce some entry and exit, which in turn would involve a change in locations, number and size of firms, and a change in the slope(s) of the representative firm's AR curve.

The instability manifested by AR > AC by r' amount and $e' > e$ is similar to that where AR > AC by r' amount but $e' < e$. In the last instance mentioned, the solution which we would expect to apply most often is the replacement of some larger firms and plants by a larger number of smaller firms and plants. Total output would increase. Also in the $e' > e$ case, a larger number of smaller firms with a greater number of plants will prevail in the long run. Total output would increase. Eventually AR > AC by the true amount of uncertainty, and all receipts would be commensurate with what—to the new firms—are energy expenditures of level e. Viewed from the variable cost adjustment approach, we would say that a stable equilibrium eventuates where AR > AC by the underlying amount of uncertainty, and where the classical functions MR, MC, and AC all intersect. Significantly, at this point, AR = adjusted AC = adjusted MC = adjusted MR.

Initially Smaller than Optimal Output

Consider by way of final example the before optimal cost production possibility. Specifically, assume entry has proceeded to the point where AR > AC by the omnisciently designated amount of uncertainty, but where the unadjusted marginal values intersection indicates less than optimal cost production.

Under the fixed cost alternative, i.e. where AC is adjusted by r amount at all q's, stability obtains when AR = adjusted AC and $e' = e$. But if $e' < e$, and tangency exists, energies e' are being rewarded with r returns. This situation is equivalent to a windfall. So new entry will take place. The AR curves, which initially would probably have been rather steeply sloped will shift to the left and flatten out because of the increased number of alternative sources of supply. But then, returns less than r will prevail and some entrepreneurs will alter the scale of their operation and others will exit from the market, in some cases being replaced by firms with smaller energy input requirements for optimal production. The larger firms which remain (and continue at the original size) will possess an allocated AR of greater magnitude than the smaller firms. Generally, to repeat, a larger number of alternative sources of supply eventuate over the space and the AR curves are gentler in slope. Stable equilibrium requires r returns for e expenditures of energy, and this eventuates where AR > AC by the omnisciently imputed amount of uncertainty and the unadjusted values MR = MC = AC.[1]

A variable cost imputation for the $e' < e$ situation, similar to that designated in the preceding paragraph, involves an adjusted MC < adjusted MR. Stated in formal algebraic terms $MC + (r+v)/q < MR + r/q$. But this inequality encourages existing firms to adjust their scale of operation. Via entry, exit, and the rationalization process, firms ultimately prevail which have AR = adjusted AC = adjusted MC = adjusted MR. These intersections simply involve e energy expenditures calling forth r revenues for the representative firms (and for all firms, be they large or small in size). This, then, is our theory. We will look into consumer satisfaction, and the

---

[1] Similar in part to classical theory, we must not (and do not) conceive of an identity of all firms. Rather, we conceive of some small and some large firms with one or several plants, ad infinitum. In the oligopolistic economy, the AR allocable to a smaller firm will be to the left of the AR allocable to a larger firm. Equilibrium prevails only when AR > AC by the right amount and the representative firm has r returns for *its* energies e.

welfare and related aspects of the relations underscoring the indicated equilibrium in the remaining chapters of the book.[1]

[1] Mr. Hiroshi Ohta proposed another format to me to describe the MR adjustment. In particular, he suggested that the r adjusted AC curve could be referred to as the required revenue (RR) curve up to output OL in Figure 5A–7. From this viewpoint, it can be shown that the classical MR = classical MC principle does not record perfectly the entrepreneur's plans or perspective. In fact, it is only when the required revenue (RR) equals the revenue commensurate with energy expenditures, i.e. the r' adjusted curve (which he proposes could be referred to as AR') that a stable equilibrium holds *and* the classical marginal values conform perfectly to the signals actually viewed by the entrepreneur.

In Mr. Ohta's verbiage, MR adjusted is a dummy concept which has nothing to do with the AR curve (or demand schedule) or the r' revenue (AR') curve, since it is really a required revenue curve at outputs < OL. Over such outputs, RR is > AR' and industrial expansion must take place. In fact, when industry expansion is indicated, even though AR is tangent to RR (hence classical MR = classical MC), the individual firm may nevertheless begin opting for a larger plant (since RR > AR' or, by analogy, MR adj > MC adj). It would only be when RR = AR' *and* AR is tangent to RR at the same output point that the subject firm would stay as it is.

At outputs greater than OL, the RR curve in Mr. Ohta's system is also known only by the entrepreneur. The RR curve over these outputs would lie well above (and increasingly above) the r adjusted AC curve, and for that matter the r' adjusted AC curve. Any price equal to a point on the r or r' adjusted AC curve is clearly unsatisfactory, as some firms would plan a smaller size operation while others would contemplate exiting from the industry. Price points above the r' (and hence the r) adjusted curves also yield unstable equilibria, particularly with respect to new firms wanting to enter. As in the case of outputs less than OL, when size of firms are greater than the optimal size, the classical MR = classical MC principle does not indicate precisely the entrepreneur's plans or perspective.

Part II

PRICES AND RESOURCE ALLOCATION

6

Unorganized Spatial Oligopoly

THREE POINTS, one on technique and two on semantics, should be kept in mind in the following discussion:

(1) A kinked demand curve is usually used throughout this chapter as a point of departure for our inquiries into unorganized spatial oligopoly. As already said, later in the book we shall formulate the limits to the use of this conception, and, in effect, replace it by other conceptions which apply to less restricted situations. (2) By unorganized (*vis-à-vis* organized) oligopoly, we mean a system of oligopolistic relations which does not involve collusive behavior between firms; in fact, we even rule out such forms of parallelism of action as *consistent* price-following by firms in an industry. (3) By a spatial market, we shall have in mind a distribution of firms in some pattern over an economic landscape. The basic conclusions of this chapter will, however, be seen to apply to any unorganized oligopoly, spatial or otherwise.

This chapter does not attempt to present a detailed picture of spatial markets; it is more an introductory "analytical" investigation of spatial competition. Nevertheless we might emphasize our belief that spatial competition constitutes a vital part of economic competition, and that its analysis may soon be so firmly established that it becomes vital subject matter for at least a one or two chapter examination in intermediate and advanced undergraduate textbooks in economic theory. In fact, we believe that some analysis of spatial competition should be included on every level of study to supplement the current emphasis on nonspatial markets, possibly replacing it as the basic explanatory mechanism in many areas of applied research, such as marketing theory. We further believe that the analysis of spatial competition will, in time, serve as the theoretical vehicle to interpret significant events in the economic history of free enterprise societies. Our present chapter, of course, cannot enter into applications of the kind proposed above. Moreover, our present analysis of unorganized oligopoly is purely introductory, being confined to determining the differences between competitively established prices in a "timed" (and otherwise dimensionless) market with those obtained in a "timed" space economy. From these comparisons, certain conclusions about non-spatial and spatial markets will be drawn.

I. SELLERS ALONE AT A POINT, ECONOMIC DISTANCE, AND PRICE

We postulate that there is a tendency of people (1) to cluster together at certain resource centers, and (2) later on to move to outlying areas. These tendencies also hold true for industrial activity, especially manufacturing establishments. Let us say that firms and industries customarily agglomerate first at established centers, where both demand conditions and cost (resources) are most favorable; subsequently, some firms (plants) and industries move to outlying suburbs and other market areas. Under the resulting distribution over space, the outlying firms tend to watch the firms at the center. At the same time, the firms in central locations learn the advantages of competing in ways other than price. Soon oligopoly develops, as our model will help explain. In the present section, however, we will confine our attention to the initial situation of sellers at a point, inquiring alone into the impacts of new entry at the same point and of distance on price.

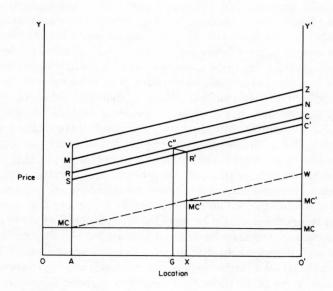

Figure 6–1: Prices over a Market Area

Basic Assumptions

In our model, we assume a small industrialized city in which all of the firms belonging to the industry are located. Freight rates are proportional to distance. Each firm is comparatively large in size and able to identify its competitors. Because rivals are involved, an attempt by any one firm to control part of the entire market cannot be considered a "live and let live" policy but is regarded as competitive action. Under the hypothesized initial spatial arrangement, firms may act either as independent oligopolists or, in concert, as followers of a price leader. In this section and throughout the chapter, we will describe only unorganized spatial oligopoly.

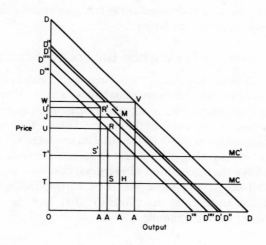

Figure 6–2: Spatial Prices

We assume specifically four sellers at the industrial center, call it A, the least-cost location. (See Figure 6–1.) But note, four firms are merely assumed for convenience in drawing the diagrams; the reader may actually regard the number as 40 or 400 or 4000, just so long as he imagines that rival sellers are able to identify one another, and are watching each other. A is the source of the raw material used by the firms, and is also an extremity of the market. Concentration at A may have been caused originally by very high costs of transportation of raw materials, a factor now supposed to be less influential because of the development of new means of transport. As further current data, assume fixed costs are zero and marginal costs are constant at A (designated by the MCMC line in Figure 6–1 and the TMC line in Figure 6–2). For a location X at the midpoint of the AO′ market (which we shall evaluate in section II of the chapter), marginal costs MC′MC′ in Figure 6–1 or

T'MC' in Figure 6–2 prevail; they are presupposed to be constant and at a level about twice that at A. Also assume that (1) each firm at A is perfectly identical in product, and each is of the same size; (2) the companies sell on a nondiscriminatory f.o.b. price basis;[1] (3) there is no consumer preference among sellers or products, save in respect to price; and (4) buyers are evenly spaced over the entire market area AO'.

The demand curves for the four sellers at A are known. They are of the form $y = b - ax$, and so similar for each seller that at *any given price* the elasticity of demand for the product of any seller is the same. The DD curve in Figure 6–2 depicts the demand for any one seller's commodity. Its intercepts are each at a distance from the origin which is two-fifths as great as the intercepts of the total market demand curve (i.e., the entire demand curve for the good) for reasons explained below.

Basic Propositions of Price when Buyers are Scattered

In traditional economic analysis, it has been well established by rules of geometry and calculus that when marginal costs are zero and the demand curve is as designated above, the profit-maximizing monopoly price is equal to half the ordinate-intercept value of the curve.[2] This we shall realize amounts to saying that sales are set at one-half the abscissa intercept value of the curve. If marginal costs were positive, price would equal half the vertical height of the demand curve above the intersection of marginal cost with marginal revenue plus the marginal costs; and sales would be correspondingly determined. We shall appreciate these rules more readily after looking into Cournot's (nonspatial) mineral springs example.

Cournot's Model: Sellers and Buyers at a Point. Cournot assumed zero costs and hypothesized that sellers will regard any rival's supply as fixed. Following the rules just noted, Cournot then holds that seller *one* would sell one-half of the total that could be sold in the market at the marginal cost (zero) price. He then observed that a second entrant would visualize a demand for his product which is half as great in ordinate and abscissa intercept values respectively as that which in total prevails. Thus, the best initial output adjustment for the second firm is the offer of one-half of the greatest amount that he would expect to be able to sell if the zero price prevailed. In other words, the second seller offers to supply only a quarter of the greatest

---

[1] By f.o.b. price system we mean the system where the price at the seller's mill is quoted with the freight to the buyer's factory either added on to the seller's f.o.b. net-mill price or else paid directly by the buyer to the transport agency.

[2] Linear demand may be expressed as $y = b - ax$; so $x = \dfrac{b}{a} - \dfrac{y}{a}$.

(a) Total revenue $R = \left(\dfrac{b}{a} - \dfrac{y}{a}\right) y = \dfrac{by - y^2}{a}$; (b) $\dfrac{dR}{dy} = \dfrac{b - 2y}{a} = 0$; (c) $y = \dfrac{b}{2}$.

quantity of the product that buyers would purchase. In turn, the abscissa and ordinate extension visualized by seller one *as his share* of the market would shrink by this quarter value, and the original seller thus would be led to contract his offering by half of the one fourth amount. But then, this contraction enlarges the sales potential viewed by the second seller to the extent of one-eighth of the total quantity that would be sold in the market at the zero price. In effect, we have the system shown in (1).

		Initial Offering	Change in Offering	Next Change in Offering
(1)	First Firm	1/2	$-1/8$	$-1/32$
	Second Firm	1/4	$+1/16$	$+1/64$

A geometric series $(a+ar+ar^2+ \ldots +ar^{n-1})$ clearly exists, with the numbers in (2′) and (2″) showing only the changes in supply that occur with the entry of the second firm; more specifically, (2′) shows the supply action of the second firm and (2″) the change in supply of the first firm.

(2′) $\frac{1}{4}+\frac{1}{16}+\frac{1}{64}+ \cdot \cdot$

(2″) $-\frac{1}{8}-\frac{1}{32}-\frac{1}{128}- \cdots$

Each series sums to $a/(1-r)-ar^n/(1-r)$ where $a = 1/4$ for the new firm and $-1/8$ for the original and $r = 1/4$ for both. Because the second term $ar^n/(1-r)$ approaches zero in either case, and the first term $a/1-r$ totals to 1/3 for (2′) and $-1/6$ for (2″), the second firm sells 1/3 and the first firm $1/2-1/6 = 1/3$ of the total demand at the zero price. That is to say, the two firms combine to sell 2/3 of the demand that would prevail at the zero price. Manifestly price, in turn, falls from $b/2$ to $b/3$ when a competitive duopoly market replaces a monopoly.

Suppose a third firm enters the market. The original two sellers were supplying 2/3 of the total market demand that would obtain at the zero price. So, the third seller will offer 1/2 of the unsatisfied portion, i.e., 1/6 of the total. But then, the other two sellers visualize a shrinkage of demand and reduce their offerings by 2/3 of 1/6 or $-1/9$. The altered supply of the original firms induces the third firm to increase its offerings by 1/18, a change in supply that causes a contraction of 1/27 by the original members of the market. The series of changes for the two firms appears in (3″) and for the third firm in (3′).

(3′) $\frac{1}{6}+\frac{1}{18}+\frac{1}{54}+ \cdots$

i.e., $a = 1/6, r = 1/3$, so $a/(1-r) = 1/4$.

(3″) $-\frac{1}{9}-\frac{1}{27}-\frac{1}{81}- \cdots$

where $a = -1/9, r = 1/3$ and $a/(1-r) = -1/6$ from the original 4/6. These two firms supply 3/6 of the total demand at the zero price after a third firm has entered the market. In other words, each of three sellers supplies 1/4 of the demand that would be satisfied by pure competitors, and this sums to 3/4 of the total market demand. It can be shown that four sellers would supply 4/5 of competitive output, five sellers would offer 5/6 of competitive output, *ad infinitum*. Assuming each firm behaves competitively, and entry is open, an oligopoly approaches the competitive output as the number of firms increases without limit.

   Introducing Positive Marginal Costs to Cournot's Model. When positive marginal costs are assumed to exist, and demand and other conditions are as defined above, the monopolist's profit-maximizing price is 1/2 the ordinate intercept value plus 1/2 of the marginal cost at the profit-maximizing output. This statement is equivalent to the assertion that the price equals 1/2 the vertical height of the demand curve above marginal costs plus the marginal costs.[1] Similar relations for duopoly and larger numbers of firms follow naturally.

   From the above rules, it follows that any one of the four sellers at A, under our broad assumption of seller homogeneity, will supply 1/4 of 4/5 of the relevant market demand. A geometrical representation of the individual seller's demand curve thus requires that it be drawn parallel to the demand curve that applies to the entire industry, henceforth referred to as the total factory demand curve; and the intercept values of the individual firm's demand curve in a four-seller market must be 2/5 that of the total factory demand

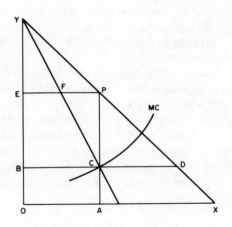

Footnote Figure 1

[1] And note the following geometrical proof, applicable to Footnote Figure 1.
Let OA stand for monopoly output. Draw BCD and EP perpendicular to the OY axis.
The area EOAP = YOAC, where YC is the marginal revenue curve.
$\triangle$YEF = $\triangle$FPC.

curve.[2] Such a drawing (following the above rules for a negatively sloped linear demand curve) will yield a price which, in our case, is 1/5 of the height of the ordinate intercept above marginal costs. Also, it will yield sales for each firm which are 1/4 of 4/5 of that which could be supplied at the marginal cost price. These effects are shown in Figure 6–2, where DD is the demand curve for any of the original sellers.

Introducing Economic Space into Cournot's Model: Buyers Distributed Over the Space. The competitive oligopoly price established in our model is equal to AV (Figure 6–2), which is half of the maximum height of the DD curve above marginal costs. At this AV price, the individual seller supplies a given quantity—let us say Z amount. Four sellers thus supply four times this amount, which, we posit, equals quantity Z'. And Z' is equal to 4/5 of the demand as found at the point of intersection of the total demand curve with the constant marginal cost line (or the marginal cost line that would be

And $\angle$YEF and $\angle$FPC are right angles.
And the opposite angles at F are equal.
So YEF and FPC are congruent triangles.
And EF = FP; YE = PC.
Hence, the rate of fall of the marginal revenue curve is twice the rate of fall of the average revenue curve.
Then BC = (1/2) BD,
YDB and PDC are similar triangles
CP = (1/2) YB
AP = AC+(1/2)YB Q.E.D.
Alternatively, since AC = OB and
YB = OY−OB,
AP = AC+(1/2) (OY−OB),
AP = (1/2) (OY+AC) or (1/2) (OY+OB)
Thus, monopoly price is equal to half the marginal cost of the monopoly output plus one-half the value of the intercept of the OY axis. See J. Robinson, *The Economics of Imperfect Competition* (London: The Macmillan Co., 1935), pp. 30, 32, 55 for this particular proof.

[2] 1/4 of 4/5 equals 1/5. Any one of four sellers will supply 1/5 of the entire market demand. We designate the entire (or total) market demand as being formed by the intersection of the demand curve with the constant marginal cost line drawn at the height of its intersection with marginal revenue. The supply of 1/5 of *this* market demand can be obtained geometrically by drawing the straight line demand curve to intersect the constant marginal cost line at an abscissa value twice that of the quantity to be sold. In other words, drawing the individual firm's demand curve to a point 2/5 of the obtained entire market demand leaves the firm with sales of 1/5 of this market demand. And similarly, its maximum ordinate value viewed from the base of marginal costs should be set at a point equal to marginal cost plus 2/5 of the difference between the highest price possible in the market and marginal costs. We see finally that the twice as great fall of MR as compared with AR yields a price and quantity 1/2 of the ordinate and abscissa points set by the firm's demand curve, as measured above and along the marginal cost line. These 1/2 values equal the 1/5 entire industry values described above. If marginal costs are positively sloped as is MC in Footnote Figure 1 instead of constant, the same results apply except that price descends a little faster with entry, and, accordingly, what is 1/5 of the relevant demand at a constant level of marginal costs is greater than that at the new level of marginal costs.

drawn as a constant at the level where marginal revenue, MR, equals marginal cost, MC, if MC were increasing).

When it is assumed that buyers are geographically separated from sellers, the amount of freight involved in each sale is an added cost, and determining the relevant amount of freight absorption is a new and intricate problem. For our present purposes, we must only observe (but see the appendix of this chapter for proof) that under our assumptions—including, let us recall, the proportion of freight rates to distance—the geometrically relevant freight rate is equal to half of the freight rate to the buyer located at the halfway distant point along a straight line.[1] (It is further shown in the appendix that where buyers are dispersed evenly over a plain rather than along a line, the geometrically relevant freight rate is equal to half of the freight rate to the buyer located at a site two-thirds the distance between the seller and the most distant point in the market.)

In Figure 6–1, we find that freight costs from site A to the market extremity are equal to MCW (shown either by the dashed line MCW or by the height MCW on the O'Y' axis). Freight cost to the halfway point of the market area (which in this case of buyers evenly scattered along a line is the relevant freight cost to be applied in a geometrical derivation of net-mill price) is equal to MCMC' on the O'Y' axis. In applying plane geometry to spatial economics, this freight cost, MCMC', may be regarded either as (a) *an increase in costs* (for example, compare TMC with T'MC' in Figure 6–2), which, in conjunction with MR, would *yield the delivered price* to the buyer located at the halfway point in Figure 6–1; or it can be regarded as (b) *a deduction from the demand curve* DD in Figure 6–2, which, with the related MR and the marginal cost of production curve considered, *yields the net-mill price* charged to all buyers. When transport cost is deducted from the demand curve DD in Figure 6–2, the net demand curve at the seller's factory becomes D'D'. In turn, this demand curve yields the *net-mill price* AM of the seller in Figure 6–2. Because of its spatial connotation we can (and by definition shall) use the term net-mill price interchangeably with f.o.b. price throughout this book.

Net-mill price AM can be compared with the nonspace price AV in either Figures 6–1 or 6–2. The latter value (AV) would have existed if there were no space assumptions—that is, if there were no freight costs. We derive, accordingly, the following propositions:

Proposition (1). When freight rates are proportional to distance, our demand assumptions are as given, and buyers are assumed to be evenly

---

[1] For an explanation of this relation in a different context, see M. L. Greenhut, "Effects of Excise Tax and Freight Cost, A Geometrical Clarification," *Southern Economic Journal*, XXI (1955), pp. 330–335. For a formal demonstration of differences in freight absorption under different assumptions of scattered buyers, see M. L. Greenhut, *Plant Location in Theory and in Practice* (Chapel Hill, University of North Carolina Press, 1956), pp. 42–47. For a more general proof, see the appendix to this chapter.

scattered along a line, the competitive price becomes equal to AM [= to OJ] Figure 6–2. This price is lower than that which would prevail in a space-less economy. (See AV [= to OW], Figure 6–2.) Even more particularly, let us note that delivered price [or f.o.b. (net-mill) price plus freight costs] to any point on the linear market is shown by the line MN in Figure 6–1. Net-mill price, AM, is less than AV by 1/2 of the freight rate to the buyer located at the halfway point of the linear market. (See Appendix to this chapter for details.) Thus, *net-mill price is equal to $b/2 - k'/2$, where k' is the freight rate to the half-way point of the linear market*. At price AM, profits become MHTJ (see Figure 6–2) for each of the firms at site A under the simplifying assumption noted earlier that there is no fixed cost of production.

II. THE IMPACT OF SELLER COMPETITION IN LOCATION ON THE PRICES OF FIRMS IN A SPACE ECONOMY

We have just observed that when sellers are at a point and buyers are geo-graphically separated from them the price will differ from the price existent in a nonspace economy. A more fundamental difference arises when a geographic separation of sellers is also assumed. This situation can be under-stood in the following expansion of the previous model.

Entry at a Distance

Assume initially that a new firm, Firm B, plans a market invasion and that it aspires to attain at least the same size as any of the firms at A. If B also locates at site A, the DD demand curve for each firm shifts laterally to the left (following the rules previously given) and hence downward to D″D″ (Figure 6–2). When freight absorption is included, the relevant demand curve becomes D‴D‴, the net-mill price for the firms at A fall to AR, with profits for each being equal to RSTU.

On the other hand, if we assume Firm B locates at X and believes that the demand for its product will be as great as it would be if it locates at A—e.g. because it anticipates that better physical relations with customers located around and to the right of X will offset the access disadvantage to the buyers located at and nearest to site A—then its allocated demand curve again will be D″D″.[1] However, the buyer halfway between Firm B and the market

[1] While the above assumption is useful, it should be pointed out that it is not integral to the analysis. Rather, the same final results would occur, we will see, if we simply presup-posed that firm B hopes for a sufficiently satisfactory demand. Note further that we may, for example, be thinking of a barber shop or manufacturing firm locating at X. And we shall find that under unorganized oligopoly these units will fix a lower price than that which previously existed for the customers living at X (and points east of X).

extremity is now at a distance half that separating A from X; thus the net demand curve for Firm B if located at the market midpoint X (i.e., the demand curve which includes freight costs as a subtraction from the non-spatial demand curve) becomes D''''D'''' rather than D'''D''' (the demand curve previously found for each of the five firms at A). With marginal costs assumed equal to T'MC' at site X (See Figure 6–2), price becomes AR' (= XR') for this firm, and its short-run profits equal R'S'T'U'.

From a practical point of view, the directors of B realize that as soon as existing contracts are terminated a coup de grâce might be accomplished. At price XR', B would supply the entire market from G to O' (Figure 6–1). This price would permit monopolization of this market segment, though it would probably invite immediate retaliation.

If the firms at A retaliated by meeting B's price over the XO' market, B's profit would be less than it could have been at location A. If B then raised or lowered his price, the result would prove frustrating. Sensing this probability, B must believe that marginal costs at X are closer to A's than is actually the case in order to locate at X. If marginal costs at X were believed to be lower than drawn in Figure 6–1, firm B would expect the firms at A either to drop out of the GO' market voluntarily, or else to be forced out by a price war.

Suppose that B adopts price XR' as part of its short-run policy. This price would lead to the monopolization of the GO' market and the repercussions would be resounding. The firms at A, having had their original profits (MHTJ) cut by a substantial amount, would lower their prices. As an important aside, we might point out here that the exact amount of the loss in profits would depend upon the extent of the market area. As the reader will appreciate by the end of Chapter 7, if the market extends to such great distance that mill price plus freight cost is equal to the *b* intercept value of the most distant buyer, 25 percent of the total sales take place over the XO' market; accordingly, the decrease in profits resulting from the loss of the GO' market can be shown to approximate 35 percent. In contrast, if the extent of the market is limited, for example because buyers in a certain very narrow climatic zone alone demand the subject product, the GO' market will represent around 50 percent of the total sales. In fact, this (last) type of assumption stands behind Figures 6–2 through 6–4 in the present chapter, as well as Figures 7–1 and 7–2 in the following chapter. Given a substantial loss in profits such as that approximating 50 percent, or of course even 35 percent, the firms at A may very well be inclined to lower their prices. If these firms lower their price below XR' plus the freight cost of B over the GO' market, firm B must obviously retaliate, and the subsequent lowering of B's price below the level set by the firms at A would inevitably result in a price war. Once the competitive price is reached, profits are zero for all firms (see the dashed line MCW, Figure 6–1). B is disappointed because his marginal costs are not so low in relation to those of the A firms as he believed they would be, but he cannot afford to raise his price. And, if the firms at A continue their competitive policy, the price remains the classical one. Any exception to this stability requires an Edgeworth type of assumption that only all sellers combined can completely supply the market. While this could cause a limited increase in price, only assuming newly-found quasi-monopolistic tendencies at both A and X would that price rise to much higher levels.

The repercussions at A may be other than those suggested above. Anticipating a price war, the firms at A may suffer the impact from B at site X by meeting his price rather than going below it. For all sales from X to O', their f.o.b. price plus freight cost may be equated with B's prices over this market length. Discrimination against nearer buyers may be the selected pattern, in which case the f.o.b. price for the buyers to the left of G remains at the old level while the price around and to the right of G is set to correspond with B's delivered price. The price set at the mill may, on the other hand, be nondiscriminatory, yet competitive against B (see SC', Figure 6–1). In either event, should B desire a price war, he can force it. He would, of course, succeed in the price war if his marginal costs were as "believed" closer to A's than that shown in the diagram.

The impact of a remotely situated firm on prices and profits may clearly be much more devastating than that suggested in models of nonspatial markets where firms are located together. The probability of this assertion rests upon the fact that the distant location is most logical when the firm selecting the distant site can substantially control its immediate market. Such a firm attains the position of a semi-locational monopolist with respect to its part of the market, but it is limited in extent and control by the price at A.

Proposition (2). When over a large range of output the production-cost level is not greater at a place(s) distant from the production center by an amount equal or larger than the freight rate to such distant site(s), a dispersion of firms results if they are willing to compete actively to gain control of markets proximate to their location. Under such assumptions, substantial localization of industry occurs only because the population is unevenly scattered, *ceteris paribus*.[1]

Oligopoly and Economic Space

The significance of the above conclusion is twofold:

1. Assume that the distant location at X *is* practical. Then, if the old firms adhere to a nondiscriminatory f.o.b. price system[2] and attempt to

---

[1] An example of what we are considering in the *ceteris paribus* is fixed costs. Another example would be a possible difference in intended size of the firm. And still another would be the willingness of a distant (smaller) firm to sell under the blanket of phantom freight, for, as we shall see in Chapter 7, the basing point system promotes localization.

[2] A spatially nondiscriminatory f.o.b. price would probably be continued in retailing. In nonretailing activities, other forms of spatial pricing may develop.

compete with the new firm, the new establishment at X can force a price war, win the whole market area surrounding its plant, and cut the economic profits of the firms at the old location to zero. A single firm located at a distance can have a devastating impact on the market price if the old firms act stupidly. But, once the outcome of that course of events is realized, the firms at the old

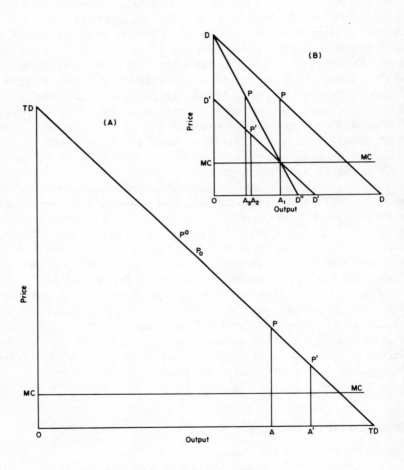

Figure 6–3: Spatial Price Competition under Oligopoly

location may either surrender this distant market area or else try to meet the price of the distant firm (e.g., by the price RC″R′C′, as in Figure 6–1). They will succeed in this policy *if* the distant firm at site X will so permit. What they certainly will not do is let this one firm (which can cut their economic profits to zero) have the same effect as if the number of firms at their site of production had doubled or more than doubled.

To visualize this in another way: If the firm located at a distance indicates its intent to control entirely its proximate market area, the demand, as measured from MC, for each of the firms at the old location, will fall. As we have noted, it will fall by approximately 50 percent, depending, of course, on the actual scattering of consumers. If the firms act in the competitive manner described earlier in our discussions of shrinking demand curves (for example, recall the 1/2 of 1, the 1/2 of 2/3, the 1/3 of 3/4, the 1/4 of 4/5 shares that arise), the new demand curve for each of the old sellers would be a miniature reflection of the old. Price would fall sharply.

Probably the original firms would realize that their old price enabled large enough sales to the buyers located nearest to their location. More fundamentally, the price arising from a fully competitive situation would not enhance sales to the old buyers sufficiently to justify competitive pricing. It would, in fact, cause a great loss in net revenues. Hence, rather than conceive of DD shrinking to $D'D'$ (Figure 6–3B) and price falling from A_1P to A_2P', those firms would conceive of their demand curve as shifting only along the horizontal axis to form DD'' (Figure 6–3B). Now, this shift leaves price at the same height, A_3P (= to A_1P), which is the best competitive price that these firms can have under the circumstances (even visually in Figure 6–3B). The only better price would be (a) the full monopoly price which we assumed they had long since left behind (see $P°$ Figure 6–3A) or (b) a widespread spatially discriminatory price which we assume is too dangerous to charge because of the excessive number of sellers and the fear of unfavorable buyer reaction.

2. Still another view of the same problem (and diagrams) may be helpful. Assume that a new firm locates at some distance from the original production point and takes over roughly 50 percent of the sales from the four firms initially in the market. Would these original firms view the new entry as if approximately as many new firms as old firms (equal in size to the original firms) had entered the market, or would they act as if an altogether different type of change had taken place? If the original firms did appraise the impact of the distant firm as the equivalent of roughly a 100 percent increase in competition, the total amount supplied to buyers would increase from OA to OA', and price would fall from AP to $A'P'$ (Figure 6–3A). In other words, the demand curve of any of the original firms would fall from DD to $D'D'$, and individual sales would fall from OA_1 to OA_2 (Figure 6–3B). A reaction of this kind would, however, completely disregard the known facts concerning demand. These facts indicate that buyers still within the orbit of control of the original firms would purchase a sufficient number of units of the good at the old price to provide greater revenue than that which could be obtained from sales at any lower price. The ordinate intercept height of the demand curve conceived by these firms tend to be unchanged by an entry at a distance.[1]

_____
[1] Actually, prices might even rise in the very short run. But we will not attempt to

Only the measurement of the demand curve on the horizontal scale would be cut roughly in half.

The impact of spatial separation of sellers makes the value of monopoly pricing obvious. This value is obscured somewhat in nonspatial economics by the fact that a new seller, seeking sales to *all* the customers of existing sellers, offers his product to *all* of these buyers. In this way, he increases the total supply to them and thus causes the price to fall. In the case of spatial separation of sellers, however, the demand of buyers located near to the original firms tends to remain unaffected by the entry of a distant seller.

We may thus summarize: (1) If the firm at distant site X permits sharing of the market, price throughout the market will level off at RC (see Figure 6–1) or perhaps become RC″R′C′, depending initially on the f.o.b. mill price policy of the new firm. (2) If the firm at X threatens, precipitates, and wins an open price war, the surrender of the firms at site A will result in price rising to near its original level, AM, or else hovering near AR (see Figure 6–1) in order to lessen the extent of the distant firms' market area. And, at the f.o.b. (net-mill) price, XR′, the firm at X will extend its sales over GO′.[1]

Price Policy under Unorganized Oligopoly in Space

Competition causes price to fall below the monopoly level (see Figure 6–3A). The firm at X would prefer, of course, to raise its price greatly but the competitive impact at A, which originally forced the price down to AM (as shown in Figure 6–1), would probably prevent an increase in the price above the indicated level, if it would even stay that high.

Reduction of price below XR′ would be feasible as a means of gaining new buyers further to the west of G in Figure 6–1 only if the firms at A would permit this encroachment without any price reductions of their own. More important than this expectation, perhaps, is the necessary assumption that the demand of buyers to the east of X is so weak that the loss in revenues from this market because of the price reduction is more than made up by bringing (and being permitted to bring) a few more buyers into the market area of the distant firm. In the practical sense, concern with the price reaction of rivals would dominate, at least for a while. Price tends to be maintained rather than steadily lowered by the entry of one firm at a distance from a production center.

The general market structure in retailing is similar in form to that described above in that the suburban department store or retail shop tends

explain this here since it involves an intricate distinction between demand by buyers located near the seller and demand by buyers at a distance. We may refer interested readers to the full development of this point in *Plant Location in Theory and in Practice, op. cit.*, pp. 70–71 and pp. 78–80.

[1] Because the firms at A generally sell over a many-sided area, the distant firm is in less danger of forcing the A firms to institute or long pursue a price war. The price tends quickly to return to or near the original level.

to keep its prices above that of the downtown stores. Its tendency toward change, if any, would be to maintain high prices rather than to lower them noticeably. An uptown store does not lower prices to bring into its orbit the buyers who are located between it and the downtown area. Instead, the impact of space, more likely than not, is to promote oligopolistic practices quite akin to price leadership. Thus price differentials between shops at a production center and those in the outlying districts favor the downtown stores.

A firm located at X, if inferior from the standpoint of costs, might either be permitted to survive at the old price levels or else be forced out of existence by a price war. If forced out, the original positions would be restored, with the number of firms in the market being sharply limited by the restricted number of sites available in the production center. Whether location is practical at a distance or whether there is no alternative to central location, a tendency to maintain prices or to follow price leadership arises. In time, the unorganized market may become organized. Whatever the case, we have again demonstrated our earlier assertions which may now be restated as follows:

Proposition (3). Economic space produces complex market-type relations among firms.

Impacts of New Location at a Distance: Conclusion. It has been shown that a location distant from an existing production point is feasible if and only if (1) any production-cost disadvantage that may hold for the distant site is offset by freight-rate savings over the market area surrounding that site, and (2) demand over this region is sufficient to warrant establishment of the new firm. It is further demonstrated that under these preconditions the distant firm may compete actively in price for markets extending from its site towards the older production point, while monopolizing those in the other direction. Any price war could be won by the distant firm given the required preconditions for its location in the first place, and this leads to the conclusion that oligopolistic relations and a short-run kinked demand curve will emerge. This kind of curve is brought about by the very fact of distance, and requires certain cost advantages for each firm distributed over the space. Small price reductions related essentially to smaller transport costs must be expected, but substantial price cuts could prove disastrous, and price increases would be a reflection of monopolistic organization. A kink in the average revenue curve of firms in a space economy may be expected generally to take form at a slightly lower level than that of the previous price. But note—as we mentioned previously— this kinked average revenue curve explains spatial pricing; it is not a rationalization which accounts for the stability of prices recognized to prevail in a world of oligopolies. This conclusion holds even though in Chapter 8, the simple one-kinked curve will be seen to give way in time to a three-section curve and, ultimately, to what effectively appears as a fully continuous, practically smooth function.

Impacts of New Location at a Production Point: Conclusion. The emphasis in this chapter on competition at a distance (i.e., seller dispersion) should
not obscure the possibility (and likelihood) of others locating in the same
general place as another seller(s) (i.e., sellers at a point). The market, we shall
later observe, is marked typically by a combination pattern of competition at
a point and at a distance. And as is intrinsic to Cournot's model, let us simply
suggest here that sellers who are located side by side tend—in the absence of
collusion, tacit or otherwise—to increase output and cause prices to fall.

Impacts of New Locations in General: Conclusion. Short-run competitive-
type impacts arise chiefly in a space economy as a result of new locations at
given production points. This is not to say that distant entry, if occurring to
any significant extent (i.e., a large number of new entrants) will not also cause
a breakdown in oligopolistic rigidities. It is, however, our intent to stress the
condition of oligopolistic *competition* resulting essentially from proximate
(identical) locations, and short-run oligopolistic *rigidities* relating essentially
to the existence of a few spatially separated firms. Manifestly, when many
firms enter in diverse directions over economic space, substantial (competitive)
price impacts at some distant points must also be expected.

III. SUMMARY

In a space economy, one market area often overlaps another, and on all sides
some compression tends to occur. Competition takes place within and from
outside a production center's market area, and the outside influence generally
leads to a complex market pattern, even though what appeared to be a simpler
market relation might have existed at one time.

Any seller locating at a distance may dominate the buyers near to his site,
and, though the firms at the industrial center may proceed by pricing competitively, the competition against the distant firm will be of no avail if the
distant location is economic. Alternatively, the firms at the center may
surrender the distant market, and, as distant sites prove profitable, some relocation will tend to occur. With firms in the outlying districts (in the new
market areas) pricing monopolistically with respect to the production center,
those firms concentrated in the center are provided with a first-hand picture
of a more profitable economic policy. As the price at the production center is
changed, the distant seller raises or lowers his price, following price leads to
his advantage and making sure that the size of market area he wants continues
to be within his control. In time, the distant seller or, even better, the firm's
own production center, may gain a position of leadership. In any case, it is
unlikely that purely simple relations will exist in the old center while strictly
complex patterns develop between it and the new. It is more likely that a
complex mix will come about throughout the market. While the condition of

space may not eliminate *per se* the simple market,[1] the simple system is less likely to exist in a space-time economy. A chainlike relation among firms dominates on all levels, extending from manufacturing to retailing. Very often it leads to *organized oligopoly*, the market pattern which we consider next in Chapter 7. If, however, formal organization can be prevented, we must ultimately expect that some slight price decrease here or there, as sellers (plants) lose sight of their own impact on the total market, will produce other breaks in price. That uncertainty continues to serve as a limiting floor is our ultimate conclusion—but these last (long-run) views belong to Chapter 8 and the chapters which follow it.

Appendix to Chapter 6
Freight Absorption Rates, Spatial Pricing, and Market Area Limits

Assume that (a) every buyer's gross demand curve is alike, negative in slope, and linear in form, (b) buyers are evenly scattered along a straight line or lines, (c) variable production costs are zero, (d) freight rates are proportional to distance, and (e) the seller under study is situated at a point on a line or at the intersection of lines.

I. THE MATHEMATICS

According to the assumptions above the following three equations are applicable:

(1) $q = b - ap$

(2) $p = m + x$

(3) $x = dK$

where q = quantity demanded at any point on a line, p = delivered price (or the price the buyers are *de facto* required to pay), m = net-mill price, x = freight rate, K = distance from the origin, i.e., from the seller's location, and a, b, d, are positive constants. For further simplification, assume $a = d = 1$.[2]

---

[1] Conceivably, we could locate people and businesses upward in space rather than horizontally and thereby have a very large number of firms at a point in economic space. Of course, some transport cost would still tend to exist.

[2] The general freight cost function may be represented as

$$(3a) \quad X = f(q, K)$$

where X stands for the total cost of shipping output q over any given distance K. Because the freight rate per unit of distance is assumed to be unity, the marginal cost of shipping output q is given as K; correspondingly, the freight rate x is also numerically equal to K. Thus

$$(3b) \quad \frac{x}{K} = \frac{X}{qK} = 1$$

$$\therefore (3c) \quad X = qK$$

$$\text{and } (3d) \quad \frac{\partial f}{\partial q} = x = K$$

Now the above equations can be reduced by simple substitutions to the general form

(4) $q = A(b-m-K)$

where A is a positive integer (which may be given here as unity). This equation indicates the quantity demanded in terms of m at a point or points over any distance K from the origin. Therefore, the aggregate demand Q obtained by shipping to the furthermost distance limit is as follows:

(5) $Q = A \sum\limits_{K=0}^{K} (b-m-K)$

or $Q = A(K+1)\left(b-m-\dfrac{K}{2}\right)$

Now, the profit-maximizing net-mill price, given any possible market extent, would be determined as follows:

(6) $R \equiv mQ = mA\sum(b-m-K)$

or $R \equiv mQ = mA(K+1)\left(b-m-\dfrac{K}{2}\right)$

(7) $\dfrac{dR}{dm} = A(K+1)\left(b-2m-\dfrac{K}{2}\right) = 0.$ The second derivative $[-2A(K+1)]$

assures maximum profits.

(8) $m = \left[\dfrac{1}{2}b - \dfrac{1}{4}K\right]$

where $K = [0 \leqslant K \leqslant k = (2/3)b]$ with the limiting value $k = (2/3)b$ obtained from (8) and (4) above,[1] and also derived later in the appendix. It must be noted here that equation (5) and hence equation (8) presuppose(s) that there also exists a buyer(s) at the seller's location. Otherwise, they must be modified respectively as follows:

(5a) $Q = A\sum\limits_{K=1}^{K}(b-m-K)$

$= AK\left(b-m-\dfrac{K+1}{2}\right)$

and

(8a) $m = \dfrac{1}{2}b - \dfrac{K+1}{4}$

on which Table 6A–1 below is based.

Hitherto K has been assumed to be discrete variable. However, it might as well be assumed that K is continuous variable, in which case equation (5) is modifiable as follows:

(5b) $Q = A\int\limits_{0}^{K}(b-m-K)\,dK = A\left\{(b-m)K - \dfrac{1}{2}K^2\right\}$

---

[1] The extreme distant value (number) $k = \dfrac{2}{3}b$ is obtained by substituting equation (8) into equation (4) and setting $q = 0$. Thus, the market extremity for the seller is at the point where the demand for his product vanishes; there exists, accordingly, a finite range for m such that $\dfrac{1}{2}b \geqslant m \geqslant \dfrac{1}{3}b.$

By similar derivation as above, the same formula of profit-maximizing net-mill price as equation (8) is obtained.[1]

A similar general system is applicable to the case of even distribution of buyers over a plain. Here our assumption (b) above must be modified. For example, let us assume that buyers are evenly scattered over the plain (and in each subset of this plain) in such pattern that their distribution within any given small space is at the same distance from the seller; this scattering is illustrated by the points of intersection of the lines on graph paper, with the seller under study being situated in the middle of the graph. We posit further that transport lines (on all routes) to any buyer follow the lines of the graph with no short-cuts available to the shipper. Other assumptions remaining unchanged, our equation (4) above would be modified as follows:

(4′) $q = AK(b-m-K)$

where A again is a positive integer whose value here is equal to 4 because of the square market area over which sales extend, and the K multiplier of $(b-m-K)$ gives further expression to the plain assumption in place of the line.[2] In turn, if no buyer is assumed to be located at the seller's site, equations (5) through (8) are correspondingly modified as follows:

(5′) $Q = A \sum\limits_{K=1}^{K} K(b-m-K)$

(6′) $R = mQ = mA\Sigma K(b-m-K)$

(7′) $\dfrac{dR}{dm} = A\Sigma K(b-m-K) - mA\Sigma K = 0$

$\therefore m = \dfrac{b}{2} - \dfrac{\Sigma K^2}{2\Sigma K}$, and from aggregation formuli[3]

$m = \dfrac{b}{2} - \dfrac{2K+1}{6}$

$\therefore$ (8′) $m \cong \dfrac{b}{2} - \dfrac{1}{3}K$

---

[1] We have $R \equiv mQ = mA\{(b-m)K - \dfrac{1}{2}K^2\}$

$\dfrac{dR}{dm} = A(bK - 2mK - \dfrac{1}{2}K^2) = 0$

$\therefore m = \dfrac{b}{2} - \dfrac{1}{4}K$

[2] Rigorously this equation should be replaced with
$$q = b - m + AK(b-m-K).$$
However, it only complicates our mathematical formulation without any effective change in our conclusion.

[3] We have
$$\sum\limits_{K=1}^{K} K = (K+1)\left(\dfrac{K}{2}\right)$$
$$\text{and } \sum\limits_{K=1}^{K} K^2 = \dfrac{K^3}{3} + \dfrac{K^2}{2} + \dfrac{K}{6} = \dfrac{K(2K+1)(K+1)}{6}$$

The solution (8′) is an approximate one.[1] The value of K is $\{(1 \leqslant K \leqslant k = (3/4)\ b)\}^2$, where the limiting $k = (3/4)\ b$ is obtained from (8′) and (4′), and also derived later in the appendix.

From our equations (8) and (8′) above and the derived values of k, it may readily be established (as will be done specifically later on in the appendix) that the profit-maximizing net-mill price in the line case and in the case of buyer dispersion over a plain drops to the minimum level $(1/3)b$ and $(1/4)b$ respectively; i.e., $m_{min} = (1/3)b$ or $m_{min} = (1/4)b$ as the seller extends his sales radius to the market extremity. It should also be clear, taking into consideration equation (3), that the maximum limit for the freight rate is $x_{max} = (2/3)b$ and $x_{max} = (3/4)b$ respectively for the line and the plain.

Our analysis may easily be extended to the case of positive and constant average variable costs. The fundamental equation (2) must then be modified as follows:

(9) $p = m' + c + x$

where c stands for constant average variable cost and where m' is the net-mill price less the cost of production c. Thus, $m = m' + c$ and (9) may be rewritten as

(9′) $p = m + x$

Consequently, the new system of our fundamental equations consists of equations (1), (9), (9′) and (3). By similar manipulation as (5)−(7), the following results are obtained:

(10) $m' = \dfrac{1}{2}(b-c) - \dfrac{1}{4}K$

(10′) $m = \dfrac{1}{2}(b+c) - \dfrac{1}{4}K$

where $K = \{(0 \leqslant K \leqslant k = (2/3)(b-c)\}$ for the line case with the limiting value $k = (2/3)(b-c)$ obtainable from (10′) and (4), and also derived later in the appendix. Further, we find, following the procedures used in (5′)−(7′), that

[1] Actually the right hand value in (8′) is the exact solution for the case of continuous, instead of discrete dispersion of buyers over the plain. To see this, suppose the buyers are evenly and continuously distributed over a circle. Then equations (4) through (7) must be modified as follows:

$$(4'')\ q = 2\pi K\ (b - m - K)$$
$$\text{and } Q = \int_0^K 2\pi K\ (b - m - K)$$
$$(5'')\ Q = (b - m)\ \pi K^2 - \frac{2}{3}\ \pi K^3$$
$$(6'')\ R = mQ = (b - m)\ m\pi K^2 - \frac{2}{3} m\pi K^3$$
$$(7'')\ \frac{dR}{dm} = -\frac{2}{3}\pi K^3 + \pi(b-m)K^2 - m\pi K^2 = 0$$
$$m = \frac{1}{2}b - \frac{1}{3}K$$

[2] Observe from (7′) that $\dfrac{d^2R}{dm^2} = -2A\Sigma K < 0$ for $K > 0$; m is, therefore, the profit-maximizing net-mill price.

(11) $m' = \dfrac{1}{2}(b-c) - \dfrac{1}{3}K$

(11') $m = \dfrac{1}{2}(b+c) - \dfrac{1}{3}K$

where $K = \{0 \leqslant K \leqslant k = \frac{3}{4}(b-c)\}$ for dispersion over a plain. The limiting value $k = \frac{3}{4}(b-c)$ is obtained from (11') and (4'), and also derived later in the appendix. [1]

From our equations (10') and (11'), and the derived values of k, it may readily be established for the case of constant costs (as will be done specifically later on in the appendix) that the profit-maximizing net-mill price falls to $m_{min} = (1/3)b + (2/3)c$ and $m_{min} = (1/4)b + (3/4)c$, respectively for the line and plain distributions as the seller extends his sales radius to the market extremity. Moreover equation (3) indicates that the maximum limit for the freight rate is $x_{max} = (2/3)(b-c)$ and $x_{max} = (3/4)(b-c)$, respectively for buyer dispersion over a line and plain. The maximum sales radius as well as the profit-maximizing m' are, of course, smaller in the case of positive production costs than zero costs.

It has been noted that our system presumes the existence of a unique distance limit. This distance limit, beyond which sales cannot be effected, is set by the value where the derived net-mill price plus the freight cost is equal to the highest price at which some demand prevails. This limit is defined by

(12) $m+k = b$

The definition given in (12) may best be understood by our re-use of selected tables first published in the *Plant Location* book. [2] Though details about the formation of these tables are described in the original source, we shall repeat here a few of their basic features.

TABLE 6A-1: THE PROFIT-MAXIMIZING NONDISCRIMINATORY F.O.B. MILL PRICE UNDER CONDITIONS OF LINEAR DISPERSION

Distance Unit(s)	Mill Price (including Freight Absorption)	Distance Unit(s)	Mill Price (including Freight Absorption)
1	$\dfrac{b}{2} - \dfrac{K}{2}$	10	$\dfrac{b}{2} - \dfrac{K}{3.64}$
2	$\dfrac{b}{2} - \dfrac{K}{2.67}$	20	$\dfrac{b}{2} - \dfrac{K}{3.81}$
3	$\dfrac{b}{2} - \dfrac{K}{3}$	50	$\dfrac{b}{2} - \dfrac{K}{3.92}$
4	$\dfrac{b}{2} - \dfrac{K}{3.21}$	100	$\dfrac{b}{2} - \dfrac{K}{3.96}$
5	$\dfrac{b}{2} - \dfrac{K}{3.33}$	1000	$\dfrac{b}{2} - \dfrac{K}{3.996}$

[1] Note that we assume a continuous variable in equations (11). Otherwise the domain of the function would be $1 \leqslant K \leqslant \dfrac{3}{4}(b-c)$ and the approximative result $m \cong \dfrac{b}{2} + \dfrac{c}{2} - \dfrac{1}{3}K$ would hold.

[2] See M. L. Greenhut, *Plant Location in Theory and in Practice* (Chapel Hill: The University of North Carolina Press, 1956), Appendix A.

TABLE 6A-2: THE PROFIT-MAXIMIZING NONDISCRIMINATORY F.O.B. MILL PRICE UNDER CONDITIONS OF EVEN SCATTERING OVER A PLAIN*

Distance Unit(s)	Mill Price (including Freight Absorption)	Distance Unit(s)	Mill Price (including Freight Absorption)
1	$\dfrac{b}{2} - \dfrac{K}{2}$	20	$\dfrac{b}{2} - \dfrac{K}{2.93}$
2	$\dfrac{b}{2} - \dfrac{K}{2.40}$	40	$\dfrac{b}{2} - \dfrac{K}{2.96}$
3	$\dfrac{b}{2} - \dfrac{K}{2.57}$	60	$\dfrac{b}{2} - \dfrac{K}{2.97}$
4	$\dfrac{b}{2} - \dfrac{K}{2.67}$	80	$\dfrac{b}{2} - \dfrac{K}{2.981}$
5	$\dfrac{b}{2} - \dfrac{K}{2.72}$	100	$\dfrac{b}{2} - \dfrac{K}{2.985}$
10	$\dfrac{b}{2} - \dfrac{K}{2.85}$		

* Minor corrections have been made from the original publication.

In deriving Tables 6A–1 and 6A–2, we assumed freight costs proportional to distance and zero variable production costs. Also we assumed that each buyer's gross demand was identical; in addition if we continue for the moment to ignore distance, his demand was negatively linear of unit slope; in other words, the gross buyers' demand curve formed an isosceles triangle with the horizontal and vertical axes. As we shall see in section II, the quantity sold is easily derived via our conditions for each extension of the market area (e.g., each increase in the sales radius, such as from distance unit e to f) whether buyers are scattered along a line or over a plain. In turn, total revenues may then be obtained, differentiated with respect to m, and set equal to zero. The profit-maximizing net-mill price, given selected market area sizes, is thereby derived.

In these tables, K is again a distance variable which, because d in (3) is unity, also may serve as the freight rate to the *most distant buyer* under the qualification that the sales radius available to the firm is limited to a point(s) short of the one set by $m + k = b$. If, of course, competitors do not limit the size of the firm's market area, the *most distant buyer* is the one at the greatest distance k from the seller who could still demand the product—given freight costs proportional to distance and the setting of f.o.b. mill price pursuant to profit-maximizing rules. When competitors do constrain the firm's market area, the *most distant buyer* is the furthermost one still buying from the seller in question; in this case, buyers at greater distance from the seller purchase the product from other sellers, even though the freight rate plus the mill price of the subject seller would be less than the b intercept price. We are, therefore, employing and shall continue to employ the symbol k whenever we wish to emphasize and refer exclusively to the "naturally limited" most distant buyer.

This buyer, let us repeat, is the buyer who is barely able (and willing) to purchase the good from the subject seller since the delivered price to his site is at the maximum value he has assigned for it.

II. A SPECIAL NOTE ABOUT FREIGHT ABSORPTION RATES AND FIGURE REPRESENTATIONS OF SPATIAL PRICING

Further explanation of our geometry and selected aspects of the tables will be of value to those who do not wish to consult the original source, but yet are interested in the derivation of prices over economic space. In this regard, it is of relevance to note that supporting the line case in Table 6A–1 are the following relations:

(A) A buyer at a unit of distance from the seller will have a demand equal to $b - m - d$, where we here use d to represent a unit of distance, with other previous assumptions and symbols still applicable.

(A') For reasons which will soon be apparent, substitute K for d to yield $b - m - K$.

(A'') Convert (A') to total revenues (R) by multiplying by mill price. Then differentiate, set to zero, and solve for m. We would obtain $R = bm - m^2 - Km$; $dR/dm = b - 2m - K = 0$; $m = (b/2) - (K/2)$.

(B) The buyer at two distance units will purchase quantity $b - m - 2d$, so in concert with buyer 1, the total consumed in the market would now be $2b - 2m - 3d$.

(B') If we convert d into K, where K refers to the distance (cost) to the most distant buyer, the total consumed in the market could be shown as $2b - 2m - 1.5K$ (since $K = 2d$).

(B'') Suppose we multiply the quantity taken in (B') by the mill price, differentiate the product, and set the results equal to zero. We would obtain $R = 2bm - 2m^2 - 1.5K$; $dR/dm = 2b - 4m - 1.5K = 0$ and $m = (b/2) - (K/2.67)$.

(C) Let a buyer be located at three distance units from the seller along the line. He would purchase $b - m - 3d$. Together with buyers 1 and 2, the total purchased would be $3b - 3m - 6d$.

(C') Converting to K, where $K = 3d$, yields $3b - 3m - 2K$.

(C'') Converting to revenues, differentiating, and setting to zero yields $m = (b/2) - (K/3)$.

The other values shown in Table 6A–1 follow readily from the above. When the freight rate per unit of distance is extremely small relative to the b intercept, such that buyers at great distances from the seller could still be within the given seller's market area, our distance units are many and the profit-maximizing price approaches $(b/2) - (K/4)$. The same price (and, in effect, geometry) directly obtains if we assume one buyer at the seller's location and others (not necessarily infinitely many) distributed evenly along the line. It is this implicit assumption of a buyer located side by side with the seller which supports the equations (5) through (8) above and the many figures in Chapters 6 and 7 (e.g. Figures 6–1 through 6–3, or Figures 7–2 and 7–3), where a modest freight cost is assumed relative to the b intercept. In other words, the deduction (K) from the total demand curve because of space is relatively small in the subject figures because the distance units involved are few; in turn, the derived price is obtainable by the $(b/2) - (K/4)$ limiting formula indicated in Table 6A–1.

The counterpart to Table 6A–1 results when buyers are distributed at selected points over a plain. Specifically, conceive of a grid (or graph papered plain) with a seller located at the center and buyer's distributed evenly at each intersection point around the seller. It is not possible in this case (as in the line case) to obtain immediately the limiting value $(b/2) - (K/3)$ by simply assuming that there also exists a buyer(s) at the seller's location. What is required instead is to assume one more buyer at the seller's location than the distance units over which the good is sold. That is to say, the equation (5') is replaced with:

$$(5''') \quad Q = \frac{1}{4} A[(b-m)\,(K+1)] + A \sum_{K=0}^{K} K(b-m-K)$$

where the first term of the right hand side of equation (5''') is new and indicates $(b-m)$ times the number of buyers at the origin for a given sales radius K. Then the formula $b/2 - K/3$ and its related figure drawings such as Figures 6–2 through 6–4 are readily derived. However, it must be noted that we already know the approximation formula (8') without resorting to the artificial assumption noted above.

It is relevant to observe at this point that because the rate of fall of the marginal revenue is twice that of the linear curve from which it is derived, the geometry of demand curve analysis requires a division by 2; hence, we rewrite $(b/2) - (K/3)$ as:

$$(13) \quad m = \frac{b}{2} - \frac{k'}{2},$$

where k' is the freight rate to the two-thirds most distant point in the market when buyers are evenly distributed over a plain.

The same general system is applicable to the case of even dispersion along a straight line or lines. Here, the limiting value for the net-mill price, we know, is $(b/2) - (K/4)$, so by the requirements of our geometry, we translate to

$$(14) \quad m = \frac{b}{2} - \frac{k'}{2},$$

where k' is now the freight rate to the halfway distant point in the market.

To obtain consistency in all figure representations involving freight absorption, one may therefore employ the formula $(b/2) - (k'/2)$, with k' equal to either $(1/2)K$ or $(2/3)K$ depending upon the spatial scattering assumed. The use of the limiting formulas $(b/2) - (K/4)$ or $(b/2) - (K/3)$, as the case be, is thus a convenient device which makes our discussions and figure representations simpler and more consistent. Most importantly, because the profit-maximizing net-mill price may readily be shown to decrease with distance, whether we use the formula-simplifying assumption of an *appropriate* number of buyers being located at the same site as the seller or apply the varying formuli (as shown in Tables 6A–1 and 2) to the situation under study, our basic comparative results are the same. When buyers are distributed evenly along a line or over a plain, we shall, therefore, think of (and make ready use of) either formula $(b/2) - (K/4)$ or $(b/2) - (K/3)$. In particular, we have seen that the latter solution holds when buyers are distributed over a circular market or discretely over a plain in the form of a square (i.e., our example of buyers located at the points of intersecting transportation lines where a set of parallel transportation lines intersect at right angles to another set of parallel transportation lines). Though they would be much less likely than the grid-square market area described here, since this market area obviously approximates many intra- and inter-urban distributions (e.g. streets intersecting at right angles), we could conceive of irregularly formed transport routes which happen to fan out in the continuing form of a triangle or hexagon. That is to say, we can conceive of a market area which grows from one triangle or hexagon of any given distance to a larger triangle or hexagon of a next larger (unit) distance size. The seller's trading radius, in other words, could be assumed to be extendable to only a larger size triangle or hexagon because the multidirectional transport routes—that must be followed to more distant buyers— just happen to add 3(d) or 6(d) more buyers with each new distance-unit extension (where d stands for the distance unit, e.g. mile or kilometer, over which the market area extends). Formula (5′) therefore applies, where A is 3 or 6, as the case be. (Incidentally, other polygonal shapes of market areas may, of course, be conceived, with A assuming these other values.) It is then readily apparent from (7′) that the A's cancel out. So it follows that in all nonlinear spatial distributions of the types described above, the profit-maximizing f.o.b. price approaches $(b/2) - (K/3)$. We shall see this principle again in Chapter 13 where, under conditions of competition, we shall also observe that the hexagonal market area proves to be the long-run equilibrium shape given a continuously-even distribution of buyers in economic space.

III. THE RELATIONS BETWEEN THE FORMULI: PRICES AND MARKET AREA LIMITS

Observe now that the maximum sales radius for a firm selling over a plain (or let us say circular market area) is set by the relation (12), $m + k = b$, where b is the maximum amount the buyer would pay, m is the net-mill price, and k is the value of the distance variable K expressed in freight rate dollars when K is at the natural distance limit allowed by profit-maximizing rules. (To recall, we have assumed that the freight rate carries unit value per unit of distance. This convenient assumption has the simplifying effect of making K in freight rate dollars or cents [i.e. x in (3)] equal to K in mileage.) Since m approaches $(b/2) - (K/3)$ when the economically greatest distance of a circular market is approached, it follows that the furthermost market area limit, $m + k = b$, is also definable by

$$(15) \quad \frac{b}{2} - \frac{k}{3} + k = b$$

where again we substitute k for the natural distance limit of K in our formula for mill price. By elementary operations on (15), we find the relation that was cited previously in the text [i.e. after equation (8′)], namely

$$(16) \quad k = (3/4)b$$

In other words, the natural limit of K under a circular (or plain) market area is at a point $(3/4)b$ in value, assuming that variable production costs are zero. Correspondingly, from the sales limit formula $m + k = b$, we easily obtain, as recorded earlier, the relation

$$(17) \quad m = \frac{b}{4}$$

So $m = (b/2) - (K/3)$ is the same as $b/4$, when $K = k \equiv (3/4) b$.

Suppose average variable cost of production (c) is constant and positive and can be covered by price (i.e. $b > c$). Then we know from (11′), or the derivations in *Plant Location op. cit.*, that the profit-maximizing net-mill price is limited to $(b/2) + (c/2) - (k/3)$ in the case of a circular market area. And we know that the maximum extent of the sales radius is set by

(18) $\dfrac{b}{2}+\dfrac{c}{2}-\dfrac{k}{3}+k = b$

So   (19) $k = (3/4)\,(b-c)$

On substituting (19) into the market area limit formula $m+k = b$, we obtain mill price in terms of production costs and b alone

(20) $m = \dfrac{b}{4}+(3/4)c$

This last result, derivable directly from the limit of Table 6A-2, is the same as the formula recently derived in the book by Martin Beckmann.[1]

Following similar assumptions, Beckmann in effect conceives of the quantity demanded as the magnitude $b-m-K$, where $b-m$ also establishes the maximum distance of K. He multiplies sales with the firms profits per unit sold $(m-c)$ at any distance and uses a density function, say, $g(K)$ with $(b-m-K)\,(m-c)$. More generally, profits over a circular area whose radius r approaches the limit $b-m$ are given by (21). (Note, in accord with previous notation, we use $2\pi K$ in (21) below in place of r).

(21) $G = (m-c) \displaystyle\int_{0}^{b-m} 2\pi K\,[(b-m-K)]\,dK$

(21′) $G = (m-c) \left\{ 2\pi \displaystyle\int_{0}^{b-m} [(b-m)\,K-K^2]\,dK \right\}$

Via integration and appropriate multiplications, total sales are obtainable.[2] Next, differentiating with respect to m the product of total sales and unit profits $(m-c)$, and setting the result to zero *directly yields* (20) above, repeated below as (22).[3] Relation (22) holds when buyers are distributed evenly over a plain.

(22) $m = \dfrac{b}{4}+(3/4)c$

In the case of buyers being dispersed evenly along a line, we have noted that *our natural distance limit formula is* $m = (b/2)-(k/4)$. Then the related distance limit to sales is set by

---

[1] *Location Theory* (New York: Random House, 1968), p. 51.

[2] Under our notation and carrying out the derivations accordingly, we find that sales would be equal to:

$$Q = 2\pi \int_{0}^{b-m} [(b-m)\,K-K^2]\,dK.\ \text{Then}$$

$$Q = 2\pi[\int_{0}^{k} (k)\,KdK-\int_{0}^{k} K^2\,dK]$$

$$Q = 2\pi\,[\dfrac{kK^2}{2}-\dfrac{K^3}{3}]_{0}^{k}$$

$$Q = 2\pi\,[(k^3)/6].$$

[3] $\dfrac{dG}{dm} = (m-c)\,2\pi\,[(k^3)/6] = (m-c)\,2\pi\,[(b-m)^3/6]$

$\qquad = [(m-c)\,2\pi\,3\,(b-m)^2]\,(-1)+(b-m)^3\,2\pi = 0$

$\therefore 3\,(m-c) = b-m$

$\qquad m = \dfrac{b}{4}-\dfrac{3}{4}\,(c)$

(23) $\dfrac{b}{2} - \dfrac{k}{4} + k = b$

So (24) $k = (2/3)\,b$

And (25) $m = b/3$

Adding nonzero constant average variable (or marginal) costs, we find because $m = b/2 + c/2 - k/4$ that the distance limit to sales is set by

(26) $\dfrac{b}{2} + \dfrac{c}{2} - \dfrac{k}{4} + k = b$

∴ (27) $k = (2/3)\,(b-c)$

In turn, we may then derive the net-mill price in terms of production costs and b alone as

(28) $m = \dfrac{b}{3} + (2/3)\,c$

Professor Beckmann derives the same result directly for the line case. He also derives other formuli dealing with discriminatory and uniform pricing over space. We shall later on in the book return to the formuli presented above in Tables 6A–1 and 6A–2 in our evaluation of work by Mills and Lav on market area stability. For the present, let us say that whereas our profit-maximizing formuli, which relate price to freight cost, point directly to the fact of freight absorption, they only point indirectly [i.e., through (16) or (19) or via (24) or (27)] to maximum distances. One may, from the opposite approach, use (16) or (19) and (24) or (27) to view directly the extent of alternative sales areas. Phrased more specifically, the relation (16) compared to (19), or (24) compared to (27) indicates that a greater distance exists between the furthermost buyer and his seller under the plain market area case than that which holds for the line case, *ceteris paribus*.[1] It would seem to follow—and we shall examine this matter in some detail in Chapter 13—that the maximum distances in market areas are a partial function of the shapes of these areas.[2]

---

[1] With respect to (20) and (28), it should be clear that $m = \dfrac{b}{4} + \dfrac{3}{4}\,c$ is less than $m = \dfrac{b}{3} + \dfrac{2}{3}\,c$ because $b > c$. Mill price when buyers are distributed evenly over a plain, is, therefore, lower than it is when buyers are distributed along a line, *ceteris paribus*, and distance is therefore greater. The significance of this conclusion will be given in Chapter 13.

[2] In a paper under preparation, this writer and H. Ohta will demonstrate that a set of prices which discriminate consistently over space against nearer buyers offers greater profits to the seller; moreover, the natural trading area of the spatially discriminating seller is the longest. However, because the principles of plant location and the micro-economic relations examined in this book are basically the same under nondiscriminatory and discriminatory price schedules, the present book uses the former in its spatial models. It may be said that in the subject paper, freight absorption rates are derived for different demand curves, concave and convex to origin as well as the linear demand curve. Again, the basic relations being unchanged, this book uses the linear demand curve assumption in most of its models.

7

Organized Spatial Oligopoly

WHEN FIRMS FOLLOW EACH OTHER'S PRICE LEADS, the demand curve for any one seller is steeply tilted, and, as a result, a decrease in price will not elicit a large increase in sales. Under price leadership or retaliatory pricing, the real demand curve for any one firm becomes a compressed reflection of the total demand curve, while, under conditions of independent pricing, the demand curve for any one firm flattens out in comparatively greater elasticity. We see

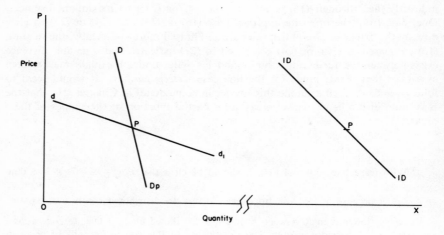

Figure 7–1: Industry and Individual Firm Demand Curves

this situation in Figure 7–1, where the IDID curve stands for the industry demand curve, the DDp curve denotes the individual firm's demand curve under retaliatory pricing (or price leadership), and the dd₁ curve depicts the demand for the individual firm's product under independent pricing.[1]

[1] The elasticity at any given price on the DDp curve is the same as on the IDID curve in Figure 7–1. But if the IDID curve were moved to the left, completely unchanged in

Inherent to any independently formed demand curve is the assumption that all other things are equal. This assumption enables us to accept "given" prices for rival firms, and we are therefore able to derive a demand curve such as dd_1 in Figure 7-1. If, however, rival firms are assumed to lower their price, say below P in Figure 7-1, in response to a lowering of price by the subject firm, the *ceteris paribus* assumption would be broken. The dd_1 curve below P would be shifted leftward as the quantity which can be sold by the subject seller will now be less than it otherwise would have been. Depending upon the expected price reactions of rivals, the results may best be illustrated by a kinked type of curve, dDp, or possibly by a curve like DDp.

Let us assume that the independent seller in question has been charging price X and that his rivals have generally held to price Y. Suppose the seller then reduces his price from X to X_1 and that this causes the other firms to reduce their price from Y to Y_1. In such a situation, the quantity sold by the price leader obviously cannot be worked out just by looking down the demand schedule (dd_1) from price X to price X_1 because price X_1 and its related quantity are relevant only when the price charged by rivals is Y. A new frame of reference is clearly required, and the lower portion of the DDp curve becomes the true function for the firm subject to downward retaliatory pricing.[1] If price following extends to upward changes as well, then the entire DDp curve is relevant. The illustration also *suggests* that under a price leadership pattern the price for the industry tends to be fixed at or near the point of maximum profits;[2] and, any departure from this price tends to require the stimulus of a definite change in economic data. This tendency toward stability makes the results of price leadership similar to those reflected in the kinky demand curve situation.

In this chapter we will examine the fundamental features of a price leadership system *over economic space*. We will first consider spatial pricing

shape or anything else except for its position on the coordinate system, the elasticity at a particular price would be increased. Although formal geometrical development is more conclusive, let us repeat here an heuristic explanation for those who so desire.

What is required in order to understand the verbal argument is simply to recall the definition of elasticity and to remember that in the following remarks we are considering two identically sloped linear demand curves. Elasticity is the measure of the relative increment of quantity caused by a relative decrement of price, and vice versa. On a curve closest to the vertical axis, the relative abscissa change as related to a given relative ordinate change must be greater than the same absolute abscissa change on the curve to the right, given the same relative ordinate change. Absolute measurements are the same because the slopes are the same. Price changes are identical, absolutely and relatively; quantity changes are equal absolutely but not relatively. The relative change in quantity is greater on the curve closest to the vertical axis. At any comparable price, therefore, the elasticity $(\triangle x/x)/(\triangle y/y)$ is greater on the curve displaced to the left.

[1] If retaliation is only to a price cut, a broken curve will be formed (e.g., dDp, Figure 7-1, with a break at P, the existing price).

[2] This point of maximum profits is found at the point of unitary elasticity when zero costs and a negatively sloping straight line demand are assumed.

without freight absorption, and then extend our discussion to the more complex cartel price practice known as the basing-point system. Finally, we will describe in general terms other forms of organized oligopoly pricing over an economic landscape.

I. ORGANIZED F.O.B. PRICING WITHOUT FREIGHT ABSORPTION[1]

Assume: (1) All sales are made at a given f.o.b. (net-mill) price with an extra charge levied against buyers according to their location and a given freight rate schedule. (2) Locational proximity to any buyer does not affect sales or the expectation of sales. (3) There are three sellers at A,[2] and, although these three firms were initially competitive in price, there has been no price competition recently nor will there be any with the entry of B.[3] (4) B is evaluating the profit potential of location X *vis à vis* location A. (5) There are no fixed costs. (6) Freight rates are proportional to distance. (7) The market is of very limited extent. (In terms of the Appendix to Chapter 6, $m +$ maximum K is much less than b.) Other assumptions will be added at appropriate places in the discussion.

Monopoloid Price Leadership

By assumption, the new entrant, firm B, neither lowers the delivered price beneath existing levels nor does it place its supply on the market for whatever price it may bring. Rather, B is in quest of sales at the prevailing price and therefore adopts as its f.o.b. (net-mill) price the current price at A plus the freight cost per unit from A to its own location.

[1] Our present discussion is much more restricted than the original which appeared in *Plant Location in Theory and in Practice* (Chapel Hill: University of North Carolina Press, 1956), pp. 65–81 and 312–314.

[2] The assumption of three sellers rather than four, as in Chapter 6, is for the purpose of simplifying the drawing of the figures to be set forth in this chapter.

[3] The assumption of initial price competition and then no further price competition is not requisite for the present model—or for any other model in this chapter. We could just as readily assume that there never was any price competition. The assumption is made here in order to pave the way for certain contrasts drawn later in this book.

A logical deductive justification for this assumption does, nevertheless, exist. It is based on the belief that price competition to a point and no further is possible, since spatially arranged firms may follow the price of a leader after a period of active competition but be reluctant to raise price for fear of adverse public opinion. If this situation is at all practical, models in economic theory may justifiably investigate cases of price competition to a point and no further in spite of such complaints as that entered by Chamberlin against Edgeworth. (E. Chamberlin, in *The Theory of Monopolistic Competition*, 5th ed. Cambridge: Harvard University Press, 1946, p. 41, observed that "... after price has been carried to its lowest point by competition, the market is split into parts so that each seller becomes a monopolist ..." The implication is that Edgeworth mixes assumptions.)

The firms at A submit to B's encroachment on sales at the prevailing price in preference to maintaining sales by further decreases in price. This policy reflects the assumption that historical developments in other markets have already taught them the lessons of Chapter 6. Each firm accepts this

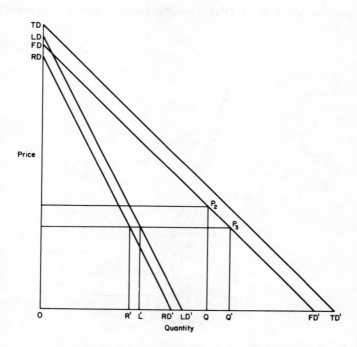

Figure 7–2: Price Derivation in Space (3 Sellers)

TDTD′ = Total demand (rural plus local).

FDFD′ = Total demand at the seller's factory; that is, the total demand less deduction for freight.

LDLD′ = Total local demand at the sellers' factory. This demand curve represents an approximation to the average demand of all buyers located between AX, as shown in Figure 6–1.

RDRD′ = Total rural demand at the seller's factory. This demand curve represents an approximation of the average demand of all buyers located between XO′, as shown in Figure 6–1.

P_3Q' = Price when 3 firms compete at A and supply an amount equal to OQ′.

P_2Q = Price when 2 firms compete at A and supply an amount equal to OQ.

OL′ = Local sales when price is set by 3-seller competition at A.

OR′ = Rural sales when price is set by 3-seller competition at A.

encroachment because the ultimate consequences of following other means of adjustment are more disadvantageous than dividing output proportionately.

Although the firms have changed over to quasi-monopolistic practices, price is not raised to monopolistic levels because of the inertia of price to any increase thereof.[1] These considerations lend credence to the establishment of a stable price lower than the monopoly price but higher than the competitive one.

Profits and Markets: A Diagrammatic View. Figure 7–2 supports Figure

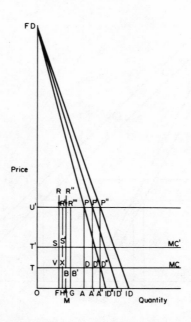

Figure 7–3: Price, Profits, and Other Relations (4 Sellers)

FDID = Individual seller's demand curve when 3 sellers locate at A.
FDID′ = Individual demand curve for the seller at A when 3 sellers locate at A and 1 seller locates at X.
FDID″ = Individual seller's demand curve when 4 sellers locate at A.
OA   = Total supply of 1 seller when 4 sellers locate at A.
OA′   = Total supply of the seller at A when 3 sellers locate at A and 1 seller locates at X.
OA″   = Total supply of 1 seller when 3 sellers locate at A.
OF   = Individual firm's supply to rural buyers when 4 sellers locate at A.
OH   = Individual firm's supply to local buyers when 4 sellers locate at A.
OM   = Individual firm's supply to rural buyers when 3 sellers locate at A.
OG   = Individual firm's supply to local buyers when 3 sellers locate at A.

[1] This price inertia is attributable partially to public opinion and to substitute products. Further, each entrepreneur must firmly believe that others will follow his price increase before he will chance the initial raise in price. The consequence of his act, if not followed by rivals, could be disastrous.

7–3. The FDID curve in Figure 7–3 is, in a sense, similar to the D'D' curve of Figure 6–2. The difference between the two is that the D'D' curve reflects completely the existence of competition, and directly yields the mill price whereas the FDID curve reflects the existence of competition only on the horizontal axis. Price must be derived from Figure 7–2; and then it may be placed on the FDID curve of Figure 7–3. As noted in the explanation to Figure 7–3, the FDID curve is the original individual factory demand curve of each of the three sellers located at A. For purposes of comparison, we may consider the TMC and T'MC' curves of Figure 7–3 to be the same as the TMC and T'MC' curves of Figure 6–2. We shall assume that the distant location suffers the cost disadvantage.

The FDID'' curve in Figure 7–3 is the net demand curve for any seller given the entry of B at location A. That is to say, it is the effective demand at the seller's factory if all four sellers (including B) are located at A. The net-mill price remains at AP, and the profits for each firm become PDTU'. All prices, demand curve magnitudes, and sales are derived in accordance with the rules established in Chapter 6, except as modified by changed assumptions here. The explanations under the figures in this chapter designate the type of competition and the number of sellers which yield the values shown therein. Our problem is to compare the situation when all firms locate monopolistically together at A with the situation when B locates at distant location X and fails to compete in price.

Suppose B locates at X and does not compete in price. Suppose further he sells only to the east of his location, in effect refusing to absorb freight on sales to the west of his location. B would thus control one-fourth of the effective demand east of X and would make no sales west of X. The decline in the sales of the three firms at A depends upon the net-mill price and the extent of the market area. If the peripheral buying point was determined by the values $m + k = b$ (see the Appendix to Chapter 6), the sales of the firms at A would only fall by approximately 6 percent. If as in the subject case (e.g., note the relatively small freight cost in Figure 7–2), the market peripheral point is much more sharply limited, then the impact on the sales of any one firm at A is much greater, in the present case approaching 12 percent. Under present assumptions, profit per firm would be cut from P''D''TU' to P'D'TU' (Figure 7–3). The decline in profits (P''D''D'P', Figure 7–3) is clearly less than the loss in profits (P''D''DP, Figure 7–3) that would have resulted if B had located at A and accepted the prevailing price. From the standpoint of the existing firms, a new rival is less competitive and harmful, under present conditions, if he chooses a location spatially removed from the production price center.

Conclusions. Under the given conditions, the new enterprise would not seek a location near the market periphery.[1] Even though a phantom freight

---

[1] Market periphery is used here in the sense of being located at the maximum trading area distance from a manufacturing center.

advantage exists,[1] profits at location X may be seen in Figure 7–3 to be only RST'U' plus SVTT' (the phantom freight); this is clearly less than the sum PDTU' which could have been realized by B at location A. Therefore, *under present assumptions*, the spatially removed location becomes feasible only when the net-mill price at A is so near the competitive level that the phantom freight is *much* more than proportionate to the decreased sales at X.

More *generally*, firm B would locate at X with the same absolute dollar profits *under full monopoloid leadership and equal investment and marginal production costs everywhere* when the following relation holds: B's mark-up above cost at X (including the phantom freight) must be greater than the A firms' mark-up above cost by an amount inversely proportional to the smaller number of sales at X as compared to A. In turn, if investment is smaller, albeit marginal production costs are the same everywhere, a somewhat smaller dollar profit will suffice. This profit must, however, be proportionate to the energy (investment) costs in order for the distant location at X to be as desirable a site as that at the production center *for a smaller firm.*[2]

II. NO FREIGHT ABSORPTION VERSUS FREIGHT ABSORPTION: LINEAR, SEMI-CIRCULAR, AND CIRCULAR MARKET AREAS

Before examining the basing-point system, it should prove helpful to discuss somewhat further a few selected aspects of monopoly pricing over space when no freight is absorbed. Probing more deeply into this special case will enable us to understand the basing-point system more readily. Moreover, though we shall observe in later discussions that there is no general *economic* reason why distant firms which follow the delivered price schedule of other firms would fail to absorb some freight, the outlines of the present model may well be found in practice. Indeed, uncertainty with respect to anti-trust policy may induce entrepreneurs at distant locations to sell only to buyers further removed than they from the production center; in effect, they would refuse to reduce their net return on any sale and be chargeable with spatial price discrimination via selected freight absorption.

---

[1] The net-mill price of the entrepreneur at X is the net-mill price of the A firms plus the freight cost to X.

[2] The broad rule presented above is applicable either when there is a complete absence of price competition or when, as in a model also included in *Plant Location, op. cit.*, pp. 65–81, there is restrained price competition. For a statistical demonstration of this assertion, as well as details of monopoly pricing over space where the distant location offers the same absolute dollar level of profits as a location at the production center, see M. Greenhut, *Plant Location, Op. Cit.*, Appendix C, pp. 201–204.

A Linear Market and No Freight Absorption

A firm which locates at a distance and accepts the price set at the production center thus charges as its own net-mill price the production-center price plus the freight cost to its own location. If it then ships most of its goods to points on the other side of its own location, further away from the production center, its net-mill price still includes the freight cost from the base point to its location so that a *phantom freight* on each sale exists. Now, the gains from phantom freight may outweigh a production-cost disadvantage at the distant location provided that the extra production costs per unit of good produced and sold is less than the cost of shipping a unit of product from the production center to the distant firm's site. However, a net residual on account of phantom freight and production costs may not justify the location, as the quantity sold by the distant firm would be less than it would have gained if it located at the production center. Effective location at a distance, under the above defined conditions, would appear to require a net gain from phantom freight which also offsets the smaller sales the firm would make.

To evaluate the situation further, let us specify the site X to be at the halfway point in the linear market running from the production center to the extreme point O'. The sales of the firm at X would be less than half that which it would have effected if it located at the production center, provided that buyers are distributed homogeneously over space and the gross demand curve of each buyer is identical. Assuming firms aspire to nearly the same profit, the net phantom-freight gain of the firm at the halfway market point would usually have to exceed the markup above costs on sales made by the firms located at the production center. This requirement, in turn, means that the freight rate from the production center to the distant location would usually have to be greater than the basic markup in the industry, with the production costs at the distant location being not much greater, if greater at all, than they are at the established center. (Note: though production costs may be unfavorable in the absolute sense, they are not necessarily unfavorable in the sense of delivered cost—i.e., production cost plus freight.) When the required combination prevails, such that the phantom freight is sufficiently positive to offset the smaller sales quantity and any disadvantage in production cost that may exist, we find that the distant site offers all the advantages necessary to enable a firm locating there to compete actively in price with the established center. Why then accept the delivered price schedule of the firms at the production center? The profits under unorganized oligopolistic competition for such a firm would greatly exceed its net expectation under spatial monopoly pricing, *ceteris paribus*, as we shall prove later on in the chapter.

Any spatial monopoly-pricing system must, accordingly, be imposed (in fact or in fancy) on a firm which locates at a distance in order for said firm to follow this system. Of course, the expectation of a long period of cutthroat competition might itself be a sufficient condition for the distant firm to accept spatial monopoly pricing. But note, this possibility establishes the spatial monopoly system of pricing as one imposed on firms located away from the production center rather than as one selected by them.

A Semi-Circular Market Area: No Freight Absorption via Sales in the Direction of the Production Center

Our principles do not change significantly if the market is arranged in a semi-circular pattern around the production center. In this case extra advantage is given the location at the production center *vis à vis* the location at the distant site, because of the *relatively* enlarged quantity of sales that is attributable to location at the production center. That is to say, the production center's sales advantage is more dominant in a semi-circular market area, though at first glance it might appear that the distant firm, itself also selling within a 180 degree arc, would require a smaller phantom freight gain. Let us examine this situation in detail:

Consider sales to any market point which would not require freight absorption by the distant firm. In particular, consider a "point" directly north (or south) of the *distant location*, this distant location being due east of the production center. Such buying point, as related geometrically to the production center point and the distant location, establishes a right triangle. Then the Pythagorean theorem becomes applicable. According to this theorem, phantom-freight gains will be found to diminish with distance. To see this, assume a unit freight rate per unit of distance and let $a^2 + b^2 = c^2$, where b^2 is the squared distance along the line running north (or south) from the distant location and a^2 represents the squared distance from the production center to the distant location. Then phantom freight a' equals $c - b$. When b equals zero, phantom freight is $a' = a = c$. When b is positive, the phantom freight gained on sales to the indicated point is less than that applicable when b is zero, for in this case $a' = c - b < \sqrt{c^2 - b^2} = a$; i.e. $a' < a$. QED.

The schedule of prices of the distant non-freight-absorbing firm therefore shows smaller gains over distances north or south of the west-east line from the production center through the *distant location*. This general result applies to all buying points for which b is positive and the locational triangle connecting the production center to the distant seller and then to the distant buyer requires a right angle or an obtuse angle at the location of the distant seller. By applying the theorem that the sum of the lengths of two sides of a triangle is greater than the length of one side, we see that the relative decrement holds for the distant firm on all sales it makes to the indicated buyers. [We would have to assume sales to the west of the distant location for different results; and then, the relative decrement converts to better results on sales made off the line north and south of points closer to the production center than the distant firm.] Given present assumptions, and assuming further that the same total sales apply to the semi-circular case as the line case, we readily see that, to warrant the distant location, any production-cost disadvantages at the distant site must be less in the semi-circular market area than in the uni-directional market.

Note, however, that if the distant location is profitable under the above designated conditions, it could be even more profitable given unorganized oligopolistic pricing. But we shall leave the details of our proof to a later point in the chapter.

The Circular Market Area Case: No Freight Absorption on Sales in the Direction of the Production Center

When buyers are scattered uniformly over a plain rather than in a semi-circular market area, the advantages of larger sales at the central location increase in importance. They make it still more likely that phantom-freight gains at the distant location would be less frequently accepted as an offset to the smaller amount of sales expected at the distant location. Production-cost disadvantages at the distant location must, accordingly, be very slight, if they exist at all, in order for the distant location to prove feasible. If these costs are high, the phantom-freight gains may well be insufficient to offset the still smaller sales that can be expected in the present case compared to the preceding ones. However, even though the distant location *under organized oligopoly* may not be feasible, the distant location under unorganized oligopoly could well be economic, *ceteris paribus*.

Freight Absorption Effects

When freight absorption is practiced, any feasible distant location tends in general to lie closer to the production center along the same line than the one we might have imagined for the non-freight absorption cases. But freight absorption features bring us to the basing-point system, and we shall now see that all of our previous statements remain generally unchanged even under the practice of increasing sales via freight absorption.

III. THE BASING-POINT MODEL

Two basic features of economic theory must be mentioned before the basing-point model can be presented; each of these is of methodological order:

(1) The abstractions used in forming scientific theories have typically been based on (and related to) geometric and arithmetic measurements. Two-dimensional planes, and three-dimensional surfaces supported the speculations of early thinkers, and this condition still holds broadly true today. Thus,

for example, before going into the methods for solving an n space dynamic programming problem, elementary study of convex sets and of convex or concave objective functions is usually presented in the perspective of two- and three-space geometry. Correspondingly, our present subject is best handled first by descriptive references of two-space order, albeit later on in the book, chiefly in Chapters 12 through 14, we shall abandon this "viewable" world. The basic mathematical foundations to be presented here are set forth in linear terms, with a figure representation (i.e., descriptive counterpart) made of the fundamental equation derived herein. Our objective, namely to provide a descriptive solution for the problem at hand, proves to be limiting only in the sense that the "specific" optimal location determined here is related to the assumed linearities in the mathematical formulation; most importantly, however, the "relative" relations derived herein will be seen to hold true in general.

(2) If realism is a desirable property for certain problems, it may be that an economic landscape ought to be considered. An implicit *hypothesis* could be formed which binds *economic space, uncertainty, and oligopoly* together. Indeed, simple empiricism would affirm the assumptions auxiliary to such hypothesis, to say nothing of the obvious relation between economic space and the identification of rivals that proves to be generative of our hypothesis. It is notable that Part II of this book has already gone beyond a "theory of limited application" (i.e., a simple hypothesis). Thus Chapter 6 has already accounted for (or, let us say, explained why) oligopolistic relations arise over economic space. Along with several additional propositions to be derived shortly, the basis for our interest in oligopoly and our policy proposals in favor of unorganized oligopoly will have been further established. Conception of the economic landscape provides, let us now propose, diverse explanatory insights into the workings of the free enterprise economy. And the basing-point price system, therefore, requires examination both for its own sake as well as for purposes of comparison with unorganized oligopoly.

The Optimal Basing-Point Location

Assume the following:

(1) A is the basing point, and O is the extremity of the market in Figure 7–4. For the sake of simplicity, we shall initially assume only one firm at A and one would-be entrant at another location.

(2) Buyers do not have any preference among sellers except as to price.

(3) Marginal costs and average costs are the same and constant everywhere. There are no fixed costs.

(4) Buyers are evenly scattered along the linear market running from A to O. Unlike previous models in Chapter 6 & 7, we assume the line to be of unrestricted length such that in terms of the Appendix to Chapter 6, $m+k = b$.

(5) The demand curve is of the straight line variety which decreases in elasticity throughout. Demand is equal in elasticity at any given price for all points in the market. Some buyers purchase more at any price than other buyers, but there is complete dispersion of these buyers throughout the market so that there is no single location which effectively offers a stronger market.

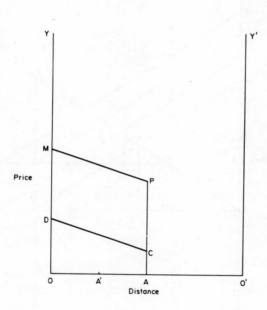

Figure 7–4: Basing-Point Locations

(6) Freight costs are proportional to distance.

(7) Any competitor can produce an identical product at identical costs.

Our model is concerned with comparing the locations and profitabilities which would exist under f.o.b. pricing and basing-point pricing. But first let us suppose that firm B plans to enter the market after a firm A and that it intends to comply with the basing-point system. Will the chosen location be with A at the basing point A in Figure 7–4 or removed to the left?

Figure 7–4 shows A'O as the half market (of AO) and AP is the f.o.b. mill price, with PM being the delivered price under the basing-point system. AC is the production cost, and CD the delivered costs.

In the more complex Figure 7–5, PM is again the delivered price, while AP is the net mill price. The triangle RPS indicates the quantity of goods sold over the market, with AS being the maximum price that could be charged for any sales at all to be made. To illustrate further, the sales at A by either of the two firms would be (1/2) PS, while the total sales of the two firms *throughout the market* amount to 1/2 [(RP)(PS)].

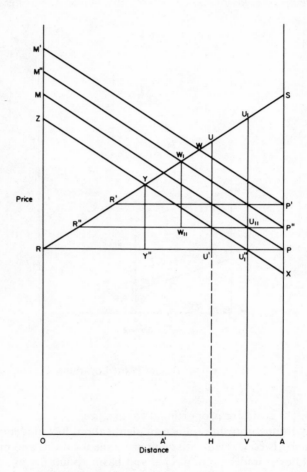

Figure 7–5: The Economic Space

It can be derived that the net profits for the "second" firm would favor its location at a distance under equal costs, where the market extends from A to O as in Figures 7–4, 7–5. In balance, a firm locating at H in Figure 7–5 gains sufficiently over the HO region to make up for its disadvantage over HA. Similar results, though not as profitable a return, hold for location A', as we shall readily see.

Sales are predetermined at all market points under a basing-point price schedule, *ceteris paribus*. Determining the optimal location under the system when buyers are distributed homogeneously over the space therefore requires only the minimization of cost.

Consider, accordingly, equation (1) below, where MC is everywhere constant and equal and there is no fixed cost. Demand, we assume, is linear with slope -1, though all conclusions would be unchanged if we hypothesized it to be $-1/2$ or -2, etc. We further assume a unit of freight cost per unit of distance, which assumption simplifies our derivations and final expressions without otherwise affecting our basic conclusions. We let x serve as a variable to measure the distance, and hence the cost of distance from the base point to the point of actual receipt (purchase) of the good. Correspondingly $\bar{x}$ is a variable which measures the distance and hence the cost of distance from the base point to the seller's actual (selected) plant site H. The number zero (O) is used in the first integral of (1) rather than A in order to distinguish the distance zero (e.g. shipment from basing point A to point A) from the place A. The symbol M in the second integral of (1) is also a distance value; it measures the distance in Figure 7–5 from the base point A to the extreme market point O. The total distance from the base point to the market extremity thus appears in (1) as the integral from O to H and then H to M, which equals M–O. Because there could be no confusion in notation, we use H as the symbol for the distance from place A to place H in (1) as well as for the place H itself in Figure 7–5.

$$(1) \quad TC = \int_{O}^{H} [(MC+\bar{x}-x)\,(z-x)]\,dx + \int_{H}^{M} [(MC-\bar{x}+x)\,(z-x)]\,dx$$

Observe the expression $\int_{O}^{H} [(MC+\bar{x}-x)\,(z-x)]dx$. If the firm is located at site H, $\bar{x}$ will have a value that is dollar-wise equal to the number of units of distance H, i.e. H–O. More simply put, we shall say in this case that $\bar{x} = H$. Now, the value x (i.e. the transport cost proportional to the distance between the base point and the purchaser's site) obviously depends on the buyer's location. If the buyer is located at a point 2/3 of the distance H, we would subtract from $\bar{x}$ the value that applies to (2/3) H. This difference $(\bar{x} - x)$ leaves a transport cost proportional to (1/3) H, which cost—along with the freight costs to other buyers located between A and H—is added to marginal costs; and similarly for the second term in (1) where buyers are located at distances greater than H–O and up to M–O with the signs reversed $(x-\bar{x})$. Because z stands for the sales that would be made if no freight costs were involved, z is equal to $b-m$, where b is again the ordinate intercept, m is the net-mill price, and each of these values is predetermined. It follows that when actual sales $z' = b-(m+x) = 0$, we are at the furthermost buying point in the market, namely at M distance from the base point. Because $\bar{x}$ stands for the distance from the base point to site H, while M has a distance value from place A equal to $b-m$, in turn equal to z, for easier computations as well as a clearer view of final results, we henceforth substitute $\bar{x}$ for H and z for M. Sales obviously decrease with distance x from A.

Let us evaluate now the initial term of the right-hand side of (1).

(2a) $\int_0^{\bar{x}} [MC(z)+\bar{x}(z)-x(z)-MC(x)-\bar{x}x+x^2]\,dx$

(3a) $= [MC(z)x+\bar{x}x(z)-(x)^2z/2-MC(x)^2/2-\bar{x}(x)^2/2+(x)^3/3]_0^{\bar{x}}$

(4a) $= MC(z)\bar{x}+(\bar{x})^2z/2-MC(\bar{x})^2/2-(\bar{x})^3/6$

And similarly for the right-hand expression in (1) where we obtain:

(2b) $\int_{\bar{x}}^{z} [MC(z)-\bar{x}(z)+x(z)-MC(x)+\bar{x}x-x^2]\,dx$

(3b) $= [MC(z)x-\bar{x}x(z)+(x)^2z/2-MC(x)^2/2+\bar{x}(x)^2/2-(x)^3/3]_{\bar{x}}^{z}$

(4b) $= MC(z)^2/2-\bar{x}(z)^2/2+z^3/6-MC(\bar{x})z+(\bar{x})^2z/2+MC(\bar{x})^2/2$
$-(\bar{x})^3/6$

Collecting all terms:

(5) $TC = (\bar{x})^2z-(\bar{x})^3/3+MC(z)^2/2-\bar{x}(z)^2/2+(z)^3/6$

Taking the derivative with respect to $\bar{x}$ and setting to zero,

(6) $\dfrac{d(TC)}{d\bar{x}} = -(\bar{x})^2+2(\bar{x})z-(z)^2/2 = 0$

(7) $\bar{x} = \dfrac{-2z\pm\sqrt{4(z)^2-4(z)^2/2}}{-2}$

(8) $\bar{x} = \dfrac{2z\mp\sqrt{2(z)^2}}{2} = z\left(1\mp\dfrac{\sqrt{2}}{2}\right) = z(1\mp.707106\ldots)$

Because the firm's profits are maximized when its costs are minimized, the positivity of the second derivative must be guaranteed,

(9) $\dfrac{d^2(TC)}{d(\bar{x})^2} = 2z-2\bar{x} > 0$

Hence only one, namely $\bar{x} = z(1-.707106)$, of the two solutions in (8) can be economically meaningful.

Recall, now, that under our unit freight cost assumption the distance M is of identically the same numerical value as $b-m$. It is further interesting to note that if we assume the freight rate (in dollars or cents) to be proportional to distance, but not on a unit per unit basis, the vector which is "approximately" (3/10) M measured vertically in terms of $b-m$ would not have the same length as the "approximate" vector length (3/10) M measured horizontally. For example, if each unit of distance carried one-half a unit freight cost, the horizontal scale OA (or RP in Figure 7–5) would be twice as long as the vertical scale $b-m$; that is to say RP would be twice SP in Figure 7–5. Relation (8) would still apply, but now in the sense that a distance 3/10 of $b-m$ measured from above P in Figure 7–5 would—by horizontal measure—be extended twice as far from P; of course, it would still be of value (3/10)M, where, however, M in dollar distance terms now requires two units on the horizontal scale for a dollar's worth of freight cost compared to every one dollar price (or quantity) unit measure on the vertical scale. Relation (8) thus holds generally under the assumption of freight rates proportional to distance. We might sum up by saying that the profit-maximizing (actually selected) site H must be approximately 3/10 of the distance M from A.

We have established the fact that when production costs are the same (or veritably the same) over an economic space, and a firm desires sales over only the market extending from the basing point to one linear extremity, net phantom freight gains are obtainable at sites away from the base point. These net gains justify a location roughly 3/10 away from the base point to the market extremity. Most vitally, we must understand that the assumption which holds that the firm will only sell over the market between points O and A in Figure 7–5 implicitly requires that we are considering a firm willing to be (and desirous of remaining) small in size. The last statement presumes that a market also extends over the opposite direction from A, and that small firms will locate at corresponding points H with reference to the market lying in the other direction. Observe finally that sites such as A′ could be more profitable for very small firms than those at A, albeit H is the optimal site for such firms under the basing-point system.

F.O.B. Compared with Base-Point Location

Consider next another small firm situation where the same magnitude of sales (i.e., production) is sought, but where the firm is willing to price f.o.b. mill at its own location. Suppose the firm is located at O; would its profits be greater or less than the firm which located optimally at H under the base-point system?

To answer this query, let us again evaluate the delivered price and sales triangle under the base-point system in Figure 7–5. We find that in a duopoly market the firm at H sells (RP)(SP)/4, or for a simpler reference we will instead use RSP/4. The firm thus earns phantom freight PP′ over the regular markup on sales R′SP′/4 and, as we shall see, approximately its regular markup above cost with respect to sales U′USP/4. The term "approximately" is required in the sentence above because the firm earns slightly less than its normal profit on sales between points HA since its net phantom freight goes down to zero at the point V halfway between H and A, and becomes negative for the larger quantity of sales existing between V and A. That is to say, between V and A a larger amount is sold than from H to V, which condition leads essentially to the italicized part of the following result:

Proposition (1). The firm at H earns an extra markup PP' on R'SP'/4, which quantity is equal to RUU'/4. It earns *slightly less than its normal profit* on that same quantity of sales U'USP/4 (which we shall see also equals RUU'/4).

To establish the nonitalicized portions of our proposition, recall our assumption of a duopoly market and the condition that equation (8) indicates optimality at H. Thus, at the location approximately .707106 from O to A, RUU'/4 (= R'SP'/4) should be realized to be (and readily computed to be) equal to RSP/8; this follows because RU' is .707106 RP and U'U is .707106 of SP. In other words, RUU' is half RSP in area. Hence, H earns PP' extra on half of its sales. In turn, it follows from this condition and previous findings that this firm earns slightly less than its basic markup over cost on the other half of its sales. This yields:

Proposition (2). The firm earns a net phantom freight *approaching* PP'/2 per unit of sales; and this return is equivalent to earning *slightly less than* a PP'' extra on every unit sold. Its basic price is, therefore, *almost equal* to AP + PP'', which value is designated henceforth as $\hat{A}P'' = \hat{O}P''$. (The reason for the qualifying words *approaching*, *slightly less*, and *almost equal* relates to the greater sales over VA compared to HV.)

A firm at O (Figure 7–5) under the f.o.b. (net-mill) price system might charge a price AP'' (= OP''). In other words, suppose it seeks a full extra markup PP'' on its sales. This firm would sell the quantity $W_{11} W_1 SP''/2$, where we use the divisor 2 simply to maintain uniform expression for all areas. (Note $W_{11} W_1 SP''/2$ is derived from R''S P''/2 − R''$W_1 W_{11}$/2, where, to repeat, such areas as R''S P''/2 are to be interpreted as a short form of (RS)(SP)/2.) Manifestly if sales quantity $W_{11}W_1SP''/2$ is equal to or greater than RSP/4, the firm at O under the f.o.b. (net-mill) price system would be earning slightly more than the firm at H, for OP'' > $\hat{O}P''$. It remains to prove that $W_{11}W_1SP''/2 \geqslant RSP/4$.

We compare areas in the equations (10)–(15), the right hand side of each of which is divisible by 2; the divisor 2 may thus be dropped from these equations for easier reference. Consider then the following, with the caveat that the development via equations (10) through (16) is tedious and that perusal of (10–13) with a skip to (15) (i.e. omitting 13a–13d, 14, 14a) should establish the basis for our conclusions sufficiently well for most readers.

(10) $W_{11}W_1SP'' = R''SP'' − R''W_1W_{11}$

Draw XZ in Figure 7–5 to establish the relation that RYY'' equals R''W_1W_{11}. Since it may further be observed that RU_1U_1'' equals R''SP''

(11) $W_{11}W_1SP'' = RU_1U_1'' − RYY''$

(12) $W_{11}W_1SP'' = Y''YU_1U_1''$

The ultimate problem then becomes a matter of determining whether the proxy for $W_{11}W_1SP''$, namely $Y''Y U_1U_1'' \overset{\geq}{\underset{<}{}} RUU'$, the proxy for one-half of RSP (the quantity which—when divided by two—would be the amount saleable by the firm under the basing-point system). If the greater than sign prevails, then the distant f.o.b. mill firm is not only netting more per unit sold but is selling more units. Let us restate this by saying we want to prove—

(13) $Y''YU_1U_1'' (= W_{11}W_1SP'') > RUU' (= RSP/2)$

To compare $Y''YU_1U_1''$ with RUU', observe first the following:

(13a) $RYY'' + Y''YU_1U_1'' = RU_1U_1''$ and in turn

(13b) $RUU' + U'UU_1U_1'' = RU_1U_1''$

Thus, if RYY'' in (13a) is less than or equal to $U'UU_1U_1''$ in (13b), $Y''YU_1U_1'' \geqslant RUU'$. We must determine whether

(13c) $RYY'' \leqslant U'UU_1U_1''$

But, we may in fact recast (13c) by noting that $RYY'' = R''W_1W_{11}$ and in turn that $U'UU_1U_1'' = U_{11}U_1SP''$. The equivalent of (13c) is then to prove—

(13d) $R''W_1W_{11} \leqslant U_{11}U_1SP''$

By inspection we readily see that W_{11} is halfway between $R''P''$. So, by well established rules, the area of triangle

(14) $R''W_1W_{11} = (1/4) R''SP''$

We further know that between VA more than 25 percent of the total sales $RSP/2$ are effected. Hence, a still greater than 25 percent share of the total sales $R''SP''/2$ is attributable to VA. Thus, $U_{11}U_1SP'' > 1/4 R''SP''$. It follows that

(14a) $R''W_1W_{11} < U_{11}U_1SP''$

and from (13d) back through (13a)

(15) $Y''YU_1U_1'' > RUU'$

This is equivalent to saying that:

(16) $W_{11}W_1SP''/2 > RSP/4$

The small firm at O which follows the f.o.b. price system, so that it adds to its net-mill price the phantom freight equivalent to that which a small firm located optimally under the basing-point system would earn on its sales, sells a greater quantity than the small firm complying to the basing-point system. In fact, we have already seen that its markup (PP'' in our example) is slightly greater than the actual phantom freight ($\hat{O}P''$) earnings of the firm complying to the basing-point system. Thus, on both actual markup and sales quantity, the f.o.b. mill gains an advantage.

We have shown that even under an extreme f.o.b. location, namely one at O, where there is *only one rival firm* in the market at the base point, the distant location under f.o.b. mill pricing is more advantageous to the small firm than is the optimal location for the firm under the base-point system. If we placed more than one firm at the base point, or selected a location to the east of O under the f.o.b. mill price system, thereby increasing sales for the distant firm, then on either count the advantage of the f.o.b. price system to the small firm becomes even more obvious. So too is the next rule clear.

Proposition (3). The small f.o.b. (net-mill) pricing firm would locate further from the base point than it would if it adheres to the basing-point system. However, exactly where firms under f.o.b. pricing do locate is the subject matter of Chapter 12 and will not be explored here. We might simply note for the present that if the f.o.b. firm went only to H and priced competitively, it would control a larger sales radius than it would if, for example, it located at A', but at not as desirable a set of prices. In fact, it can be shown that its sales (not sales radius) would also be less. As a basic rule we have:

Proposition (4). The base-point system is imposed on the small seller who dares not chance a war with the firms at the production center.

IV. OTHER COLLUSIVE PRICE SYSTEMS IN SPACE

There are several other price systems over economic space that approximate collusion *per se*. Their effect is either to block entry or to encourage excessive entry if doors are left open and security in business seems to exist. *A priori*, these systems tend to distort location. Since their locational effect is generally similar to that of the basing-point system, we will not at present go further into the matter, although we shall reopen the subject in Chapter 8. Just a few brief thoughts appear to be necessary at this point.

Uniform Prices over Space

One often collusive-spatial system which deserves mention is the uniform price system. Under this price policy, the seller's net return varies on each sale, being greater on sales close to his mill and smaller on distant sales. The seller, of course, discriminates between buyers.

To the extent that all sellers price identically and uniformly, an approximation to the purely competitive market may seem to exist; but this is clearly misleading. Pure competition involves a regular shading in price by sellers as buyers shift from one trader to another and entry by new sellers occurs. On the other hand, in a complex market, a seller who practices price discrimination may permanently lose the buyer against whom he discriminates. There is no continuous shading of price towards a uniform level in this market. Rather, the movement of prices is sudden and complete. Sometimes, uniform pricing over space reflects the existence of insignificant transport costs, though this condition unfortunately is neither necessary nor sufficient. Quite often, uniform pricing reflects a parallel action type of price leadership, or possibly active collusion.[1]

Uniform Prices by Zones

In an alternative system the seller divides the country into zones, within and

---

[1] The so-called practice of "postage stamp pricing" in which the f.o.b. mill absorbs more and more freight with greater shipping distance, say for the purpose of enabling buyers to resell at the uniform resale price, often involves oligopolistic competition in pricing among manufacturers. Whatever the basis be for the practice, however, retailers and wholesalers in a given market area always *appear* to be in collusion.

between which he discriminates against buyers. This practice may or may not reflect collusion, depending upon the location and price policy of competitors. If competitors are located nearby and establish similar zones with similar price gradations, the prevailing uniformity of price smacks of simple price following or agreement. If rivals are located at distant points, but zones are worked out so that common price levels prevail, collusion probably exists. However, if both locational differentiation and price differentiation exist, so that each seller seeks to control or dominate the market over which he has an advantage, we have unorganized oligopoly (i.e., oligopolistic competition). This type of relation between sellers prevails even though other sellers, in trying to prevent another from dominating the market areas nearest to this firm's plant, absorb in some nonproportional way larger and larger amounts of freight over the particular area in question. What determines the extent of competition in this case is the degree of uniformity. If phantom freight is substantial, the situation smacks of collusion. Otherwise, it points to oligopolistic competition.[1]

Multiple or Plenary Base-Point Systems

Finally, multiple or plenary and other variations of the basing-point system may also be found in use by firms which sell over distances.[2] Since a detailed analysis of price practices in a space economy, as distinct from locational impacts, belongs more to books devoted solely to this subject, we shall let the analysis offered earlier suffice for our purposes. Later on we shall examine the efficiency of the several spatial distributions that are brought about by the different pricing patterns and market types considered here.

V. SUMMARY

In this and the preceding chapter, we have presented diverse models to illustrate many relationships and sides of the oligopolistic market in a space economy. There are three basic conclusions which should be kept in mind:

1. A distant competitor may spoil the market of an old production center if firms compete *very* actively in price. Because of this possibility, the firms at

[1] Tangible evidence of collusion generally has been required in the courts as the claims by prosecuting counsel of a *per se* violation have tended not to be successful. Today, however, substantial identity in price pattern may serve as *prima facie* evidence, and this, in effect, could yield a *per se* violation.
    We might observe further on this matter of spatial price discrimination that if a practice is competitive, the firm that acts so competitively as to absorb nonproportionately larger amounts of freight in *certain* places may find itself in violation of the law, especially if the firm is a significantly large one. For example, see *U.S. v. United Shoe Machinery Corp.*, 110 F. Supp. 295, 1953.

[2] By *plenary* we mean that system in which all production points become basing points.

the production center soon learn that if a distant location possesses advantages over the established center, in so far as selected parts of the market are concerned, their best policy is to permit a distant firm to compete in price— but not too actively. Kinky demand curve oligopoly tends to result in the short run.

2. When the advantages of the distant location, even with respect to selected market segments, are not too clear, or when the market is already organized, the distant location appeals only to very small firms. This is true regardless of whether the state of organization involves monopoloid price leadership with or without freight absorption, or some other variant of it.

3. Dispersion of firms proceeds more readily and fully under oligopolistic competition than under organized oligopoly. Indeed, undue localization is encouraged by the basing-point and related systems since, among other things, sales to buyers in the established production centers are increased by the price and contact advantages they receive. Some glamour (or prestige) is also gained by the sellers located at such center, as compared with the seller located at a distance. Organized oligopoly just does not promote an efficient distribution in space. We will discuss this matter further in later chapters.

4. For the purposes of this book, we have not gone into the full details of organized oligopolistic pricing in a space economy, as our objective is to stress the oligopolistically competitive economy. We might, however, elaborate here on one point. Consider the principle established early in this chapter that a firm locates with economic advantages away from a production center *under organized oligopoly* only when the phantom freight it gains offsets the smaller amount of sales which accrue to it at the distant location. But remember that it is just when relative costs over the distant portion of the market area are favorable that oligopolistic competition would be still more profitable for the firm in question, *ceteris paribus*.[1] Manifestly, if it accepts the state of organized oligopoly, it does so because the *ceteris paribus* assumption does not hold. The firms at the production center may just not behave in accordance with the ethics economists would like to see established under the principle of comparative costs. The small firm locating at a distance thus accepts organized oligopoly because there is security in doing so. This proposition, in turn, presumes that the system of monopoly pricing over space already exists.[2]

---

[1] See the author's *Microeconomics and the Space Economy* (Chicago: Scott, Foresman, 1963), pp. 130–145. Also see *Plant Location, op. cit.,* Appendix III, pp. 301–304 for specific illustrations of the extent to which phantom freight gains must exist to warrant selection of a distant site under organized oligopoly rather than location at the production center under such pricing system.

[2] Manifestly, regional economic growth is influenced by spatial pricing patterns and regional disparities in income are partly explained thereby. How to evaluate its significance is another matter. And see, G. Borts and J. Stein *Economic Growth in a Free Market* (N.Y.: Columbia University Press, 1964), esp. Chapter 3.

8

Product Prices and Efficiency

We shall present in this chapter the idea that a noncollusive, open entry and exit oligopoly economy moves relentlessly to the point of technological efficiency. At the same time, we shall find that consumer satisfactions tend to be maximized in this economy and that a determinate (stable) equilibrium condition holds. If, as one friendly critic suggests, we inveigh later on against norms or policies associated with pure competition, let it so be, for our conclusion will focus on the kind of error which economists make when they rely on models that neglect the dimension of space. We shall develop our case by examining the path along which the oligopoly economy moves.

I. THE DYNAMIC PATH TO EFFECTIVE MARKET RESULTS

Consider a space economy in which people and resources are unevenly scattered, in which plant size (including research, machines, etc.) indivisibilities prevail, in which collusion between firms is not permitted, but in which there are risks and uncertainties attributable, among other forces, to consumer capriciousness, changing technology, and competitive business policies. In this economy, firms are able to identify their rivals and a competition develops between them wherein one finds only a few sellers competing for a given market even though there may be many sellers in the industry scattered over the nation. The market type we visualize is, therefore, one in which sellers are tied to other sellers as if by a chain.[1] The result is oligopoly, not pure competition, since each firm or plant selling to a given market tends to be comparatively large and important, not atomistic as in classical economics.

Now, the theory of pure competition and the oligopoly theory that results from the spatial dispersion of sellers and buyers are based upon different assumptions. For example, the former visualizes business units that are atomistic relative to existing demands. Moreover, homogeneity of sellers

[1] E. H. Chamberlin, *The Theory of Monopolistic Competition*, 5th ed. (Cambridge: Harvard University Press, 1946), see Appendix C.

and buyers, fully flexible prices, ready access between sellers and buyers, even perfect knowledge and the like are typically postulated. In the latter theory, each seller is relatively significant in size. We can, if we wish, postulate heterogeneous products and imperfections in knowledge, in price movements, and in access between traders. Notwithstanding the differences in assumptions, the consequences of the two theories have certain basic similarities. Each market type approaches a more efficient resource allocation through free entry and free exit. Also, though the image of the firm that is drawn in pure competition may be less realistic than the image drawn in space oligopoly theory, neither are close reflections of existing enterprises. Indeed still other highly comparable characteristics prevail.

The striking similarity between pure competition and what would be its counterpart oligopoly form may readily be visualized through a model which traces the early development of a space economy in which entry is free and competition between firms is strong. Through these forces, we shall see that the space economy achieves a close approximation to "classical" efficiency, resource allocation, and prices.

Cartel Development *vis-à-vis* Competition from Entry

Conceive accordingly of a new product, a given market area, and an original seller. Next assume a new competitor or two. Accept a kinked average revenue curve as a rough reflection of the price competition initially engaged in by these firms.[1] Then note that as new market areas develop and new firms with new plants begin to dot the economic landscape, the kinked average revenue (or demand) curve visualized by the original duopolists, or by the few original oligopolists, shifts to the left for each seller (cf. Dd' to Dd in Figure 8–1).

By way of contrast, in the case of a cartel confronted by open entry, the cartel directors would visualize for each firm only a leftward shifting of the average revenue function along the horizontal axis as new firms enter, provided new entrants do not disturb cartel solidarity. Thus figure 8-2 suggests price maintenance in cartelized markets. In contrast, under competitive entry in unorganized markets, the leftward shift of the average revenue function proceeds *along both axes*. Indeed, with enough entry, the

---

[1] According to this conception, collusion or tacit price leadership practices is a necessary prelude to willingness to change prices regularly, upward or downward, in response to changes in demand. In contrast, competitive duopolists or oligopolists tend to maintain a given price. They change their price only when convinced that demand itself has changed so greatly that the old price is out of line with present realities. This disparity may arise with continuing entry.

And see F. Machlup, *The Economics of Seller's Competition* (Baltimore: The Johns Hopkins Press, 1952), pp. 154–157 for support of the kinked AR curve in a space economy. But note, in classical oligopoly theory the kinked demand curve does not explain how price is determined: the theory states that with entry all firms' demand curves shift to the left and somehow or other kinks are formed. More than this is required in theory.

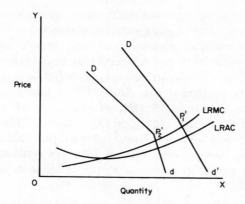

Figure 8–1: New Entry-Unorganized Oligopoly

displacement to the left may be such that the kink in the curve could take place at a lower value than that previously assumed by the seller, while a flattening of the curve may be conceived to have taken place above the kink of the curve (cf. Figure 8–3 and 8–1).[1]

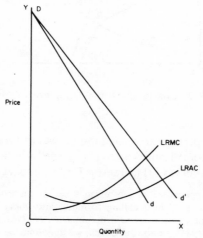

Figure 8–2: New Entry-Organized Oligopoly

[1] Let us remember here the suggestion made earlier that we will shortly break away from what in effect is the Cournot version of the impact of entry on price and quantity sold. We will note that—as viewed by the individual firm—the demand curve not only becomes a miniature of the original, but flattens out in form. That is to say, we will justify a more flattened curve Dd than that of Figure 8–3. And see Z. S. Gurzynski, "A Theory of Spatial Realities," *South African Journal of Economics*, March 1966, pp. 68–81. Also see M. L. Greenhut, *Plant Location in Theory and Practice* (Chapel Hill: University of North Carolina Press, 1956), Chapter II, Section 3, and Chapter VI.

The new entry of unorganized rivals, who may not revise prices upward with increases in price by a given seller, and who may also be expected to ignore minor reductions in price by older firms, induces an earlier seller to view a somewhat different-shaped AR curve than he did before the entry. Thus, any seller conceiving of unfavorable impacts should he increase or maintain his price would be inclined to lower his price, at least in time. By this act, he would maintain adequate sales. (E.g., cf. sales at price P'_2 on demand curve Dd' with sales at P^2 on Dd' and P_2 on Dd, Figure 8–3.) In effect, industrial homogeneity increases with new entry, for the differentiation between firms attributable to location and other matters decreases as the number of alternatives open to the consumer increases, and price tends to fall accordingly.

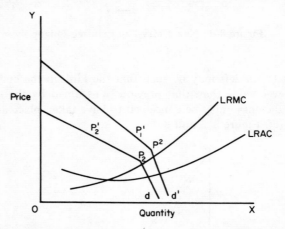

Figure 8–3: Continuing Entry-Unorganized Oligopoly

New entry in unorganized oligopoly, we propose, generally causes increases in the demand elasticities over both the lower and upper portions of the oligopolists' AR curves.[1] The reason for the impact on the lower portion

[1] The decreasing importance of any given seller in space as the number of rivals increases may be readily seen by recalling to mind, and going beyond August Lösch's conception of spatial competition, as recorded in *Die räumliche Ordnung der Wirtschaft*, (Jena: Gustav Fischer, 1944). Following Lösch, we may imagine initially an entrepreneur who is unaffected by any seller and who sells over a circular trading area. But then let a rival enter the industry with a location selected at a not too distant place from the subject firm. When this entry occurs, a duopolistic market prevails, though the distance between the firms may be such as to leave them with little or no competitive impacts on each other. As other firms enter, differentiating themselves spatially from the original firms, the trading areas of all, sooner or later, become sharply compressed. The circular area of any one seller, and the subsequent broken circles which may have occurred for some, give way later on to polygonic areas such as the triangular market area. At such point in time, any given seller would be subject to *close* competition from three sellers, as three rivals, in effect, surround him. But with still further entry, the triangle could be compressed into the form of a square,

of the curve is that the greater the number of rivals, the relatively smaller will be the reaction to a given (price-lowering) seller by these rivals since said seller will be less important than he used to be. Indeed, a small range of price freedom ultimately arises which converts the original kinked demand curve into a three-section curve (see Figure 8–4). If it were possible for the number of firms to increase without limit, i.e. $n \to \infty$, the kinks would have become less and less pronounced so that in time the curve would have become smooth and differentiable throughout. We shall restate below in nonmathematical terms our concept of the three-section average revenue curve. This review may, of course, be skipped without loss of continuity of thought.

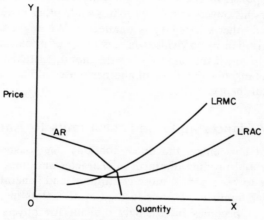

Figure 8–4: Three-Section AR Curve

The Three-Section Average Revenue Curve Reviewed

Our three-section curve has a slightly sloping (in fact highly elastic) portion that prevails above a certain price. This high elasticity belongs to the top section of the curve. Here we find that the contract, service, name and product advantages which a concern may have are insufficient over the relevant range of prices to provide it with many sales *if rivals' prices are maintained and*, at the same time, *are relatively low*. The third or lowest section of the curve is the

or the pentagon may have arisen. In any case, Lösch tells us the hexagon sooner or later appears and proves ultimately to be the equilibrium market-area shape. With this polygon, we have six *close* identifiable rivals. It is significant that the impact of any one firm on the others tends to be comparatively small now, much smaller than was the case when firms were fewer in number. We assert, therefore, that the entry of firms in a space economy, as in the classical nonspatial competitive conception of the capitalistic economy, pushes the demand curve for a firm to the left and raises the elasticity of demand for the product of any given seller more and more over time. Add a few extra firms at each production point, introduce some product differentiations, conceive of substitutable industry products, and one begins to visualize the economy ultimately to be described in this book.

steeply sloping (in fact highly inelastic) portion of the curve. The setting of prices over this part of the average revenue function would provoke sharp reaction from some rivals and would lead to but small increases in sales. Between the upper and lower portions of the curve, we find the part of the curve which resembles in appearance the average revenue function usually drawn to illustrate the monopolist's—or the monopolistic competitor's —average revenue function. Over this range of the average revenue (AR) curve, the oligopolist has some effective price freedom. That is to say, adjustments in his price do not compel reaction; upward revisions do not cause substantial loss of sales nor do downward revisions occasion price wars. The oligopolist, in effect, is insignificant over this range of price, for over these values his buyers remain with him while other buyers are basically uninfluenced and other sellers largely unaffected. We might suggest that the seller has lost his identity to rivals over this range of prices, being in a sense "infinitesimal" in much the same way as the monopolistic competitor of the Chamberlinean tangency theory or in another sense "alone," as is the mono-polist of classical theory.

Indivisibility—Uncertainty and the Limits to Entry

With additional new entry, the differentiations due to space, name, and possibly service and product diminish in character and importance, causing the entire curve to become still more continuous and generally flatter. With larger and larger numbers of firms located at all points in the market and over all areas, it becomes increasingly difficult for buyers to distinguish between them. If it were not for the limits placed on numbers by indivisibilities and uncertainties, the market would convert into a many seller market in which each firm becomes so small and so much like its rivals that downward changes in price stimulate large increases in sales for any given firm without causing great inroads on the sales of any particular rival. The relative size of each firm would approach the atomistic market type in this event, and the inroads on service, product, and spatial distinctions would make for a purer and purer competition.

But the conditions of indivisibility and uncertainty do exist. They place natural limits on entry, with geographical indivisibilities combining with technological indivisibilities to restrict entry; so too do these indivisibilities cause and merge with uncertainties.[1] Thus, let us henceforth, as we did often

---

[1] We might observe here in note for readers concerned with this matter that we shall go into details about indivisibility and uncertainty later in the chapter. For the present, we should note that indivisibility, for example, in finance, freight rate making, and the like alter the uncertainty pattern that otherwise would exist: it becomes an inseparable part of the total package. Significantly, these indivisibilities do not cause arbitrary results. But *there are* indivisibilities related essentially to natural phenomena, such as demand, tech-nology, research, etc., which may *in an extreme case* be conceived to be extra to (rather than to blend with) uncertainty. When what we have referred to here as natural phenomena

in the past, simply refer to these forces as uncertainties, except for a special discussion which distinguishes between them later on in the chapter. We must at this moment simply add the thought that these uncertainties are magnified by the intense competition that develops from the situation of identifiable rivals.

Profits Prevail in the Long Run

The existing uncertainties lead occasionally to price wars, advertising wars, branch-plant competition, *ad infinitum.* New entrants offer new product lines, although at a still later point in the industry's development, new enterprises tend to be replacements, not additions to the market. The number of firms is limited, and the Chamberlinean tangency solution where economic profits disappear is thus revealed to be inconsistent with the forces of uncertainty. The market adjusts itself to a return called *profits* and this return ties up with the natural limitations (such as limited space) that exist to entry.

Oligopoly not Monopolistic Competition

We should repeat that if it were not for uncertainty the many firms-differentiated market type would be conceivable. However, these limiting forces do prevail, and, as a consequence, we experience at best a limited number of firms which can enter any given market area over a given period of time. By encouraging as much entry as is possible, the influence of these constraining forces is kept to an effective minimum.

It is a basic lesson in pure competition economics that entry of efficient firms and exit of inefficient firms lead ultimately to a market pattern in which technological efficiency is gained and factor returns are based on competitive imputations. Correspondingly, a *substantially similar efficiency and set of returns arise when competitive entry and exit are maintained in oligopoly.* For the present, the aphorism should suffice that if entry of new firms is encouraged, efficient firms ultimately will replace inefficient ones while all surviving units

indivisibilities are added to prevailing uncertainties so as to limit entry *sharply* (for example, demand is very limited with respect to efficient output, a state of surplus or windfall for a firm could continue for very long periods of time. We would distinguish this state from all others (i.e. where entry is limited, but not sharply) by setting forth as a general guideline the idea that if an omnipotent cartel director headed an industry which ideally should contain two or more firms, and he had the power over the firms to establish the ideal number of plants, with each of ideal size, so that cartel profits would, accordingly, be at their maximum, he could not so act. The indivisibilities, we assume, are so limiting and rigid that some firms and some plants of a single firm cannot even approach optimal size. These indivisibilities, though natural, would be of the kind which bring into the market oligopolists possessed of sharply different opportunity cost levels. Distinction between uncertainty and indivisibility is desirable in this case. In all other instances of unorganized oligopoly, indivisibilities and uncertainties can be treated as one, especially *in the long run.* Phrased broadly, *we may generally expect less constrained entry to evolve in time* as a result of indivisibility.

will tend to rationalize their plant(s) and company size towards the ideal, provided that further competition is maintained.

It is also a basic lesson in pure competition economics that not only is technological efficiency maintained but "resources are allocated perfectly in full compliance with consumer demands." As an aside here in Section 1, though considered in detail in Section V of this chapter, let us observe that similar results hold for oligopoly. That is to say, resources *are* allocated perfectly in full compliance with consumer demands when there exists an unorganized open entry and exit oligopolistic economy.

Finally, it is a basic lesson of classical economics that monopoly leads to higher prices and to poor resource allocation. Remembering our previous statements about organized oligopoly, we can repeat our assertion that a competitive oligopoly market—in which entry is free—approaches classical results though the organized oligopoly does not. But let us move on now to the proofs of our several claims.

II. EFFICIENCY

We have said that the parameters of an unorganized economy—subject to conditions of free entry and exit, and formed over an economic landscape—in time acquire corresponding values to those of the purely competitive economy. We shall support this assertion as briefly as possible in our present statement.[1] We trust that the argument to be presented in our next subsection, which draws in part on previously proven relations and in part on propositions to be established at a later point, will be understood (and accepted) to be a special formulation designed to show how our theory reflects classical theory. First we shall show the correspondence between classical theory and our theory by reference to classical concepts and analysis. Then, we shall present the framework of thought sketched previously in Part 1 of this book. Throughout the present discussion, we shall assume a linear demand curve of decreasing elasticity at lower prices, and justify this curve on the grounds that its main alternatives, a constant or increasingly elastic curve, would be unlikely and exceptional.[2] In any case, as we shall realize later on in this chapter (namely in Sections III and IV), our conclusions would be unchanged should other demand functions be assumed. As a final related preliminary note, we

---

[1] For an early and detailed discussion of the competitive properties of a space oligopoly, albeit a less formal one than the present, see M. L. Greenhut, *Microeconomics and the Space Economy* (Chicago: Scott Foresman, 1963), especially Chapter 8.

[2] The writer is not unmindful of the increasing use of curves of constant elasticity in econometric theory, though he suggests that their *raison d'être* is chiefly mathematical simplicity. His own preference for the negatively sloped linear demand curve relates to a belief in its greater generality; but fortunately, we shall find that the arguments of Sections II and III of this chapter do not depend on this or any other "intuition" as to most relevant demand curves.

use the reference MC throughout Section II, though we intend it to be always understood as long-run marginal cost, not short-run marginal cost.

Price and Marginal Cost

Take the purely competitive norm of $P = MC$. In the space economy, average revenue curves tilt, hence the equilibrium—if efficient—would require $P > MC$. But will $P > MC$ be comparable from firm to firm? Our answer is yes, as can readily be shown.

(A) Let profits be arranged in an hierarchical order reflecting degrees of uncertainty. This hierarchical arrangement, we assert now (though *later* in the Chapter we *evaluate in detail*), is based on exactly the same foci as are the differential rents of classical theory which relate to differences in risks and skills. So let us next assume, though we again shall also later prove, that each firm produces at or near its optimum cost position. P will then exceed MC— which approaches equality with AC—by the amount of profit differential attributable to the existing varying degrees of uncertainty throughout the system. If then we regard uncertainty as an opportunity cost to society, we might well treat it as a competitive return along with the returns long accepted in economic theory, as we explained in Chapter 5.[1] And if we do regard uncertainty as a functionally limiting constraint to production (i.e., as a cost), $P > MC$ actually amounts to $P = MC$, as is readily viewed when uncertainty is assigned to a variable input status.

(B) We may look at the same relations somewhat differently. Suppose the average cost level for a *given industry* is lower in one market area than another and suppose also at first that the same linear market demand curve prevails in each. Greater profits will clearly prevail in the low-cost area; so, with open entry, relatively substantial competition will develop in that area causing the average revenue curve for each plant to shift significantly to the left. Comparing the average revenue curve for a plant in the low cost area with the average revenue curve of a plant in the high cost area uncovers a lower elasticity at any given output (assume the ideal output in each market) for the low cost area plant. If our mensuration ended here, divergent $AR > AC$ ratios would prevail at the given output in the two markets. But profits in an industry tend to be equated from plant to plant and market area to market area. This equation is derivable from long established rules of competition and open entry. It follows that *intra-industry* returns on investment tend to be proportionate; in equilibrium, the shapes of the AR curves in the two areas

---

[1] See F. Machlup, "Competition, Oligopoly and Profit," *Economica*, N.S. IX (1942), pp. 1–23 and 153–175 along this line. And note that under our conception we could view the classical tangency position as involving full returns to all productive factors, and the counterpart oligopolistic position as involving a higher level of average cost, with the difference between the two average costs, in equilibrium, representing the social opportunity cost of uncertainty.

are altered with the elasticity at the defined output in the low cost area tending to be the same, not less, as that in the high cost area.

On an *inter-industry* level, any ratio divergence of AR with MC reflects
the difference in uncertainty. In effect, what thus may appear as a divergency
actually amounts to a set of corresponding proportions as profit hierarchies
are directly related to the alternative amounts of uncertainty that prevail in
the market.

Technological Optimality

We must now account for the assumed classical approximation between MC
and AC in the equilibrium, since if substantial and varying inequalities prevailed, some firms would not only be producing inefficiently but the ratio of P
to MC would vary even after differentials for uncertainties are added to
costs.[1] Here too we find a salutary effect from open entry. What competition
means, as was noted before, is a leftward moving average revenue curve, so
that at any given price the elasticity along the compressed curve is greater
than at that price on the original curve. The development of more readily
substitutable goods (productwise and/or locationwise) further raises the
elasticity at any given price as the whole shape of the curve is altered. The
slope of the related MR curve becomes gentler. And with the limit set to
entry by the requirement of an hierarchical set of profits related to the prevailing uncertainties (as are differential rents for the different levels of risks
and skills), the likelihood is great (in fact, we shall find it approaches unity)
that MR will equal MC at points where MC = AC.

Following the above, consider this next force. If production appears to be
stabilized at a point short of the optimum cost position, a stability seemingly
marked—we assume—by a P > AC by just the amount of the uncertainty that
prevails in the market (i.e. by r as defined in Chapter 5), then P will be
sufficiently greater than unadjusted AC to warrant entry by new firms. In
contrast, if production appears to be stabilized at a point after the optimum
cost position (i.e., P > unadjusted AC by an amount which provides a return
r, as defined in Chapter 5), the entrepreneur will exit from the market or
realize that by rationalizing the size of his operation (e.g., setting up optimum
size branch plants in place of the larger than optimum size plant(s) he
currently has) his position will be improved. In time, rationalization and replacement must continue to the point where returns exactly commensurate
with energy expenditures and uncertainty obtain.[2]

---

[1] The proportionality between P and MC does not suffice by itself to yield optimal
resource allocation, as was shown by L. McKenzie, "Ideal Output and the Interdependence
of Firms," *Economic Journal*, Vol. LXI, December 1951.

[2] If we treated uncertainty as a variable cost, we would have observed that in this case
of greater than optimum size initially, P in effect is < adjusted MC and contraction in size
must occur. (See the Appendix to Chapter 5 for details of treating uncertainty as a variable
cost.)

A Restatement of the Above Propositions Based on the Appendix to Chapter 5*. Assume that maximum profits (i.e., $MR = MC$) involve $P > AC$ at the optimum classical cost position and that P is greater than AC at this point by exactly the amount of uncertainty which omniscient knowledge would tell us is applicable to the given activity in the market. By re-using Figure 5A–7 as 8–5, we observe that if we add the indicated uncertainty (which

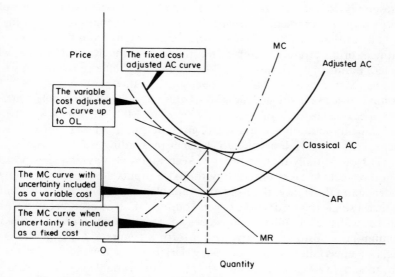

Figure 8–5: Optimality and the *r* and *r'* Adjusted AC Curves

by Chapter 5 terminology equals r/q) to the classical AC curve at the classical optimum point, we would find $P = AC$ adjusted. And if we also allocate uncertainty r/q to MC, we would find at the equilibrium point where classical $MC = AC$ that the ascription of uncertainty to marginal cost must be identical with that added to average cost. To complete our introductory statement, if the same amount *r* of uncertainty is ascribed to AC and MC at some other output point, such as at a *q* where classical average cost inclusions show greater than optimum output, any AR value which also happened to equal AC adjusted at that point would be < the MC which includes the *r* uncertainty, and vice versa for points of less than optimal output. What we are pointing to is simply (and only) the *uniqueness* of the optimum cost position, as will be further apparent in the following remarks.

We found in Chapter 5 that the cost of uncertainty may be added as a

---

* Readers who skipped the Appendix to Chapter 5 on a first reading may omit this section without loss of continuity. However, sufficient details are provided here to make this section stand alone, and thus its reading is recommended for all.

variable cost to MC or ascribed as a fixed cost. The variable cost transformation—it may be recalled—involves an opportunity cost r' that is commensurate with the actual e' expenditure of energy. This r' return is distinguishable from the return r which would be earned given an optimal performance elsewhere (or given the required receipt of r regardless of whether the optimal expenditure e or some e' energy was used up). Because of the importance of this particular relationship, we shall focus attention on the uncertainty which corresponds to the energies ($e' \gtrless e$) actually expended and the absolute returns ($r' \gtrless r$) commensurate with these energy expenditures. By doing so, we shall see that the adjustment to MC which results from the variable cost treatment of uncertainty requires, in turn, an adjustment to AC which, when effected, points to a determinate solution; and we shall also see that if we fail to adjust MR as well as MC, the operational value of the classic MR, MC relation is lost. As in the appendix to Chapter 5, we shall for simpler verbiage often speak henceforth of applying r or r' to MC, AC, or MR when, of course, the imputation process at any given output involves r/q or r'/q; when exact specification is desirable, no shortcut in wording will be taken.

(1) Note initially that, in order to keep Figure 8–5 as simple as possible, we do not include extra uncertainty for extra inputs associated with outputs greater than OL. Hence, the fixed and variable adjustments to the AC curves produce a single (merged) curve beyond output OL. However, because we also wish to evaluate in full the properties of production beyond the classical optimum cost position, we are setting forth a Figure 8–6 which shows the effects of uncertainty as an increasing variable cost beyond output OL. In turn, to simplify Figure 8–6, we only record the variable cost picture of uncertainty, thus leaving Figure 8–5 for readers who wish to view the fixed cost approach for values beyond output OL. We are in fact attempting to keep the study of our figures within manageable limits. So Figure 8–5 depicts the alternative ways of treating uncertainty up to output OL while presenting only fixed cost transformation beyond output OL; and Figure 8–6 only depicts the variable cost view over all outputs. In brief, Figures 8–5 and 8–6 must be used together (or separately as the case be) to consider outputs beyond OL.

(2) Conceive of an absolute "payoff" r for an uncertainty attributable to engaging in a business venture. This payoff r is based upon what would be an optimum performance in said venture and its best alternative. Add to it a component value v that is tied directly to the size of an investment, greater or less than optimal. In other words, conceive of some value r *plus* a variable value v, where the magnitude of the latter is based, for example, on the rule that the greater the investment in excess of the optimum, the greater is v,. and vice versa, with v assuming negative values over less than optimum output. (This rule follows, of course, from the idea of an investment total formed by a greater (or less) than optimum output multiplied by its related average cost.) In this way any artificial adjustment to the classical technologi-

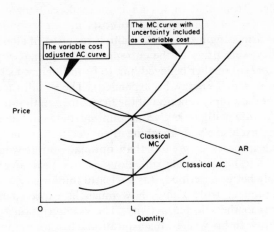

Figure 8–6: The *r'* Adjusted AC Curve

cal cost curves on account of uncertainty would be based in part on the size of output (input).

(3) Apart from instances of obvious profit or loss, where entry or exit will occur, there are five instances where the returns to the firm may appear to be at an equilibrium level, but in fact are not. Three of these instances are found at points before optimum cost production and two at greater than optimum cost outputs. An artificial adjustment to MR is especially helpful in revealing the instability of the last two cases. This adjustment involves ascribing *r* (not *r* + *v*) to classical MR; that is, our revenue adjustment reflects the optimum transformed opportunity income of the factor not the actual value of the energy expended by the factor.[1] In general, the artificial MR adjustment enables us to maintain the conceptual value of the MR↔MC relation when uncertainty is treated as a variable cost, and yields the same result as in the fixed cost case.

As noted above, the MR adjustment is largely artificial. Without it, the variable cost approach would fail to yield significant conclusions. With it, the marginal values point to an identical set of results as that of the fixed cost approach. An alternative framework (and view) of the interdependence of firms is thereby provided. We might further observe here for those who have not read the Appendix to Chapter 5 that the MR adjustment enables us to consider the decision-making process from the entrepreneur's viewpoint. His

[1] We might also recall from the Appendix to Chapter 5 the assertion made there that we impute the uncertainty "cost" (*r* + *v*) to the AC and MC of a given investment because all costs must be defrayed in the long run if the plant (firm) is to survive. But we ascribe only the uncertainty "cost" (*r*) to MR since the requirement for a viable, truly efficient system does not, *ipso facto*, select the particular firms that survive.

view often differs from that of his advisory staff, call them engineers. To illustrate: the r' $(= r + v)$ adjustment to costs in our system points to the income that the firm's engineers would claim is required of alternative outputs provided (a) they were privy to the entrepreneur's optimal opportunity cost ratio (i.e. R_0), *and* (b) further believed him to be indifferent as to how long he worked (i.e. how much energy he expended). The r' adjusted cost curves, therefore, reflect the supply function of the firm, albeit in the strictest sense the engineers work only with objective accounting data and use the classical marginal values exclusively in reaching their decisions. The adjustment to revenues (which in cases of greater than optimal output would make MR adjusted $>$ AR, and hence appear ridiculous) is, to repeat, an artificial adjustment, or possibly better described, it is a wishful thinking type of adjustment. Only the entrepreneur truly knows how much he expected he would earn (or had to earn) in the selected activity. The r/q ascription to his revenues therefore ties up with his wishes, his aspirations, his hopes, and most vitally his expectations of things to come. When the adjusted marginal values are unequal and the entrepreneur's decisions conform to the sense of the inequality, i.e. he expands his operation when his MR adjusted $>$ MC adjusted, and vice versa, we shall see that he tends to move towards a better position. When he ignores the inequality, he is in the process of exiting from the industry. That the MR adjustment provides values which de facto do not exist is, therefore, of no consequence. The adjusted value must be interpreted for what it is—a conjectured (required) return which some entrepreneurs expect will happen and, accordingly, follow to resolve their decisions, while others believe it should have already happened and hence no longer expect to occur. The full significance of (and basis for) the MR adjustment will be evident in the last two instances (cases IV and V) described below.

Three Instances of Less Than Optimum Cost Outputs. (I) AR may be greater than AC by the amount r/q at an output where energy expenditures are less than the optimal expenditure level, i.e. $e' < e$. And if tangency prevails, classical MR = classical MC.[1] Outsiders will readily identify the existence of a high rate of return in the industry, and entry will take place under conditions of unorganized oligopoly. Increased competition causes the AR schedules to shift leftward and to flatten. The shifting may be such as to cause the AR schedule to fall between the r and r' adjusted AC curves of Figure 8–5. Indeed, to avoid unnecessary repetition, we shall assume that this situation happens to arise, and turn attention, accordingly, to the second instance where equilibrium may appear to exist in a space economy.

(II) AR, we assume, is greater than the r' adjusted AC curve but less than

---

[1] When AR is tangent to r' adjusted AC, MC $<$ MR since adjusted MC = MR. Let us also observe here that v is negative for outputs less than the optimal output and positive for outputs greater than the optimal output, as will be demonstrated later (pp. 173, 174) in a more general way than was done in the Appendix to Chapter 5.

the r adjusted AC. For simplicity, assume it is tangent to what we shall call the hypothetical AC adjusted curve, which curve happens to lie somewhere between (and reflects in part each of) the r' and r adjusted AC curves up to output OL in Figure 8–5. We readily deduce, as we shall indicate below, that classical MR > classical MC at any output where AR is tangent to such hypothetical AC adjusted curve. From an engineering standpoint, we see that firms will expend their output. But let us go behind the assertion that classical MR > classical MC at the indicated output.

Consider four AC curves: the classical, the r' adjusted curve, the hypothetical, and the r adjusted curve. It is well-known that the MC value may be viewed by drawing a tangent to the classical AC curve at the relevant output, next drawing a curve marginal to it at twice its rate of fall, and observing finally the marginal curve's value at that output. [For the numerical counterpart, note that in equilibrium MC $= P(1 - 1/e)$, with e easily determined by reference to the tangent to the AC curve.] The classical MC value is, of course, the same as that applicable to the r adjusted curve. We further know—in accordance with our assumption that r' for uncertainty is a linear function of energy expenditures—that the r' adjusted AC curve is the reflection (on a higher level) of the classical AC curve. Adjusted MC for r' adjusted thus is > classical MC at the given output. In turn, if hypothetical AC is a cross between the r and r' adjusted AC curves, and if AR is tangent to hypothetical AC at the given output, it possesses a marginal value at that output which falls somewhere between the values of the marginal costs applicable to the r and r' adjusted AC curves. So its MR, i.e. classical MR, is > classical MC. It follows that even though some entrepreneurs may consider the higher rate of return for energies expended to be sufficient offset for the lower returns than r, instability prevails as engineers will be recommending an expansion of output. Three main possibilities may then be identified: (1) If the AR curve that is tangent to the hypothetical AC happens to be the one actually drawn in Figure 8–5, the unstable position of any input-output less than OL may soon be ended, with the long-run equilibrium position quickly reached. (2) If the AR curve lies above the one drawn in Figure 8–5, some net entry will take place. (3) If the AR curve lies below the one drawn in Figure 8–5, some net exit will take place.

(III) Let AR be tangent to the r' adjusted curve. For reasons mentioned above, classical MR > classical MC so that no stability at all exists in even the classical sense. Output expansion by some firms to the profit-maximizing level is indicated by the present situation. But note, a net exit of firms must also occur to raise AR to the position shown in Figure 8–5. The long-run equilibrium position may be reached directly. Or, as we shall see later on in this chapter after we have presented the multi-plant, multi-LRAC curve possibility for firms in economic space, the exit of some firms may lead to entry by a larger number of smaller firms. It follows that a new combination of smaller size firms, larger number of alternative sources of the good, decreasing product differentiation, and greater output would arise; in turn, this set of changes would produce leftward-shifted and flattened AR curves, as these are formed coterminously with the leftward-shifted AC curves of the new firms. But, for the moment, it must suffice to say that equilibrium—in any case—eventuates at the point of optimum costs on the firm's r' adjusted AC curve. (See Figure 8–6.)

Two Instances of Greater Than Optimum Cost Outputs. (IV) AR may be greater than classical AC at a point beyond optimum costs by the amount r/q. Classical MR may equal classical MC, but adjusted MR is obviously less than adjusted MC. It is, therefore, manifest that this particular situation is not an equilibrium state. Equally apparent is the slight likelihood of finding the present case in practice, except conceptually on the part of misguided decision makers. This follows because a return equal to r for $e' > e$ energies implicitly requires an industry where firms are unduly large in size considering the extent to which competition has already taken place. The present situation may, therefore, be expected to apply only to the early stages of an industry's development, where firms are too large and too few in number, but where engineers visualize a sharply kinked (i.e. two section) AR curve, and the firm prices accordingly. Contraction in scale of operation for some firms (or plants) is indicated, as is possibly the exit of others. The very flat, rather elastic AR schedule—which is implicit to this case—will then be conceived to shift, and actually *does shift* upward becoming steeper in slope for the reason that the AR curve allocable to the smaller size firms (plants) must be more desirable than before. The myopia for excessively large size having been ended, windfalls will arise for the now optimum size firms. But these surpluses must also be short lived as competitive entry soon occurs to cause the AR curves (now conceived, let us propose, in three section form) to shift leftward and downward to the intersection (or tangency) point of AR and the r' (or r) adjusted AC curve, as shown in Figure 8–5.

(V) Let AR be greater than classical AC by the value r'/q at an output greater than the optimum output. Even though classical MR might also equal classical MC, the firm is in an unstable position. We easily recognize this condition by noting that adjusted MR is less than adjusted MC. Indeed, the present case is even more extreme than the preceding one in the sense of probably involving a still earlier stage of industrial development than that of Case IV. Rather significant profits are obtainable if the firms reduce their operations to the optimal scale. The representative firm could, in fact, reach the size where the allocated AR schedule happens to yield both the engineer's objective of classical MR equal to classical MC and the entrepreneur's objective of an equality between adjusted MR and adjusted MC. Profits would then exist which are greater than those applicable to case IV after the rationalization process applicable to that situation had taken place. The entry of new firms is thus promoted, and ultimately the equilibrium depicted in

Figure 8–5 must hold. As with case IV, the initial situation assumed here is quite unlikely, for it requires excessive size firms which face (or conceive of) very-very elastic (and flat) AR schedules above the kink. Moreover, these firms produce a larger total of goods at a lower price than that which should have been expected of them. Most significantly, perhaps, when firms are initially of the excessive size of our present case, the true allocable AR schedule should be expected to have been *much greater* in magnitude and slope than that visualized; in such case, windfalls via higher prices are possible, and the room for entry immediately obvious.

Cases IV and V suggest that there are other possible instances where larger than optimal size firms and plants may prevail. But these instances will generally reflect economic advantages. They would occur when demand conditions, and the number of firms are such as to enable entrepreneurs to earn much greater than r' for $e' > e$ energies. The rule of adjusting MR by r and adjusting MC by $r + v$, and then comparing the adjusted values to determine the entrepreneur's satisfaction with his firm's output does not apply perfectly to these circumstances since a return noticeably in excess of r' for e' energies exists. The difference in the perspective of entrepreneurs and their engineer "advisors," which is reflected in the inequality of the adjusted MR and MC values, first arises forcefully after sufficient entry has taken place. Indeed, when classical MR = classical MC at a point where energies e' are $> e$, returns must probably fall to r' or almost to r' before the MR, MC adjustment serves as an adequate guide to entrepreneurial differences with their engineers and their willingness to overrule them. As we observed above, some rationalization of firm and plant size will then tend to occur. In turn, the ordinate intercept point on the allocable AR curve is next conceived to rise and the slope of the curve steepens. This rationalization restores the state of profits (windfalls) and, in time, induces new entry. Ultimately, the AR curve shifts leftward and tends to flatten, though it *must be steeper in slope* than that required by cases IV and V where r or r' returns applied to energies $e' > e$ at the point where classical MR = classical MC.

Most vital to any situation of production at a greater than optimal output point is the fact that regardless of whether the firm correctly or incorrectly conceives of its AR curve, profitable production *is* possible under the initial conditions of cases IV and V. If competitive entry is assumed, the AR curve must shift leftward in time. If it cuts the r adjusted AC curve from above at points short of output OL in Figure 8–5, profits still exist and new entry will occur. If it intersects the r adjusted curve at output OL from positions below AC adjusted rather than lying tangent to it at output OL, classical and adjusted MR are respectively > classical and adjusted MC; then, output will be increased, economic losses will take place, and some firm(s) will exit. Eventually AR must be tangent to the r adjusted AC curve *and* intersect the r' adjusted AC curve at output OL. This tangency to the r adjusted AC curve requires classical MR to equal classical MC; correspondingly, the adjusted marginal values are also equal to the classical least cost position. Either this particular AR curve must eventuate or else economic production under competitive conditions is impossible. Alternatively phrased, if production is possible at all under conditions of competition, it must be possible (and in the limit is possible) at the minimum point of classical AC. It is only under conditions of simple monopoly or organized oligopoly that higher cost production would continue indefinitely over time in a system formed by economic space.

III. THE OLIGOPOLY AND PURE COMPETITION EQUILIBRIUM: MORE ABOUT EFFICIENCY

The equilibrium conditions and positions of firms in a space economy are, therefore, counterpart to those in a purely competitive world. The differences in words that are used center around the terms: (a) discontinuities in average revenue curves (a condition which is primarily important in short-run analysis); (b) indivisibilities in space and production, another essentially short-run condition which nevertheless causes us to use the word "approach" rather than to speak dogmatically of complete identities; and (c) the existence of multi-plant or large plant oligopolists rather than single-plant atomistic firms.

There are three fundamental long-run properties of the efficient space oligopoly which can be specified: (1) production in conformance with consumer wants; (2) production guided by an hierarchical pattern of rent and profit returns commensurate with risk, uncertainty, and, let us at this point re-employ the word, indivisibility; and (3) prices marked up above cost in accordance with the natural exclusionary (shortage) effect of uncertainty and indivisibility. The required hierarchical pattern of returns, viewed coterminously with competitive entry and exit of firms, provides the basic regulatory force of the system: they lead to fair pricing and the satisfying of consumer wants. Our thesis can be summarized as follows:

> A capitalistic economy, formed along oligopolistic lines, approaches an *efficient* one provided entry and exit are kept free and the organization of oligopolists is outlawed.

Difference Between Indivisibility and Uncertainty

Our theory regards indivisibility as ultimately blending (more or less completely) with uncertainty because, as with uncertainty, (1) institutional indivisibilities, such as in finance, freight rating by zones, etc., and (2) natural indivisibilities, such as in demand, technology, economic space, etc., elicit a nonprobabilistic range of returns for the firm. Indeed, they actually alter the uncertainty that otherwise alone would have prevailed. Even certain types of indivisibilities, such as those imposed or set up by government (e.g. patents, their duration, the likelihood of receiving one, etc.), tend to have this blending impact with uncertainty. Moreover, as we shall shortly see, the possibility of mixing small and large firms over economic space adds a continuity to the system that makes indivisibility essentially just a modifying influence on uncertainty. Notwithstanding this blending process, there is an advantage in separating the two and examining their individual impacts on entry. The full significance of the relation between indivisibility and uncertainty will become increasingly apparent as the present analysis unfolds.

Slight Indivisibility–Uncertainty Restraints on Entry

If entry is generally open, albeit not unlimited, many firms may exist in the market. Should the number of entrants be so large that the representative firm is producing at some point short of the optimum cost point on the r' adjusted LRAC curve, an exit by some and rationalization by others of size of plants and firms must take place.

There are, of course, alternatives to $AR > AC$ by just the amount r'/q. So, if instead of being greater than AC in proportion to energies expended, the firm's AR is greater than the relevant AC by r/q, or by more than the opportunity cost of the indivisibility and uncertainty applicable to the industry, the change of plant and firm size towards the optimum would proceed initially from new entry, and subsequently from rationalization, without any exodus being repuired. If, on the other hand, the differential was less than r'/q, a great exodus would occur. And finally, to repeat, if AR was greater than AC by r'/q, rationalization and exit by existing firms would take place. In any case, we ultimately reach the point of optimum size if the restraints to entry are slight.

Sharp Indivisibility–Uncertainty Restraints on Entry

Let us imagine a market in which there is room for only two firms. (The case of a pure monopoly will be discussed in Chapter 13.) We might then accept a short-run kink in the AR curve, and a scale of production the locus of which is formed over the rising portion of the LRAC curve. But, with unorganized oligopoly, either additional entry tends to arise directly, or, if AR happens to be greater than AC by only the "normative" amount at the given "greater than optimal output," the proper inclusion of indivisibility and uncertainty as an adjustment to costs and revenues at this output would indicate that the existing firms have an excess of MC over MR. [The MR adjustment, to recall, is based on the optimal performance elsewhere (i.e. r) while the MC adjustment $(r+v)$ is based on the same optimal (ratio) performance plus the extra for the additional investment (energy) expenditure that is actually involved in the activity under analysis.] This condition would lead to a contraction in the size and/or number of the plant(s) belonging to the firm, as the average size of firms will be decreased over time.

Two problems arise under this last situation: (1) Would the $AR > AC$ differentials that are obtainable when duopolists rationalize to optimal size yield a sum sufficiently greater than the normative amount required by the industry's indivisibility and uncertainty to attract other entry? Can we be sure that during (or after) the rationalization process, entry will take place in the presence of *sharp* indivisibility and uncertainty restraints so that, in turn, the prevailing $AR > AC$ differentials would not be excessive? Related to this query is another problem which we have previously tended to avoid. In fact, before we can resolve the above question, we must ask (and answer) the next question. (2) How should we conceive of the LRAC curve in a space economy where single as well as multiple plant firms exist? We must also discuss (a) the conditions under which the energy investment expenditures of the firms are to be conceived to increase with an increase in the *number* of the plant(s) of the firm, and (b) whether firms of different size may arise in the market such that the economy would ultimately have the equivalent of, say, 2 and 1/2 or 2 and 3/4 optimal-size units in the given activity. To answer the two main questions posed above and those related to them, let us proceed initially with question 2 and first define the LRAC curve for a space economy.

The Set of LRAC Curves. We conceive of a set of LRAC curves for each firm, the subsets of which are ordered on different levels. Each of the levels includes all practical sizes of plants—as in the classical conception of the LRAC curve. Each subset level is determined by the overall size of the firm, itself partially a function of the number of plants conceived to comprise the firm. We suggest, then, the possibility of a firm having a central "office" or "plant," one plant of a certain size, or two or several plants of the same size, alternative sizes being possible of course. We assume that in certain industries marked economies are obtained from centralized operations in purchasing, selling, accounting, finance, labor relations (negotiations), and research; while, in other industries, the general manager(s) of a particular plant(s) in a single or multi-plant firm might conduct one or several functions on his own, in consultation with staff members in a general office located elsewhere or in his own plant.

One LRAC curve may pertain to a single plant operation, with all relevant sizes of the single plant firm shown along the curve. A lower level LRAC curve may be identified which depicts the same firm with alternative plant sizes. The lower level curve will then relate to the existence of more than one plant of the given size, with the implicit assumption that selected economies are obtained from some specialization (and centralization) in buying, selling, finance, accounting, research etc. Still lower levels of the LRAC curves are identifiable up to a point beyond which the addition of another plant of a given size means an addition to the cost of communication, the cost of coordination of effort, the weakening of the initiative of managers, etc., which exceeds any further gains from centralization of selected activities. Thereafter the LRAC curves rise to higher levels, ultimately to ridiculous values.

It is conceivable, of course, that a firm may have plants of varying sizes, so that one of its nonoptimal-size plants bears a cost which places it on the very lowest level possible. But we specify this level as being the same as that obtainable when all the plants of the firm are of the same nonoptimal-given size. We do this because we gain nothing by conceiving of a lower level for a nonoptimal-size plant in a family of alternative size plants (in alternative market areas). That is to say, nothing is added that is not conceptually allowed for by the simplifying assumption that all nonoptimal-size plants of the firm (in all market areas) are of the same size. To understand our point, consider the following.

Accept as conceivable the situation that a given nonoptimal-size plant might appear on the very lowest *possible* LRAC curve if it were part of a family of different sized plants rather than of plants of identical nonoptimal size. But this possibility is theoretically unnecessary. The very idea that alternative sizes of plants may be combined in such a way as to produce a lowest LRAC value for a given nonoptimal-size plant, a value which is lower than the related low point on the LRAC curve formed by identical non-optimal-size plants, implicitly attests to the greater technological advantage of the optimum-optimorum. And because we have already seen that any non-optimal-size operation tends to provide returns that are not commensurate with the indivisibility-uncertainty cost of the activity under analysis, only the optimum-size plant ultimately prevails. Nothing is, therefore, gained analyti-cally by the inclusion of the unequal size plant situation in our conception. It suffices that a similarly shaped LRAC curve is drawn which assumes for a multi-plant firm that each of the firm's plants is of the same size. This assump-tion is a simplifying one and does not affect the conclusions of our theory.

The Investment (Energy) Expenditures along the LRAC Curves. One final matter must be handled now before we may proceed with the answer to the other main and sub question. How do we know that the investment (energy) expenditure of the firm changes as one moves to the right along any LRAC curve, and correspondingly as one moves to LRAC curves of a different level? In answer, we repeat from the Appendix to Chapter 5 our proof that the investment or energy expenditure is less at outputs smaller than the optimal one and greater at larger than optimal outputs. It will readily be shown that this same proof also applies to the multiple plant firm, specifically the move-ment from one level to another in the set of LRAC curves.

Consider a given LRAC curve. Let I_n be the optimum-size plant in its optimal performance (x_0) and let I_0 refer to a smaller than optimum output (x_n) produced by the same plant. Then, let II_0 be the plant of optimal size for the smaller than optimum output (x_n). Plant size II_n thus appears on the LRAC curve for output (x_n), while I_0, of course, establishes the optimal cost level at output x_0. We know that AC = TC/X. So, total cost (TC) for plant operation I_0 is greater than or at the least equal to what would be the corresponding total cost of the *same plant* in the production of x_n. This relation follows because if x_n is less than the optimal output, and the total cost in producing and maintaining this quantity exceeds the total cost in producing and maintaining x_0, the optimal quantity could be produced with the difference $x_0 - x_n$ stored or discarded. Thus total cost of $I_n \leqslant$ total cost of I_0. But plant size II is more efficient in producing x_n than is I; hence, total cost of II_n is less than I_n. It follows that total cost (investment or energy expenditures) decreases with smaller than optimal-size plants. Similarly, if for x_t, which we shall assume is $> x_0$, the total cost of production (i.e., the investment or energy expenditure) is stipulated to be less than x_0, plant I_0 could not even be optimal in producing x_0, as we assumed it is. Manifestly, if I_0 is optimal in producing x_0 and x_0 is the optimal output, the cost of producing x_t (where $x_t > x_0$) must be greater than that of producing x_0.

The proof that energies expended increase from left to right along a given LRAC curve is readily applicable (and extendable) to the set of LRAC curves. Thus, if the LRAC levels fall from smaller firms to larger firms, the lowest level curve at any given plant size must still involve a greater energy total than that which holds for each previous (higher level) curve; in fact, the higher level LRAC curve otherwise would cease to exist as the greater quantity would be produced with the difference stored or discarded. It further follows that when the movement proceeds from a given plant size on the lowest level LRAC to the comparable plant size on higher level (greater quantity) curves, costs continue to rise.

We may view the situation of multiple plants and energy cost expenditures in an alternative way. Let L_3, L_2, L_1 run in descending order from a given point involving the smallest (one-plant) firm to the larger [two-(L_2) and three-(L_1) plant] firm. It follows that L_3 is at the highest level of cost with L_2 and L_1 respectively being at the lower levels of cost. Let L_0 (the n plant firm) have the lowest of all LRAC curves for any given size of plant. Total firm energy expenditures, at any comparable output point on curves L_3, ..., L_0, must be the highest on L_0; if it were not, the higher level curves (L_3, L_2, L_1) would not exist, as the firm would use the larger number of plants, letting each produce it own output x_0, with a portion of the total output $n(x_0)$ being stored or discarded. The larger firm producing the larger total output must expend the greater energies even though the *representative* plant, as shown along the LRAC curve, produces on a lower level than any other representative plant.

It follows further that with L_1, L_2, L_3 next representing firms which have a larger number of plants than n (i.e. these firms are larger than L_0), the energy expenditures clearly increase. In brief, the greater the number of plants of any given size, the larger is the firm size and the greater are the related energy expenditures. This is not to say that a nonoptimal size plant(s) which is part of a small firm cannot ever be found expending greater energies than the optimal—optimorum size plant(s) and firm(s); but this and other cases are readily subsumable within the comparisons we are able to make along the lowest "economic" level LRAC curve for small and large firms, since when a small (or large) firm is wasteful of energies, said firm must disappear in the long run. More generally phrased, all uneconomic representative plants are to be considered to have been dropped from all LRAC curves. Thus, for example, if one large plant (or two small plants) is able to produce a greater output or the same total output at a lower cost than can two small plants (or one large plant), the uneconomic size plant(s) is to be dropped from the LRAC curve to which it otherwise would belong. It follows that not only are aggregate outputs and aggregate investment energy expenditures to be conceived of as increasing with increases in the number of plants (as we go from L_3 to L_2 to L_1 to L_0 then to L_1 etc.), but this relation holds regardless of the particular (and possibly different) plant sizes being compared.

It is most important to note at this point that our previous analysis in terms of r returns for energy expenditures e, and all of the related diagrams that were used, were made to appear to center on the one firm—one plant situation. Yet our analysis actually applied to the multiple plant, multiple level cost curve set described above. To see this, consider the following:

By definition, the firm whose manager(s)-owner(s) have opportunity cost r are ready to expend energies e. If they earn r for smaller (or larger) energies e', or earn $<r$ for preferred energies e, either entry or exit will occur. The rationalization process intrinsic to effective economic performance must lead the firm to the lowest cost level possible, such that if the lost opportunities applicable to its members happen to be r, energies e must be applied. There will be similar results for firms whose members have different alternatives from r, provided that these other firms prove to be economically necessary and become a viable part of the industry. But this last point can be best analyzed later on in the development of our theory. For the present, we will conclude our discussion of sets of LRAC curves by recasting our production function in mathematical form, after which we shall provide answers to the remaining questions posed above.

Mathematical Formulation. Let the production function of the spatial firm with one plant of size m be defined as

(1) $q_m = F_m(x_1^m, \ldots, x_n^m), (m = 1, \ldots, y)$

where x_i^m stands for the i_{th} input by the firm with plant size m.

By conventional presentations, the slope of the isoquant for any output q_1 in a two factor world is given by

(2) $q_m = f_m(x_1^m, x_2^m)$

The MRS between the factors becomes

(3) $-\dfrac{dx_2^m}{dx_1^m} = \left(\dfrac{\partial q_m}{\partial x_1^m}\right) \Big/ \left(\dfrac{\partial q_m}{\partial x_2^m}\right)$

The cost of production, as in conventional presentations, is given by the linear equation

(4) $C_m = g_1 x_1^m + g_2 x_2^m + a_m$

where the g's stand for input prices, and a_m is the fixed cost.

Productive efficiency may change as a result of centralized research, accounting, buying, etc. Accordingly (2) through (4) is convertible to multi-plant functions, where m' below refers to an alternative "set" of branch plants $(1, \ldots, v)$ of sizes m.

(5) $q_{m'} = f_{m'}(x_1^{m'}, x_2^{m'}), (m' = 1, \ldots, v)$

Substitute m' in (3), and let (4) become

(6) $C_{m'} = g_1' x_1^{m'} + g_2' x_2^{m'} + a_{m'}$

where $a_{m'}$ is now the fixed cost allocable to a plant, and g' depends on regional factor prices for the m' branch plants.

For any given cost $C_{m'}$ (defined by the required and purchased input combinations), we find—solving (6)—the relation

(7) $x_1^{m'} = (C_{m'} - a_{m'})/g_1' - (g_2'/g_1') x_2^{m'}$

The slope of the isocost line is the negative of the input price ratio and must be tangent to the isoquant curve under output-maximizing conditions. Of course, maximizing output for a given cost is equivalent to minimizing cost for that particular output, and we have, in effect, set forth above the plant size and plant number requirements for producing a given quantity at lowest cost.

By applying a multiplier m to (5), alternative outputs may be considered and an expansion path, based upon plant size and number of plants, traced. The long-run cost curve for the alternative representative size plants ($m = 1, \ldots, y$) under any given size firm ($m' = 1, \ldots, v$), in turn, could then be derived. Total cost is, accordingly, designatable as

(8) $C_{m'} = \phi_{m'}(mq_{m'}) + a_{m'}$

The average cost of producing output q under plant size m thus varies with the size m' of the firm. Of course, there is an optimal size plant and firm for output $q_{m'}$ given by the tangency of the relevant isoquant and isocost lines.

Correspondingly, there is an optimal size plant and firm for other outputs.

The production function of the multi-plant firm in economic space may be summarized in slightly different form. By letting m apply only to a given size plant of a firm with a given number of plants, tangency of isocost and isoquant is established by equating (g_2/g_1) and $-\left(\dfrac{\partial f_m}{\partial x_2{}^m} \middle/ \dfrac{\partial f_m}{\partial x_1{}^m}\right)$. But there exist alternative size plants in the family of alternative number of plants. In implicit form $H[C, q, m, m'] = 0$. Treating m' parametrically, it follows that when partials are taken with respect to m for all given g (assuming they are practically continuous) and set equal to zero, the long-run envelope curve which envelopes the LRAC curves given by a fixed m' is obtained. [E.g., see Figure 8-7D infra.] If partials are taken with respect to m, m', and q the optimal-optimorum is derived. But note, the very lowest curve which may actually be found in the industry depends on (a) the demand that exists over the entire economic space, for this influences the number of market area subdivisions that will arise, and (b) the cost conditions over the space, for this influences the sizes and number of plants in the respective market areas and the related costs of a particular output. Ipso facto, (a) and (b) in concert determine the lowest level possible of the LRAC curve at any given output, hence all outputs. Of course it may be that demand and cost conditions are so constraining that the firm which would have the optimal–optimorum plant cannot exist in the long run; only other firms with smaller opportunity cost requirements, producing at their own optimal–optimorum position may be able to survive. But more about this below where, however, to avoid confusion, we shall reserve the term optimal–optimorum for references to the very lowest LRAC possible in the industry, and simply speak of the optimal-optimorum cost position for (any) other firm(s) as the optimal position.

Rationalization, Excessive Profits and Sharp Restraints to Entry: Size and AR, AC Differentials. The answers to our remaining questions will now be seen to fall readily into place.

Assume that sharp restraints to entry, coterminous with a rationalization of plant sizes by each duopolist, ultimately bring about an $AR > AC$ by a sum greater than the indivisibility and uncertainty which actually underscores the activity in question. What will happen?

Suppose we conceive initially of the optimal LRAC curve for each duopolist as not including the salary of the manager, nor any (other) skill, risk or uncertainty imputation required in theory. Then compare the LRAC curve for the optimal-optimorum duopolist with that of a hypothetical firm which, because it is small in size (i.e., it controls a smaller number of plants), happens to have a higher LRAC curve. This hypothetical firm, we assume, would be directed by managers satisfied with a smaller (effective) energy expenditure.

Now it should be recalled that just as the investment energy cost of a firm increases to the right along any LRAC curve, the total investment energy cost of a firm must rise with increasing size of the firm. The remuneration required by managers who invest lesser (effective) energies than others, *ceteris paribus*, will be less than that required by those investing more, though, of course, to each man in each set of men, the individual return must be equivalent to or greater than his optimal opportunity return. By ascribing the required remuneration for management (or in the case of single proprietorships the implicit cost of the entrepreneur), we see, for example, that a firm of one-half the size of another, with a higher LRAC curve level than the other, may nevertheless prevail in the market.

It is significant that all firms within any given uncertainty classification are at the same level of average cost after the service energy imputation is made. This is so even though many of the plants (firms) have their optimal point at a larger (or smaller) output than the plant that happens to be drawn as the representative plant. Ascribing the risk on capital and then the uncertainty on equity investment to the common level, as established by the services and risk imputation, leaves a still higher, but continuing common level for all surviving firms in the industry. It is the residually added component which makes the tangency between LRAC adjusted and a negatively sloping AR curve possible without giving up classical technological efficiency.

A few related observations should be included here. Firms not of the optimal-optimorum size (i.e. higher cost firms *before the service-risk imputation process*) can conceivably be squeezed out via price wars by firms that are closer to the optimal-optimorum size firm. So the trend in the market is towards a divisible continuous system which is the most efficient one possible given a limited number of factors of production, including managers and entrepreneurs. Indivisibility, in effect, tends to be a short-run constraint; correspondingly, $AR > AC$ may be excessive in the short run only. We shall see in Chapter 13 that the entire system is also possessed of Pareto optimality features.

IV. A DIAGRAMMATIC REPRESENTATION OF THE EQUILIBRIUM OF A SINGLE OR MULTI-PLANT FIRM IN ECONOMIC SPACE

We may present our theory both schematically and generally by diagramming the equilibrium conditions for the multi-plant firm in economic space. Manifestly, the single-plant firm is a special case falling within the general theory and view presented here. Such classical firm was analyzed diagrammatically in Chapter 5, although the reader was also left free to visualize a multi-plant firm if he desired.

The Set of LRAC Curves in 3D and 2D

Figure 8–7A depicts the total cost of a firm with an alternative number of plant possibilities. Each additional plant increases fixed costs; total costs rise also with increased output. Significantly, the vector from 0 to a given total cost curve decreases up to plant number 3, indicating that average costs fall up to the three-plant situation and increase thereafter.

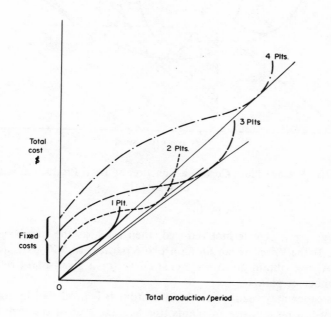

Figure 8–7A: Total Costs—Multi-plant Firm

The elementary ideas presented in Figure 8–7A may be recast in the three-dimensional drawing of Figure 8–7B. Let us focus attention within the hammock-shaped portion of the figure. By design, the hammock extends away from the YZ plane as plant numbers greater than one are conceived, for otherwise we would be including within our focus the extremely small (irrelevant) output case (closest to or along the YZ plane) and assigning to this microscopic output a varying (increasing) number of plants. The hammock thus depicts increasing output with increasing number of plants as one reads from left to right *away from points C and B*.

Consider cross section BB′ in Figure 8–7B along the shaded plane parallel to YZ. The resulting BB′ curve shows that, given some large production rate,

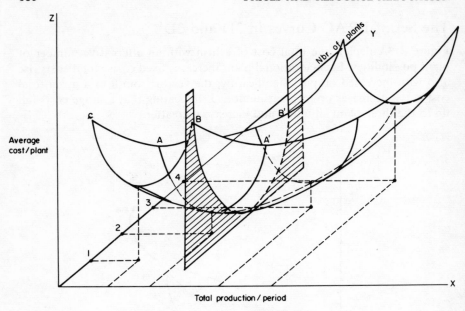

Figure 8–7B: Average Plant Cost as a Function of Total Production and Number of Plants

the average plant cost is first reduced, then rises, as the number of plants increases. If the "tire" is cut along a plane parallel to XZ, such as through points AA′, we obtain an average cost curve for a given plant related to a given number of plants.

The reader may readily see that if output B is produced by too small a number of too large a size of plants, the average cost of the firm would be substantial. In contrast, output B could be produced by a larger number of smaller size plants at lower average costs. Clearly, there is an optimal output for which an optimal size and number of plants exists.

By placing the hammock of Figure 8–7B parallel to the YZ plane, and then looking directly at it from a position behind the XZ plane, i.e. the view from the fourth quadrant in the upper floor of our system, Figure 8–7C appears. The set of LRAC curves that are shown in Figure 8–7C involves some slight distortion of average costs, especially at very small outputs; however, it does enable us to view the multi-plant cost relationships reasonably well in two dimensions. The set of LRAC curves are thus to be interpreted as average cost per plant for a given quantity of goods produced by a given plant (and number of plants). We see that costs decrease up to a given size of firm and then increase. The curves LRAC′ and LRAC″ can be viewed as two of many curves representative of small and large size firms, with the LRAC‴

curve viewed as the cost curve of the optimal size firm. Figure 8–7C is thus the counterpart to the cost curve set described in section III, and we could relabel the curve LRAC′ as L_3, with LRAC″ becoming L_2, etc.

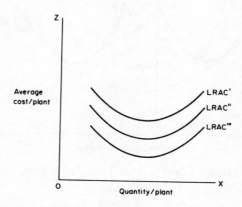

Figure 8–7C: The LRAC Set 2D

We may recast Figure 8–7B alternatively as 8–7D, which view would again be gained from a position behind the XZ plane. This time we do not place the hammock parallel to the YZ plane but leave it as drawn. However, let us view the plant numbers in a more continuous pattern than is referenced in Figure 8–7B, such as, for example, 41, 42, . . . By recognizing, in turn, that the size of the firm is not only a function of the number of plants the firm has but also of the number of offices it has throughout the landscape (e.g. regional purchasing, accounting, sales offices), Figure 8–7D would reappear in a still more continuous format.

To fully appreciate this particular view of costs, suppose we compare the LRAC curve of a firm which has the optimal-optimorum representative plant with the LRAC curve of a firm whose optimal cost requires the same size or a slightly smaller size plant, but which firm, in any case, is slightly less efficient than the most efficient one. Suppose no long-run payments for owner(s)-manager(s) have been included (or imputed). The difference between the LRAC levels would then reflect the difference in the opportunity cost (i.e. the desired (and relevant) income values and energy unit expenditures) of the owner(s)-manager(s) of the firms. Though Figure 8–7D might imply that only the firm which we may refer to as the optimal-optimorum firm produces at its least cost, a comparable diagram obtains for all other firms with (some) changed numbers and/or levels being applicable. In other words, the next

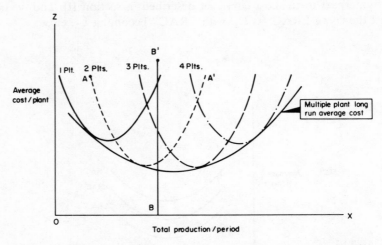

Figure 8–7D: Average Cost/Plant vs. Total Production, Multi-plant Firm

size firm to the optimal-optimorum firm has its own bell-shaped long-run average cost curve which (before any imputations are made) would be on a slightly higher level than that of the optimal-optimorum firm. This curve would either be (a) displaced slightly to the left of the optimal-optimorum firm, which condition exists when the capacity of its owner(s)-manager(s) is slightly less than that of the owner(s)-manager(s) of the optimal-optimorum firm, or (b) it would be above the optimal-optimorum firm, which condition occurs when capacities are identical but their organizational ability, etc. is slightly different. When it is capacity which is less, the differences also may relate to the nonoptimal-optimorum firm having a smaller set of regional offices, which set in turn reflects the smaller energy expenditures optimally ordered by (and for) its owner(s)-manager(s). For reasons explained previously, if this firm exists, its production will proceed at its optimum cost level, not before or after this point. We shall, in fact, shortly find that this firm *may* survive in the long run, regardless of whether or not there is also room in the industry for the optimal-optimorum firm.[1]

[1] The high cost firm whose optimal production point involves smaller size than the optimum-optimorum firm is not to be confused with the producer described in Chapter 5 who is high in cost because his preferred energy expenditures fail to conform to the existing technology. The high cost in the initial case relates to relative inefficiency and hence relatively low opportunity costs. In the latter case it relates to noncompatibility and hence inadequate long-run returns because the entrepreneur violates his own best job position. If we had wanted to include noncompatibility possibilities in the text above, we could have referred to less efficient firms which were smaller *or larger* in size than the optimal-optimorum firm, rather than just referring to smaller firms.

Efficiency in Production

Both the classical and spatial theories recognize high and low cost producers, and both theories relate cost to efficiency. For example, consider a classical case, such as that of Firms A and B whose average cost curves are shown in Figure 8–8A. Firm B is presumed to have lower production costs due to more

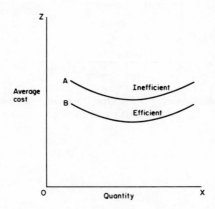

Figure 8–8A: Single-Plant Firms: One Possibility (Before Imputations for Risks and Skills)

efficient operations, at least before imputations are made for manager's services and capital investment. After the imputation, the curves for B and A will be on the same level, merging perfectly or otherwise as the case may be. Now assume two multiplant firms, Firm A and Firm B, in economic space. Again assume that Firm A (the smaller few-plant firm) is the inefficient firm before the imputations are made, as shown in Figure 8–8B.

Then suppose both firms in Figure 8–8B survive in the long run, a co-existence made possible under imputations for differential skills. By ascribing the appropriate r_A and r_B for the services given and the risks undertaken by the managers and investors in the two firms, the lowest cost level on the curves A and B will become the same. Thus Figure 8–8C is drawn under the assumptions that both firms are covering their risk and skill opportunity costs and will survive in the long run. When uncertainty on investment is also ascribed, the curves move together to a still higher level. Figure 8–8B then reappears as Figure 8–8D.

We might emphasize with respect to Figure 8–8D that the less efficient firm, Firm A, is the higher costing firm before opportunity cost "service and

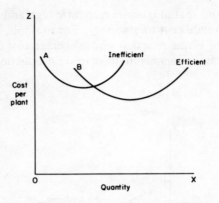

Figure 8–8B: Multi-plant Firms: One Possibility (Before Imputations for Risks and Skills)

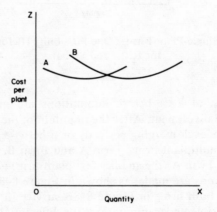

Figure 8–8C: The Multi-plant Firms of Figure 8–8B (After Imputations for Risks and Skills)

capital risk" imputations are ascribed. After these imputations are effected, the adjusted curves are on the same level. Firm B is, of course, inefficient in producing the lowest cost output of Firm A. However, if Figure 8–8D were to include the LRAC curve for Firm B, presumably different size plant (and plants) for Firm B would provide it with an average cost in producing Firm

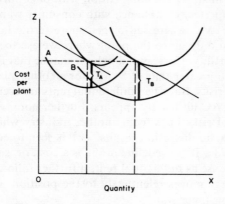

Figure 8–8D: Varying Opportunity Costs

A's best output which (though higher than B's average cost in producing its own optimal output) is nevertheless lower than the respective average cost of Firm A. Imputing lost opportunity costs, however, clearly raises the adjusted average cost curve of Firm B for that output to a level above that of Firm A. So, regardless of the plant it uses, if the initial conditions are that AR is tangent to the AC adjusted curve of Firm A, as recorded in Figure 8–8D, this AR curve would still be below the adjusted curve applicable to Firm B. Firm B can prevail if and only if its optimal-optimorum output is possible. It follows that if production under competitive conditions is feasible, Firm B may very well be part of the long run, and so too may Firm A.

Note finally in Figure 8–8D that an R for uncertainty is conceived to have been applied to the cost curves in the form of r's at the relevant output levels. These lost r-values represent long-run profits. Significantly total $r_B > r_A$ but since $e_B > e_A$, the final equilibrium position of both firms is at the same average cost. We have a case here where a large firm can exist side by side with a small firm. Similarly, the theory allows the coexistence of multi-plant with single plant firms as the viable number and size of firms depend on short-run happenings, the prevailing technology, demand, availability of entrepreneurial skills to this and other industries, and other forces recorded previously in the book.

V. WANT SATISFACTION AND DETERMINATE EQUILIBRIUM

It has long been said that if P > MC somewhere in the economy and P = MC somewhere else in the economy, production will not conform to consumer wants. Apparently, mixing pure competition with oligopoly and with monopoly, etc., yields imperfect compliance with consumer wants. But notice, in classical theory $P > MC$ where self-owned more fertile land is used rather than less fertile land only up to the point where we ascribe differential rents for differences in fertility. Correspondingly, it maybe that $P > MC$ for a one plant (firm) and still greater than $P > MC$ for an other plant (firm) because of different skills or risks. But when differential rents are ascribed, the classical trilogy $P = MC = AC$ ultimately appears. Furthermore, when one industry subject to one set of risks buys from another industry which is subject to a different set of risks, no distortion results, as P is seen to equal MC after the imputations are made. If we redefine profit as a cost, or, shall we say, regard profit in the same sense as differential rent, it further follows that production in the defined society moves relentlessly to the position of being in perfect compliance with consumer wants.

We are, therefore, asserting that the oft-levied charge against oligopoly theory, namely that of being indeterminate, is wrong. Rather than being indeterminate, the long-run market policy, price, and price reaction practices of the members of the oligopoly economy are as precise, exact, and predictable as any set of corresponding order that may be claimed for pure competition. Only at a moment or for short-run periods is the charge appropriate. Sooner or later the oligopolist either behaves in the fashion described, or it appears as if he so behaved in a viable economy.

This result is analogous to the classical ideal that any set of returns (profits) must be commensurate with the precise set of differentials prevailing in the market (in our case uncertainties). Then, if some firms have a plant(s) in each market area(s), too small compared to the optimal-size plant, and others have too large a plant and/or group of plants, while some are just right, the viable free enterprise economy elicits a change in size. The return earned by the optimal-size plant(s) and firm(s) establishes a relationship with the prevailing uncertainty in the given industry(ies) to provide that plant(s) and firm(s) with the greatest possible profits. Firms with too small or too large a plant in other industries would find their profits inadequate for the uncertainty to which they are subject. Market entry or exit must take place as the firms are drawn to the size and payoff position that justifies their existence. In each market (industry), that output, price, technology, size of plant(s) and firm(s) is brought about which dovetails with (i.e., matches) the hazards of engaging in the activity in question.[1]

[1] The outline of an existence proof of the oligopolistic equilibrium is available in the language of mathematical programming. In this regard, observe that realism requires us to conceive of nonlinear costs, hence nonlinearity of constraining region. Oligopoly requires us to conceive of negatively sloping demand curves for each firm and diminishing returns with output (i.e., declining revenues) over the whole system. The objective function is, therefore, concave. Mixing nonlinear (convex) constraining regions with a concave objective function is admissible; so, any local maximum is a global one and a unique

VI. SUMMARY AND PREVIEW

We have established the equilibrium conditions and properties of the oligo-polistic firm, noting in the process the correspondence between it and pure competition. But in spite of our references to a space economy, our theory has been developed in terms of oligopoly per se. We have found that com-petitive output and price effects stem initially from the competition of new firms locating near others; alternatively, entry at a distance tends to yield tacit (if not organized) price following, that is until sufficient competitive inroads over the space have occurred. So, again, the normative oligopoly theory developed thus far has been formed as a general theory, though we have not yet defined in any way the spatial configuration(s) that relate to the long-run equilibrium of the oligopolistic economy. In Chapters 10, 11, 12, and 13 we shall set forth the spatial configuration(s) which directly relate to the normative theory of oligopoly just established. But before entering upon this field of analysis, the factor pricing side of the oligopoly economy in equili-brium should be presented. This will be done in Chapter 9.

Appendix to Chapter 8
A Note (Digression) on Positivism and Realism

Many polemics have been expressed against the model of pure competition, and in William of Occam fashion we shall not try to compete. One of the more funda-mental attacks is to demonstrate the unrealistic qualities of the kind of competition described in the model, and in its place to present a more precise formulation of competitive activity.[1] The approach followed in this book has been somewhat different. We have proposed the easier application of more realistic (albeit still generalizing) models of the economy, and in the process stressed the determinate-ness and existence of the oligopolistic equilibrium, as well as its efficiency and want-satisfying characteristics. Open entry or exit and noncollusion of firms are the fundamental requirements for the effectiveness of an oligopolistic economy. To keep entry open, large firms might have to impart their technological know-how to new entrants, and even to license others under their patent. But this and related prag-matic exercises, we leave to others.

There remains, of course, the natural query "what does an oligopoly model add that is not already made quite clear by the classical one?" This query demands, of course, a complete discussion of methodology, and anything less would have little value. A detailed discussion of instances where the classical model fails could then be appended to any discussion on methodology. And a word or two in this regard *is* indicated here.

equilibrium solution prevails. (See G. Hadley, *Nonlinear and Dynamic Programming* (Palo Alto: Addison-Wesley, 1964), esp. p. 123 "... if the functions f_i, s_{ij} have the proper convexity-concavity properties, then any local maximum ... is also a global maximum."

[1] For example, see the weighty attack of this kind by P. W. S. Andrews, *On Competition in Economic Theory* (London: The Macmillan Co., 1964).

We propose that an oligopoly model could help, among other applications, in regulating the public utility, in understanding the impact of the trade union on the free enterprise economy, in analyzing the incidence and effects of taxes, and in the regulation of industry via anti-trust laws. But we shall content ourselves in this appendix with only short, generalizing statements on the anti-trust laws, chiefly to indicate one instance where the classical model does not serve as an efficient vehicle for establishing economic policy.

I. POSITIVISM, PURE COMPETITION, AND THE ANTI-TRUST LAWS

As formulated in the so-called area of "positive economics," it might be expected that the deductive consequences of models in economics, such as the market's performance, would serve as the cornerstone for any anti-trust policy pronouncements made by public officials. Instead, however, it seems that the usual practice of officials—guided by economists who wish to do more than just observe and explain—is to claim that intent, or the market structure of the industry is the crucial test. We assert that the basis for this ambivalent position among members of the economics fraternity is the confusion in applying pure competition theory, though the theory itself is hardly to blame.

Consider in this regard the thesis that the intent of a corporate official is irrelevant to any litigation involving an economic offense against the general public. However, check the decisions on anti-trust in the United States or even the writings of economists who eventually subscribe to the doctrine that "intent" must be determined.[1] Is not intent an important factor only in private litigations or in non-economic offenses against society, including, of course, torts, felonies, or other predatory practices? The benevolence or malevolence of the butcher, baker, and the candlestick-maker, we were once told, should be of no vital interest to us.[2]

Consider, also, the idea that certain kinds of market structure are an economic offense against the public. But surely attempts to measure departures from atomistic competition, which speak in terms of degrees of monopoly, must remain an unholy exercise. Degrees of monopoly, as determined by AR, MR differentials, or as derived from estimates of the total sales of the largest two, three, or four firms, are highly arbitrary procedures, and more the reflection of industry differentials than of good or bad oligopoly. The proper yardstick for evaluating economic actions cannot relate to the postulations in an economic model any more than do the *assumptions* in a theory of the physical universe serve as the basis among physicists for their prescriptions as to how best to conquer space. Assumptions, hypotheses, or postulations should be left where they are, as the basic beginning points in con-

[1] See A. E. Kahn, "Standard for Anti-Trust Policy," *Harvard Law Review*, 1953, reprinted in E. Mansfield's *Monopoly Power and Economic Performance* (New York: W. W. Norton, 1964), pp. 144–164.

[2] If our sense of fair play and ethics causes us to consider as an objectionable business practice not only an offense against another private individual but an offense against society, then a statute could be passed against such activity (e.g., the acts regulating business practices in the United States and Great Britain). Of course, the common law of unfair competition would, to some extent, be available. In any case, nothing stated above should be construed as relating to statutes safeguarding the ethics of citizens.

structing a theory. Correspondingly, benevolence or malevolence are *extras* in economic theory. Attempts to measure degrees of monopoly are similar to trying to determine intent; they represent endeavors to apply economic theory without appreciating, understanding, and being able to make the leap demanded by the extremely abstract framework of pure competition.

It is with respect to the consequences of the theory that we alone gain the requisite material in economics for defining and measuring the effective and the ineffective, the good or the bad. Accordingly, we do not agree with the frequent references in economic policy-making regarding intent, market structure, and their like. Results alone (unless ethics demand regulatory statutes) should serve as the proper benchmark for evaluating an activity in the economy. And it is the objective of this book to formulate a theory which provides a ready basis for recognizing whether the result of the firm's activity and that of the economy is or is not as good as possible. The theory proposed is that of unorganized oligopoly and the prescriptions are simple: Maintain open entry and exit and prevent cartelization or other comparable organizations of oligopolists. In the broad sense, the anti-trust policy in the United States is more in keeping with the theory of this chapter than has been the monopoly policy in Great Britain, though each stress intent and structure rather than the practices which would assure the economy of maximum efficiency. Specific changes in anti-trust practices will be suggested by our theory, and Chapter 15 will be used in part to go further into this matter.

9

Factor Prices and Efficiency

WHAT IS THE IMPACT OF OLIGOPOLY ON FACTOR PRICES, both hired and entrepreneurial? This basic question, with focus particularly on the long run, underscores our present investigation. Unfortunately, however, as is so often the case, new avenues of speculation give rise to the need for some definitions. We shall provide these before proceeding with our basic question.

We define the sale value of the marginal product of the input factor (i) as the average revenue times the marginal product (i.e. $SV_i = AR \times MP_i$). The marginal cost of an additional variable unit of input is defined as marginal cost times the marginal product (i.e. $MC_i = MC \times MP_i$). Though the concept marginal revenue product (of the input) is often used in the literature on factor prices, and hence is well known, we shall nevertheless herein define it formally as the marginal revenue times the marginal product (i.e. $MRP = MR_i = MR \times MP_i$).

The marginal rate of substitution between the factors of production (MRS), sometimes referred to as the marginal rate of technical substitution, must be distinguished from the marginal revenue rate of substitution (MRRS). The former involves the ratio between the marginal products of the factors, and the latter relates to the ratio of the marginal revenue products of the factors. In the process of reaching the long-run equilibrium, the pure competitor equates the marginal product ratio of the factors (expressed in dollar-terms) with the corresponding ratio of factor prices; in turn, the oligopolist equates the marginal revenue product ratio of the factors with the corresponding factor price ratio. These relations, as well as some other background material, may be developed easily as follows:

Consider the production function $q^0 = f(x_1, x_2)$, and let costs be defined as $C = p_1 x_1 + p_2 x_2 + \alpha$. Form next the Lagrangian expression—

(1) $V = p_1 x_1 + p_2 x_2 + \alpha + \lambda [q^0 - f(x_1, x_2)]$

Taking the partials and equating to zero yields—

(2a) $\dfrac{\partial V}{\partial x_1} = p_1 - \lambda f_1 = 0$

(2b) $\dfrac{\partial V}{\partial x_2} = p_2 - \lambda f_2 = 0$

(2c) $\dfrac{\partial V}{\partial \lambda} = q^0 - f(x_1 x_2) = 0$

From (2a) and (2b), we find—

(3) $\dfrac{p_1}{p_2} = \dfrac{f_1}{f_2}$

Minimizing cost under an output constraint requires ratio equality of factor prices and marginal products.

Consider again the production function $q^0 = f(x_1, x_2)$. Regard q^0 as fixed (i.e., as an isoquant) and take the total differential—

(4) $dq = f_1 dx_1 + f_2 dx_2$

Because dq is zero along an isoquant—

(5) $-\dfrac{dx_2}{dx_1} = \dfrac{f_1}{f_2} = \mathrm{MRS}$

which we know from elementary economics is the $\mathrm{MRS} x_1 x_2$.[1] In concert, (3) and (5) establish the principle that costs are minimized when the isocost line is tangent to the isoquant. The impact of oligopoly on long-run factor prices may now be viewed.

I. FACTOR PRICES IN UNORGANIZED OLIGOPOLY

We assume pure competition in buying and define profits for an oligopolistic firm as follows—

(6) $\pi = P_z Z - P_x X - P_y Y - \alpha$

where output Z is $f(X, Y)$ and $P_z = g(Z) = g[f(X, Y)]$
Then—

(7) $\dfrac{\partial \pi}{\partial X} = P_z \left(\dfrac{\partial Z}{\partial X}\right) + Z \left(\dfrac{\partial P_z}{\partial X}\right) - P_x = 0$

$\qquad\qquad = P_z \left(\dfrac{\partial Z}{\partial X}\right) + Z \left(\dfrac{\partial P_z}{\partial Z}\right) \cdot \left(\dfrac{\partial Z}{\partial X}\right) - P_x = 0$ (the function of function rule)

---

[1] C. E. Ferguson, *Microeconomic Theory* (Chicago R. Irwin & Company, 1969), revised edition, p. 158, note 7, observes that in formal usage the consumer $\mathrm{MRS}_{x\ for\ y}$ is written as $-\dfrac{dy}{dx}\bigg]\ du = 0$ with the subscripts reversed when writing the producer's technical substitution, i.e. $\mathrm{MRS}_{y\ for\ x}$ is $-\dfrac{dy}{dx}\bigg]\ dq = 0$. We shall not follow the latter practice.

$$= P_z MP_x + Z\left(\frac{\partial P_z}{\partial Z}\right) MP_x - P_x = 0, \text{ where } MP_x = \frac{\partial Z}{\partial X}$$

$$= MP_x\left[P_z + Z\left(\frac{\partial P_z}{\partial Z}\right)\right] - P_x = 0$$

(8) $MP_x\left(\dfrac{MR_i}{\partial Z}\right) = P_x$, where $MR_i = P_z\partial Z + Z\partial P_z$

(9) $\dfrac{MR_i}{MP_i} = \dfrac{P_x}{MP_x}$, where $MP_i = \partial Z$

(10) $MR_i = MC_x.\ MP_i = MC_i$, where $MC_x = \dfrac{P_x\partial X}{\partial Z}$ and $MC_i = P_x\partial X$

In turn—

(7′) $\dfrac{\partial \pi}{\partial Y} = P_z\left(\dfrac{\partial Z}{\partial Y}\right) + Y\left(\dfrac{\partial P_z}{\partial Y}\right) - P_y = 0$

(10′) $MR_i = MC_y.\ MP_i = MC_i$, where $MC_y = \dfrac{P_y\partial Y}{\partial Z}$ and $MC_i = P_y\partial Y$

From (10) and (10′), we obtain—

(11) $\dfrac{P_x}{MP_x} = \dfrac{P_y}{MP_y}$

which conforms to (3). The profit maximizing oligopolist produces *somewhere* along his LRAC curve. Indeed, we also obtain—

(12) $\dfrac{P_x}{MP_x} = \dfrac{P_y}{MP_y} < P_z$, since $AR > MR$

In the long run, we must have—

(13) $P_z = AC \text{ adj.} = AC + \left(-Z\dfrac{\partial P_z}{\partial Z}\right)$

And when (13) holds, there exists—

(14) $\dfrac{P_x}{MP_x} = \dfrac{P_y}{MP_y} = P_z + Z\dfrac{\partial P_z}{\partial Z} < P_z,$

where $P_z + Z\dfrac{\partial P_z}{\partial Z} = $ classical AC. Note finally from (10) and (10′) that $MRRS_{x\ for\ y} = MR_x/MR_y$, where we substitute MR_x defined as MR_i/MP_i in (10) and MR_y defined as MR_i/MP_i in (10′) for MC_x and MC_y.

Following the above paradigms, we note that in any (short-run) kinked

AR function an imperfect identity would prevail between $MRRS_{x \; for \; y}$ and P_x/P_y because $MR_i \neq MC_i$ in (10) and (10'). More than a classical change in the factor price line is necessary to assure the tendency towards full employment of the factors of production. Significantly, for reasons already noted in Chapter 8, inequalities and lags disappear in the long run, and then changing factor supplies in the long run move the isocost line to tangency with the highest isoquant possible.

In unorganized oligopoly, the returns to land, labor, and borrowed capital are relatively less than in pure competition (e.g. $P_i = MR_i < P_z \partial Z$). At the same time, total output and the real satisfaction of all factors differ under conditions of heterogeneous unorganized oligopoly from that which would apply to the purely competitive market.[1] Manifestly, the full extent of the differences between relative factor prices in oligopoly and pure competition requires a detailed examination of the long-run profits which accrue to oligopolistic entrepreneurs. Before turning to this vital topic, however, some aspects of oligopsony must be considered. In our discussion below, we shall also include references to buying market types other than oligopsony.

II. FACTOR PRICES IN UNORGANIZED OLIGOPSONY

It is well established that, relatively speaking, monopsonized factors will be used in a smaller proportion than are competitively bought factors. In effect, the marginal rates of substitution of the monopsonized factors are lowered because the marginal expenditures of the monopsonized factor (for additional factor inputs) rise rather than stay constant, as in the case of pure competition. Since monopsonized factors are used less, their factor prices are lowered in the relative sense. Therefore monopsony of one factor tends to reduce the proportionate employment of that factor, *ceteris paribus*, with competitive factors tending to be in stronger demand by the industry in question.[2]

It follows that we may typically expect extra profits to be received in the short run when monopsony conditions prevail because each firm in the industry tends to produce less. In turn, relative differences exist in factor returns. In the long run, too, relative differences in factor returns are to be expected when some factor or factors are monopsonized while others are not. In general, under conditions of heterogeneous buying, many monopsonized agents shift to other uses.

[1] If heterogeneity means extra satisfactions, these conceivably could be greater in the complex market, with the entrepreneur probably receiving at least the lion's share of the extra satisfactions. Whether or not the gain is proper will be considered later in the chapter. For a detailed discussion of the different factors' shares, see the author's *Microeconomics and the Space Economy* (Chicago: Scott, Foresman, 1963), Appendix A.

[2] Note that when a seller has monopoly controls, a subtraction from the marginal product curve, *in effect*, takes place. On the supply side, an addition to the factor pay curve, *in effect*, occurs under conditions of monopsony.

It is a short step from the aforementioned thoughts to the observation that most of the results of oligopsony are similar to those of pure monopsony and monopsonistic competition. The essential difference in the markets is the tendency for greater price rigidity to prevail under oligopsony in reflection of a possible inequality between $MRS_{x\ for\ y}$ (or $MRRS_{x\ for\ y}$) and the marginal expenditure relation (i.e., ME_x/ME_y) because of the buying discontinuity in the short run. We will henceforth employ the term monopsony in a generic (all inclusive) sense, using specific verbal reference to pure monopsony when only monopsony is being discussed or special reference to oligopsony when this market alone is to be stressed.

Monopsonistic buying "of all kinds" and purely competitive buying are distinguishable in the sense that in monopsony the marginal rate (or revenue rate) of substitution is made inversely equal to marginal expenditures (not inversely equal to the factor prices). To see this, define the monopsonist's cost equation as—

(15) $C = P_x X + P_y Y + \alpha$

Then—

(16) $\dfrac{\partial C}{\partial X} = P_x + X \dfrac{\partial P_x}{\partial X} = ME_x$

and—

(17) $\dfrac{\partial C}{\partial Y} = P_y + Y \dfrac{\partial P_y}{\partial Y} = ME_y$

Since each $X\dfrac{\partial P_x}{\partial X}$ and $Y\dfrac{\partial P_y}{\partial Y}$ is positive, the marginal cost of, let us say, labor exceeds its price. Then from (10 and 10'), we obtain for monopsony—

(18) $MR_i = MC_i$ or $\dfrac{P_z \partial Z + Z \partial P_z}{\partial Z} = \dfrac{ME_x}{MP_x} = \dfrac{ME_y}{MP_y}$, $i = x, y$

Let us assume for simplicity that the ratios of the ME's to the corresponding supply prices are respectively constant, e.g. $ME_x/P_x = ME_y/P_y = m$. Then utilizing (18) leads to—

(19) $\left(X\dfrac{\partial P_x}{\partial X} \bigg/ Y\dfrac{\partial P_y}{\partial Y} \right) = \dfrac{P_x}{P_y} = \dfrac{MP_x}{MP_y}$

which result corresponds to the relation between the average and marginal values associated with the tangent drawn to a demand curve. In turn—

(20) $\dfrac{ME_x}{MP_x} = \dfrac{ME_y}{MP_y}, \dfrac{P_x}{MP_x} = \dfrac{P_y}{MP_y}$

Thus the profit maximizing monopsonist also produces at some point of least cost along his LRAC curve. However, we shall see that substantial differences distinguish monopsonistic buying from purely competitive buying notwithstanding the profit maximizing monopsonist's production at some point of lowest cost.

(I) Though the monopsonist remains on his lowest LRAC via $MRRS_x$ $_{for\ y} = ME_x/ME_y$, his optimal cost (including his optimal-optimorum cost) is above that of the pure competitor, provided we assume full employment for both economies and identical dollar payments to all functional inputs, with all other things except final product prices and size of firms equal. Given these provisos, the theorem follows directly from (20). In other words, because ME_x is greater than P_x and ME_y is greater than P_y, the $MR = MC$ position involves a higher MC at their optimal cost positions for the monopsonist *vis-à-vis* the competitive firm, *ceteris paribus*. It follows that the optimal input use of the monopsonist is therefore less because his fixed costs (assumed the the same) are not allocated as efficiently as in the competitive firm. Thus the lowest cost of the monopsonist is higher than that of the pure competitor and real income is decreased, *ceteris paribus*.

(II) *In a mixed economy* the impact of pure monopsony is largely analogous to the impact of pure monopoly. An undesired differential exists between commodity prices and factor prices, the extent of which depends upon the degree of monopsony. Clearly, some factor prices will show a greater relative decrease in price than will others.

(III) The short-run impact of monopsony in a mixed economy is to provide extra profits to the monopsonistic entrepreneur, for it makes him act like (or more like) a monopolist.

(IV) If land, labor, and capital are monopsonized to the same extent, the impact of monopsonistic conditions is obscured. Generally a decrease in total output takes place, and the monopsonized factors share this loss if at full employment levels they accept relatively lower payment than they would in pure competition because of the existing differentiation.[1]

---

[1] The monopsonized factor does not receive the whole marginal physical product. But, the extra sum that the monopsonist receives in the long run does not appear as profits, because, if sellers' competition eliminates economic profits, the extra shares the monopsonist receives from his factors merely may offset the decreased efficiency of his operation. The fact that entrepreneurs may receive more than the residual amount that equals his marginal physical product contribution is not the same as exploitation (see Appendix A. *Micro-economics, op. cit.*). But most vitally, even when this condition exists, the operations may be unprofitable. Of course, when the hired factors receive less than what would be the competitive marginal product contribution, they suffer some loss from monopsony. It is, however, possible for the hired factors to receive exactly the same real sum at full employment under monopsony as they would under a purely competitive buying situation. In such case, it is the entrepreneur (and, of course, the consumer) who will suffer the loss from inefficiency. Manifestly, there is no a priori reason for this result ever to occur, and, usually, a combination loss exists. Everything ultimately depends upon the "utilities" the factors obtain from differentiated buying conditions and the standard rate of return society is required to leave its entrepreneurs.

III. UNORGANIZED OLIGOPOLISTIC PROFITS—WINDFALL OR RENT

We know that economic profits equal the difference between revenues and explicit plus implicit costs. In turn, profits can be said to equal the difference between revenues and opportunity costs, by which we assume an identity between both explicit costs and implicit costs *and* their related opportunity costs. There are, of course, exceptions to these identities: One exception occurs when a person is more proficient as an entrepreneur than as a salaried manager, in which case the real implicit costs to the firm are greater than opportunity costs. Another exception occurs when purely psychic satisfactions obtain (i.e. satisfactions which have no bearing on the skill, health, working lifetime, etc. of the factor) and alone justify continued service; in this case the real implicit charge to the firm on the account of the entrepreneur is less than his opportunity costs. A third exception exists because duopoly and oligopoly necessitate a divergence between implicit and opportunity costs. The fourth exception is the most important; specifically, a natural rent may apply because of extra (special) factor skill in the subject activity over other alternatives. We will reserve our discussion of this last exception to a later point in the chapter.

The first exception involves a rent-like return. Because it is so rare, it is usually considered irrelevant in economic analysis and, hence, can be readily ignored. The second exception is similar to the claim that some people are willing to work as hard as others but nevertheless will accept a smaller monetary return; accordingly, they are able to accept what amounts to less than the prevailing return. This situation is short run for any firm.

Exceptions one and two may or may not be included in the theory of profits, depending on the objectives of the researcher. The issues they raise are comparatively unimportant, and their inclusion carries short-run significance alone.

The third exception simply reflects the limited number of alternatives open to duopolists and oligopolists, *ceteris paribus*. Thus, a rental-like premium is ascribable as a cost over the true value of the lost opportunity. Let us imagine, under conditions of oligopoly, the existence of a limited number of alternative investments of identical (or nearly identical) kind. The entrepreneur's capital, if invested in the next most similar opportunity, would entail an extra high price, which can be considered as a premium or complex market rent over the opportunity cost alternative. This premium should be added on to opportunity costs in imputing costs to the firm. Manifestly, the complex market rent is as trivially unimportant as the two first exceptions; no further statements about it are required.[1] (As we have said, we shall discuss the fourth exception in detail later on.)

[1] See *Microeconomics, op. cit.*, p. 224, n. 28, for further discussion of the complex market rent.

Who and What is the Entrepreneur?

Economists have generally dodged the question of who or what the entre-preneur is,[1] not having defined him consistently as a person, as management, as a stockholder, or as anyone else. Yet to explain profits, one must have a clear-cut identification of entrepreneurship. We will not consider the entre-preneur, as has often been the practice, as a person(s) employed in his own business who is not salaried but who would receive monetary or equivalent rewards for identical work performed elsewhere.[2] For directing such a business, as well as for managing a corporation, the return that is due (and received) is classified in this book as a cost or rent. The word entrepreneurship, when employed henceforth, will be used narrowly; it will refer only to the equity investment of the owners of a business, such as the stockholders of a corporation, and will not include proprietory services.

This definition of the entrepreneur means that any uncertainty which is related to the owner's (or a manager's) services will be treated as a cost or rental that is intrinsic to the owner's (or a manager's) performance.[3] An owner or manager of a business will be treated as a hired factor except that explicit payments will be ignored and instead long-run imputations to cost will be made for him just as in theory they are made for the single proprietor who uses himself in his business. Though uncertainty may be tied up inextricably with the manager's occupation, this uncertainty is not to be considered of the same order as that ascribable to equity capital. Uncertainty in the following pages, therefore, will only mean the uncertainty that is related to capital invest-ment, not the uncertainty which shrouds the service performance of the wage earner, the salaried employee, the single proprietor, or the partner.

The next question arising from our definition is whether the *distribution* of funds between lenders and owners should be considered. Does it matter whether for some firms and industries the loan-equity proportion is higher than for others? One might, in fact, ask whether a normative yardstick should be employed, possibly one based on the proportion between risk and un-certainty which underscores the activity.

Our answer to this query is a relatively simple one. As economists, we are not concerned with a particular real-world company, but rather with the representative firm. To the extent that certain real-world investors may increase the spread between their expected and lowest likely returns via the financing techniques pursued by them (and their company), a divergence will

[1] For an exception to this remark, see the fine discussion of M. Bober, *Intermediate Price and Income Theory* (New York: The Ronald Press Company, 1955), pp. 422–428.

[2] The nonsalaried owner in free enterprise economies is typically the proprietor (owner) or a partner in the business.

[3] Wages of management and the return for assuming risk (not uncertainty) are treated herein as imputed costs; they differ from profits. Manifestly, by regarding the entre-preneurial and managerial services together as functional performances, any related uncertainty is, therefore, also a cost.

exist between underlying business risks and uncertainties and the spread countenanced by investors in the specific company. We contemplate, however, no difficulty from this condition since we assume each industry has its own character and that for each "character type" there arises a more or less identical financing pattern. As has been pointed out before, an industry to us is not necessarily a set of firms producing a similar product; instead, we defined an industry as a set of firms subject to the same risk and uncertainty. It follows from the definitions and assumptions we have made that the hierarchical pattern of risks and uncertainties which underlies the business would be matched monotonically by the financing differences that arise among (and become accepted parts of) the industries in the system. Our concern is only with the underlying economic returns in the economy, not the financing techniques which modify them in particular instances; the basic risk and uncertainty underscoring the activity remains unchanged. It is in light of this condition that we may broadly refer to the uncertainty on capital investment rather than to the uncertainty on the owner(s)' investment, as is more precisely the case.

What are the Opportunity Costs of Oligopolists?

The answer to what are the *opportunity costs* of oligopolists (including here— in our reference to opportunity cost—both management and equity invest- ment) is not a simple one, as we learned in Chapter 5. Certainly it is not so clear-cut as is the answer to the same question raised with respect to other market types. This is so in part because firms are few and restrictions on entry are many in the oligopolistic economy. Thus, if an individual entrepreneur has funds to invest, he does not have an unlimited number of firms among which to choose. In fact he has so few choices (in any one industry) that he may be unable to invest in any existing oligopolistic firm except at a premium. If the oligopolist wants to consider alternative job opportunities of a similar kind, he too has relatively few choices available. Most significantly, the oligo- polistic firm operates under uncertainty. But having already covered both the matter of complex market rent and the impact on the LRAC curve of uncer- tainty on the capital investment, we need go no further into these aspects of opportunity costs.

Service Energy Expenditures and Opportunity Costs

In Chapter 5 we described how the alternatives an individual faces may relate to activities which involve comparable or dissimilar risks and uncertainties. At first glance, one might have expected that any individual's true opportunity costs would apply to activities of highly similar order, for otherwise we would appear to be ascribing as a cost that which an individual *could* earn but possibly would never want to earn, given the risk and uncertainty to which he would be subject. Our concept of energy cost combined with the discount involved in the transformation function R bridges the gap in question. Let us review the concepts briefly.

Energy units and our Transformation to Opportunity Costs. There are aspects of imputing a rent to management which differ sharply from the classical problem of imputing a rental return for land, simply because in the one we deal with the human being, and in the other with inanimate land. Thus, the true opportunity cost of land is based on the best alternative foregone, whatever its use may have been (comparable or not, such as in the production of wheat compared to, say, cotton, *etc.*). In the case of human beings, the most comparable alternative would appear to be the requisite point of departure. However, we may avoid the pitfall of comparing unlike activities by tying ourselves to the fundamental roots of any activity—the energy expended (including butterflies—ulcers, *etc.*, as you will) in any performance.[1]

Every individual has a certain lifetime total of energy units to use. This total is based only partly on the sum he acquires from his business position. Thus, the cost of business X cannot be said to be equal to the alternatives foregone in Y *in the same period of time*, as time becomes relative with people. Indeed, for any one person, time is relative to the particular job he "may" have. This is why theoretical precision requires us to employ the ratio method when we compare unlike activities, and then to alter it according to the lifetime the individual would have in the subject employment. In contrast, when we compare like activities, we may apply the absolute alternative earnings method.

Differential rent can be founded on either energy units in unlike activities or on lost opportunities in a highly similar alternative employment, if such exists. The basic analytical process will be the same under either method, the limiting requirement being the need to select the "best" alternative. That the analytical process is the same is especially apparent when we realize that the concept of energy units is quite broad. In terms of services, for instance, it includes the physical energies expended in work plus the mental ones, such as the certainty and the risk-uncertainty feelings associated with the individual's position. Thus psychic satisfactions which reappear in the income/energy cost ratio must be counted. [Indeed, besides the dollar and cent items which go with every earned income, the *purely* psychic satisfaction of prestige, belief in importance or work, and the like (which are not part of the expected income/energy computation, having no effect on energy expenditures) could be included in the comparisons. However, in order to maintain the same emphasis on the profit motive that has been previously employed in this book, we will not take this path. We will exclude purely psychic satisfactions that

[1] See M. L. Greenhut, *Plant Location in Theory and in Practice* (Chapel Hill: University of North Carolina Press, 1956), pp. 290–291, for an earlier use of this idea.

do not relate integrally to the income/energy utils computation.] This means that the best ratio of energy utils received and expended will be applied to the work in question, with purely psychic factors being considered as short-run elements not basic to our theory; this is especially in order since purely psychic factors relate to owner(s)-manager(s) who may have started the firm but are not part of it in the long run.

Two final matters must be noted here: Use of the ratio method means that we must eliminate windfalls from cost imputations on capital to view the classical average cost curve. Moreover, because our definition of entrepreneurship excludes the person, no windfalls are included in the service income/energy ratio. The more distant income-annuity values which form part of the ratios would then be considered to be limited by the simple competitive market returns, that is up to the point where we impute uncertainty on the owner(s) investment in drawing the adjusted average cost curves. Corresponding treatment, we shall shortly observe, applies to the uncertainty portion of the ratio dealing with the owner's capital investment.

Equity Capital Expenditures and Opportunity Costs. The returns proffered in the best alternative use of equity capital serve as the base for the rental-cost imputation attributable to equity capital. However, two vital constraints apply: (1) the imputed rental cost (not windfall sums) attributable to equity capital must be set by a "rate-transform" based on the risks in and magnitudes of alternative investments. In effect, we conceive of a hierarchy of risks, each level of which warrants a return. The return attributable elsewhere to the degree of risk involved in the subject activity is the basis for the imputed rental cost. (2) Because economic lifetimes are scarcely affected by the different risks or uncertainties of investment, the "rate-transform" tends not to involve a substantially different period over which the lost opportunities may be evaluated. Nevertheless, to the extent that the lifetime over which an investor would make a capital investment varies according to the risk and uncertainty he accepts at a given moment, a further adjustment similar to that effected for managerial services would be required. Given the imputed rental cost of equity capital, the extra return received by the entrepreneur compared with what would be received in the best alternative under the relevant *transformed* uncertainty would govern the selection of the investment as well as identify the actual short-run surplus returns that are made in the chosen activity. (3) The imputation for uncertainty which establishes the adjusted costs must also be predicated on values extending from the short to long run. An imputation based on the best returns expected this period alone in some alternative activity would typically eradicate some part of (if not all of) the short-run profits one may conceive of in a given activity. In other words, the set of annuity values which mark the opportunities foresaken typically must be conceived as falling in value in the long run before the time discount is applied. The assumption in Chapter 5 of a set of identical i's over the factor's working lifetime should, therefore, be recognized as only a simplifying device pursued at the time our theory was first being sketched.

Final Notes about Opportunity and Implicit Costs and Profits

Equity capital is subject to different risks in different lines of activity. This is true even in the purely competitive market in which free entry means zero economic profits in the long run but not identical returns on capital. Risk is a cost, and different risks exist among industries. These risk differentials elicit (and require) diverse returns. For any particular company, the opportunity rental cost of equity capital must typically be based on the risk return on comparable investments.

When entry is limited (e.g., in oligopoly) so that the returns to capital appear very large, part of the returns may be for risk, and part may be for something else. We must distinguish in practice between the returns for different degrees of risk and the returns for different degrees of risk plus uncertainty. It is the uncertainty factor which limits entry *sharply* and leaves economic profits.[1] This profit, let us recall, can be identified by assigning the oligopoly to a risk without uncertainty category that ties the rental portion of its return to that which in effect would have been earned in a simple competitive market.

Similar in character to equity capital is the implicit cost of entrepreneurial service. Because service requirements (including uncertainty) differ among trades, the best opportunity cost for any owner-manager involves the transformed rate of what would have been earned by the factor in his other (best) alternative. In addition, a differential rent for extra skill in the subject activity may also be ascribed. Significantly, to repeat, the returns to management (including the single proprietor or partner) are considered here as costs not profits. Profits apply only to the uncertainty component of the equity investment of the owners of the business.

To sum up briefly: cost ascriptions involve a transformed rate and absolute sum formed by the best alternative foregone (no matter how different it is) plus any relevant differential rent for scarcity. [We shall explore the full meaning of the differential rent for scarcity later on; for the moment, let it suffice to say that it is a cost attributable to natural scarcity (extra skill) in the subject activity distinct from a scarcity attributable to uncertainty.[2]] In the case of equity capital, the most similar alternative in terms of risk forms the basis for the rental-cost imputation. The profits are similarly identifiable,

[1] An uninsurable risk exists that is insurable only on the basis of one gamble among other gambles. This uninsurable risk (uncertainty) differs from an insurable risk. The insurable risk is predictable objectively by reference to its own set of data; the uninsurable risk requires reference to outside data before a value can be even approximated. See M. Colberg's discussion on risk and insurance in Colberg, Bradford, and Alt, *Business Economics*, rev. ed. (Homewood, Ill.: Richard D. Irwin, Inc., 1957), pp. 6-7.

[2] See *infra*, pp. 203, 204

except to say that they are the return for uncertainty and that any short-run excesses thus represent windfalls which disappear over time. As for individuals, the readiest and simplest technique is to use the approach which recognizes that an individual's lifetime is limited. Working with energy units, one may derive the opportunity costs from the alternatives foregone. The return to individuals, let us repeat once more, is defined herein as a rent (i.e. as a cost).

Are Profits Unearned in Oligopoly?

Any long-run economic profit is justifiable on several grounds. For one thing, there is great uncertainty in entering a complex market, as the tasks of innovating and combining indivisible productive factors are intricate. Analogously, the problems of successful competition are many. Finally, space limits the entry of new firms. These forces combine to make long-run profits an integral return in oligopoly.

Oligopolistic profits, we have claimed, are attributable to uncertainties. These profits reflect (1) the innovating genius of the owner(s)-manager(s) operating under (2) the gamelike intensity and uncertainty of competition that exists when only a few participants are involved in a play of strategic moves, and where (3) the system is marked by the natural exclusion of space and other indivisibility-induced uncertainties. In a sense, the complex selling market is like the competition found among prize fighters as distinct from the tug-of-war between fraternities. Any bonus left over as a result of the great intensity of the competition (i.e., the uncertainty in the market) is, according to this view, not unearned.

Economic Value in Oligopoly. Economic value must include all costs in the long run. It must equal the aggregate of the salaries paid and the workers' wages, the land rent, the natural rents, and, in the complex market type, the complex market rent, and the economic profit of the entrepreneur. The extra problems and strains in oligopoly, we therefore contend, require a greater premium in the long run than that demanded by other market types.[1]

Rents and Profits

We are now at the point where we are able to discuss rents and profits in a somewhat different way from the above. We shall try to give a bird's-eye

---

[1] Oligopoly might be further compared with pure competition in a similar way to that in which equity capital (stocks) and borrowed capital (bonds) are compared. The opportunity cost of equity capital relates, we know, to the foregone alternative of loanable funds. But the extra hazard of being a noncontracted-for return sets up a premium over and above the loan "interest rate" return. Moreover, the complications of stock ownership which make it a residual-unpredictable share in all respects, including loss, reflect a sharp, long-lasting note of uncertainty which carries profits or losses to the holders of stock.

summary type of view of our preceding analysis of profits at the same time.

For present purposes, note that rents (i.e., the rentlike returns to factors) are divisible into four main kinds: land rent, quasi-rent, monopoly rent, and natural rent. Of these, land rent is the simplest to describe. It is paid to the owner of a scarce resource which is relatively fixed in supply, the element of fixity giving the return to land its distinctive characteristic.

Quasi-rent refers to the return paid for a factor temporarily fixed in supply. Quasi-rents are not permanent because the factors are only in fixed supply for a short time. As soon as other units can be trained or adapted for comparable use, quasi-rents are ended.

Monopoly rent is a much more important concept. It refers to an artificially created return in excess of the factor's opportunity costs.[1] Monopoly rents may be permanent. They reflect barriers against entry of new enterprise or against the use of needed resources. In both cases, product scarcity results. Extra returns due to license restrictions and trade union exclusions are examples of monopoly rents. In any form, however, monopoly rents are not proper parts of the average cost curve of the factor receiving the bounty, though, of course, they are part of the costs paid out by a factor using a productive agent in receipt of monopoly rent.

Natural rents are similar to quasi-rents in that they reflect the existence of a scarce resource. They differ from quasi-rents because the duration of the scarcity is indefinite in time and, in fact, may be permanent; also, they represent a return which is not closely tied to opportunity costs—in which respect they resemble monopoly rents. Any fundamentally significant distinction between monopoly and natural rents must be related to the cause rather than the amount of the extra return.

Natural rents are found mainly in two forms: one occurring on the hired factor level and the other on the managerial level. On the hired factor level, a given group may possess some unique skill which is applicable only in the industry which uses that skill. The cost to the buyer includes the factor's opportunity cost plus its natural rent. On the managerial level, we may find a person whose efficiency is greater in the role of owner-manager than of employee-manager. Hence, that part of the return in excess of the foregone opportunities is the natural rent.[2] We also find a natural rent element in oligopoly when the lower opportunity cost (i.e. the complex market rental premium) must be brought up to the competitive level for comparative analysis.[3] Also, special (extra) skill may apply as with lower echelon employees.

[1] If implicit costs are greater than opportunity costs, differential rents prevail. If monopoly rents also exist, we would say that the total returns are greater than opportunity costs plus the natural rent differential.

[2] Compare R. Triffin, *Monopolistic Competition and General Equilibrium Theory* (Cambridge: Harvard University Press, 1940), pp. 173–177; and K. E. Boulding, *Economic Analysis* (New York: Harper & Brothers, 1941), pp. 229–232, 442–444.

[3] A natural rent created by a hired factor may be received by the entrepreneur. Thus, because of factor immobility, the pay to the hired factor may be less than its contribution. This

What we call *profit* refers broadly to the return for innovating in an economy subject to uncertainties. Because firms may have to be of a certain minimum size (i.e., with multiple plants), a market large enough for three and one-half no-profit firms would provide profits for three, and this short-run indivisibility may clearly be spatial as well as nonspatial. A similar and more permanent effect obtains for the element of uncertainty. Because of the intense cutthroat competition, a market otherwise large enough for four firms may contain only three firms.

The product of short-run indivisibility tied up with uncertainty is, therefore, scarcity. But we must distinguish *natural scarcity* (and its counterpart, rent) from the scarcity traceable ultimately to uncertainty (and its counterpart, economic profit). In the first case, the scarcity relates to unique ability.[1] In the second case, the resource (or talent) exists, but it does not move into the industry.[2]

Orthodoxy and Oligopoly

The views on long-run profits presented here conform much more closely to orthodox economic conceptions than may first appear to hold.[3] Certainly, the similarity of long-run trends in the different markets deserves mention and illustration. For example, theory concludes that economic profits are eliminated in the long run of pure and monopolistic competition, and correspondingly, we have observed, substitute goods will eliminate extra profits (windfalls) in oligopoly. Obviously, long-run economic profits must differ from firm to firm, just as the returns for different risks must vary. New entry— and substitute goods—therefore play a similar role in complex markets and simple markets. When excess profits prevail, substitute goods will be produced; and when profits are too small, substitutes will disappear. The long run in

condition might relate to the restricted entry of rivals, enabling the oligopolistic firm to pick up the natural rent from its factor. However, since natural rent is not received by its originator, it is really an "extra" or monopoly rent in the hands of the receiver.

[1] When managerial *ability* is scarce, it earns differential rents. This is true for all markets.

[2] Another comparison between natural rents and profits, as related to uncertainty and spatial indivisibility, might be made here. Suppose a market requires Y number of firms for purely competitive results, but, because of uncertainty, only X number of firms compete in the market. Natural rents exist for the firms in accordance with differential abilities, and profits will also prevail. The natural rents measure the difference between the most efficient firm and the marginal (or Yth) firm which would have set up purely competitive zero-profit conditions. The amount attributable to uncertainty—that is, the profit sum— equals what is left after natural rents have been added.

Similarly, the advantages of location set up natural rent differentials. And when, *in addition*, a spatial indivisibility causes long-run uncertainty which yields only X number rather than Y number of firms, economic profits exist. Natural rents, therefore, are additive to the point where purely competitive zero-profit conditions would have prevailed; then, any extra above natural rents measures the profits attributable to uncertainty.

[3] F. Knight, *Risk, Uncertainty, and Profit* (Boston: Houghton Mifflin Co., 1921).

oligopoly yields payloads for its factors that measure, and are commensurate with, the risk and uncertainties of engaging in economic activity. The world of capitalism and the principles of orthodoxy remain effective under space conceptions. The new idea does not supplant but rather embraces the old. Space economics takes form by building upon the perfectly valid foundations of classical economics; in doing so it helps shed some light on selected complex realities of our time.

Part Three

SPATIAL DISTRIBUTION

IO

The Urban Setting (Intra-Urban Spatial Efficiency)

IN COMPARISON WITH RURAL AREAS an urban complex is often characterized by higher income, more modern facilities and practices with respect to sanitation, housing, education, transportation, and communication, as well as by what is said to be a more democratically oriented political administration. These attributes, combined with the availability and greater variety of employment opportunities in the urban area, tend to pull the rural worker and his family to the city. It is in the cities where manufacturing industries concentrate, and where the establishment of one manufacturing industry leads often to the establishment of others. Indeed, research in location theory suggests that it is in the urban center that the maximum advantages of agglomeration are found. These agglomerating advantages appear typically in the form of a large scale unit providing localization economies which are reflected in lower costs of transportation, production, and/or distribution. Finally, incomes and real standards of living tend to be higher in the city, as the proximity of one person to another produces the basic requirements for division of labor and specialization.

We find that industrial workers tend to purchase retail goods and services locally. These purchases add another stratum (the tertiary sector of the economy) to the primary-secondary sectors so frequently basic to the early days of the city. An extremely complex network of relations between individuals and firms develops in time, helping to differentiate the urban center from the small town or hamlet located at some distance from it.

The whole urban spectrum of attraction of people, division of labor, and specialization so interact that eventually the very large cities appear to support themselves, with their inhabitants servicing one another. The localizing of economic activity, at least in the largest cities, extends to the location of such specialized forms of economic activity as operatic performances and professional athletic programs, a reflection of the advantage of size. The measurement of a "full urban economic potential" is, at the same time, rendered both difficult and complex to define. How industry distributes itself in the city and region, i.e., efficiently or inefficiently, is thus only one side of the entire theme we shall examine in this and the following chapters of Part 3 of our text.

As we approach the fundamental welfare question of economic effectiveness, we must study certain features of the urban economy, a subject too long ignored by most economists. Economic efficiency is not simply a matter of producing at the minimum cost point of some LRAC. Rather—as we noted previously in the book—there are alternative sets of LRAC curves that may be applicable. We shall establish in this and the following chapter the thesis that locations *within* and *among* cities are analogously determinable; moreover, on each level, the fundamental relations and principles—which were established in Chapter 8—apply once again. We shall, further, find that the interdependency between firms, people, and their cities establishes the relevant LRAC curve under the free enterprise system, and that this LRAC curve is the lowest possible curve given the technology, the want structure, and the limited resources that exist.

I. THE CITY—GENERAL REMARKS

A city may be defined as a large physically contiguous mass which occupies a relatively small area of the earth and is possessed of a high population density in comparison to nearby rural areas. The residents of the city engage in activities which differ noticeably from those of rural areas. Substantial employment is customarily found in the services, commercial, transportation, and financial trades of the city. Linkages and spill-over effects extend the urban activity from its core area to the rather remote-peripheral borders of the city; however, the pattern of economic activity begins to change noticeably at such places.

Five definitions of urban areas were cited by the Bureau of the Census in the 1960 Census of Population: (1) the *urban place*, which refers to a collection of 2,500 inhabitants or more, (2) the *city*, which contains a population of at least 25,000 inhabitants, (3) the *urbanized area*, which requires at least one city having 50,000 inhabitants or more, (4) the *standard metropolitan statistical area* (SMSA), which consists of a county or group of contiguous counties, containing at least one city of 50,000 or more inhabitants, and (5) the *standard consolidated areas* (SCA), such as New York and Chicago, which are significant metropolitan complexes.

An extension to the SCA has been referred to as *megalopolis*! But no matter how named, the idea of the SCA is simply that of a supermetropolitan area. In turn, the term megalopolis may be employed to describe an urban unit network, such as the one scattered along the Atlantic seaboard in the northeastern part of the United States from Baltimore through Washington extending to New York and Boston, a continuous stretch of urban and suburban areas of some 600 miles in length and containing some thirty million people (Figure 10–1).[1] This concentration results from the coalescence

---

[1] J. Gottman, *Megalopolis: The Urbanized Northeastern Seaboard of the United States* (New York: The Twentieth Century Fund), 1961.

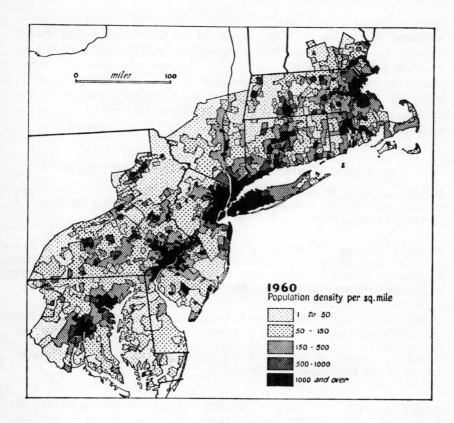

Figure 10–1: The density of population according to the 1960 Census, by minor civil divisions. Reproduced from J. Dottman, *Megalopolis: The Urbanized Northeastern Seaboard of the United States* (New York: The Twentieth Century Fund), 1961.

of a chain of metropolitan areas, each of which developed around a substantial urban nucleus. A megalopolis is also developing in the Chicago area, along an L-shaped axis extending from Milwaukee to Chicago Heights to South Bend, pushing itself north toward Detroit, south to St. Louis, and west to Omaha. In the far west, megalopolis is developing along the coast, with major nuclei at Los Angeles, San Francisco, Portland, and Seattle. Elsewhere in the world, definitions of cities or urban masses are similar to the definitions used in the United States.

Some Further Background

Two contributions to the subject of urban classification warrant mention at this point, for they help us to understand the forces determining spatial efficiency. In the one, a study by C. D. Harris in the 1940's, it was recognized that cities differed in functions. He proposed a simple quantitative method to analyze the following subtypes of United States cities—manufacturing, retail, diversified, wholesale, transportation, mining, university, and resort and retirement. (See Table 10–1.) He used arbitrarily selected percentages as the bases (or criteria) for determining the classification of a given town.[1]

TABLE 10–1: CRITERIA USED IN CLASSIFYING CITIES[2]

Manufacturing Cities M' Subtype. Principal criterion: Employment in manufacturing equals at least 74 percent of total employment in manufacturing, retailing, and wholesaling (employment figures).

Secondary criterion: Manufacturing and mechanical industries contain at least 45 percent of gainful workers (occupation figure). *Note:* A few cities with industries in suburbs for which no figures were available were placed in this class if the percentage in the secondary criterion reached 50.

Manufacturing Cities M Subtype. Principal criterion: Employment in manufacturing equals at least 60 percent of total employment in manufacturing, retailing, and wholesaling.
Secondary criterion: Manufacturing and mechanical industries usually contain between 30 and 45 percent of gainful workers.

Retail Centers (R). Employment in retailing is at least 50 percent of the total employment in manufacturing, wholesaling, and retailing and at least 2.2 times that in wholesaling alone.

Diversified Cities (D). Employment in manufacturing, wholesaling, and retailing is less than 60, 20, and 50 percent respectively of the total employment in these activities, and no other special criteria apply. Manufacturing and mechanical industries with few exceptions contain between 25 and 35 percent of the gainful workers.

Wholesale Centers (W). Employment in wholesaling is at least 20 percent of the total employment in manufacturing, wholesaling, and retailing and at least 45 percent as much as in retailing alone.

Transportation centers (T). Transportation and communication contain at least 11 percent of the gainful workers, and workers in transportation and communication

---

[1] C. D. Harris, "A Functional Classification of Cities in the United States," *Geographical Review*, XXXXIII (January, 1943), pp. 86–99.
[2] Reproduced from C. D. Harris, *op. cit.*, p. 88.

equal at least one-third the number in manufacturing and mechanical industries and at least two-thirds the number in trade (occupation figures). (Applies only to cities of more than 25,000, for which such figures are available.)

Mining Towns (S). Extraction of minerals accounts for more than 15 percent of the gainful workers. (Applies only to cities of more than 25,000, for which such figures are available.) For cities between 10,000 and 25,000 a comparison was made of mining employment available by counties only with employment in cities within such mining counties. Published sources were consulted to differentiate actual mining towns from commercial and industrial centers in mining areas.

University Towns (E). Enrollment in schools of collegiate rank (universities, technical schools, liberal-arts colleges, and teachers colleges) equalled at least 25 percent of the population of the city (1940). Enrollment figures from *School and Society*, Vol. 52, 1940, pp. 601–619.

Resort and Retirement Towns (X). No satisfactory statistical criterion was found. Cities with a low percentage of the population employed were checked in the literature for this function.

Following along this line of research, H. J. Nelson[1] in the 1950's attempted a more sophisticated service classification of American cities. He based his classification on the idea that cities do not perform vital services in the same proportions. Nelson was concerned with determining, by use of standard deviations, the point at which an economic activity in a city becomes sufficiently important to be of special significance. He classified 897 United States cities according to one or more of the following census activity categories— mining, manufacturing, transportation and communication, wholesale, retail trade, finance, insurance and real estate, personal service, professional service, and public administration. Such data, he found, are not normally distributed. Instead, the distributions are skewed (Figure 10–2).

The studies of Harris and Nelson, notwithstanding their rather arbitrary design, provide us with an (intuitive) impression of the relative functional importance of United States cities. They stress the functional forms that cities may take, although they fail to provide either a fundamental theory or operational model; but this failure merely reflects the general nature of most of the pioneering work done in the area of urban economics. Recent studies are attempting to classify cities analytically, and this may lead to a possible advance from a single quantitative study of cities to a precise meaningful measurement of different types. We shall examine selected phases of the kind of urban-regional economic study we have in mind later, chiefly after we have probed into what may be called micro-urban location theory.[2]

[1] H. J. Nelson, "A Service Classification of American Cities," *Economic Geography*, XXXI (July, 1955), pp. 189–210.
[2] A friend who prefers anonymity suggested that I should follow a classification of location theory as micro- and macro-location theory. What is included in these concepts will become clear in the next section of this chapter. I further acknowledge to this friend the great help given me in the formulation and writing of the early pages of this chapter.

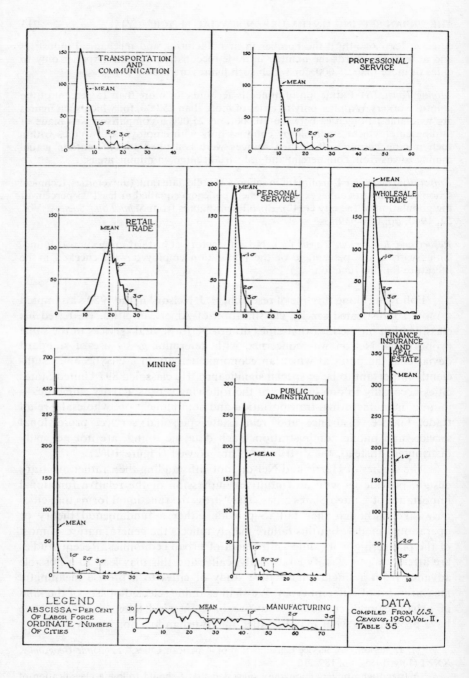

Figure 10–2: Distribution of City Types compared to a Normal Curve. Reproduced from H. J. Nelson, "A Service Classification of American Cities," *Economic Geography*, XXXI (July, 1955).

II. INTERNAL URBAN FORMS AND EARLY MICRO-URBAN LOCATION THEORY: A REVIEW OF THE LITERATURE

In the 1920's, Colby[1] wrote that centrifugal forces towards the periphery reflect rapid obsolescences in the central places and tend to push the city outward. On the other hand, centripetal forces, he said, stem from the "convenience" factor. In effect, the advantages of proximity pull many economic activities towards the center.

Colby suggested that of these two forces the centrifugal ones often prevail, with cheaper land, larger areas for development, the use of the automobile, and the like all combining to push functions outward in a massive sprawl. His work was a precursor to the development of three major theories of internal urban forms. These theories, we shall see, are micro-type explanations, in the sense that they deal with the locations of particular activities or units in the *urban* land mass rather than with some conglomeration of activities or units. Thus they speak in terms of particular transportation facilities, different residential housing units, various public and quasi-public buildings, the manufacturing plants of companies or industries, and commercial properties *individually* and even in relation to each other. They evaluate these units in the light of general economic principles, but they do not view them as an agglomeration *vis-à-vis* some other agglomeration. Urban growth—as a gradual expansion of *particular* functional units from the center towards the periphery—is the micro-side of a theory of the urban economy.

The Concentric Zone Urban Theory

The first of these urban theories presented the idea of the concentric zone, as depicted in Figure 10–3a. The theory in question was proposed by a sociologist, Burgess, to explain the distribution of urban functions and land use in Chicago in the 1920's.[2] His was essentially an adaptation of von Thünen's location model for agricultural land use. By analogy, he let the central business district serve as the core, and around this core circular zones exist. These zones include: (1) a zone of warehousing and light manufacturing; (2) a zone in transition within which are located the blighted areas where commercial and industrial land uses encroach upon residential districts; (3) a zone of workingmen's middle-grade homes; (4) a zone of better resi-

---

[1] C. C. Colby, "Centrifugal and Centripetal Forces in Urban Geography," *Annals of the Association of American Geographers*, V. 23 p. (1933) 1020.

[2] E. W. Burgess, "Urban Areas," in *An Experiment in Social Science Research* (Chicago: The University of Chicago Press, 1929), pp. 113–138, T. V. Smith and L. D. White (eds.).

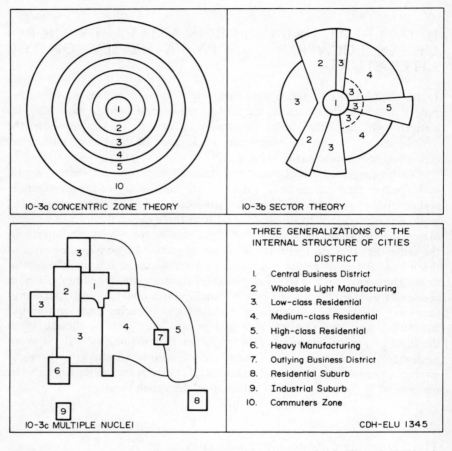

Figure 10–3a, 3b, 3c: Generalizations of internal structure of cities from C. D. Harris and E. L. Ullman, "The Nature of Cities," *The Annals of the American Academy of Political and Social Science*, V, 1945, p. 281. The concentric-zone theory is a generalization for all cities. The arrangement of the sectors in the sector theory varies from city to city. The diagram for multiple nuclei represents one possible pattern among innumerable variations.

dences; and (5) a commuters' zone beyond which are found nonurban-like uses of the land. Each successive "new" circular ring derives from each previous inner zone as the city grows. Beyond the major functional urban-built-up area lies the "urban-rural fringe," a transitional zone between urban and rural uses which is functionally difficult to define. Increased usage and ownership of the automobile has contributed to the complexity of land uses. Only occasionally does one still find a sudden (abrupt) change from the urban community to the rural area, as for example in Czechoslovakia where it is possible to observe an immediate difference between city and farm land uses on the outskirts of Prague.

Some shortcomings of this model are rather obvious: (1) Chicago served as the reference point for Burgess, but unlike other United States cities, even in the early twenties, Chicago had a very definite central business district whose growth was and still is constrained by limited public transit access, e.g., the elevated trains or highways. The Chicago central business district remains quite confined and appears as a commercial anachronism in an age where central business district growth has often sprawled in all directions. (2) The model fails to take into account spatial differences in topography, including drainage and slope, though most of the more recent theories abstract similarly. At the same time, as a pre-World War II model, it did not take into account the full impact of the automobile on present urban land use, structure, and growth. (3) Burgess' emphasis was on residential activities more than on commercial and manufacturing activities. He, therefore, did not provide an analytically based theory of the kind required by economists.

A number of salient features, however, stand in its favor. Though the concentric zone theory is not a detailed description of reality, it does represent a "good first approximation" to the actual distribution of urban functions and land use patterns. Moreover, the theory represents an ideal form for examining urban problems. It is useful, furthermore, in the design of comparative urban studies, since most cities probably contain vestiges of concentric zones.

The Wedge or Sector Theory

Homer Hoyt,[1] studying real estate problems in the 1940's, hypothesized that urban structure and growth followed a wedge, or sector pattern. He stated that a series of wedges of various land uses could be observed extending outward from a commercial core (see Figure 10–3b). Growth was assumed to proceed in the case of residences along transportation routes toward high, flood-free grounds, and along the waterfronts. With respect to commerce and industry, growth tended to avoid movement in dead-end directions.

According to Hoyt, the highest densities of development were found along the wedges served by the best transportation routes and facilities. The best grades of residential areas, in turn, occupied wedges favored by water frontage, or other unusual features. These lands tended to have a premium

[1] H. Hoyt, *The Structure and Growth of Residential Neighborhoods in American Cities* (U.S. Federal Housing Administration, Washington, D.C. 1939), and see his "Recent Distortion of the Classical Models of Urban Structure," *Land Economics*, V. 40, 1964, pp. 199–212.

placed upon them. And once set forth in a particular direction, urban growth would gain momentum along the given wedge.

The general form of the city becomes stellar or diamond shaped in time, according to Hoyt, depending upon the number of major "radiation" routes. He selects this form rather than the circular design that was stipulated by Burgess. His analysis provides additional insights.

More than the Burgess theory, the sector theory considers: (1) The importance of the increased use of the automobile, and its impact on land uses and values, for along certain wedges access is easier than in others. The theory, accordingly, introduces transportation directly as a factor in determining the location of urban activities. (2) The model incorporates rent as a basic factor in explaining location, implying that a close relationship exists between types of transportation facilities and types of residential activities. In that transportation breaks down the "friction of distance," so that the access of people to "selected" goods is improved, the wedge model proves to be a better approximation to the real world than the concentric zone theory. (3) Also the stellar or fragmented form produced by the wedges conforms more closely to the real shape of most cities than does the Burgess concentric model. (Even in the Chicago of the 1880's, the days of the horse-drawn buggy and electric train, the city structure and growth pattern conformed more to a stellar pattern than to a circular one, as the transportation routes represented the major axes around which sectoral growth occurred.) (4) The wedge model is more complete than the Burgess model in that it not only considers the important sociological aspects of urban form (i.e., residential forces), but considers the economic explanations for urban form (rent, transportation, the locations of non-residential units, and the alternative uses of land). (5) Special physical features, such as the effects of the distribution of water and other natural and unusual features which account for land use and rent, may also be taken into account in the wedge model. The model is, accordingly, more realistic than the Burgess model. And finally, even though it was not recognized by Hoyt, (6) the stellar shape is a close fit to Christaller's hexagonal model of urban distribution (to be discussed in the Appendix to Chapter 11). If one assumes, as have Isard, Berry, and others, that intra-urban commercial activities conform closely to a hexagonal model, it is quite possible that Hoyt and Christaller, while theorizing independently, were proceeding along much the same lines at about the same time.

A number of arguments against the model may be raised here, some of the most important of which are: (1) the model did not account for activity in the interstitial areas. That is to say, activities on land lying between transportation routes, the high-rent districts, and the commercial areas were all ignored. (2) The model did not describe reality in detail nor accurately, as it considered only transport, land rent, and upper-income residential variables. Its failure to include prices, economic rent in general, profits *et al.* rendered the theory a *special*, not general explanation of the space economic form.

(3) Related to the above, Hoyt's model failed to describe or account for cities which do not conform to stellar shapes, but which appear instead as enormous sprawls, each unique, and each seemingly defying generalization. Hoyt's stellar or wedge theory does not provide a general theory of urban inter-dependence structure nor does it impart sufficient insights into the question of intra-urban micro-efficiency. A more general formulation—with more far-reaching analytical powers—is required. Nonetheless, an urban micro-theory was evolved, moving from a rather static concentric zone model to the more dynamic wedge model, a dynamism emphasizing the increasing significance of the transport media. Let us, accordingly, proceed to even more advanced models, all in a way stemming from the wedge theory of urban structure.

Multiple-Nuclei Theory

A third contribution to *early* urban micro-location theory was presented in the 1950's by C. D. Harris[1] and E. L. Ullman[2] who formulated the multiple-nuclei theory. This theory assumes that each of the major classes of "related" land use activities requires specialized facilities and thus special locations. Each class of activities forms a nucleus with others which are most closely related. So we find, in practice, nuclei of entertainment, warehousing, manu-facturing, government functions, education, etc., which, because of their special functions and interdependencies, tend to cluster near each other on sites that best meet their special requirements. Figure 10–3c illustrates this theory.

The advantages of the multiple-nuclei theory are many: (1) It is a more advanced system of thought than the two preceding theories; indeed a more realistic appraisal of the transport and land rent variables may be derived from it by relating these costs to the agglomerating (production) cost advan-tage provided by some activities when located side by side. In effect, a fairly comprehensive set of economic rents has, therefore, been included as a basic part of the model. (2) The theory emphasizes the location of economic activities rather than residential locations, thus providing an economic model less restricted and in some ways more dynamic than the preceding theories. (3) The theorists also recognize the relationships between population densities and transport facilities by focusing attention on the importance of passenger transit routes.

The weaknesses of the theory, on the other hand, include: (1) Failure to provide a quantitative-correlative treatment of the population density variable with the other variables that are stressed in the study. (2) The absence of any verification of some of the fundamental assumptions of the theory,

[1] C. D. Harris, "Suburbs," *American Journal of Sociology*, V. 49, 1943, pp. 1–13, and then, C. D. Harris and E. L. Ullman: "The Nature of Cities," *The Annals of the American Academy of Political and Social Science*, V, 1945, 242.

[2] E. L. Ullman, "The Nature of Cities," *op. cit.* with C. D. Harris.

such as the need for entertainment facilities to be side by side. In fact the authors fail to provide a rigorous quantification of the basic, underlying premises and conclusions of the theory. And (3) only the cost side, not the demand side, of location was considered as we shall later see. In the language of Chapter 8, long-run prices and economic profits were not considered.

A more recent contribution to "classic" urban micro-location theory along the same lines is that of Berry.[1] Building on Christaller's hexagonal model of the distribution of settlements, and on Isard's extension of this theory to a micro level, Berry demonstrated empirically how the location of urban business activity corresponds to the hexagonal model. He observed and exemplified the development and growth of the hexagonal spatial patterning around substantial sized metropolitan areas. This patterning, he noted, involves a hierarchy of types of business districts distributed much as the settlements in central place theory. Thus the hierarchy consists of the central business district, the major outlying regional shopping centers, the more distant neighborhood shopping centers, and the "ribbon" commercial development areas.

Berry's model, although not avowedly an urban micro-locational model in that it did not focus on a particular activity (or set of activities) within the urban mass, nevertheless has certain attributes which enable it to explain individual commercial locations in the city. Where Berry's model fails is in not accounting sufficiently—in the formal analytical sense—for residential and industrial types of land uses and locations. We are led to visualize a hexagonal arrangement with a nucleus consisting of inter-related activities. But we are not advised of the size(s) of the hexagon nor the unit efficiency of the members of the space.

III. INTERNAL URBAN FORMS AND RECENT CONTRIBUTIONS TO MICRO-URBAN LOCATION THEORY: A REVIEW OF THE LITERATURE

The earliest attempts to explain urban development were preoccupied with assuming a shape and stressing—albeit not analytically—the location and the nature of a "particular" activity or sub-sets within that shape. Neither the general principles governing all locations nor the location of specific kinds of activities were examined in depth. Two significant ways of analyzing the micro-location problem, however, did evolve in recent years. And it is to these developments that we now may turn.

[1] B. J. L. Berry, "The Impact of Expanding, Metropolitan Communities upon the Central Place Hierarchy," *Annals of the Association of American Geographers*, V, 50, 1960, pp. 112–116, and see his "A Note on Central Place Theory and the Range of a Good," *Economic Geography*, V. 34, 1958, pp. 304–311, with W. L. Garrison.

The Nearest Neighbor Method

One formulation consists of a composite of urban micro-macro location theory seeking to explain the location of particular commercial activities against a screen of generalized activity. This formulation is attributable to Garrison and others working at the University of Washington during the late 1950's.[1] Their research was largely descriptive, although designed to analyze the location of certain kinds of commercial activities in shopping areas together with the location of doctors' offices. Borrowing techniques from botanists, they analyzed locations according to a model known as the *nearest neighbor method*. Their study referred to three kinds of distributions—random, uniform, and hexagonal. And by using selected formulas, they tried to ascertain whether the data conformed to the random, uniform, or hexagon pattern. The result from one point of view is macro: namely, the aggregative aspect of a hexagon, in the center of which a full set of activities could be found. But also some attention was placed on the question whether consumers tend to purchase from their nearest neighbors, and whether or not certain "particular" types of commercial activities locate near similar (or different) kinds of commercial activities.

The Spatial Interdependence Approach

This writer[2] and others have worked along still another line of approach. Instead of being concerned with the shape itself, as in the studies noted previously, the emphasis has been on determining the "general" relations within a shape.[3] Variables such as profits, prices, costs, distances, and other market considerations are recorded in order to ascertain the optimal location of "any" particular firm. While the theory extends to the macro level, as we shall see later in the book, we are able to identify certain micro-extensions. But before we do this, some additional preparatory words are in order.

The Descriptive Empirical Approach. Most of the descriptive-like inquiries into the urban economy, such as those recorded previously in this chapter,

---

[1] W. L. Garrison, B. J. L. Berry, D. F. Marble, J. D. Nystuen, and R. L. Morrill, *Studies of Highway Development and Geographic Change* (Seattle: University of Washington Press, 1959).

[2] See M. L. Greenhut, *Plant Location in Theory and in Practice* (Chapel Hill: The University of North Carolina Press, 1956), Chapter II.

[3] In this respect, it is important to mention here that, although some significant research has started in the area of micro-locational theory, there have been few implementations of real-world problems. Studies have been conducted of the location of supermarkets, tire stores, drug stores, and others by locating services and commercial establishments; in addition, research of a similar kind has occasionally been performed by academicians. But these efforts have tended to lack analytical substance. We actually have some pretty powerful tools of analysis available, but are not using them to solve the location problem.

have dealt with *a priori* assumed shapes of market areas, and, to some extent, the forces which attract certain types of consumer and commercial activities towards each other. This approach has followed the methods of other scientists rather than the marginal analysis, programming or game strategy models of the economist. Nonetheless, we hope to prove that these inquiries can be integrated with economic principles. If they can, we would have a general theoretical picture as well as be armed with empirical subsets of the theory.

The Analytical Approach. There are two analytically designed approaches to *location theory* (not really urban location theory) which *relate* to the descriptive-empirical studies of the *urban economy.* One is called the "market area" school; the other the "locational interdependence" school. The studies by location theorists which attempt to explain the size and shape of the firm's "market area" provide a macro-economic view of the spatial economy. These studies, accordingly, are the subject matter of Chapter 11. On the other hand, the studies by location theorists which stress the locational interdependence of firms provide a micro focus that enables us to consider the efficiency of locations within the city, rather than the efficiency of the city location within the region, as holds for the macro approach. Because the subject of locational interdependence is a complex one, needing the full analysis given it in Chapters 12 and 13 (conforming *there* with theories previously developed in Chapters 5–8), we can only present here *the outlines* of locational-interdependence theory. And we do this with the further caveat that the "synthesis" between micro-location theory and intra-urban locational efficiency is only a precursor of the more formal, analytically detailed extension of the "synthesis" that will be made in Chapter 13.

IV. THE MICRO-LOCATION THEORY OF THE FIRM

The inquiries into the spatial interdependence of locations began with Hotelling.[1] By assuming (1) an even spatial scattering of consumers, (2) an infinitely inelastic demand for the product of an industry, (3) equal costs of procuring and processing raw materials at all locations, (4) the same freight rate on the final product at all locations, (5) a perfectly competitive market except as regards space, and (6) sale of goods on an f.o.b. mill basis, Hotelling reasoned that firms would concentrate at the mid-point of the entire market area. From this vantage point, each firm could supply buyers located at the extremities of the entire market area while not surrendering locational advantage to rivals. The assumption that the transportation cost on the final product could never lessen the amount of sales accounts for this result.

Locational dispersion is encouraged when the buyers' demand for a

[1] H. Hotelling, "Stability in Competition," *Economic Journal*, XXIX, 1929, pp. 41–57.

product is characterized by some elasticity numerically greater than zero.[1] With this precondition, freight costs become a limiting factor to sales. By locating at the center of the entire market area, any one firm could minimize freight costs and thereby maximize sales. But as soon as more than one firm is admitted to the conceptual picture, departure from the mid-point is seen to be profitable. Thus, if (1) consumers are assumed to have identical demands and to be scattered evenly over an area shaped in the form of a square, (2) the demand curve of each consumer is in the form of a straight line, negatively sloping, (3) the other assumptions listed earlier in this section are still applicable, and (4) a line is drawn horizontally across the square bisecting the sides, one of two firms would locate at the first quartile point on the line and the other at the third quartile point on the line. From these vantage points, each firm would monopolize half of the entire market area. Such locations are the most profitable ones, for they maximize sales by minimizing transportation costs.[2]

A spatial scattering of sellers is therefore the rule under the above assumptions. But when all factors influencing locational interdependence are considered, especially uncertainty and any related initial localizing of firms, long-run concentrations at a few production centers may be explained. Moreover, the clustering type of dispersion based on uneven demands and compensating costs may be traced. The theory points, then, to an oligopolistic clustering—yet dispersion—over a landscape, or within a city, which proves to be efficient from the locational viewpoint as well as the product and factor price viewpoints already set forth in Part II of this book. Of course, the dynamic concepts to be stressed in Chapter 13 will acknowledge that in many ways the economy tends to make the best of whatever took place in the past. But though we do not intend to probe deeper at present into dynamic aspects, we can say a little more about spatial interdependence theory below, leaving analytically formulated *proof* of the following assertions for Chapter 13.

The Maximum-Profit Location

Under the locational interdependence framework, we are able to visualize as

---

[1] See A. Smithies, "Optimum Location in Spatial Competition," *Journal of Political Economy*, XLIX, 1941, pp. 423–439.

And similarly, if a finite limit to an inelastic demand is assumed, firms will tend to disperse. See A. P. Lerner and H. W. Singer, "Some Notes on Duopoly and Spatial Competition," *Journal of Political Economy*, XLV, 1937, pp. 145–186.

[2] These locations are at the same points as those which would be selected by the bi-plant monopolist. Such locational selections are termed "quasi monopolistic." See A. Smithies, *op. cit.*, p. 429. But if great uncertainty exists, for example, regarding the competitor's choice of a quartile location, because the duopolists have long been extremely competitive in price and location in other market areas, both firms will be found at the center of the subject market.

part of the locational process not only the cost factors of location (such as transport cost, labor cost, etc.), but also the demand factors, that stress the inroads on the sales of one firm due to selected location(s) by rival(s). The inclusion of cost and demand factors in a single model points out the need for a broader statement of the determinants of plant location than one which holds that firms seek the location offering the largest market area, or one which concludes that firms seek the location of least cost. This need is ful- filled by the concept of the maximum-profit location.[1] By definition, this location relates to that site from which a given number of buyers (whose purchases are required for the greatest possible profits) can be served at the lowest total cost.[2] And while the lowest level of average production cost at this site may be higher than that which exists at alternative ones, the mono- polistic control gained over a larger number of buyers (spead over a market area) makes it the maximum-profit location at the optimum output.[3]

This definition of the locator's objective recognizes the fact that one location may offer lower manufacturing-unit costs at a given output than another, but that the relative positions may be reversed as the market area of the firm expands and differentials in transport cost appear. For example, high cost manufacturers who extend their operations by water transportation may gain lower total unit costs to distant buyers than competitors linearly nearer to these buyers who are forced to use the railway or highway networks. (Viva the sector theory!)

The concept of the maximum-profit location does not have to be con- fined to an analysis in which the demand or cost factor is held constant. It lends itself readily by definition to an examination of cost and of locational interdependence. (Viva the multiple-nuclei theory!) When uncertainty prevails, implicit modification of the concept is, however, required. A maxi- min-minimax force arises which cannot accept the more daring movement to the quartile, sextile, octile, etc., where a bi- or multi-plant monopolist would locate his plants. We shall analyze the impact of uncertainty on short-run spatial distribution in detail in Chapter 12.

The maximin-minimax principle tends, because of uncertainty, to draw firms together in the short run. In fact we shall see in Chapter 12 that the strategy of games produces a short-run concentration albeit a dispersion eventually results. Indeed, the theory of Chapters 8 and 9 has already suggested that a long-run dispersion, taking underlying cost and demand

[1] This maximum-profit location concept is many-sided. Essentially, it excludes purely psychic income factors.

[2] Empirical evaluation of market area demand *vis-à-vis* lowest cost is possible. See. for example, M. L. Greenhut, "Size of Markets vs Transport Costs," *Journal of Industrial Economics*, VIII, 1960, pp. 172–184.

[3] Weber's least-cost location fits the above definition in part; it is limited, however, because Weber's least-cost location must emphasize the cost of procuring, processing, and distributing goods to a *given* buying point and thus it cannot convey sufficient spatial implications.

differentials into consideration, must arise in time. And Chapter 13 will prove this point. For the present, let us simply state that the generic maximum-profit location theory is adaptable not only to manufacturing-plant location but also to retailing and individual locations. On all levels, a long-run efficient distribution must arise, provided a profit-seeking economic location policy is a relevant goal, and is an effective force in competitive free enterprise economies.

Intra-Urban Micro-Locations: A Concluding Statement

Our maximum-profit location theory gives an insight into an objective of plant location. It analyzes the ways and means by which plant managers seek to achieve this objective in their selections of plant sites. And the following main economic conclusions are derived: (1) When firms sell to a given buying point, they seek the least-cost location in reference to this consumption center and ignore the locations of rivals in selecting their plant-sites. (2) When firms sell over a market area, their site-selections are influenced greatly by the location of rivals. (3) In selecting a plant site, each firm seeks the location which offers a particular sales output at the lowest cost possible so that all lost opportunities are, at least, covered in full. (4) When firms sell over a market area and unequal costs exist at alternative locations, uncertainty is increased; the maximin-minimax force of concentration thus becomes a likely part of short-run locational patterns. (5) When firms sell over a market area, we shall see later in the book that the tendency to disperse depends upon the height of the freight cost, the elasticity of the demand function, the characteristics (slopes) of the marginal costs, the degree of competition in location, the degree of competition from substitutable products at the various locations, and the homogeneity or heterogeneity of the firms belonging to the industry.

Market Imperfections and Other Considerations

Such market imperfections as time of delivery, personal contacts, custom, equalizing and other types of discriminatory price systems all influence the localization of industry and distort the findings listed above. These market imperfections tend mainly to yield special theories of location, and do not provide the general theory necessary for an understanding of underlying trends.[1] They appear to suggest, however, that different ethnic and religious groups could set up unique factors of consideration that might distort any theoretical presentation of the location of individuals founded on general cost and utility functions alone. But nevertheless, to the economist who is interested in intra-urban, inter-urban and regional economic locations in general,

[1] And see M. L. Greenhut, "A General Theory of Plant Location," *Metroeconomica*, VII, 1955, pp. 57–72, for an example of rejection of certain special locational data and subsequent derivation of a more general theory.

our outline of locational interdependence implies that there is an underlying force leading towards spatial equilibrium and efficiency. (Our last two chapters in Part III will, to repeat, probe deeply into this assertion.) We must only point out now that what will be proven to hold true over a regional landscape must, of course, hold true over an intra-urban landscape. In other words, although the locational interdependence (and maximum-profit location theory) that has just been outlined was set forth, to analyze location along a line or over a plain and not within a city or urban land mass, the line or plain may be understood to lie within the confines of the SCA, or the SMSA, whenever one's interest centres on the urban form.

It should be clear that whether the empiricist observes multiple nuclei, a wedge, or even a concentric circle, the urban economy in a free enterprise system must consist of that set of activities which conforms to the topography, the resources, and the want structure of the urban mass and its surrounding region. His conception must relate to a maximum profit function that holds in a world (and economic space) framed by uncertainty. Manifestly, if our basic economic theory holds, the planner's task is to identify the resource and want structure of the system. Planners should encourage, as quickly as possible, the kind of urban mass (e.g., wedge sector) that best fits the culture and landscape under study.

V. LOOKING AHEAD

The location "market area" type of analysis to be presented in the second section of Chapter 11 disregards previously mentioned forces of concentration. Its framework assumes that firms are never attracted to sites near to those of their rivals. Accordingly, it does not adequately explain (1) the situations where the market areas of firms are identical, nor (2) the situations where the market demand is largely concentrated at a point. In other words, the macro-location perspective of Chapter 11, which describes the boundary lines separating the market areas of firms, does not consider the imperfectly competitive nor the pure location factors so basic to the theory of spatial interdependence. Because of this, the market area school of thought customarily has presented too limited a view. Yet, it is in its context that one best describes changing market areas and the dynamic relations between freight rates and mill prices over time. We shall see in the next chapter that market area (macro)-location theory has, in fact, recently moved towards a pictorial representation of a general spatial *equilibrium*, and thereby is approaching the same end as micro-location theory [i.e., the spatial (or locational) interdependence theory]. We shall still later find that the "market area" approach is able to depict, although so far only in the mind's-eye, not only the macro picture of an economic landscape but the particular sizes and shapes of market areas which establish an efficient economic *equilibrium* over the total space. In many ways, Chapter 11 actually assumes knowledge of and acceptance of the theorems of still later chapters. But, because it deals in such detail with aspects of the urban mass, it was felt that it would best be placed to follow this chapter on the urban economy rather than be presented after the proofs have been set forth.

II

The Urban-Regional Setting (Inter-Urban Efficiency)

TO UNDERSTAND THE LOCATION HIERARCHIES throughout a landscape one must employ certain tools applicable to the theory of locational interdependence and stress the macro features of that theory itself. This theory and its extensions contain micro-macro properties which are transitional in nature in so far as concerns our objectives at this point; they will lead us later in this chapter to a purely macro view of the urban-regional economy. In Chapter 13 we shall set forth the precise form of the spatial equilibrium which complements the equilibrium properties of Chapter 8. Our present study begins with the indicated "transitional" materials.

I. FROM MICRO- TO MACRO-LOCATION THEORY

A general formulation of land-use patterns to include agricultural, commercial, residential and industrial use is possible. All that is necessary is a brief recall of selected tools of microeconomic theory.

Let the curves I_o, I_1, ..., I_n in Figure 11–1 stand for isoquants of increasing output size while the curves I'_o, I'_1, ..., I'_n in Figure 11–2 are consumer indifference curves, similarly ordered. Let costs be set by the ordinate intercept values in the figures. Factor price lines, such as AB and CD in Figure 11–1 occur at two different locations (locations 1 and 2); they relate respectively to the total cost and factor prices applicable at locations 1 and at 2. Isocost line EF is included to indicate that expansion paths, such as ST (or MN), may readily be traced. In corresponding manner, budget lines of similar form may be added to Figure 11–2, and a consumer satisfactions path traced.

Related to Figure 11–1 is a total cost curve applicable to each alternative site. This total cost curve is identical in shape to any such function usually conceived in nonspatial economic theory; it would yield bell-shaped average and marginal cost curves.

What about total revenues? In answer, observe that the framework of thought and theory presented in Chapter 8 suggests that *for certain purposes*

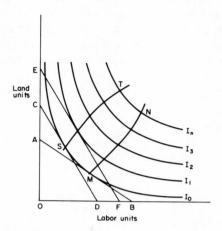

Figure 11–1: Isoquants and Expansion Paths

the concepts of our theory of oligopoly might well be substituted for those of pure competition. But the opposite pattern must also hold. More specifically, because the oligopoly theory that was formulated and proposed in Chapter 8 is simply a transform of pure competition economics, *for present purposes* a reverse mapping from oligopoly theory to the purely competitive framework

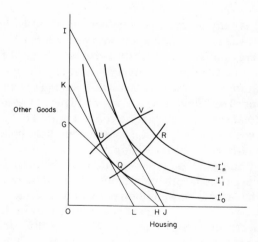

Figure 11–2: Indifference Curves and Consumer Satisfactions Paths

may (and will) be applied. Accordingly, let us assume that all buyers are located at a point. Then the total revenues, net of the transportation costs which apply to the firm's location, may differ from the total revenues at any other location only by the cost of the difference in distance. With total revenues taken as data, and total costs derived from Figure 11–1, Figure 11–3 emerges to characterize the *long-run* total revenue and total cost curves at the two different locations.

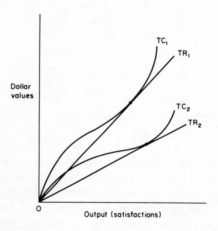

Figure 11–3: Long-Run Total Revenues and Costs at Different Locations

Figure 11–3 is fully general: As was demonstrated earlier in the book, individuals may engage in alternative activities with alternative income receipts related to the energy units used. But as we also saw there, the income/energy ratio may be expressed in absolute dollar values, e.g. the income value r. In turn, the expenditure of income may be divided among several goods yielding given satisfactions. The indifference curves of Figure 11–2 are thus derived. And then, with total energy costs taken as data, Figure 11–3 emerges in terms of the revenues, costs, and satisfactions of the household unit. It then reflects Figure 11–2 similarly as it reflects Figure 11–1.

Figures 11–1 and 11–2 are representations of the optimizing process. In the former, the expansion path points out the greatest output at different levels of costs. The income-consumption path, in turn, establishes the greatest satisfactions for different levels of income. As noted above the total costs of different outputs are derivable from Figure 11–1 for different locations, and revealed in Figure 11–3; correspondingly, the total revenues at alternative locations for different satisfactions may be mapped from Figure 11–2, over to

Figure 11-3, with the horizontal axis of Figure 11–3 now to be read as satisfactions rather than output.

The price of the final product, hence the total revenue of the *firm* shown in Figure 11–3, is exogenously given. The energy costs of the household unit are comparably given in dollar terms when Figure 11–2 serves as the basis for 11–3; in contrast to Chapter 5, we here assume that energy *costs* (indicated by total costs) are curvilinear with respect to input units, decreasing relatively up to a point and then increasing as energy inputs increase.

The *firm* is in equilibrium at a particular location when TR is tangent to TC. The ultimate selection of a location is influenced by the total investment desired. Thus, Figure 11–3 suggests that the selling price is higher at location 1 either because of the paucity of competition there or because a significantly strong consumer want prevails for the good in that market; in turn, if a comparatively substantial investment is desired, the high cost location 1 would be selected. It is significant to observe further with respect to Figure 11–3 that unlike the representations in previous chapters, where energy *units* were conceived to increase linearly with greater output, our present assumption of different cost areas requires that energy expenditures be considered as a function of other costs, not outputs. It should then be clear that if $TR > TC$, new firms will enter, while if $TR < TC$ they will exit.

The *individual* is in equilibrium at a particular location when TR is tangent to TC. In contrast to the firm which may sell at high or low prices, so that either a high or low cost location may be feasible, Figure 11–3 yields only one feasible location for the individual. To appreciate this difference, realize that the cost of living is implicitly considered in the revenue curves of the individual since these curves are relevant only at the point of tangency with a given level of satisfactions. Since real income is the same at given abscissa values along TR_1 and TR_2 in Figure 11–3, while energy applications measured in total costs are obviously less along TC_2, location 2 alone is feasible. Of course, if TC_1 was compressed nearer the vertical scale (or extended rightward) such that tangency with TR_1 occurs at lower cost and smaller satisfactions (or higher cost and greater satisfactions) than for location 2, the household unit could be indifferent between the two. In terms of our sketch of opportunity costs in Chapter 5, the discounts applicable to the different uncertainties, energy expenditures, working lifetimes, etc. that apply to the different (jobs) and places, could happen to yield equally desirable alternatives. We may generally expect, however, that in the conjectures of a decision maker, TR is tangent to TC for only one of many alternatives.

The other basic forces comprising Figure 11–3 apply to the individual without variation from their application to the firm. Thus if $TR > TC$, new individuals will seek similar sites, while if $TR < TC$, alternative opportunities are not being matched and the individual rejects the location (job) accordingly. On Darwinean-like grounds (i.e., desire to survive), we assert for practically *all* individuals that there must be at least one $TR \geq TC$. However, only in the rare case of indifference because of equal-alternatively satisfying opportunities would the final decision involve a play of chance.

The Rental Function

Some household units derive relatively greater satisfactions from better housing facilities than do others. Some are able to pay greater amounts for their homes. To economize on the cost of traveling to work is counterpart to economizing on the cost of shipping goods to the market. Depending upon the individual (or the firm), large or small sums may be offered for a given location. In the equilibrium, a noncost outlay case may or may not prevail, with rents for housing having risen in accordance with the much greater demand by household units for space and shelter than is required by the commercial, industrial, etc. demand for a particular space, or vice versa.

A simple rental function may easily be derived. Recall initially that the TR curves are net of transportation costs. Thus it may be that TR_2 is less than TR_1, simply because of the cost of distance to the market (or to the place of employment). Borrowing next from the more specialized perspective of Dunn,[1] let us conceive of alternative *agricultural* uses of land which provide a higher rent per acre for some agricultural use of land than is possible under other uses. More specifically, if transport costs on a particular product rise sharply with increasing distance, the slope of the rental cost curve in Figure 11-4 is steep with respect to distance (cf. BD with AC), and the rental sum rapidly approaches zero away from the market point. Between OE, the particular agricultural use related to line BD results, whereas between E and C an alternative use is able to provide the higher rent. Correspondingly, if distance from the market center is considered to be great in cost by the individual household units of a given culture, residential use may prevail over the landscape between points O and E, leaving manufacturing units to occupy lands at distances beyond OE. Manifestly, the urban development in one place may differ from another as resources, cultures, etc. differ.

The Economic Landscape

By extending the above frames of reference (i.e., Figures 11-1 through 11-4) so that they refer specifically to all extractive activities, to all professional and commercial uses (retailing and wholesaling), and, in addition, to all industrial

---

[1] The format here and in Figure 11-4 is drawn from E. Dunn, Jr., *The Location of Agricultural Production* (Gainesville, Florida: University of Florida Press, 1954), which, in turn, is traceable to J. H. von Thünen's *Der Isolierte Staat in Beziehung auf Landwirtschaft und Nationalökonomie* (Berlin, Schumacher Zarchlin, 1875), Part 1. Also see, R. G. Muth, "Economic Change and Rural-Urban Land Conversions," *Econometrica* (1961), pp. 1–23; and A. Alonso, *Location and Land Use* (Cambridge: Harvard University Press, 1964), pp. 37–42.

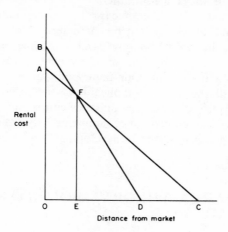

Figure 11–4: A Rent-Distance Map

uses as well as all residential rent alternatives, an identification of the profit-maximizing (and satisfaction-maximizing) uses over the entire landscape may be set forth. Then by rotating the rental gradient that includes all alternative rent vectors around the vertical scale, a concentric zone theory of land use would be obtained. If, however, uneven transport surfaces, different soil conditions, nonubiquitous raw materials, agglomerating advantages, shopping good features, and other forces of this kind are assumed to apply, land use patterns in the form of wedge-shaped and multiple-nuclei arrangements would be seen. Indeed, the forces of spatial interdependence already outlined, and which will be dealt with in detail later on, point to a still more specifically formulated spatial hierarchy. This hierarchy is shown in our theory of the equilibrium sizes and shapes of the market areas of all firms. This theory implicitly includes all household units as well as business firms, for the "buying" area of the household is the theoretical inverse of the "selling" area of the firm.

To appreciate the generality of our theory, we must turn to the remarks that follow about certain elementary aspects of market area sizes and shapes. These will form a background for explaining the basic relations existing between the locations of cities and the general theory of spatial equilibrium. Only when our theory has been completely stated will we be able to reconcile and view analytically both the fact that in some cities and regions households may outbid industry for certain lands, and *vice versa*, but also that they cluster together in wedge-shaped or, for that matter, concentric circle formations, etc. Indeed, only then will we be able to appreciate the condition that both the sizes and shapes of cities and economic regions may differ, even though all units which form them comply with the same set of spatial equilibrium forces. It will not be a contradiction that business units may—in the long run—be assigned to the economic (profit-seeking) main category, while individual household units may best be characterized as utility maximizers. With regard to the household, purely psychic income may be assigned a number which subtracts from cost, an adjustment similar to the classical addition to cost of natural rent. Our theory of spatial equilibrium as ultimately set forth will therefore be applicable to the urban community (i.e. household units) as well as to business units. Of course, since the fundamental emphasis of this book is on general economic activity over economic space, only the sketch of a theory of urban development and location will later be presented herein.

II. MARKET AREA THEORY—BOUNDARY LINES IN SPACE

The size of a firm's market area suggests the wisdom with which its plant location has been selected. Thus, if (1) buyers are assumed to be evenly scattered and to have identical demand schedules, (2) the market is imperfectly competitive *because* firms are geographically dispersed, (3) all rivals charge a net-mill price which is marked up above their cost by the same sum, (4) the product is sold on the f.o.b. mill basis, and (5) the freight rates on the final product are the same for all sellers, the least cost producer will quote the lowest mill price and thus will capture the largest sales territory, i.e., market area. Under these assumptions, locational efficiency may be ascertained by investigating the size of the firm's market area: the larger it is, the wiser has been the locational choice.

Boundary Lines and the Price and Freight Rate Systems

The sales price and the freight rate on the final product are the immediate determinants of a company's market territory under the f.o.b. mill system of pricing. Any decrease in either the freight rate or sales price of a firm widens the market area controlled by the firm; any increase narrows this area.[1] It follows that two sellers, located in different sectors, divide an entire market area equally between them, if their locations are symmetrical to the entire market area, and provided further that they are subject to the same freight rates, charge identical net-mill prices, and sell a homogeneous product.[2] This

[1] Hans Ritschl, "Reine und historische Dynamik des Standortes der Erzeugungszweize," *Schmollers Jahrbuch fur Gesttgebung*, LI, 1927, pp. 813–870, and see pp. 814, 815, 816, 846, 848, where Ritschl repeatedly stresses the fact that a lowering of freight rates increases the market area of a firm.

[2] Frank Fetter, "The Economic Law of Market Areas," *Quarterly Journal of Economics*, XXXIX, 1924, pp. 520–529, 527. It is deserving of special mention that Fetter is accredited

division produces a straight line separating the markets of each producer. (See MN, Figure 11–5A where the entire market area is assumed to be in the form of a circle.[1])

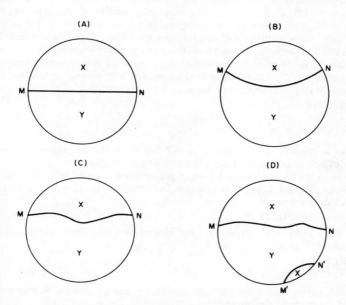

Figure 11–5: Some Market Area Boundary Lines

By positing (1) heterogeneous duopoly *because* the firms are geographically separated, (2) an entire market area circular in form, (3) f.o.b. mill system of pricing, (4) transport costs proportional to distance, (5) net-mill prices marked up above cost by the same sum, and (6) either a higher net-mill price and/or freight rate on the finished product for one enterpriser as compared to

by many as the writer who stimulated interest in market areas. Before Fetter, John Bates Clark in his *Control of Trusts*, 1st ed. (New York, The Macmillan Co., 1914), pp. 104–112, had inquired into this problem by describing the indifference line separating the market area of competitors. In fact, much earlier than this, a German writer (Launhardt) combined an analysis of cost orientations and market areas. Launhardt's lack of reputation in the United States is due principally to the fact that his book is out of print and not generally available in this country. (Wilhelm Launhardt, *Mathematische Begründung der Volkswirtschaftslehre* (Leipzig: B. G. Teubner, 1885).

[1] Each firm (X and Y) is located at a point which minimizes the transport distance over the half-circle surrounding its plant. It can be shown that this point is at a distance $4r/3\pi$ from the center of the circle on the perpendicular bisector of the diameter of the circle.

his rival, the straight boundary line dividing the entire market area gives way to a curve. This curve bends backward towards the plant which pays the higher freight rate and/or is burdened with higher costs of production. (See MN, Figure 11–5B).[1] Freight and/or production cost disadvantages narrow the market area of a firm.[2] In fact, the firm's entire market may be destroyed

[1] Erich Schneider, "Bemerkung zu einer Theorie der Raumwirtschaft," *Econometrica*, III (1935), pp. 79–101, 83–89, sets forth the above proposition and related ones by means of elementary mathematics. For readers interested in the basis for the statements already made and to be made in the text above, consider the following proofs of Schneider:

Let Z_1 and Z_2 refer to the distance from the customers to producers 1 and 2 respectively; II_1 and II_2 are the factor prices for the respective producers; F is the constant freight rate on the final product, which is assumed to be the same for both sellers. Schneider then solves for the isostante (the indifference line between the competitors).

(1) $II_1 + F(Z_1) = II_2 + F(Z_2)$

(2) $Z_1 - Z_2 = \dfrac{II_2 - II_1}{F}$

If the prices at the factories are equal, $Z_1 = Z_2$. If $II_1 \neq II_2$, a hyperbolic curve results which bends backwards towards the factory charging the higher price.

As soon as the constant freight charges are assumed unequal (e.g., because of shipments by water, railroad, highway, or rate policies of the different carriers), the equation for the indifference line becomes

(3) $II_1 + F_1 Z_1 = II_2 + F_2 Z_2$

If $II_1 < II_2$, and $F_1 < F_2$, producer 2 has control over only the regions comparatively close to him. If $II_1 = II_2$

(4) $\dfrac{Z_1}{Z_2} = \dfrac{F_2}{F_1}$

The isostante, in this case, is inversely proportional to the freight rate; it, therefore, takes the form of the circle of Apollonius.

[2] It is worthy of note that when one firm suffers a freight cost or production cost disadvantage, the long-run location of each firm may not be at the points described in note 1, p. 237. For example, if it is assumed that (1) costs of production are equal at all locations, but the freight rate on the final good is higher in one zone than the other, (2) the cost of transporting the final good is not too significant a part of delivered-to-customers cost, and (3) demand is highly inelastic, the firm in the higher-rated zone gains by moving to a location near the center of the entire market area. This move increases its market area while not causing significant losses in sales to buyers situated far from the plant; further, this relocation forces the rival firm to move to a site proximate to its competitor. The actual short-run locations may well be together in the lower-rated zone.

The locational significance of American freight-rate structures may be seen also by reference to the practice of establishing rate advantages for freight moving in a particular direction. This type of system produces results similar to those described above. Firms minimize transport costs by sending more freight in the direction favored by the carrier rather than *vice versa*.

If the curve in Figure 11–5B is due to production-cost differentials rather than freight-rate inequalities, firms may move near to or at the center of the market. More definite determination of their long-run locations depends upon the costs hypothesized for the several locations, the conjectural beliefs of the locators as regards their rival's plans, and other factors evaluated in Chapter 12 but too numerous (and intricate) to record (and examine) at this point

if its net-mill price plus freight costs (to any and all buyers) exceed those of the other firm.[1]

The boundary separating the markets of two firms may take irregular shapes when transport costs increase at variable decreasing rates over longer distances. Mathematical determination of the nature of the curve depends upon the rates of change in the prices charged by each carrier and the values assigned to the constants (the freight rate applicable to the first unit of distance of each carrier). These freight rate progressions, which may produce equal freight charges for varying distances within particular mileage brackets, as well as lower mileage charges over longer distances, could yield a curve such as that shown by the MN line in Figure 11-5C. Further, if a cheaper method of transport to parts of the entire market area is assumed to exist for one firm, a highly irregular boundary becomes possible, and an invasion of territory quite near to the plant of a competitor may occur. (See MN and M'N', Figure 11-5D.)

Carriers often use "basing points" or "basing lines" in order to meet competition of rival transport agencies. This practice further distorts market areas of firms, for when rates are reduced to certain points, the firm that is so located as to reap this advantage gains an expansion in its market area. The straight line that separates market areas, when net-mill prices and freight rates are equal and products are homogeneous, gives way to indentations following the outlines of carrier's "basing areas." (See MN, Figure 11-6A.) Similarly, a wave-like type of boundary appears if one carrier uses the group rate system of generally decreasing its rates with distance though charging a constant sum for given distances along its route, while the carrier in the other sector establishes freight mileage rates which not only decrease relatively but also continuously over distance. (See MN, Figure 11-6B.)

The price policies of firms also distort market areas. Thus, where duopolists are heterogeneous *because* firms are geographically separated, and the lower-priced seller uses a constant net-mill price under the f.o.b. mill system of pricing while his rival adopts an identical net-mill price for proximate buyers but reduces this for distant buyers, the boundary separating the firms scoops out as a soup bowl, even though freight rates are equal. (See MN, Figure 11-6C.) If two sellers who use the f.o.b. mill system vary their net-mill price so as to discriminate against nearer buyers in a similar way, a straight line divides the entire market area in half, assuming freight rates are equal and their alternative net-mill prices are the same.

Overlapping of Markets. Market overlapping may occur. Thus, if both sellers use an equalizing delivered-price system (all customers pay the same delivered price regardless of location) the boundary between the sellers will be completely eliminated, *except* when (1) marginal production costs plus

---

[1] Fetter, *op. cit.*, pp. 522, "Both markets can exist so long as the price difference of the two markets is less than the full freight difference."

freight on the final product limit the range of operations of one or both firms, and/or (2) contact advantages and the importance of time-of-delivery form a market ring around a factory which cannot be penetrated by a distant seller.

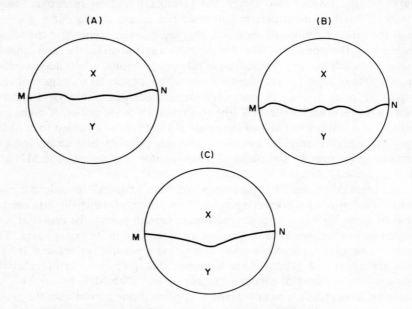

Figure 11–6: Other Market Area Boundary Lines

A sharp spatial division of markets is, similarly, precluded by the single or multiple basing-point systems of pricing, *except* when (1) the total delivered-to-customers cost of a firm is in excess of the price quoted at a given point(s), or (2) contact advantages and/or the impact of time-of-delivery create a market ring around the rival's plant. In the first case, a seller may voluntarily give up this buying point(s) to his rival, rather than sell at a delivered price(s) which does not cover his costs. In the second case, a seller may find that he cannot invade the market area adjacent to his rival's factory without violating the basing-point system of pricing.

Such monopolistic features as (1) heterogeneity of products, (2) spatial price discrimination whereby both sellers quote the same delivered price to buyers within given mileage brackets, and (3) identical group-rate systems by carriers prevent the MN lines drawn in Figures 11–5 and 6 from always being sharp and distinct. A zone of transition or indifference is found when markets are imperfectly competitive for reasons in addition to space and number of sellers. Within this zone, some buyers (assumption 1 above) are indifferent to slight price differentials, or all buyers (assumptions 2 and 3 above) are indifferent to sellers. In other words, an overlapping of market areas exists.

This overlapping can be caused by freight absorption either by the buyer,[1] the seller, or the transfer agency.[2] The dashed lines in Figure 11–7 define a zone of indifference. Obviously, if our focus is either intra- or inter-urban but the sellers (e.g. retailers) do not deliver or price in any way except f.o.b. their shops, these assumptions are largely inapplicable. A sharp line may then divide the sectors within the city or between the cities, as the case be.

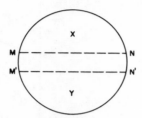

Figure 11–7: Overlapping Boundaries

Boundary Lines: Costs and Population

The models presented above emphasize the influence of two forces (namely, the freight rate on the final product, and the sales price) on the size of market areas and the shape of the boundary line. But they do not help us to understand the cost and demand limitations on the maximum extent of a firm's (or a city's) market area, nor do they help to define the necessary minimum size of

[1] See E. M. Hoover, *The Location of Economic Activity*, 1st. ed. (New York: McGraw-Hill, 1948), pp. 58, 59, where differentiation as to product is cited as a cause of market overlapping. Also see A. Lösch, *Die räumliche Ordnung der Wirtschaft* (Jean: Gustav Fischer, 1944), p. 8, wherein he cites heterogeneity as a cause of overlapping. The buyer, in effect, may willingly absorb freight on the preferred product.

[2] Market overlapping due to the practice of the transfer agency occurs when freight rates are used which, in a relative sense, tend to ignore distance. One special case of this kind may prevail when one seller is able to use a different form of transport or is otherwise favored by the carrier. To illustrate, recall from note 1, p. 238 that if $\Pi_1 = \Pi_2$, the isostante defined by $F_1 Z_1 - F_2 Z_2 = 0$. Upon squaring, a quadratic appears. But further recall that Z_1 and Z_2 are distances; respectively, they can be written as $\sqrt{(x+a_0)^2 + y^2}$ and $\sqrt{(x-a_0)^2 + y^2}$. By appropriate substitutions and rearrangements, the general equation for a conic section appears $Ax^2 + Bxy + Cy^2 + Dx + Ey + F = 0$. The discriminant $4AC - B^2$ may be $\gtreqless 0$, and hence an ellipse, parabola, or hyperbola obtains. It can be shown that when $\Pi_1 \neq \Pi_2$, and the freight rate charged to the product of one seller is substantially higher than that charged another—regardless of the direction in which the goods are shipped—the market area of the seller subject to the high freight rate is elliptical. The other seller may thus sell to places quite distant from it in the direction of the other seller, as one firm's market area would surround the market area of its rival.

the market area, the localization and/or dispersion of industry, and the number of producers (and cities). One step towards an explanation of these problems was undertaken in the late 1930's by Edgar M. Hoover.[1]

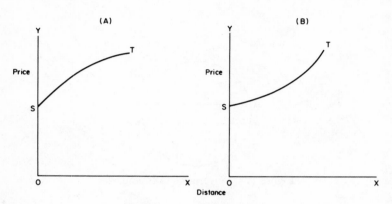

Figure 11–8: Margin Lines

In Hoover's study, emphasis was given to the slope of the "margin line" (see ST, Figures 11–8 A, B), the line which represents the increase in delivered prices with growing distance from the mill. Any influence tending to cause convexity from above this line, as in Figure 11–8A, due to decreasing unit cost with increasing scale of production, and/or nonproportionality of freight rates with distance, diminishes the number of independent sources of supply; at the same time, it promotes an extension of the firm's market area. On the other hand, a concave margin line promotes the use of a larger number of different sources and leads to a smaller market area for each.[2] Thus, as in Figure 11–8B, the margin line first rises slowly and then sharply, thereby indicating that though freight rates are proportional to distance, or even increase at diminishing rates with greater distance, the expansion of output (i.e. the market area of the firm) causes marginal production costs to rise so much as to produce a margin line which is concave upward.

Apart from marginal production costs and freight, Hoover claims (1)

[1] *Location Theory and the Shoe and Leather Industries* (Cambridge: Harvard University Press, 1937), pp. 12–23.

[2] Hoover points out that returns to scale (increasing and decreasing) play a more variable role than freight rates. "So long as extension of the market lowers costs, the slope of the margin line will be less steep than that of the transport gradient. In fact it may be negative." *Ibid.*, p. 20. And see F. Mossman & H. Morton, *Logistics of Distribution Systems* (Boston, Allyn & Bacon, Inc, 1965), pp. 76–83.

that the distribution of consumers helps to determine the slope of the margin line. Should there be a concentration of buyers at a given distance from the seller's plant, the steepness of the margin line would, if costs are increasing, be augmented at this point; and contrariwise. (2) The elasticities of demand of buyers who are located at given distances from the seller also affect the slope. This slope would increase with a smaller elasticity and tend to flatten out with greater elasticity, if costs are increasing.[1]

According to Hoover's analytical pattern, it may be concluded that if (1) heterogeneous duopoly relations exist *because* firms (cities) are geographically separated, (2) rivals are situated at a distance from each other, though close enough to compete at points equidistant from their plants, (3) the entire market area is being supplied by the existing sellers, (4) the freight rate on the final product is equal for each seller and proportional to distance, (5) the final product is sold on the f.o.b. mill basis, and (6) marginal costs of one firm are rising less rapidly than those of the other firms as production is increased, then attempts to expand sales (e.g. by selling in other directions) will cause the net-mill price of the cost-increasing firm to rise relatively compared with the other and the boundary line between the two will retreat and bend backwards towards the firm whose costs are rising the most. Expansion will, of course, be carried out if and only if the increase in sales to buyers located far from the seller's factory is sufficient to offest the loss in revenues on sales to nearer buyers. To generalize in terms of macro-urban location theory, if marginal costs in one city rise less rapidly with increases in output, the inter- as well as intra-urban boundary line(s) will move and bend away from that expanding unit *vis à vis* the other, *ceteris paribus*.

Boundary Lines and Area Shapes: Inter-Firm, Inter-City

While Hoover's analysis provided an insight into the forces determining the

[1] *Ibid.*, p. 21. "If the demand is highly elastic, so that a great deal less is bought in such a case, then the extension of the market area may bring comparatively little increase in output and comparatively little rise in prices . . . Elastic demand, then, is a factor tending to localize extractive industries."

While Hoover's solution of the effect of an elastic demand on the slope of the margin line is patent, one can question the applications he makes for his deduction. Firms *might* localize (or, shall we say, a single firm may not have enough incentive to establish a branch plant) and they would sell over a larger market area, but, more probably, and according to the school of writers which stresses the location interdependence of firms (see Chapter 12), the existence of an elastic demand promotes dispersion. Probably, the contradiction in theory is due to the difference in emphasis among the writers in question. The type of approach used by Hoover takes location as datum, and, accordingly, is concerned primarily with the size and shape of the firm's market area; the locational-interdependence school stresses the impact of demand on location, thereby confining its interest largely to the factor which causes firms to be attracted to or repulsed by each other. The extent and shape of the market area is of lesser interest to these writers than are the locational techniques for maximising demand.

number of producers, and the size of the firm's market area, the problems of
minimum size, maximum size, and localization or dispersion remained largely
unsolved. An endeavor in these directions was made a few years later by
August Lösch, in his *Die räumliche Ordnung der Wirtschaft*.[1] Lösch sought to
define further the economic region, a concept popularized by Ohlin,[2] and in
the process derived his "ideal economic region."

Lösch postulates a broad homogeneous plain with uniform transport
features in all directions, and with an even scatter of sufficient raw materials.
Furthermore, the agricultural population is uniformly distributed over this
plain, each individual having identical tastes, preferences, technical knowledge,
and production opportunities. The result of these assumptions is the dotting
of the plain with completely self-sufficient homesteads.[3]

Lösch begins his analysis by inquiring into the situation in which a farmer
considers supplying beer to others, besides to himself. Though limited by
freight costs, this would-be entrepreneur gains the advantages of larger scale
of operations and of specialization. If the demand is sufficient, the farmer can
sell advantageously over a circular area; if the demand is too small compared
with costs, this would-be entrepreneur gives up his plan.

Assuming that the market is imperfectly competitive *because* firms are
geographically scattered, and that the demand curve for the individual farmer
exceeds his costs at some levels of output, production is immediately profitable. But in time the entrance of competitors makes the circular area smaller
and smaller. This decrease in sales reflects the leftward shifting of the demand
curve, which continues according to Lösch until the Chamberlinean tangential
point is reached. Before the tangency is reached, other changes must first
take place.

The market areas of firms cannot remain circular; for, even though these
ideal shapes are close enough to touch each other, perfect merging is impossible. Accordingly, profits continue and new firms enter; it is only when the
circular area is reshaped in the form of a hexagon that the equilibrium conditions can be satisfied. Lösch depicts the hexagon as the most perfect market
area shape. It has the advantage of being most akin to the circle, and, therefore, as compared to other polygons, such as the triangle and square, shipping
distance is minimized, and, accordingly, demand is maximized. It has the
advantage over the circle in that the number of independent producers is the
largest possible, while the elimination of the empty corners maximizes the
demand of the entire population.[4] The balance in spatial competition is finally

[1] A. Lösch, *op. cit.* See, in particular, pp. 71–94.

[2] B. Ohlin, *Interregional and International Trade* (Cambridge: Harvard University
Press, 1935).

[3] A. Lösch, *op. cit.*, p. 72.

[4] *Ibid.*, pp. 74–77. "Zusammenfassend können wir festellen, dass das regelmässige
Sechseck um so mehr die vorteilhafteste Gebietsform wird, je grösser und abgerundeter das
Gesamtgebiet, je elastischer die Nachfrage an der Gebietsgrenze und je näher die not-
wendige Versendungsweite der möglichen ist," p. 78.

realized only when the hexagon is so reduced in size that profits are completely eliminated.

Lösch's equilibrium is determined by a system of equations for which the first condition is (1) that each producer maximizes his gains. This condition involves equality between marginal revenue and marginal cost. The next three conditions require the number of independent existences to be maximized. Thus, (2) all areas must be served by at least one firm. This leads to the third condition, (3) all extraordinary profits must disappear, for, under the competitive free-entry assumption, new rivals will eventually eliminate all surplus incomes. This condition requires (4) that the area served by each individual be the smallest possible, for, if the area served by it is too large, profits would exist. The last condition of equilibrium requires (5) that any consumer on a boundary line be indifferent to the possible sources from which he can obtain a given commodity at minimum cost. Without this condition, the boundaries would overlap and the points of indifference would take on zonal qualities.[1]

After establishing the hexagon as the ideal market area shape, Lösch views the trading area of the various products as nets of such hexagons. Depending upon the nature of the product, the respective sizes vary from very small hexagons to very large ones. By turning the nets around a common center, 6 sectors are obtained where production centers are most frequent, and 6 others result where production centers are scarce. The coincidence of many of these centers minimizes the freight burdens and perforce enhances the consumer demand by enabling purchases from many local mills. It signifies inter-industry localization. This is then the reason why Lösch maintains that though the firms within an industry disperse, each trading over its own hexagonal market area, there will be some agglomeration of industries. In turn, how many self-sufficient systems come into existence depends upon the commodity having the largest necessary shipping radius. These self-sufficient regions are styled the ideal economic region.[2]

Once Lösch drops the assumption of continuous settlements, the door is reopened to other polygonic irregular conceptions of the market area. These imperfectly shaped economic areas are due to the fact that sales to one community may be insufficient to make production feasible. Sales to a more distant community are, therefore, necessary to cover costs. But, in fact, because this more distant community may contain a large number of buyers, its inclusion within the firm's market area may bring profits.[3] Obviously, if

[1] See Lösch, *Ibid.*, pp. 65, 66.

[2] See *ibid*, pp. 84–90. Also see François Perroux, "Economic Space: Theory and Application," *Quarterly Journal of Economics*, LXIV, 1950, pp. 89–104.

[3] *Op. cit.*, pp. 82, 83, "Als wichtigstes Ergebnis aber folgt aus dem Vorhergehenden, dass bei diskontinuierlicher Besiedlung auch die mögliche Grösse der Marktgebiete und die Zahl der von ihnen umfassten Siedlungen diskontinuierlich wächst. Das wiederum ermöglicht Sondergewinne. Denn wenn beispielsweise der Absatz in 32 Siedlungen notwendig wäre, damit eine bestimmte Fabrikation sich lohnt, nach dem zu kleinen Gebiet

spatial concentrations of consumers (coterminous with uncertainty) make profits possible (unjustified in Lösch's system but justified in ours), and if intra-industry dispersion is required, a network of regular-identical size hexagons would not exist; moreover, they would not be minimum in size in the Chamberlinean sense. Nevertheless, we shall see in Chapter 13 that the *spatial* system which evolves in practice is efficient in a general Löschian form notwithstanding profits and unevenness. For the present, however, we must branch off into another line of inquiry, namely that of determining what other scholars (namely those interested in focusing on the urban economy alone) tended to say about sizes, independent existences, etc. After this review is complete, we will be able to synthesize macro-location theory with the theories of the urban economy. But first, let us recast in summary form the message which general economic theory and macro-location theory provides to all who are interested in "urban" economics.

Urban Location Theory and General Economic and Macro-Location Theory. Given the location, the boundary separating the trading areas of firms depends upon price policies, costs, the prevailing freight rate practices and transport lines. Moreover, space economic theory (e.g. Chapter 8) suggests that rents determine industrial locations. Since a theory of residential location involves utility maximization, which we know from our analysis of opportunity costs is just the other side of profit maximization, the same substitutions and decisions are made in households as in industry. [Let it be recalled here that even our treatment of the purely psychic income seeker is symmetric. That is to say, as defined in Chapter 2, the profit and utility maximizing concepts practically merge under conditions of uncertainty with the former being more restrictive only in the sense that such persons as the manufacturer who is obsessed by gambling instincts in the decision process, or is impelled by purely personal environmental preferences which have no bearing on his energy expenditures, is excluded from the former category albeit not the latter. Including them would not affect our theory noticeably since in the long run the related business fails to exist. Most importantly, irrational persons are excluded

Nr. 13 mit 31 Siedlungen aber ohne Übergang gleich das unnötig grosse Gebiet 14 mit 36 Siedlungen kommt, so muss der Absatz sich eben auf 36 Siedlungen ausdehnen. Die Nachfragekurve schneidet dann die Kostendurve, statt sie nur zu berühren und damit enstehen Sondergewinne in dieser Branche. Solche mässigen Gewinne sind geradezu die Regel, denn es ist ein Zufall, wenn die Nachfragekurve auf ihren Sprüngen die Kostencurve eben noch berührt."

For other discussions on Lösch's theory, see W. Stolper, "Book Review," *American Economic Review*, XXXIII, Sept. 1943, pp. 626–636.

Also see W. Isard, "The General Theory of Location and Space Economy," *Quarterly Journal of Economics*, LXIII, 1949, pp. 476–506, 495–502.

Also see G. Ackley, "Spatial Competition in a Discontinuous Market," *Quarterly Journal of Economics*, LVI, 1942, pp. 212–230, wherein the central thesis is that spatial discontinuities induce monopolistic price behavior and offer profits.

from each as the irrational entrepreneur or irrational individual who is guided in his residential preferences by non-utility maximizing considerations would have only short-run impacts on the landscape.] The same basic analysis pattern thus applies to residential patterns as to industrial location processes. It further follows that just as the theory of spatial interdependence sets forth conditions which cause firms to localize or disperse, corresponding analysis applies to residential patterns.

Market imperfections may also affect prices, rents, etc. and dominate the situation. Thinking now essentially of industries and cities, let us recall that whether or not we view an ideal dispersion in the Löschian sense or as a clustering type of dispersion in the multiple nuclei sense, the division of trading areas between centers may well approximate the outline of a hexagon (and a net of hexagons), as in fact we shall demonstrate in Chapter 13. The viewpoint of market area theorists, then, is macro, in the sense that the location(s) is (are) given, and the relations and interdependencies between firms and industries are not specified. At the same time, however, the penultimate finding of the market area school is micro, and the full micro-macro statement of the representative firm's equilibrium requires only the addition to Lösch's theory of the forces which bring together or repel selected firms in selected industries. This ultimate joining of theories—in Chapter 13—will complete our view of the urban and regional landscape. At this point, however, we must turn our attention directly to a special aspect of urban macro-location theory, which was formulated recently by a few economists. This attention recognizes the condition that urban location theory, in effect, requires the market area school to specify the boundary limits to all sub-stratums of the economic space under examination. In the following pages, we shall deal with this requirement.

III. THE REGIONAL HIERARCHY

Except for relatively minor modifications, this book accepts Lösch's system of hexagons as the spatial pattern which should be mapped onto the theory of Chapter 8. But first, a simple extension of Lösch's conception, presented originally by Beckmann a few years ago,[1] is needed to draw attention to the relation between the *cities* of a region. Once these relations are understood and the economic landscape, in effect, is bounded, we reach the point where the particular location forces within the region (disregarding the number and sizes of the cities contained therein) can be examined so that the *equilibria shapes* in economic space can be identified.

[1] M. J. Beckmann, "City Hierarchies and the Distribution of City Size," *Economic Development and Cultural Change*, Vol. 6 (April, 1958), pp. 243–248.

Beckmann's Model

Assume a homogeneous universe and a set of self-sufficient economic regions. Then let Lösch's hexagonal networks or the outlines thereof be fitted together so that, from the largest prevailing market area size (i.e. an economic region) down to the smallest hexagonal size, there exists within each exactly "s" market areas of the next smaller size (or order, as it is referred to in the literature). Each (and every) central place *of a given size* throughout the homogeneous universe then contains the same number of coincident market centers, and, accordingly, produces and sells the same products.

Assume next that the population of each central place within an economic region is proportional to the population throughout the market area served by the central place. That is to say, the population of each city is assumed to be in some proportion "k" of the total population which it serves. A table such as 11–1 thus obtains, where we assume that each larger central area contains 5 sub-centers in its area (i.e., $s = 5$) besides its own central city, and where $k = 1/2$. Note that the rural population in Table 11–1 is the same as the city population in each order because $k = 1/2$; since we shall have need later on for a related statistic to k, let $r = $ the rural population of order 1.

TABLE 11–1: System of Cities

Order	City Population (C_n)	Total Population (P_n)	Number of cities in order ($s = $ the multiple 5)
1	1,000	2,000	625
2	10,000	20,000	125
3	100,000	200,000	25
4	1,000,000	2,000,000	5
5	10,000,000	20,000,000	1

In Table 11–1, the smallest cities (and areas) are called the first-order place. There are five orders of cities and areas shown in the table. A place of the fifth order serves 5 places of the fourth order, . . . , and 625 places of the first order. It is implicit to the table that the population of each place in each order is a multiple $s/(1-k)$ of the next lower order place.[1]

[1] Let $n = $ the order of the place. Let P stand for the total population served, and C_n the city population served, with r designating the rural population served by a first order place, and k and s having the meaning given in the text above. Then—

(1) $C_n = k(P_n)$

(2) $P_n = C_n + s(P_{n-1})$

(3) $P_n = k(P_n) + s(P_{n-1})$

(4) $P_n = \dfrac{s(P_{n-1})}{1-k}$

Because from (3) $P_{n-1} = k(P_{n-1}) + s(P_{n-2}) = (s/1-k)^2 (P_{n-2})$, we find by substitution in (4) that—

By conceiving of $s/(1-k)$ as the *mean value of a random variable* $[s/(1-k)]$ the population of each larger order city *would average* to $s/(1-k)$. Higher orders would produce greater variations [see exponents in (5), note below], and some overlapping of city sizes may be expected to occur. The hierarchy of cities within a region approaches, in fact, a continuous distribution.

Rank-Size Rule. The rank-size feature of the spatial hierarchy presented above may be recognized quite readily. Following Table 11–1 we would find that a city halfway in the third order would be larger than others to the extent that there exists one larger city in the fifth order, five larger cities in the fourth order, and twelve larger cities in the third order. The rank of the subject city is, therefore, $1+s+s^2/2 = 18.5$. Note that the number assigned to rank increases as we move to a lower order while the city size decreases by the inverted multiple of $s/(1-k)$ as we proceed toward lower orders. In opposite reference, a fifth-order central place in Table 11–1 carries the lowest number rank, namely one, while it contains the largest population, namely the equal of $\dfrac{kr(s^{n-1})}{1-k^n}$.[1]

It follows from the above that a large k implies a large relative urbanization. In the limit where the proportion k approaches unity, the city would equal the region and there would be no lower order (higher-ranked) cities. In contrast, the more the populace of the region is oriented to rural life, relatively speaking, the smaller is k, the smaller is the size of the city, *ceteris paribus*, and the closer is the rank-size of cities to a constant proportion of the

$$(5) \quad P_n = \left(\frac{s}{1-k}\right)^2 (P_{n-2}) = \ldots = \left(\frac{s}{1-k}\right)^{n-1} P_1$$

We know that $P_1 = r + C_1$ and $C_1 = k\,(P_1)$, or in turn $C_1 = k\,(r + C_1)$. So, we find both—

$$(6) \quad C_1 = kr/(1-k)$$

and

$$(7) \quad P_1 = r + \frac{kr}{(1-k)} = \frac{r}{1-k}$$

Substituting in (5), we then obtain

$$(8) \quad P_n = \left(\frac{s}{1-k}\right)^{n-1} \left(\frac{r}{1-k}\right) = \frac{r(s^{n-1})}{(1-k)^n}$$

and from (1),

$$(9) \quad C_n = \frac{kr(s^{n-1})}{(1-k)^n}$$

The first order place, therefore, has a population equal to $kr/(1-k)$. And each place of order n has a population equal to $s/(1-k)$ times the population of the $n-1$ place.

[1] See (9) in note above. In numbers, where $k = 1/2$, $r = 1,000$, $s = 5$ and $n = 5$, we have $\dfrac{1/2\,(1000)\,(625)}{(1/2)^5} = 10,000,000$, as in Table 11–1.

size of the largest city.[1] In turn, the smaller is s, the smaller is the population of the higher order city of a given order, and, *ceteris paribus*, the greater is the area of that order in terms of the number of acres allocable per thousand of people.

Evaluation of the Model: Its Löschian Roots. There are many short-comings which may be noted in connection with the rank-size model presented above, such as the claim that it applies chiefly to retailing, wholesaling, and related activities whose input prices do not vary appreciably over the space. Overlapping and irregularity of market areas, as described in section II of this chapter, have also been somewhat ignored in the model. Significantly, however, all weaknesses of this kind stem from Lösch's opening assumption of a homogeneous plain and an initial even distribution of population. We shall later on in the book visualize the full meaning of these assumptions, and in the process derive a more realistic, less restricted approach to market areas in economic space. When this is done, the main advantages of the altered theory

---

[1] Remembering that in *ranking* cities, we move from higher to lower orders, it follows that we must subtract from the largest order the order number necessary to place us in the class size under evaluation. For example, let N equal the highest order in the system; also let n equal the order in question running from the lowest to the highest order $(1, 2, \ldots N)$; and let m relate to the class rank in question and m' the city rank, each running from the higher to the lowest rank, respectively from $(0, 1, \ldots N-1)$ and $(1, 2, \ldots)$. Then it follows that if we are interested in the rank of the largest city in order n, we are equivalently seeking to determine the first ranking city in class rank $m+1$ where $m = N-n$. The first ranking city in class order n is, therefore, ranked $1+s+s^2+s^3+ \ldots +s^{m-1}+1$. By well-known rules, this sums to $[(s^m-1)/(s-1)]+1$. The rank (R) of the city halfway in a given order may be given as $[(s^m-1)/(s-1)]+(s^m/2)$, which is further approximated by

(1) $R = s^m \{(1/2)+[1/(s-1)]\}$

From N we shall subtract m ranks of cities in order to establish the size of the city in the n_{th} order. In conjunction with (9) in the note on p. 249, this yields the (population) size of the subject city, as indicated by—

(2) $S = C_{N-m} = \dfrac{kr(s^{N-m-1})}{(1-k)^{N-m}} = \dfrac{kr}{s}\left(\dfrac{s}{1-k}\right)^{N-m}$

The product of the rank (R) and the size (S)—not s—of the city halfway in the n_{th} order is—

(3) $(S) (R) = C_{N-m} \{s^m [(1/2)+1/(s-1)]\}$

$= \dfrac{kr}{s}\left(\dfrac{s}{1-k}\right)^{N-m} \{s^m [(1/2)+1/(s-1)]\}$

$= \left[\dfrac{kr}{s}\left(\dfrac{1}{2}+\dfrac{1}{s-1}\right)\left(\dfrac{s}{1-k}\right)^N\right](1-k)^m$

$= K(1-k)^m$

where K is a constant. When k is small $(1-k)^m \to (1)^m$, and the size of the city times its rank (or, in alphabetical arrangement, the rank-size of cities) approximates that of a constant. The rank-size rule states that the size of the m'_{th} city approximates one/m'_{th} the size of the largest city; Beckmann, *op. cit.*, p. 246.

will be seen to lie in the varying number of settlements that may be contained within a place of higher order. It is because our final view will admit of resource endowment discontinuities and differences, and ultimately, in fact, permit as a market area shape the hexagon or outlines of the hexagon (i.e. some irregular form of the hexagon) that we arbitrarily selected for s the value 5 in Table 11–1, rather than 6 which might have suggested our complete acceptance of the Löschian form. Incidentally, had we implicitly let each place of higher order coincide with one place of the next lower order, our $s = 5$ would, of course, be equivalent to a Löschian $s = 6$ even though only 5 lower order settlements were distinguished. The (empirical?) regularity suggested by the rank-size rule is compatible with the hierarchies of market areas suggested by Lösch. But, this also means that the model presented above is limited by Lösch's postulates, and, accordingly, as in all good theory only depicts real world relations in the mind's-eye.

Empirical Findings. In Lösch's celebrated *Southern Economic Journal* paper,[1] he recorded the similarities between the theoretical results of his system and some actual spatial relations which he found in the Mid-west region of the United States. For obvious reasons, Lösch's distribution over space appears in a more discrete grouping than that described by Beckmann. As Nourse[2] points out, statistical examinations, such as those by Singer[3] and Allen,[4] which fit the population of urban places by logarithms,[5] have not worked out well partly because of the difficulty of defining (and counting) the people in a city. The urbanized central place may be over or under estimated throughout the space, and the predictiveness of the model held to be faulty due to no shortcoming of its own.

IV. AN ECONOMIC THEORY OF THE URBAN AND REGIONAL ECONOMY

In a general sense competition for space takes place between business firms and households with each required to outbid the other in all cases except those where government regulation (e.g. zoning) may otherwise rule. In corresponding manner, competition for space takes place between the members

[1] A. Lösch, "The Nature of Economic Regions," *Southern Economic Journal* (1938), pp. 71–78.

[2] H. Nourse, *Regional Economics* (New York: McGraw Hill, 1968) p. 48.

[3] H. W. Singer, "The 'Courbe des Populations', A Parallel to Pareto's Law," *Economic Journal*, 46 (1936), pp. 254–263.

[4] G. R. Allen, "The 'Courbe des Populations' A Further Analysis," *Bulletin of the Oxford University Institute of Statistics*, 16 (1954), pp. 179–189.

[5] For example, $\log R = \log C^h - a \log C_i$, where previously used notation holds, and the superscript h indicates the next higher order of city while the subscript i refers to any particular order of city.

of each sector. Thus the rental cost imposed on one sector by the other sector may not serve as the full rental cost required of the purchaser of the space. Rather, the *rental* cost to the user may include the intra-industry *differential* payment which has long been recognized as a cost (albeit called the noncost outlay case in classical formulations before the natural rent concept was fully developed). A theory of the urban economy is therefore the particularized counterpart to our theory of the firm in economic space. Page limitations which defer to the essential interest (and purpose) of this book indicate, however, that only the outlines of a theory of the urban economy can (and should be) presented here.

The Outline of the Theory

We have derived the thesis that different size firms (single and multi-plant firms) will be found scattered over an economic space in the long run. Corresponding part of our theory was the thesis that uneven resource endowment combined with a limited number of most efficient entrepreneurs available to any one industry would cause different cost levels (and efficiencies) to obtain prior to imputations of differential rents. Between industries, risk and uncertainty differentials would also exist, warranting in their turn a payment which defers to the differential hazards of engaging in economic activity. All firms which survive in the long run would maximize their own rents (profits), i.e. be efficient *vis-à-vis* those which fail, and, in the process, earn the maximum rent (profit) to which they are entitled. Opportunity costs are thus covered in full in the long run. Firms (and individuals) with greatest needs (and income) can pay the highest land rents, *ceteris paribus*.

Some Details of Urban-Regional Microeconomic Theory

A simple extension of the theory of the firm in economic space applies to the urban economy and the regional landscape. The differential payments earned by the individuals who own the firm may enable them to outbid others for land as, all other things equal, the greater the individual's income the greater is his ability to acquire goods which provide him with utility. Only in the short run do business establishments possess similar advantage with respect to competing for land against other business units. In the long run, rental imputations for skills, risk, and uncertainty have been made, and businesses can compete successfully for a particular space *vis-à-vis* other business units only to the extent that a particular property (or resource endowment) enables the firm to offer a greater rent for the space than may other firms. Because monopoly and quasi rents *are*, however, *obtainable* in the short run, some firms not only may compete successfully for space compared to other firms— apart from product and technological requirements—but may capture some of the accoutrements yielded by the space for themselves (again, as a monopoly rent or quasi rent, as the case be).

Besides governmental, environmental, and geological differences, it is *essentially* because of (1) the competition for space which prevails among individuals, and among individuals and firms, and (2) the varying short-run advantages from region to region of some firms in a given industry over other firms in the same industry that differences in urban places arise. But even over and above intra-industry differences from place to place, item (1) above would alone promote differences in size and value of residences as well as of size of residential and industrial areas from city to city. The short run intra-industry variations in rents (and windfalls) in turn add on to (3) the inter-industry differences in requirements of space to produce significant variations in urban landscapes from region to region. Still more fundamentally, if the above-mentioned forces could be abstracted except for attention being centered on the variation in size of trading areas among firms, and industries, it becomes clear that whereas firm A of industry A may often locate its plant next door to (or nearby) a plant of firm B of industry B, there will be places where only the one plant of the one firm will be found. Simply put, we may expect the trading areas of the plants of one industry to be somewhat different in size than the other. The number of individual plant units over the landscape is partially a function of the technology, the general cost conditions, and the distribution of demand over the economic space.

Notwithstanding the natural economic forces which generate intra-urban differences, a basic (systematic) regularity applies over the landscape. Competition for land reflects the opportunity costs of potential users of the land, and considering all business and household units together, it is clear that those units which have the greater "rental income" will, *ceteris paribus*, compete successfully in the short run for a given space. Short-run patterns established, selected long-run advantages (e.g. agglomerating advantages) arise which often enable some cities to develop a greater intra-industry localization than is elsewhere the pattern in the industry. By including governmental, environmental, and geological differences—to say nothing of foreign government entanglements and geographical variations *etc.*—the full complex of forces accounting for intra- and inter-urban variations is at hand. *But* urban and regional microeconomic theory is, nevertheless, predictive, at least in the same sense as is all of microeconomic theory. What type of regulations should be applied to the urban-regional landscape, what impacts do excise and property taxes have, and similar questions, all involve the same tools of analysis as in the classical set of micro-economic problems. The prices, profits, rents, economic orderliness, and equilibrium properties, as well as the differences which underscore (the theory of) firms in economic space, are of analogous order to what a detailed development of urban and regional economic theory would reveal. Why one city more than others evidences a concentric zone development rather than a wedge, sector, or multi-nuclei type of development is a question which involves essentially the same forces and tools of analysis as do other questions in microeconomic theory. The task of the urban and regional economist is therefore in many ways essentially descriptive, for analytically he must simply borrow the tools of general microeconomic theory in order to explain what happened in the past, what could happen if . . . , and what future modifications appear to be desirable under selected value judgements.

V. FINAL ASPECTS OF URBAN AND REGIONAL ECONOMIC THEORY—CONCLUSIONS AND SUMMARY

The rental function of Figure 11–4, when extended to include all alternatives, must reflect rather closely the idea of substitution between land rents and transportation costs. A competition for space arises between firms and individuals which yields differences from city to city and region to region. Moreover, uneven distribution of resources, topographical discontinuities, and, in addition, boundary limits for cities based on political differences eventuate in an "into" not "one to one" mapping of land rents and transportation. Thus, for example, carrier basing lines alone may yield discrete, not perfectly continuous, relations between land rents and distance. In fact, smog, riots, insurance costs, traffic congestions, taxes, indivisibilities (terminal costs, etc.), and other natural and institutional forces lead to a broken type of rental function over space. Because institutional forces do not remain steady, we would even find a continuous shifting in land uses as well as varying gradients of land rents with respect to distances. We could, indeed, expect that the cities and suburban landscape would yield a picture like that shown between points 0 and K_8 in Figure 11–9. In turn, between cities of higher and lower orders, the entire landscape from 0 to K_{12} would, in general, obtain. The intensity of land use in the inner core compared with the extensive use of land on the outskirts is well indicated in studies of the city,[1] apart from being evident to the casual observer.

The theory presented here thus suggests that the economic region is bounded by the largest effective trading area of the (oftentimes largest) firm (or city). But note, because the largest trading area of a firm and the effective radius of the city may not be identical, distinction between regions may (and should) be made depending upon the objective of the research. A slightly different specification of the region, namely on the basis of the highest order city, may be advantageous to economists interested in urban economics. Or, again, in more general formulation, the choice between defining the economic

---

[1] For example, see E. M. Hoover and R. Vernon, *Anatomy of a Metropolis* (Cambridge, Harvard University Press, 1959). Also see, W. R. Thompson, *A Preface to Urban Economics* (Baltimore: The Johns Hopkins Press, 1965), esp. Chapter 10.

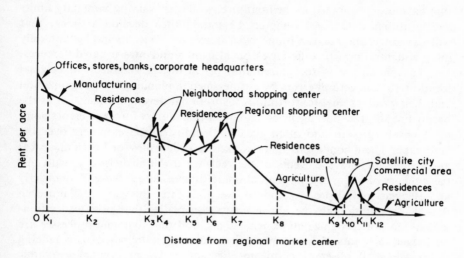

Figure 11–9: Reproduced from H. Nourse, *Regional Economics* (N.Y.: McGraw Hill, 1968), p. 120

region by the largest firm and city, or on some other basis, such as factor analysis,[1] must depend on the particular focus of the researcher. From our standpoint, it is the particular firm and the particular industry that matters most in the long-run equilibrium theory presented herein. Whether located in a high or low order place or in identical manner in each region is superfluous to us. Our main concern is to propose a general theory which points to forces that prevail in different degrees in each market area, the main requirement being that they produce the same final profit-making result.[2] When this is so, we can delineate the equilibrium market areas that typically arise among the firms in a given industry *vis-à-vis* other industries, and we shall do this in part of Chapter 12. The appendix at the end of the present chapter is also along these lines, although its principal focus is on some fine points of central place theory. In the appendix to this chapter we shall discuss different types of cities

[1] M. Megee, "On Economic Growth and the Factor Analysis Method," *The Southern Economic Journal*, pp. 215–228, 1965; and B. Olsen and G. Garb, "A Factor Analysis of Characteristics of the South," in *Essays in Southern Economic Development* (Chapel Hill, UNC Press, 1963), pp. 293–319, eds. M. L. Greenhut and W. T. Whitman.

[2] Empirical findings of this writer indicate, in fact, that though some firms and industries may tend to localize, a dispersion (and differences over the landscape) nevertheless will obtain in each case. See, for example, M. L. Greenhut "An Empirical Model and a Survey," *Review of Economics and Statistics*, XLI (November 1959), pp. 433–38 and M. L. Greenhut and M. R. Colberg, *Location of Florida Industry* (Tallahassee: FSU Studies 36, 1962). Also see, P. Sargent Florence, *Investment Location and Size of Plant* (Cambridge, England, Cambridge University Press, 1949). The diverse studies by others on localization coefficients point to similar results: e.g., see H. Nourse, *op. cit.*, pp. 64–66.

that have been examined in the literature, with their varying boundary limits and locational differences. Chapters 12 and 13 then develop a theory that will explain economic variations over space *and time*, including not only inter- and intra-industry differences, but also inter- and intra-urban differences.

To sum up: it is recognized that (a) historical "chance" in original location, (b) conjectural errors by businessmen in planning their organization and their product mix, (c) fortuitous institutional developments, such as the basing lines of transport agencies, and other momentary forces or errors point to stochastic growth and often accidental industrial development over the landscape. These conditions make rank, size order rules (or Löschian space) an extreme limit to the events of the real world. Nevertheless, as with our basic theory of oligopoly, we shall ultimately claim the existence of an orderly and efficient spatial process. Indeed, we shall enter this general claim even though, in addition to the above errors, we realize that private decision-makers do not recognize all external signs, and that dynamic processes are misjudged (or wants of the future are ignored or not anticipated). A balancing force—we shall observe—permeates the space. Given political-economic wisdom, and given a people sufficiently industrious and capable of anticipating the future, the micro (and macro) path actually pursued by the economy, as it moves towards the long-run equilibrium, will be understood to be one of the highest paths available to the people. The spatial equilibrium properties of the system will then be seen to prevail in the same general pattern (i.e. subject to the same limitations and errors) as are the efficiency-consumer want-satisfying properties of the classical spaceless economic market. Indeed, because of resource and cultural differences over the nation's landscape, and, in turn, because of the possibility that risk and uncertainty may differ from market area to market area, in what otherwise would appear to be the same industry, not only will we actually find plant-size variations within a firm, and plant- and firm-size variations among sellers of similar products, but the market area size of firms (and cities) will differ. In turn, from one economic region to another, variation in rank-size rules, number of orders, *etc.*, also must prevail in practice.

Appendix to Chapter 11
The Urban Setting

To understand urban economic problems one must also understand the factors which explain the location of economic activity. By analyzing these factors one can anticipate, plan for, and control the location of new economic activities within and outside the central place. We shall in this appendix *sketch* selected aspects of location theory which will help us to understand the urban economy. But the appendix is only included for those readers interested in probing deeper into urban-location theory. Others may turn directly to pp. 261ff. for the main gist of what we have to say here, or may omit the appendix entirely. In Chapter 12, we shall go into general location theory, which is fundamental to our theory of the firm in economic space.

I. THE CITY: AN AGGREGATIVE VIEW OF URBAN-LOCATION THEORY

Walter Christaller published his central place theory in 1931.[1] This theory was designed to explain the location of cities, their sizes, and their distributions. However, Christaller was not the first urban economist to recognize the connection between spatial patternings and urban location. In the 1880's Kohls attempted a theory to explain the size and distribution of cities and transportation networks. Later, in 1916, Sombart[2] wrote that the size of a town was related to the "surplus production of its supporting region," while Bobeck,[3] in 1938, wrote of the importance of the "additional product" and the "additional demand" generated by the region in determining the actual size of the urban center. Though early urban model builders favored a scientific theory of urban growth which would not deviate too far from reality, Hassert[4] asserted that nature was too diverse for schematizing, generalizing, and model building.

Central Place Theory

Christaller's work has served as the basis for most of the recent theoretical works on the urban center. Others following in this line of thought in the 1940's were, as we have seen, August Lösch,[5] who formularized some of Christaller's ideas, by providing them with mathematical representation and sophistication, and E. Ullman,[6] who recorded Christaller's contributions in English. Empirical studies along this line were also presented in the 1950's by Berry and Garrison.[7] These scholars expanded some of Christaller's major ideas about hierarchies and shapes of networks. In turn, Hoover[8]—through his concept of margin lines—emphasized what Christaller referred to as the range of a good, while Reilly[9] contributed to central place theory by adding the idea of trade area limits to the urban center following Christaller's work.

Central place theory seeks to explain the hierarchies of marketing, transport,

[1] W. Christaller, *Die Zentralen Orte in Süddentschland* (Jena: Gustav Fischer, 1933).

[2] W. D. Sombart, *Der Moderne Kapitalismus*, V, I (München and Leipzig, n.p. 1916).

[3] H. Bobeck, "Uber einige funktionelle Stadttypen und ihre Beziehungen zum Lande," *Comptes rendus de congres international de geographie* (Amsterdam, 1938), 2, pp. 88–102.

[4] K. Hassert, *Die Stadt Georgraphisch betrachtet* (Leipzig: n.p. 1907).

[5] A. Lösch, *Die räumliche Ordnung der Wirtschaft* (Jena: Gustav Fischer, 1944).

[6] E. Ullman, "A Theory of Location for Cities," *American Journal of Sociology*, V, 46, 1941, pp. 853–864.

[7] B. J. L. Berry and W. L. Garrison "Recent Developments of a Central Place Theory," *Papers and Proceedings of the Regional Science Association* 4 (1958), pp. 107–120, and see their "A Note on Central Place Theory and the Range of a Good," *Economic Geography*, V, 1958, pp. 304–311.

[8] E. M. Hoover, *Location Theory and the Shoe and Leather Industries* (Cambridge: Harvard University Press, 1937), pp, 12–23.

[9] W. J. Reilly, *The Law of Retail Gravitations* (New York: Pilsbury Publishing Inc., 1953).

and administration networks found in urban areas.[1] Essentially, the theory begins with space and population—the geographic and demographic variables which serve respectively as the source and object of production. The theory stems from the conception in the physical sciences of the crystallization of mass around a center. This elementary form is of centralistic order. And if such order can describe human cells and inorganic matter, it could well describe social behavior, such as the ordering of settlements, and its impact on spatial agglomeration patterns. That the location of all urban settlements exhibits systems of concentration and dispersion, much in the pattern of the human cell, is broadly evident in the world around us.

The Ideal Urban System. The ideal urban system, conceived by Christaller and extended by Lösch, with its visual appearance of an hierarchy of inter-connecting, hexagonally-shaped complementary regions and settlements, is shown in Figure 11A-1. Here the hexagon constitutes the ideal equilibrium form; moreover, it suggests the minimum number of central places necessary to serve a given area, with no place lying outside the system. Squares and triangles, as mentioned in our discussion of Lösch's spatial equilibrium theory, fail to maximize demand as they increase the transport mileage from the central place to the outlying districts, while other polygonic shapes create voids or gaps; specifically, such regions as the circle do not account for interstitial areas.

In reality, it seems that no particular shape uniformly characterizes a trade area and its trading center. For while six lines of traffic might be economic in an equilibrium system of central places, a layout of six converging traffic lines will result only if there are six distant places each of such importance as to necessitate a transportation line between a given center and its neighbors. The transport facility, then, plays an important role in the theoretical framework, being the ultimate mover of goods and services. And this is what one might have expected, since the root of location economics lies in the vital matter of transportation—or distance if you prefer.

Other Aspects of Central Place Theory. Christaller derived his ideas deductively from empirical studies involving the analysis of such data as those obtained from physicians and from the records of the installations of telephones in southern Germany. He recognized a system consisting of ten orders of settlements, which he classified according to the centrality of the settlement. The population size, order, kind, and number of *central goods*, as well as the number of *central places* of smaller sizes included in the overall trading area of a given center, were fundamental parts of his system. Smaller places, he suggested, tended to have small surrounding regions, while large places offered a greater number and variety of goods, having larger trading areas. Within the large place one finds numerous smaller places and smaller sales areas. As the larger places grow, they attract a greater number and variety of commerce. The presence of a larger market allows for the development of more specialized retailing, as well as personal services and general facilities. Moreover, a larger sales area enables the central place to expand to include previously nonexisting kinds of economic performances. Large places also tend to become a

[1] More generally, see E. Smykay, D. Bowersox, and F. Mossman, *Physical Distribution Management* (New York: The Macmillan Co., 1961).

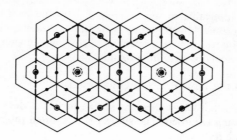

Figure 11A–1: A Hexagonal Network: Two main economic regions are shown above, though others are presumed to exist outside of the figure. The dashed-lined large-size hexagon depicts the grid with the largest trading area. One finds also within the largest central place an industry which sells its wares over the continuous dark-lined hexagon. The industry within the smallest hexagon is also found in the largest central city shown above.

tourist, a financial, a wholesale, and/or administrative center, besides quite often being the center of a manufacturing complex. Cumulative-like growth occurs over time.

Urban economists such as Christaller often theorize that, in the last analysis, it is not the functional attributes but rather the geographic relationships which determine the existence of a discrete system of central places. And because industrial and administrative centers are more than just agglomerations of people, such that, for example, the smallest county seat may offer more centralized social and political functions than a large residential community, he concludes that size of population is an insufficient guide to the functional performance of the city, being less important than the geographic factor in accounting for the number of independent "central" places. But though we recognize that utility maximization differs slightly from profit maximization, our theory of economic decision-making may readily be extended to include household choices. Such conception complements the geographic approach.

Under uncertainty, what some writers would call personal considerations actually merge with pecuniary values so that the two are inseparable. Economic men—in the broad sense—are utility maximizers. Indeed, subjectively rooted estimations of one's energies and one's economic lifetime are fundamental in determining real opportunity costs in the economic universe. Our theory, therefore, rules out only one extreme kind of personal (or psychic income) motivation: namely, the *motivation* that is so unique to an individual that it is virtually certain his firm would be replaced in the long run; let us say, the firm he manages (or owns) will not prove viable as psychic incomes do not offset economic losses in the long run.

It is, however, noteworthy that even though the profit maximizing theory of the firm excludes purely psychic income seekers while utility maximizing theory does not, the general analysis and theory of this book could easily be recast to include noneconomic relations. In developing a theory of the central place, one may "loosely" substitute pure utility maximization for our form of profit maximizing under conditions of uncertainty. This substitution would mean that when purely personal psychic income is applicable to the individual, it would be given a dollar value commensurate with some "given" utility scale; in turn, subtracting this value from what would otherwise be too high a schedule of costs would yield the representative "individual" in the social system under study.

Central Places and the Law of Retail Gravitation

About the same time that Christaller was setting forth his views, "the law of retail gravitation" was being recorded. The subject thesis, often referred to as a gravity model, stipulates the following:

Two cities attract retail trade from any intermediate city or town approximately in direct proportion to the population in the two cities and in inverse proportion to the square of the distances from these two cities to the intermediate town.[1] This statement can be expressed mathematically as follows:

$B_A/B_B = (P_A/P_B)/(D_B/D_A)^2$, where B_A is the proportion of retail trade from the intermediate town attracted by city A, B_B is the proportion attracted by city B, P_A is the population of city A, P_B is the population of city B, D_A is the distance from the intermediate town to city A, and D_B is the distance from the intermediate town to city B.

A second formula, known as the "breaking point" formula, is useful in estimating the range of a good, or the extent of the retail influence of a given center. It is expressed mathematically as:

$$D_B = \frac{D_{(A \to B)}}{1 + \sqrt{P_A P_B}},$$ where $D_{(A \to B)}$ is the distance from A to B and D_B gives the

breaking point distance of retailing for city B compared with city A.

It is possible to convert this model into a small multiple regression model, where the breaking point of retail trade between two cities is taken as the dependent variable. But this and other extensions are only of tangential interest to us and should be left to other writings. As we observed in Chapter 11, precise formulas of this kind can at best be tenuous approximations to reality.

The Central Place in Gravity Models

A number of empirical studies have utilized the gravity or potential model in studying problems of economic development. These models use formulas of the kind $V = P_j/d_{ij}$. They join with many of the studies noted above in Chapters 10 and 11 in making the theories of urban development an intrinsic part of the subject of the locational efficiency of the central place.[2] In the subject studies, mass has been measured in terms of a number of indices: population numbers, employment, income, volume of retail sales, the number of establishments, number of families, capital investments, car registrations, commodity output, and value added by manufacture—depending on the problem to be studied, the data available, and related considerations. Similarly, distance has been (and can be) measured in a

[1] W. J. Reilly, *op. cit.*, p. 7, and for further details on the Reilly Model, see R. Murphy, *The American City* (New York: McGraw-Hill, 1966) pp. 60–64 or F. Mossman and N. Morton, *Logistics of Distribution Systems* (Boston: Allyn and Bacon, 1965), pp. 231–235.

[2] W. Isard, *Location and Space Economy* (New York and Cambridge: John Wiley and Sons and the Technology Press of MIT, 1956).

variety of ways, such as physically along a straight line in terms of miles, or in terms of transport cost (*economic distance*), the latter being especially useful if industrial location is being analyzed. Exponents other than unity may be used; for example, if the value d^2 (or more generally, d^n) appears to be applicable, it could be used.

In addition to the important studies which apply the gravity model to the analysis of location, transport distances, and the size of administrative areas, there are many other studies which offer comparable hypotheses, yet significantly different formulations. Some of the more important have dealt with spatial prices. For example, Warntz[1] reasoned that the supply and demand approach of traditional economics requires refinement in terms of a spatial continuum. He studied price variations over a space which, for practical purposes, may be considered as continuous. He considered demand and supply to be spatially continuous variables, and he derived a product-supply space potential for each of a set of commodities whose spatial variation he explained statistically. He thus introduced an economic variable into the study of the geography of prices. More specifically, Warntz posed the hypothesis that the price of a good "h" in region V is directly proportional to the demand for it and inversely related to its supply. He tested his hypothesis, and presented it by maps showing the supply potentials for the same good. He substituted general income potentials on the implicit assumption that demand increases with income. His statistical tests via regression analysis yielded less than fully encouraging results. But, in any case, an interesting avenue of spatial relations was opened up for examination. (See Figure 11A–2.)

II. THE URBAN CENTER: CONCLUSION

From Christaller to Reilly through Isard, Harris, Chinitz,[2] Perloff,[3] Thompson[4] and others, the conception has been derived of a central place originally formed because of selected resource advantages. It is clear that climate as well as topography comprise basic parts of the resource advantages of different places—especially in early times or in underdeveloped areas. And so a city develops, grows and spreads, with some cities, given their kind of resource advantages, developing into financial and service centers and others emphasizing manufacturing activity. Because some are built along waterways, others on islands, while still others are land locked, the micro components described in Chapter 10 tend to vary from central place to central place.[5] Even the macro extension of the theory which is characterized by different size central places and hence different size trading areas for the urban mass must speak in terms of varying "possibilities". Thus the trading area for the urban mass—in the form of a large or small hexagon, or even some irregular polygon—will

[1] W. Warntz, "Geography of Prices and Spatial Interaction," *Papers and Proceedings of the Regional Science Association* V, 3, 1957.

[2] B. Chinitz, "Contrasts in Agglomeration: New York and Pittsburgh," *American Economic Review*, 51, 1961, pp. 279–289.

[3] H. Perloff, *et al.*, *Regions, Resources, and Economic Growth* (Baltimore: Johns Hopkins Press, 1960), e.g., pp. 419–420.

[4] W. R. Thompson, *A Preface to Urban Economics* (Baltimore: Johns Hopkins Press, 1965).

[5] R. Muth, "Urban Residential and Housing Markets" in *Issues in Urban Economics* (Baltimore, Johns Hopkins Press, 1968) (eds. H. Perloff and L. Wingo, Jr.), pp. 285–333.

vary from place to place, as the superstructure of activities formed in any city must be linked with the resource advantages and specializations which prevail at any one time.

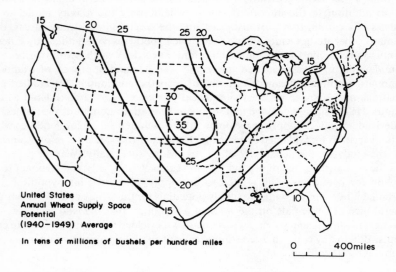

Figure 11A–2: Warntz Space Potential Map. From William Warntz, "Geography of Prices and Spatial Interaction," *Papers and Proceedings of the Regional Science Association*, V, 3, 1957, p. 122.

Agglomerations and deglomerations marking industrial activity also help define the central place. The related polygon forms must interact with the social and psychological peculiarities of individuals and groups, inducing some people to move toward the central place while others stay far from it. Where important wants cannot be satisfied because the consumer is too distant from the supplier, either new sources of supply must arise or the consumer must relocate himself. Over time a merging of needs, abilities, and capabilities must obtain. And the central place must expand or contract as new wants and resources appear.

Let us say that the growth and decline over time of cities and towns reflect the growth in the primary, secondary, and tertiary sectors allocable to the city.[1] In turn, this growth reflects the resource and want base of the region, a base which in its own right will influence and be influenced by the social and psychological habits of the inhabitants of the area. Central places, therefore, vary at different times, with different patterns of places being identifiable. Nevertheless, we shall shortly discover that there is always a tendency toward spatial economic efficiency, seen from both the inter-intra *urban* views presented in this and the preceding chapter, and the entire intra-inter *regional economy* aspect of the following chapters. It is because of

[1] And see B. Harris, "Quantitative Models of Urban Development: Their Role in Metropolitan Policy Making," *Issues, op. cit.*, p. 394.

ideas still to be presented in this book—as well as past material about the central place itself—that we repeat our statement that divergent variances occur over space and that no two central places will (nor need) be perfectly alike. It is, of course, at this point, where we speak of imperfect identity between central places and of the related differential importance of location forces among industries, that the spatial inter-dependence side of micro location theory comes into play. Its stress on intra and inter industry dispersion as well as on the concentration of firms, each limited by profits for uncertainty and indivisibility, is vital to urban economics. It is, in other words, but a short step from Lösch's macro location spatial equilibrium system to the micro equilibrium system described earlier in the book and the spatial equili-brium system yet to be discussed. That the two location theories actually converge *in their long run view of spatial interdependence* will then be obvious.

III. A NOTE TO THE PLANNER

To understand the full limits to specific economic planning in the spatial sense, and yet, at the same time, to present the general policies of the urban-regional structure, we must turn to Chapter 12 where the details of the main trends in location theory are presented. These details will provide us not only with a picture of factor and product price efficiency over space, but they will indicate the spatial equilibrium of *all industries* (and all cities) over the entire intra and inter urban landscape. Chapter 13 will tie up the product and factor price theorems of Part II with the location theory formulated throughout Part III. For the present, we must simply observe that the gravity models (which, in effect, point out the boundary lines between cities) do not, in themselves, designate any optimality of city size, of city location, and of inter-city relations. The spatial equilibrium of the firm in economic space, already alluded to in Chapters 10 and 11, carries in itself this logical extension i.e., to the entire urban and regional mass. Our conclusions in Chapter 13, via the materials just dealt with and the more general investigations of Chapter 12, will be seen to hold true not only for the firm and its industry but, as previously proposed, for the individual and the group. Simply put, this individual unit and the aggregation of units constitute the urban and regional mass; alternatively, the theory of the firm in economic space is a theory of the form and structure of cities distributed over economic space.

12

Urban-Regional Concentration and Dispersion

IN CHAPTERS 6 AND 7 we assumed homogeneous production costs over the economic space. Similarly, our models were simplified via the assumption of linear demand. Our purpose there was simply to compare the basic (general) effect of market organization on spatial ordering. And we saw that if price competition prevails, large firms would tend to disperse more readily, while, if price is regulated, small firms only would move quickly to distant and obscure locations compared to small f.o.b. mill-pricing firms which would move even farther from a production center.

Obviously prior investigations were incomplete and a more general study of the spatial oligopoly is required. We must not only compare the willingness of firms under unorganized and organized oligopoly to locate at a distance from an established center, but we must inquire into what causes particular firms in any market to fail to economize on distance. Then we should find out whether the resulting pattern is efficient. This multiple-sided question, which stresses the spatial patterns of unorganized oligopolists, serves as the basic concern of this chapter and the next. First we shall review and develop a theory of plant location, after which we can determine the efficiency of the deduced location patterns. Though long-run locations are mentioned from time to time in this chapter, its chief focus—contrary to that of the next chapter—is the short run. Readers who already have a general knowledge of the development of location theory, or are otherwise uninterested in the early history of this theory, may turn directly to page 277ff. These last pages of the chapter, giving an overall perspective, are self-contained.

I. LOCATION THEORY: THE COST APPROACH

Interest in the theory of plant location may be attributed to three Germans: Launhardt,[1] von Thünen,[2] and Weber.[3] These men (particularly von Thünen

[1] W. Launhardt, *Mathematische Begründung der Volkswirtschaftslehre* (Leipzig: B. G. Teubner, 1885).

[2] J. H. von Thünen, *Der Isolierte Staat in Beziehung auf Landwirtschaftslehre und Nationalökonomie*, 3rd ed. (Berlin: Schumacher Zarchlin, 1875).

[3] A. Weber, *Theory of Location*, Trans. by C. J. Friedrich (Chicago: University of Chicago Press, 1928).

and Weber) set the stage for what is today referred to as the least cost theory of plant location.[1]

The Least Cost Theory of Plant Location

Of these three theorists, Launhardt is the least known in the United States; in fact, his influence on American writers is chiefly indirect for his book is not generally available in this country. Launhardt, according to many accounts,[2] explained the location of industry as being determined on the basis of two variables: differences in cost and differences in demand at alternative locations.

The second writer, von Thünen, was concerned primarily with agricultural locations. His theory, though designed to explain the type of crops that would be grown at varying distances from the market, can be applied to manufacturing locations. The location decision rests upon the differences in the cost of a given crop (commodity) at alternative sites. In turn, the cost differences are due to the land rent and the transportation expense.

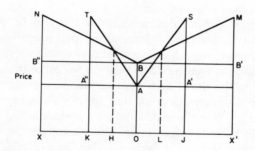

Figure 12–1: Transport Costs and von Thünen Rings

Von Thünen's theory may be illustrated simply. Assume that, in Figure 12–1, O is the consumption point, OA is the production cost of a dollar's worth of potatoes at any point in the space and A'S (A"T) is the cost of transporting the potatoes over a distance of OJ (OK) miles. OB represents the production cost at any location of a dollar's worth of wheat, and B'M

---

[1] Of course, traces of location theory may be found among many economists, including Smith, Ricardo, and Mill.

[2] T. Palander, *Beiträge zur Standortstheorie* (Uppsala: Almqvist und Wiksell Boktryckeri, a-b. 1935), pp. 139, 140, 231, 247; E. Schneider, "Bemerkungen zu einer Theorie der Raumwirtschaft," *Econometrica*, III (1935), 79–101; A. Lösch, *Die räumliche Ordnung der Wirtschaft* (Jena: Gustav Fischer, 1944) p. 6.

(B″N) represents the freight charge on wheat over a distance of OX′ (OX) miles. Clearly, the freight rate is higher on potatoes than on wheat. (Compare slopes AS and AT with slopes BM and BN.)

Von Thünen's assumption of a uniform homogeneous plain means that labor and capital are equal in unit rate and productivity at all locations and that the cost of production (exclusive of transport cost) is the same everywhere. The land rent and the cost of transporting the goods therefore become the effective codeterminants of location. The producers of potatoes will be found in the OL (OH) region, while wheat will be grown in the LX′ (HX) region.[1]

Weber's theory of location is procedurally the opposite of von Thünen's. In von Thünen's scheme, the location is given and the type of production is to be determined; in Weber's theory, the branch of industry is given and the location is sought. Von Thünen assumes a homogeneous land surface and one consumption center; Weber assumes spatially uneven deposits of fuel and other raw materials and several consumption centers. In practice, however, Weber confined his geometrical representations and general discussions to a given buying point.

Weber's approach, like von Thünen's, is from the cost angle. In his theory, the entrepreneur selects the plant site which minimizes the sum of all expenditures. The location decision thus involves finding the optimum in substitution between the factors of cost.

There are three general determinants of location in Weber's theory: transportation, labor, and the agglomerating (deglomerating) force. Transportation and labor are regarded as general regional factors; the agglomerating force is classified as a general local factor. The cost of transportation tends to draw industry to the site of least transportation expense, while the cost of labor may cause displacement from that site to one where the savings in labor cost are larger than the additional transportation cost. The decentralizing tendencies of these two factors are either counteracted or intensified by Weber's third consideration: the agglomerating force (marketing advantages, proximity to auxiliary industries, economies of scale) and its corollary, the deglomerating influence (land rent). These location determinants either draw industry closer together or disperse it, depending upon the respective strength of each force.

Weber's theory, like von Thünen's, involves substitution between transport cost and nontransport cost factors. A series of isodapanes (points of equal transport costs) are conceived to surround the minimum transfer cost point with the curve farthest away from the minimum isodapane representing

---

[1] Compare with Lösch, *op. cit.*, pp. 25–39; Palander, *op. cit.*, pp. 71–103; and E. M. Hoover, *Location Theory and the Shoe and Leather Industry* (Cambridge: Harvard University Press, 1937), pp. 30–33. And see A. H. Leigh, "von Thünen's Theory of Distribution and the Advent of Marginal Analysis," *Journal of Political Economy*, LIV (1946), 481–502. Also see von Thünen, *op. cit.*, Part 1. Note: von Thünen relaxes his assumption of equal wage payments in the third part of his treatise. This change in assumption permits consideration of the effects of varying labor costs on location.

sites of highest transfer burdens. The isodapane which exceeds the least cost transfer point by an amount equal to the maximum nontransfer cost economies obtainable at an alternative site is the critical isodapane. If the site offering lowest nontransport costs happens to lie inside the critical curve, the non-transfer cost advantage is worth more than the difference in transport costs. If it lies outside the critical isodapane, the economy in production is less than the extra transport cost that would exist.[1] Obviously, each location, when compared to other locations, has certain transfer cost advantages or disadvantages and certain nontransfer cost advantages or disadvantages.

Weber's analytical framework is that of pure competition. All buyers are assumed to be concentrated at given market centers, and each seller locates at the lowest cost site with respect to some buying point. Each seller has an unlimited market, for price is a datum and demand for the output of a firm is infinite relative to its supply. There are, therefore, no monopoly gains derived from location. Weber not only follows this type of abstraction from demand (i.e., assumes a market type in which demand does not exercise an active role in determining location), but he also disregards institutional costs, such as taxes and interest. These omissions arise from his desire to formulate a general theory of location applicable to all economic systems.[2]

Proponents of the Least Cost Theory

Weber, in particular, had great influence on plant location economics. A school of writers followed him in asserting that manufacturing locations were determined by the desire to locate at places of least cost. Some of these writers, such as Palander[3] and Hoover,[4] were interested in the size of the market area and, therefore, in a sense, were concerned with the demand factor. The majority, however, disregarded demand in the von Thünen-Weber tradition. Thus, Predöhl[5] was interested solely in developing a substitution

[1] For a discussion of contour systems, see Palander, *op. cit.*, pp. 212; Lösch, *op. cit.*, p. 12; and Hoover, *op. cit.*, pp. 32–55.

[2] Interest, insurance, taxes, climate, and management are all excluded from Weber's system because they are institutional in origin and/or because they are of such special nature that they influence only a few plant locations.

[3] *Op. cit.*; in discussing von Thünen and Weber, Palander stated (p. 221) that the mutual connection between market and location has been neglected.

[4] *Op. cit.*; in particular, see Chapter III. Also see E. M. Hoover, *Location of Economic Activity*, 1st ed. (New York: McGraw-Hill Book Co., 1948), Chapter IV.

[5] A. Predöhl, "Das Standortsproblem in der Wirtschaftstheorie," *Welt Wirtschaftliches Archiv*, V (1925), 294–321. Also see G. Cassel, *Theoretische Nationalökonomie*, 3rd ed. (Leipzig: W. Schall, 1923) pp. 83–96. For an interesting discussion along these lines, see W. Krzyzanowski, "Review of the Literature of the Location of Industries," *Journal of Political Economy*, XXXV (1927), pp. 278–291. O. Engländer, "Kritisches und Positives zu einer allgemeinen reinen Lehre vom Standort," *Zeitschrift für Volkswirtschaft und Sozialpolitik*, V (1927), 435–505. A. Predöhl, "Zur Frage einer allgemeinen Standortstheorie," *Zeitschrift für Volkswirtschaft und Sozialpolitik* V (1927), 756–763. W. Isard, "Distance Inputs and the

cost analysis. Ritschl[1] inquired into the historical changing pattern of cost and location. Linke[2] and other students of Weber attempted to explain and to measure industrial displacements from transport centers as the result of labor and agglomerative influences. Holmes and other writers discussed industries in terms of their orientation to materials, labor, market, and other cost factors;[3] Dechesnes[4] was similarly inclined.[5]

Conclusions

The significant features of the von Thünen-Weber type of theory are: (1) the emphasis on the search for the least cost site; (2) the assumption of a given demand at a particular buying point which remains unaffected by a seller's choice of location; and (3) the inherent disregard of the uncertain, gamelike locational interdependence of firms. Each of these three aspects brings out the basic limitations of this school of thought, for: (a) site selection involves substitution among not only the cost but also the demand factors of location at alternative places, (b) market demand (and the utility gained by the individual) is a variable, significantly affected by, and affecting, (c) the locational interdependence of firms (and people). We will now consider objections (b) and (c) to the von Thünen-Weber type of theory, and then we will analyze the initial complaint.

II. LOCATION THEORY: THE DEMAND APPROACH

The von Thünen-Weber theory is applicable to agricultural locations and to certain manufacturing locations, especially where small-scale manufacturers

Space Economy: Part I: The Conceptual Framework," *Quarterly Journal of Economics*, LXV (1951), 181–198.

[1] H. Ritschl, "Reine und historische Dynamik des Standortes der Erzeugungszweige," *Schmollers Jahrbuch für Gesetzgebund*, LI (1927), 813–870.

[2] A. Linke, *Die Lederindustrie (Erzeugende und Verarbeitende)* (Tübingen: n.p., 1913). See Hoover, *Location Theory and the Shoe and Leather Industry, op. cit.*, p. 119.

[3] See E. Holmes, *Plant Location*, 1st ed. (New York: McGraw-Hill Book Co., 1930). Also see the empirical type of studies of E. Hedlund, *The Transportation Economics of the Soybean Processing Industry* (Urbana: University of Illinois Press, 1952); and D. C. Hague and P. K. Newman, *Costs in Alternative Locations: The Clothing Industry*, National Institute of Economic and Social Research (London: Cambridge University Press, 1952).

[4] L. Dechesnes, *La Localization des Diverses Productions* (Brûxelles: Les Éditions Comptables, Commerciales et Financières, 1945).

[5] The cost factors described by recent writers are not identical to those considered by Weber. Weber's original interest lay in the evolution of a theory applicable to all economic systems. Other writers, such as Holmes, Hoover, Palander, and Dechesnes, stress the free enterprise economy and thereby include institutional factors within their framework. The ultimate objective of these treatises is the formulation of a system that includes all factors of location in a free enterprise economy.

sell to large wholesalers. But the increasing awareness during recent years of the limitations of the von Thünen–Weber purely competitive framework led to another approach to the problem of plant location. Under the influence of Fetter,[1] Hotelling,[2] Lerner and Singer,[3] Smithies,[4] Chamberlin,[5] and other writers, interest has centered upon locational interdependence. This conception was based on the theory of duopoly; it disregarded cost[6] and explained the location of firms as the endeavor to control the largest market area. The methodology and conclusions were in contrast with Weber's technique and findings, but the problem was essentially the same.

In Weber's framework, price is given and buyers are assumed to be concentrated at a point. Because there are no sales-price advantages offered at alternative locations away from the selected market, the location decision, in reference to a given market center, rests solely upon cost. In the Fetter-Hotelling framework, delivered price varies with location, for buyers are assumed to be scattered over an area. Each firm [subject to identical costs and quoting the same f.o.b. (net-mill) price] is able to sell to proximate buyers at delivered prices lower than those of its rivals. This industrial pattern excludes competitors from the market area surrounding a seller's plant and makes the location of each seller dependent upon the number of consumers he can monopolize. The attempt to control the largest number of buyers (largest market area) at prices yielding the greatest returns is the driving force behind orientations to spatial market areas. Under this framework, the size of the market area belonging to a firm is determined by the locational interdependence of the firms.[7]

The assumption that plant location can be determined by the attempt to control the largest market area has prompted the writers on locational interdependence to evaluate the forces which influence the conjectures of a locator as to the likely locations of his rivals. As we noted in Chapter 10, their general findings were that, even if the freight rate is significant, an inelastic demand curve over-rides the friction of distance, as duopolists would tend to locate at the center of the market; simply put, economizing on freight costs is un-

[1] F. Fetter, "The Economic Law of Market Areas," *Quarterly Journal of Economics*, XXXVIII (1924), pp. 520–529.

[2] H. Hotelling, "Stability in Competition," *Economic Journal*, XXXIX (1929), pp. 41–57.

[3] A. P. Lerner and H. W. Singer, "Some Notes on Duopoly and Spatial Competition," *Journal of Political Economy*, XLV (1937), pp. 445–486.

[4] A. F. Smithies, "Optimum Location in Spatial Competition," *Journal of Political Economy*, XLIX (1941), pp. 423–439.

[5] E. H. Chamberlin, *The Theory of Monopolistic Competition*, 5th ed. (Cambridge: Harvard University Press, 1946), Appendix C.

[6] These theories assumed that the costs of procuring and processing raw materials were equal at all locations.

[7] Each seller becomes a locational monopolist when consumers are scattered and firms practice f.o.b. selling. In Weber's system, as in perfect competition, sellers compete actively for the same market.

necessary under infinitely inelastic demand. On the other hand, a very elastic function would disperse industry.

Locational interdependence is much more complicated than these simple rules suggest. It requires a detailed appraisal of the influence on site selection of (1) the basic character of the demand curve, (2) the nature of the marginal cost curves, and (3) the height of the freight rate. These factors influence the hypotheses which entrepreneurs accept about their rivals' location policies; along with other factors, such as the industry's history of competition in location, they determine the degree of dispersion when conditions of sale are competitive (in the classical sense) except for space and the number of competitors. We shall evaluate the impact of these forces on theory in the following chapter. For the present, we require only the final conclusions of the model presented there.

Locational Interdependence Forces in an Unorganized Duopoly Market: A Descriptive Statement

(1) When demand is concave upward (i.e. from a position above the curve), the impact of distance on delivered price will be shown to be greater than when demand is linear or convex from above. There is then less doubt as to whether one's rival will seek to economize on distance, for obviously the market extremities may not be serviceable from a central (very distant) site; the firms, accordingly, will tend to disperse (away from the market center), and so economize on distance.

(2) When demand is convex upwards, delivered price over any distance from a seller will be found to be less than it would be if demand is linear or concave upward. It is doubtful, therefore, whether one's rival will necessarily seek to economize on distance. The cost of shipment added to price does not preclude a firm from selling to distant points as readily in this case as in others. Thus location at the central site *may* be selected by a rival, and, if so, the other duopolist will have been proven to be foolhardy if he moved to a site somewhere off center. Uncertainty as to the need for economizing on distance, *ceteris paribus* is great in this case, and the duopolists would therefore tend to localize.

(3) When demand is linear and negative in slope, the curve *per se* does not dominate in any significant way at all the overall conception as to which type of site(s) would maximize profits. In a broad sense, the demand curve is neutral, and other forces will be more likely to control the actual location.

(4) We shall show later that a rising marginal cost curve in a space economy will lead to relatively low delivered prices, compared to the situation of constant marginal costs, or declining (long-run) marginal costs. Localization of firms may well result.

(5) Declining marginal costs in the long run—in effect high level costs today—will be shown to induce a firm to expect an attempt by its rival to

economize on distance. Options on land distant from the market center, and, in fact, purchase thereof could well be foreseen in this case.

(6) Constant marginal costs have a neutral effect on any duopolist's conjecture as to the likely behavior of his rival. Other forces are likely to dominate the move away from or towards the market center.

(7) The freight rate itself plays a role in locational patterns along with diverse other forces mentioned later in this chapter and evaluated in Chapter 13. It should suffice for the present simply to say that the higher the freight rate, the greater will be the dispersion of firms *ceteris paribus* and *vice versa*.

Locational Interdependence Forces in an Unorganized Oligopoly Market: A Descriptive Statement

Differing opinions have been expressed concerning the location of three or more firms under inelastic demand. Hotelling[1] offers the view that the sellers would locate at the center of the market. This thesis, however, has only slight merit under game theory; and while it is possible that firms would concentrate, we shall find in Chapter 13 that the probabilities of the situation suggest *some* immediate dispersion.

Indeed, once the assumption of an infinitely inelastic demand curve is dropped, it becomes apparent that the firms will disperse in a more ideal way. Their locations will follow the limitations set by a finite demand. And if, in fact, in addition to demand elasticity, the cost of transport and the marginal costs of production are assumed to be high, the scattering of firms will proceed even more quickly in closer conformity with the location of buyers. Each firm, especially if it is establishing a branch plant in a new market area, would be induced to announce its plans for a location away from the center without waiting to play cat and mouse with its rival.

Conclusions on Locational Interdependence and the Unorganized Complex Market. While economists generally have postulated equal production costs at alternative locations, the above analysis can be broadened to include the case of divergent production costs. However, this type of model will be considered more usefully later, so we shall at present simply sum up the main findings of locational interdependence theory and nothing more.

Locational interdependence theory points to the following main conclusions: (1) The tendency to disperse depends upon the height of the freight costs, the elasticity of the demand function, and the characteristics (slopes) of the marginal costs. These factors, along with historical practice, determine the degree of competition in location. (2) Each seller seeks to control the largest market area, and his choice of location is determined by the type of interdependence between sellers and rivals that exists in the industry. (3) Each

[1] *Op. cit.*

seller becomes a spatial monopolist when sellers and buyers are separated geographically from rivals and when the selling industry uses the nondiscriminatory, f.o.b. mill-price system. (4) Effective demand varies at alternative sites because of freight costs and the location of rivals. (5) The basic theory is designed mainly for manufacturing plant location where raw materials and labor skills are fairly ubiquitous and where demand is the vital variable factor within the control of the firm. The overall theory is probably also highly relevant for locations of functional middlemen and those of certain specialty good wholesalers and retailers. In fact the individual who derives his satisfactions (religious, social, climatic—including amount of space and air— entertainment, etc.) over an area is in a position very similar to that of the firm. Like the business establishment, he jockeys for the right location within a landscape of diverse costs and utilities. (6) Three or more firms do not locate exactly the same as do two. All other things being equal,[1] the force of dispersion becomes stronger as the number of firms increases. As the firm locates, so too does the individual in a broad sense. As the firms and individuals locate, so does the city.

Locational Interdependence and the Organized Complex Market

In order to recognize how the described forces affect location under organized oligopoly, we should realize that the "number" of base points is determined by the different conditions just mentioned. At the same time and by way of further model building, note that the size of the freight rate determines the significance of the gains from phantom freight. If these gains are large, firms may no longer desire a great volume of sales and accept instead a position which gives them a high unit profit and low volume sales at distant sites. They may even establish multiple branch plants and scatter them over the market area. The organized oligopoly practice of no price competition actually may be viewed in reverse by visualizing the distance economizing factor when a downtown department store establishes an uptown "exclusive" branch in a high-priced district of the city. The greater the "freight rate" (or cost of distance), the greater the tendency to establish such a branch.

As a final observation, consider the limitation of the theory of locational interdependence. By design, it abstracts from procurement and production costs in much the same way as the least cost theory abstracts from demand. It is, therefore, only a one-sided theory which presents a special type of explanation of the underlying forces of location in space. In the following section, we will attempt to avoid specialization in assumptions. We will treat cost and demand as fully variable factors governing the selection of sites and, in the

---

[1] An example of inclusion in the *ceteris paribus* assumption is the type of produce being sold, shopping good or convenience good.

process, we will uncover the intense uncertainty that develops over rival strategies.[1]

III. THE THEORY OF THE MAXIMUM PROFIT PLANT LOCATION

Although it is difficult to predict his ultimate influence on theory, August Lösch reached the core of the "location" problem in his book, *Die räumliche Ordnung der Wirtschaft*.[2] From Lösch, perhaps more than from any other writer, the theory may be advanced that the location of a manufacturing plant depends upon its production costs at alternative locations and the market area it is able to control from each site. However, while Lösch explicitly recognized variability in costs and demand at alternative locations, and emphasized long-run competitive adjustments in location which minimize freight cost, he did not combine in his analysis an investigation of cost with an appraisal of locational interdependence. In fact, Lösch really gave only lip service to the cost factor of location, largely disregarding it in his basic model by assuming a homogeneous land surface. He was not, in fact, concerned with the principles of interdependence described above. Let us briefly review his theory of location in the following paragraph.

In the long run, each firm sells over a hexagonic market area, for this shape minimizes the total distance from its center to all points within the market area.[3] Because the trading area of each firm is in the form of a hexagon, a system of hexagons (all firms and industries) exists. When rotated around a common center, this system creates a plain (or surface) marked by six sectors that are relatively open (barren) and six sectors dotted by concentrations of individuals and industries (full). The gains from this pattern lie in the inter-industry and inter-consumer advantages of agglomeration. In turn, within given industries, the entrepreneurial scattering (and hexagonic market area) maximize the total effective demand for each product. Thus, in Lösch's theory, the agglomerating cost factor promotes inter-industry concentration, but the demand factor leads to a honeycomb type of dispersion of firms within an industry.

Although highly informative, Lösch's postulation that attempts to

[1] In the forthcoming sections, we will see more clearly why space and uncertainty go hand in hand.

[2] (Jena: Gustav Fischer 1944), Chapters 1–15. To look at the point of lowest cost is as wrong as looking for the point of highest sales. "Jede solcher einseitige Orientierung ist falsch. Richtig ist allein die Suche nach dem Ort Grössten Gewinns" (p. 19).

[3] In generalizing his picture of the ideal size and number of firms, W. A. Lewis, "Competition in Retail Trade," *Economica*, XII (1945), pp. 202–234, deduces the hexagon as the market area that yields the ideal stable equilibrium. For a demonstration of, and specification of, the size of the hexagon yielding this equilibrium, see pp. 205–206 of Lewis' article.

maximize effective demand lead to a hexagonic type of intra-industry dispersion of firms is, for several salient reasons, clearly inadequate as a general explanation of plant location in a private capitalistic economy. (1) He ignores cost differentials other than those attributable to advantages of agglomeration and transportation; (2) he fails to carry to its real-world result the full impact of agglomerating advantages on the locations of firms belonging to a given industry; (3) he consequently does not combine an analysis of cost and demand factors in one model; and, thus, (4) he disregards the uncertainty forces which cause extraordinary concentrations of homogeneous business units. We shall first investigate the third complaint by presenting a model in which both cost and demand are treated as variables at all locations. The other criticisms will be taken up later in this chapter, along with the question of whether past and present location theory adequately explains site selections in a free enterprise or a highly regulated economic society. (In Chapter 13, we shall return to selected details of Lösch's theory of location.)

Cost and Demand

Suppose that location B (Figure 12–2 at the center of the market) is the least cost position and that other sites entail greater procurement and production charges. Where will firm A locate?

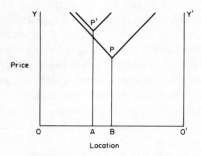

Figure 12–2: One Feasible Location

If the costs of production and procurement at locations other than B exceed transportation savings from these sites to any buyer, no location other than B is feasible, as shown in Figure 12–2 where the BP and AP′ stems include equal markups above cost. As a general rule, then, where P_b (price of B) plus T_b (transportation cost from B to any buyer's site) is less than P_a plus T_a, the firms must locate at B.

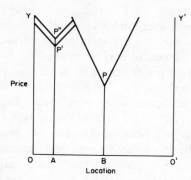

Figure 12–3: Alternative Location

If the procurement and production costs are significantly larger at other locations but there is an untapped segment of the market which can be supplied most economically by a nearby plant, a location at A in Figure 12–3 is feasible. The firm may even charge a higher markup above cost so as to extend stem AP′ to AP″. The choice of a high cost location because of such a market segment is generally made by a small-sized plant.[1] An owner who plans a large-scale enterprise must compete actively at or near B in order to attain the maximum profit objective (see Figure 12–4).

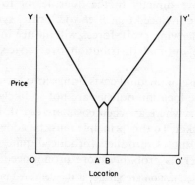

Figure 12–4: The Impact of Uncertainty on Location

[1] Ritschl, *op. cit.*, pp. 813, 829, 848, 870. Very distant sellers can exist even though they have higher production costs and a smaller sales radius, for the freight rate protects these firms.

Assuming equal costs and linear or concave upwards demand, quartile positions may be expected to result initially, and, in the long run, if one of two firms assumes any price or location it adopts will be automatically followed by its rival. However, if costs are not identical at all locations, the short-run quartile movement, in particular, may not take place. The determining factors are the sales, the net-mill prices, the costs at the two locations, and the hypotheses accepted by the locators.[1] Significantly imperfect knowledge of each other's costs arises when costs differ over space. The combination of the above factors introduces a special element that must be considered in theory.

The essential difference between the cases of equal and unequal cost is the element of extra doubt. Although past performances may have reflected quasi-monopolistic location policies, the future might suggest opposite inclinations. Quasi-monopolistic location practices are based upon economic advantages gained by firms which expect the site-selection of rivals to be perfectly conceived. But B, if convinced he could lose more at the quartile location, may choose greater competition by location in the center of this particular market. This conviction would be based on the belief that the high costs at the quartile or other locations *may not be* made up by the savings in freight, the consequently smaller freight absorption in deriving the f.o.b. mill price, the anticipated lower average delivered price, and the expected increase in sales; indeed, if this is what the owner of firm B anticipates, then firm A's owner is likely to have a similar view and might locate at the site offering lowest procurement and production costs. The consequence would be that even though the quartile sites may still be the most profitable, the optimistic maximax criterion which may have previously governed locations in the industry no longer applies. In effect, firm B has too much to lose and too little to gain by location at a site away from the central (least cost) site. Correspondingly A will move directly to the quartile, or to a location near the quartile point, only if convinced that B *always* locates symmetrically. Chapter 13 will show that underlying profit forces will induce in time a movement to new positions and to optimal distribution over space, perhaps via branch plants.

The important case of unequal costs brings into focus two new principles: (1) quasi-monopolistic location policies are not so likely to be adopted when costs are unequal everywhere as when costs are equal, because of the added uncertainty in the market. To this principle must be added a new one; namely, (2) rivalry from substitutable products (produced quite possibly at the lowest production cost center) is probably more pronounced and more influential

[1] Sales at the quartile location are greater if the delivered price to a large number of buyers is sufficiently lower from this location than the delivered price from the least cost site. The comparison between delivered prices depends upon the extent to which savings in freight compensate for the higher production costs. Finally, the net-mill price and associated sales must be large enough to reflect a net-average revenue curve which is raised sufficiently to offset the higher production costs. An increase in sales alone does not make it profitable for firms to locate at sites of higher cost.

and is, therefore, a determinant of location when costs are unequal at alternative locations.

A Related Model.[1] Define cost as the unit delivered price of factor inputs multiplied by their rate of utilization at any given site for any given plant process. Let unit delivered price of inputs (mill price + transportation cost) be influenced by (a) the competitive structure of the factor market, and (b) transportation rates that change with (i) commodity classification, (ii) quantity of movement, and (iii) distance of movement, with the rate increasing less than proportionately as the distance of input shipment increases. Next, determine the rate of "intensity" of input utilization at each site for a particular plant under a given production process and production function. Consider all inputs variable, including capital or plant at each prospective site, so that the plant location decision is seen to involve a long-run commitment. This approach, Professor Churchill argues, is more in keeping with the profit-motivated decision-maker who must determine the best sizes of plants for the different locations prior to the actual site-selection.

To incorporate plant size as a variable input into the model, Churchill employs a stock-flow production function which relates output to given quantities of inputs, all of which are variable including capital. Capital is treated as a stock value (size of plant, number of machines, etc.) at each site, the use of which, however, is variable along with other traditional variable inputs (labor, raw materials, etc.) according to the scale of output.

Churchill then defines an optimum cost expression that determines the minimum cost associated with any level of output at any production site. He uses a simple linear cost equation ($C = P_1 V_1 + P_2 V_2$) based on delivered inputs, and constrains it by a Cobb-Douglas production function ($V_1{}^a V_2{}^b$) which in Lagrangian form is added to the cost equation. By setting all partial derivatives equal to zero, the author derives the site which minimizes cost. Churchill concludes that the optimum "least cost" location and size of plant (output) will vary for a given process (plant) according to the "productivity" (as reflected in higher values for the exponents a and b) and "abundance" (as reflected in lower delivered prices P_1 and P_2) of factor inputs.

After expressing minimum costs in terms of input utilization for each level of output at a particular production site, Churchill completes the analysis by deriving a total revenue function. He assumes, somewhat unnecessarily, that buyers are located at a point in the region in which the seller may locate,

[1] The model sketched here is that of G. Churchill "Production Technology, Imperfect Competition, and the Theory of Location: A Theoretical Approach," *Southern Economic Journal*, XXXIV, July 1967, pp. 86–100. According to the author, his model is a take-off of L. Moses "Location and the Theory of Production," *The Quarterly Journal of Economics*, May 1958, pp. 259–272 and my own maximum profit location theory recorded in *Plant Location in Theory and Practice* (Chapel Hill, UNC Press, 1956) and originally in "Integrating the Leading Theories of Plant Location," *Southern Economic Journal*, XVIII (1952), pp. 525–538.

but introduces imperfect competition into the product market by assuming a negatively sloped demand curve for the product according to buyers' tastes and preferences. In Churchill's model, any change in the location of rivals (from one static optimal solution to the next) would involve a small upward or downward shift in the total revenue function of the other seller, depending upon whether rivals locate more or less distant from the "assumed" buying center. This same impact could have been viewed (as could the conception of buyers dispersed over space) by imposing a variable highest possible delivered price which the seller could charge, depending on the location of rivals; that is to say, treating the highest possible price a seller could charge as a parameter would have brought the locational interdependence of firms directly into the model rather than indirectly.

To conclude the analysis, the maximum profit location for a given plant of given size (i.e., its long-run level of output) is determined at the site where the spread between total cost and total revenue is the greatest. This differential is influenced significantly by product shipment costs, which, in turn, are influenced significantly by the location of competitors.

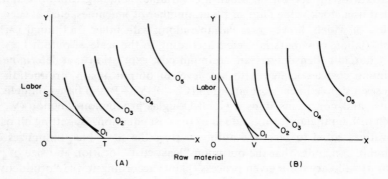

Figure 12–5. Economies and Diseconomies at Different Locations

A Diagrammatic Representation of Maximum Profit Location Theory. Diagrammatic characterization of maximum profit location theory may be presented easily. In doing this we shall draw in part on our earlier Figures 12–2, 3 and 4, on the representations in the paper by Leon Moses,[1] and on the analysis of Gilbert Churchill. Accordingly, assume in Figure 12–5 that the production function is not homogeneous to the first degree and that slightly different kinds of raw materials and labor are available at different locations.

[1] *op. cit.*

We, therefore, find in Figure 12–5A or 12–5B, respectively applicable to sites A & B, that a varying separation (hence varying input requirement) exists between outputs $O_1, O_2, \ldots, O_5$ notwithstanding an assumed constancy in the first differences of their total output values; i.e., $O_3 > O_2$ by the same amount as $O_2 > O_1$ etc. The shapes of the isoquants are also different at the two sites reflecting the added condition that the inputs are slightly different from place to place. If input factor prices are also different, such that, for example, raw materials are relatively lower in cost at site A, any superimposed isocost line of identical total cost would be flatter in Figure 12–5A than that of Figure 12–5B. (Cf., ST and UV, where each is defined to represent the same expenditure.)[1]

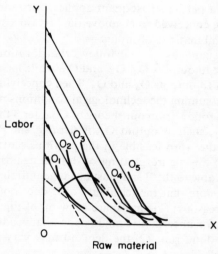

Figure 12–6. Feasible Long-Run Locations at Different Costs

Though technology is assumed to be the same over the economic space, differentials in factor input skills (or quality) and the resulting different processes imply slight discrepancies in the shape and level of the unadjusted LRAC curve from place to place. That is again to say, the separation between isoquants will not be identical at sites A and B. Selecting certain isoquants from the two Figures 12–5 and sketching in the full set of isocost curves applicable to each site (albeit, to repeat, not the full set of isoquants) yields Figure 12–6.

[1] See C. E. Ferguson, *Microeconomic Theory* (Chicago: Irwin & Co., 1966), Chapter 7, in particular pp. 140–152, for a lucid explanation of input substitution and optimum technology. And see H. Siebert, *Regional Economic Growth Theory and Policy* (Scranton, Pa., International Textbook Co., 1969), pp. 28–31 for an analysis of the interdependence between spatial structure and rates of return to factors.

In Figure 12–6, each isocost line of a given slope starting from zero cost at the origin is assumed for simplicity to involve the same dollar cost for the two locations; in turn, the same cost increase is assumed to apply from line to line for the site to which the cost pertains. For diagrammatic simplicity, only one complete isocost line has been drawn for each location (i.e. with intercepts on each axis), namely the first. But again note, each isocost line, whether continued to the other axis or not, still carries the same cost as the corresponding line drawn for the other site: specifically, the fourth line above O emanating along the vertical scale involves the same cost as the fourth line to the right of O which begins on the horizontal scale. Observe now, that the isoquants drawn are only those belonging to the site for which the minimum isocost tangency to a particular isoquant applies; for example, the isoquant O_1 for site A is to be conceived to lie above the first isocost line applicable to that site over all combinations of inputs.

Taking the isoquants as data, it follows that location B is the optimal cost site with respect to outputs O_1, O_2, and O_3, while location A is the more efficient with respect to outputs O_4 and O_5. Then conceiving of many alternative locations, and assuming the technological conditions provided in Figures 12–5 and 6, it would follow from our theory of Chapter 8 that if production of some small quantity, such as output O_1, is *feasible*, site B at least would be used. Significantly, the word feasible in the previous sentence is a vital one, for it means that in any figure plotting of dollars against output, the total revenue curve applicable to the B site must be tangent to the total cost curve at output O_1. Finally, note that the feasibility of B does not exclude the feasibility of A for two reasons: (1) an n space blow-up of Figure 12–5, including all costs and profits for uncertainty, might show that production is warranted at both sites in the long run; (2) the demand may vary over the economic space, such as described next.

Conceive for the sake of simplicity a linear demand curve of decreasing elasticity; assume, in fact, that the demand triangle is isosceles. At locations very distant from the seller, buyers will purchase smaller quantities than would buyers located proximate to the seller, *ceteris paribus*. Given homogeneous transport conditions, the portion of the demand curve above market price, when rotated around the vertical scale, yields a cone showing the quantity of the good sold at any point k in the space. (See Figure 12–7.) With uniform density of population, the quantity of output sold is the volume of the cone times the population density. Manifestly, differentials in population density may prevail for site A *vis-à-vis* B. The related sales volume and total revenue curves would, therefore, differ, and site A could alone prove to be the long-run profit-maximizing site. Indeed, population trends (or changes) could ultimately establish A as the real least cost site, with site B eventually proving to be uneconomic. What would otherwise appear to be the lower cost production point, i.e. site B, may thus prove to be the noneconomic alternative. We shall have more to say about this set of relations in Chapter 14 where

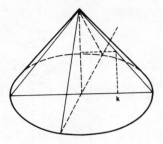

Figure 12–7: A Demand Cone over Economic Space

we shall also develop formally the corollary principle that firms and plants need not be of the same size over an economic space.

Special Subcases

Heterogeneity. The assumption that the official who resolves a company's location problem is able to identify the least cost location in a market area suggests that his counterparts—in similar *industries*—may find that the same site also minimizes their costs. We would expect as a general rule that the problems and computations of officials in similar industries are much the same. If we may further presuppose that the least cost location for the industry in question is also the least cost location for other industries, particularly those producing similar goods, the problem of substitutable (heterogeneous) products becomes of vital importance as a factor in location. This locational factor may be understood and evaluated with the aid of Figure 12–8.

In Figure 12–8 quartile locations would result in an increase in price between X′ and Z′ as compared to the price that would exist if a central location were adopted. This increase in delivered price will cause losses in the district between X′ and Z′. However, additional losses may be traced to the very high cross-elasticity of demand which would be likely to exist at the central site.[1]

---

[1] Our general discussion can be readily understood by noting that locations at A′ and B′ raise the selling price between X′ and Z′ considerably above that which would exist if the optimum cost locations at B were chosen. Significantly, the more effective utilization of the X′O and Z′O′ districts, *ceteris paribus*, may or may not compensate for the loss between X′ and Z′, depending upon which segments of the market have the higher cross-elasticities. To the extent that point B represents a highly industrialized location, the loss to rival industries may be greater than the gains from the hinterlands. On the other hand, when costs are equal, the problem of substitutable products is most pronounced at the market periphery. This is because rival industries may locate elsewhere under equal costs and

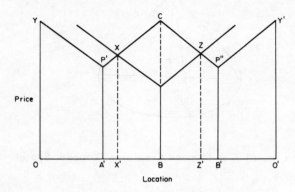

Figure 12–8: Price, Location and Market Area

A related case arises when heterogeneity exists *within* an industry. Here, too, we find a smaller probability that any given firm (industry) producing a substitutable product will locate symmetrically (disperse) with its rivals, because the custom formed by differentiating rather than duplicating a product encourages greater independence of action and increases the uncertainty as to how a rival will locate. This means that it is less likely that heterogeneous (as compared to homogeneous) firms will pursue quasi-monopolistic location policies with respect to each other when costs are equal over the economic space.

Large and Small Firms. When firms are large and costs vary widely among locations, the firms tend to concentrate, *ceteris paribus*, in the particular city or district which is least in cost, in relation to the whole market area.[1] These firms are following sound policy in emphasizing the location of their rivals. Only the foolhardy dare chance the initial move if doubt exists as to the probability of symmetrical locations. According to our reasoning, the location of the smaller firm is somewhat more flexible. These firms seek smaller segments and, therefore, may locate at the least cost position in reference to a particular segment of the entire market. In this respect, the smaller firms can

delivered prices are highest there; the applicable demand is therefore more elastic at places most distant from the seller's factory. Equal costs indicate quartile locations for homogeneous firms within an industry; unequal costs do not suggest the same result.

[1] See P. S. Florence, *Investment Location and Size of Plant*, National Institute of Economic and Social Research, Study VII (London: Cambridge University Press, 1938), p. 84. The large firms within an industry concentrate at given points. Also see his *Post-War Investment, Location, and Size of Plant* (London: Cambridge University Press, 1962), p. 18 for similar findings.

choose their sites with greater freedom, and since they are more ready to avoid locations near competitors, *a priori*, they often are found in the less industrialized areas.[1]

IV. CONCLUSIONS

The inclusion of cost and demand factors in one model points out the need for a broader statement of the determinants of plant location than one which maintains that firms seek the location offering the largest market area. This need is fulfilled by the concept of the maximum profit location.[2] By definition, this is the location where a given number of buyers (whose purchases are required for the greatest possible profits) can be served at the lowest total cost. Even though the lowest level of average production costs at this site may be higher than that at alternative sites, the monopolistic control gained over a larger number of buyers (spread over a market area) makes it the maximum profit location at the optimum output.[3]

This definition of the locator's objective recognizes that one location may offer lower manufacturing unit costs at a given output than another, but that the relative positions may reverse as the market area of the firm expands and differentials in transport cost appear. For example, high-cost manufacturers who extend their operations by water transportation may gain lower total unit costs to distant buyers than competitors who are linearly nearer to these buyers but are forced to use the railway or highway networks.

This concept of the maximum profit location is not only relevant when the demand or cost factor is held constant but when both are treated as variables. By definition, it lends itself readily to an examination of cost and of locational interdependence. When uncertainty prevails, however, implicit modification of the concept is required. Then a maximin force may arise which makes the daring movement to the quartile site unwise. We propose, accordingly, that the strategy of games may, in a rough sense, be applicable in some cases and *may* suggest concentration when dispersion otherwise would result. We observe also that maximum profit location theory appears adaptable not only to the general type of manufacturing plant location but also to locations on other levels, particularly retailing and the individual.

[1] This statement does not include service companies. For statistical vetification of this deduction, see *ibid*. Small plants disperse comparatively more than the large firms, frequently locating in the less industrialized areas.

[2] This maximum profit location concept contains many sides. Essentially, it excludes the strictly psychic income factor.

[3] Weber's least cost location fits the above definition only in part because it emphasizes the cost of procuring, processing, and distributing goods to a *given* buying point and thus does not convey spatial implications in full.

V. LOCATION THEORY SUMMARY

Location theory, as described above, deals essentially with unorganized markets. It points to several main conclusions: (1) When firms sell to a given buying point, they seek the least cost location in reference to this consumption center and ignore the locations of rivals in selecting their plant sites. (2) When firms sell over a market area, their site selections are influenced greatly by the locations of rivals. (3) In selecting a plant site, each firm seeks the place which offers the optimum sales output at a cost that cannot be matched elsewhere. (4) When firms sell over a market area and there are unequal costs at alternative locations, the maximin force of concentration plays a significant role in determining the locational patterns. (4) When firms sell over a market area, the tendency to disperse depends upon the height of the freight cost, the elasticity of the demand function, the characteristics (slopes) of the marginal costs, the degree of competition in location, the degree of competition from substitutable products at the various locations, and the homogeneity or heterogeneity of the firms belonging to the industry. Of course, market imperfections, such as *time of delivery*, *personal contacts*, *custom*, *equalizing and other discriminatory price* systems, influence the locational pattern of the industry and modify the above findings. These market imperfections tend to yield special theories of location; they do not readily lend themselves to a general theory giving information about underlying trends.[1] At the same time, they suggest that different ethnic and religious groups will have unique beliefs and objectives which would require modification of any theoretical presentation of the location of individuals based solely on "general" cost and revenue functions. These forces, along with externalities and with dynamic conditions which reflect the fact that historical "chance" may not have been coterminous with omniscient inspiration, indicate that the best of all worlds may still be ahead for all of us. But an epilogue at this point which further summarizes briefly where we have been and where we must still go is now in order.

VI. EPILOGUE

We may trace and then retrace the direction taken to this point in the book. From the conception of maximum profits under uncertainty, and the relation drawn between oligopoly, uncertainty, and economic space, we derived a theory of long-run equilibrium in which zero windfalls prevail. But this equilibrium not only satisfies efficiency principles, it also involves complete

---

[1] See M. L. Greenhut, "A General Theory of Plant Location," *Metroeconomica*, VII (1955), pp. 57–72, for an early paper on the rejection of certain special locational data and subsequent derivation of a generalized theory.

fulfillment (satisfaction) of consumer wants. Competitive entry and exit are market requisites, as a spatial monopolist, just like the classical monopolist, would charge rather high prices, acquire long-run surpluses, and select locations which often entail excessive use of the transport facilities, hence bringing about excessive costs. Through competitive action only are we assured of the lowest cost of production practical. But we must recognize that by the lowest practical cost of production we mean the lowest cost before imputations, which in turn depends on the availability of entrepreneurs. It is thus the case that by the end of Parts 1 and 2, we had not proven that any given industry would be characterized by, and in effect employ, the lowest cost curves possible for it before all imputations; rather, we had only proven that each firm (in *all industries*) would produce at the lowest cost point on its lowest LRAC curve and that after the imputation, the lowest (total) costs would prevail *given the location of firms*. It was thus conceivable that all firms in all industries could be poorly located, and the average cost curves relevant to each firm would thereby belong to the nonoptimal set. In other words, even after the imputation process which otherwise indicates lowest cost given the skills and resources available to the economy, a still lower cost might be possible for that country. It was in this light that Part 3 of the book began, and we, accordingly, investigated the location of individuals and cities besides that of firms.

To the present point in Part 3, we have learned that the locations of individuals and cities belong within the same general analytical framework as that applicable to the firm. We have, in fact, observed that the location of the firm is of the same analytical order as the (microeconomic) evaluation of product and factor prices. In reverse sequence, it should be clear that the inquiry of this book could have begun with the least cost theory of location after which the theory of the maximum profit location could have been examined, and the question tackled whether firms locate optimally. Then, since maximum profit *location* theory is just a special aspect of the theory of the firm, the other basic question immediately arises: does the spatial firm produce efficiently and maximize consumer satisfactions?

It is probably clear to all readers that "the maximum profit" concept applies to plant location in a way similar to the conclusions of Chapters 5 and 8, and, accordingly, the same income/energy optimality proposed previously will apply to locational distribution. But, it is another thing to prove *within the theoretical framework of location economics* that (1) the optimal distribution of firms and industries would arise over space, and that (2) each unit would sell over market areas of optimal size and shape. In the absence of this proof, Parts 1 and 2, as is true of all of nonspatial economic theory, simply assume that viable firms and industries are drawn to their lowest possible LRAC curve. It is as if they assumed Detroit is the automobile capital of the world because it *is* the best located city for this product. But micro-theorists interested in economic space cannot take this assumption as an implicit departure point. Rather, they must determine the propriety of the assumption, for otherwise microeconomic theory simply proposes that *given* the LRAC curve (or given the set of LRAC curves) for a firm and industry, maximum profit behavior leads to optimization by the surviving units. Regardless of how we had begun the book, we would have been drawn to this problem sooner or later. Chapter 13 is designed to resolve the query whether the spatial distribution of competitive firms is or *is not* economically optimal.

Appendix to Chapter 12
Spatial Pricing and Efficiency: Selected Details

The spatial distribution of an organized oligopoly, as described in Chapter 7, can suitably be reviewed here with a very brief discussion of organized pricing over space. Then we shall have a quick look at a basic finding of Chapter 6 with reference to the spatial pricing patterns of unorganized oligopolists. The appendix thus serves essentially as a departure point for our evaluation in Chapter 13 of the locational effectiveness of an *unorganized* oligopoly economy.

I. THE SPATIAL PATTERN UNDER ORGANIZED OLIGOPOLY

Consider the different kinds of spatial price systems that may exist:

(1) The Equalizing Delivered Price System

Under a system of uniform price quotations throughout the country, or, at any rate over large areas of it, firms are able to sell to distant buyers regardless of location and without limit *insofar as prices are concerned*. Aided by state fair trade laws and the federal government's Miller-Tydings and McGuire Acts, the equalizing delivered price system makes location depend essentially on costs. Any firm seeking a plant site visualizes a vast market area at its command, regardless of the location it chooses. Accordingly, with sales potential constant, the matter of location boils down to finding the best cost site for effecting the particular sales distribution visualized by company officials.

In practice, firms tend to concentrate at places where population is centered and, indeed, will locate near the center of the whole market, provided the production costs there are satisfactory. Since freight costs are usually low under this price system, the degree of distortion due to the extra agglomeration of firms is slight. The distortion is confined to a greater use of transportation (a cheap resource for this industry) than otherwise would be employed.

(2) The Single Basing-Point System

When freight costs on the finished product are not negligible but firms desire extensive market areas for sales, the basing-point price system may be used. Under this system, large firms tend to concentrate at the base point and generally sell over the whole market area. In contrast, small firms which, by definition, do not plan or seek sales to all market points, generally locate at a distance from the base point but not so far away from the central site as would small firms under the f.o.b. price system.[1]

Under basing-point pricing, firms locate, therefore, where costs are least. That is to say, when a firm selects a certain sales total, it will look for the site offering its predetermined sales potential at the lowest net cost. Under equal procurement costs everywhere, those (small) firms subject to relatively limited production and selling capacity tend to locate at the site where phantom freight is maximized. When costs are unequal, the small firm may, of course, accept a smaller phantom freight.

We may conclude our discussion of this case by noting that the system's objective of permitting sales to distant markets has the effect of discouraging large firms from locating near those markets. The result is an undue use of transportation facilities. Unlike the equalizing delivered price system in which the location distortion reflects a relatively unimportant wastage of transport facilities, this system requires harsher condemnation.

(3) Noncompetitive Price *and* Location Policy

Before we turn our attention to the multiple base-point system, let us examine noncompetitive price *and* location policy.

By definition, noncompetitive price *and* location policy refers to that situation in which firms locate side by side and adopt the same (or generally the same) base mill price plus freight rate schedule to all distant points. By further definition, a distant firm with a noncompetitive price competes only in location when it adheres to the delivered price schedule of the firms at the production center. It follows, in contrast, that a distant firm which resorts to its own f.o.b. mill price might eliminate its rivals from selected portions of the market, thereby altering market area potentials. This firm is actually pricing and locating competitively.

Noncompetitive price policy relates essentially to either the equalizing delivered price system, or the single basing-point price system or some variant of these. In turn, noncompetitive price and location policy refers, as noted above, to the situation in which all firms are located side by side and adopt comparable prices, in effect establishing the basing-point system if other firms comply therewith. In all of these cases, demand is not an effective and meaningful variable of location because unit sales, in effect, are fixed *over the whole market area*. Some cost element must be the governing factor of location of the firms.

Transport lines are always lengthened by noncompetitive price or location practices, a situation especially damaging to effective economy since it appears to tie up with the formation of excessively large plants by large organized oligopolists. Of course, here, as in all our discussions, we have disregarded time of delivery and the possible importance of close contact between buyers and sellers.

(4) The Multiple Basing-Point System

Our pattern of locational forces begins to change somewhat with the multiple basing-point system. Here demand and not cost may be the deciding factor in industrial location. Recall in this context our discussions in Chapters 6 and 7 that, when new base points are created, competition in price and location takes hold at a

[1] See A. F. Smithies, "Aspects of the Basing Point System," *American Economic Review*, XXXII (1945), pp. 705–726.

distance. This competition has the effect of squeezing market areas into different shapes and magnitudes so that the demand potential from area to area may vary. Accordingly, the size of markets (i.e., one of the two aspects in which the demand factor of location is evident) may be the chief variable in location.[1] Given the size of the market, cost will then guide the firm in its choice of a site.

The multiple basing-point system reduces, of course, the amount of distortion found under the single basing-point system. Nonetheless, within each base point area, the same locational pattern develops as under the single base point system.

(5) Other Price Systems—The Border Between Organized and Unorganized Oligopoly

Some other price systems produce the situation in which demand may vary from area to area. Under the plenary price system, for example, all plant sites become base points, and each plant absorbs freight if it desires to sell to buyers near a competitor's location. Any variant between the plenary and f.o.b. mill price systems, such as sporadic freight absorption, or equalizing delivered prices over a zone with freight additions to more distant zones, will cause demand to vary within and from area to area. Unlike, say, the basing-point system, in which demand affects the locational pattern only if close physical contact with selected consumers is important, these systems permit demand to be a locational factor even from the standpoint of the shape of the demand curve. Certain shapes, we have noted, induce firms to locate at a distance from each other, and to monopolize market segments; others do not. Whether the industry is organized or unorganized depends essentially on the extent of the systematizing of prices over space.

II. THE SPATIAL PATTERN UNDER UNORGANIZED OLIGOPOLY

F.o.b. mill pricing and all close variants modify the total market potentials existing in an industry. The upshot is that, within certain well-defined limits of price differentials, any plant locator tends to visualize different-sized market areas over the economic landscape. Sometimes these areas overlap, but usually they are distinguishable because of competition, population, or consumer concentration and topographical features. While the firm may sell its wares over much of any given area, regardless of its location in that area, sales to other market areas often prove to be sharply limited, if not impossible. When pricing and location are competitive, cost and demand are co-determiners of location. But what is the locational efficiency under f.o.b. pricing?

Under the general conditions of decreasing or near constant long-run costs, relatively high freight rates, elastic demand, two, three, or, better yet, many sellers, homogeneity within an industry, importance of time of delivery or personal contacts, and a history of experience in price and location, firms tend to spread out over space in accordance with consumer dispersion. In contrast, unequal costs and heterogeneity between industries—and the other elements opposite to those listed above— tend to induce concentration, *ceteris paribus*. It follows that in a free enterprise economy some firms and industries will concentrate unduly, especially we shall see in the short run, while others will obey the rules of efficient location. It is, however,

[1] See M. L. Greenhut, "Size of Markets vs. Transport Costs in Industrial Location Surveys and Theory," *Journal of Industrial Economics*, VIII (1960), pp. 172–184.

only when markets are organized that firms regularly fail to disperse effectively in space, for the tendency to equalize profit from market area to market area (see Chapter 8) which induces an efficient long-run dispersal of the plants of unorganized oligopolists does not exist in this market.

What we have, therefore, finally suggested is this: Even though marginal costs increase and demand is quite inelastic, and even though producers are quite heterogeneous and other elements are promoting localization, the tendency over time is for firms to learn and relearn the advantages of dispersing, especially if there are more than two firms in the industry. As we shall see in Chapter 13, the game of location is not a constant-sum game, and the effect over time is for firms in an industry to deglomerate. It follows that the underlying trend is toward greater and greater efficiency in the alignment of firms and industries over economic space. The main exceptions to this, without considering organized markets, would be when unequal costs or shopping good items are involved. Under unequal costs, the economic location for all firms may be the low production cost site, though if the disparity is not too great small firms (and, in time, even large firms) will gain advantage in dispersing. In the case of shopping goods, the consumer *wants* his suppliers to be located side by side. Sales are magnified (and satisfactions maximized) when firms in this particalar kind of trade locate together.

What is basically required for efficient location is therefore unorganized oligopoly, a market in which competitive pricing and location takes place at a distance whenever intra-industry dispersion offers advantage to the consumer. Our basic proofs in support of this vital conclusion and others recorded in Chapter 12 and this appendix will be given in the following chapter.

III. FINAL NOTES

We have proposed that consumers influence the location of suppliers, as, in turn, their own locations are influenced by the skills they possess and their job opportunities. The prevailing interdependence between all economic units is expressed in a spatial distribution which complies both with the resource advantages of different places and the demands (including whims) of consumers. While totalitarian states may try to ensure that there is intra-industry dispersion, except where cost differentials exist, a free enterprise society naturally attains this result except when consumers prefer otherwise.

The difference between free and regulated economies is simply that consumers in the free enterprise economy wish to be able to compare goods offered for sale next door to each other. In regulated economies, the standardization of goods and the state control of products make this form of shopping impossible. The free enterprise society gives its people what they want; the totalitarian society obtains what its framework is designed to produce. The efficiency of the respective societies must be argued on other grounds: politics, ethics (the good life), the query that asks "which system elicits the best effort among people", religion, and social psychology. The issue is just not economic, for the framework of each society tends to lay down its own unique values.

13

The Spatial Equilibrium of the Firm in Economic Space

WE HAVE OBSERVED THAT August Lösch[1] presented the view that a system of rational locations requires an intra-industry dispersion of firms and an inter-industry localization of firms. In systems characterized by uncertainty and locational interdependence, it would seem, however, that some intra-industry concentrations must occur. If so, Lösch's system would apply to planned economies alone and, indeed, this was broadly the view of the present writer some years ago.[2] We shall reconsider this idea here, employing Lösch's theory as a point of departure in moving towards our general theory of the firm in economic space; we use the word general to include market area configurations as well as the price equilibrium properties set forth in Part II of this book.

Here we shall both modify a position we previously took, and yet emphasize that view. Section I of this chapter analyzes some fine points of the theory of locational interdependence which were only glossed over in our earlier chapters. Proof will be given that there are forces other than those attributable to spatial differences in tastes (demand) and resource endowments (costs) which encourage the localization of homogeneous plants and firms. The question will then arise whether these forces point to a major error in Lösch's theory of location.

Section II of the chapter will show more specifically how, over a landscape in which distance is important, Lösch's derived system of spatial relations contradicts or ignores the theory of locational interdependence. One could for a while surmise that Lösch actually erred and that notwithstanding his claim, his theory does not apply to free enterprise systems.

In sections III, IV, and V of the chapter, we shall observe that the locational interdependence forces which induce intra-industry concentration —again apart from any natural differentials in demands and costs in space— are actually only short-run forces. We shall show that Lösch's perfect intra-industry dispersion of plants actually should result in the long run *in any*

---

[1] A. Lösch, *Die räumliche Ordnung der Wirtschaft* (Jena: Gustav Fischer, 1944).

[2] *Plant Location in Theory and Practice* (Chapel Hill: University of North Carolina Press, 1956), pp. 270–272.

economy and that modifications thereof are to be attributed only to special features, such as uneven distribution of demand and resources. Moreover, in spite of the recent critique of Mills and Lav, as detailed herein, we shall find that the hexagon is the basic market area shape under a competitive spatial equilibrium. We hope then in this chapter to outline a general theory of the firm in economic space such that when the spatial properties of this theory are joined with the previously established price equilibria properties of the oligopolist, as will be done in Chapter 14, the price and location practices of firms in a free enterprise economy will have been integrated fully.

I. ANALYSIS OF LOCATIONAL INTERDEPENDENCE

We assert that firms in an industry will be induced to locate towards the center of the market area whenever the following conditions prevail: (1) the demand curve of a buyer at a point in the market is convex, or even linear (2) marginal costs of production are rising, (3) the freight rate is small relative to other costs, (4) there prevails very little close competition from any one industry for the proportion of the consumer's dollar normally spent on the subject product, (5) the products of the firms in the subject industry are slightly differentiated, and (6) a long history prevails of highly competitive price and location practices in the trade. If we adopt the above conditions, and if, for simplicity, we consider two sellers and assume they are supplying a set of buyers who are scattered along a line and who, except for location, are homogeneous, we find that the duopolists will locate at or near the center of the line. Let us see why this is so!

Demand Curves and Locational Interdependence

Consider first a monopolistic firm that is subject to a linear demand curve. Let freight rates be proportional to distance, a dollar unit per distance unit. Assume a constant marginal cost of production curve and raise it by the freight rate allocable to each unit of product sold in the market. And let b stand for the value of the price intercept, i.e. the highest price buyers would pay for the good. Recall from the Appendix to Chapter 6 (though we review the highlights briefly here) that the spatial price to the halfway market point will be greater than the nonspatial monopoly price by half of the freight cost per unit of goods shipped to that point.[1]

---

[1] To see this result most easily, consider the case of a monopolist. Let demand be $y = b - ax$ or $x = (y-b)/a$. Total Revenues $(R) = xy = (y^2 - by)/a$. Then $dR/dy = (2y-b)/a$ which, when set to zero, yields $b/2$ for the price. If we then take any constant level of costs, e.g. zero, and add to it the freight rate to a certain point in the market, the delivered price to that point in the market may readily be seen to equal $(b/2) +$ half of the freight rate to that point in the market. (Note we shall provide further details in note 2, pp. 290–291 to prove this claim beyond the present level of intuition.)

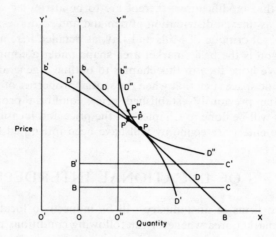

Figure 13–1: Alternative Demands and Freight Absorption

Price P is the price on D, D' and D'', given marginal production cost BC.

Price P' is the price on D' with freight costs BB' added to marginal production cost BC.

Price $\hat{P}$ is the price on D with freight costs BB' added to marginal production cost BC.

Price P'' is the price on D'' with freight costs BB' added to marginal production cost BC.

The above principle can best be appreciated when we observe that if all buyers were located with the seller at an end point of a line, and costs were zero, the profit-maximizing (and, in effect, delivered) price would equal $b/2$. If all buyers then move to, let us say, the halfway point along the given line, price would equal $b/2 + k'/2$, where k' is the freight rate to the specified halfway point along the line.[1] If all buyers were dispersed evenly along this line, the delivered price to the halfway point in the market would again be equal to $b/2 + k'/2$.[2] If costs are positive, as BC in Figure 13–1, the MR = MC

[1] If all buyers are at the same freight rate distance k' from the seller, costs per unit of sales must rise by k' and delivered price would be $b/2 + k'/2$ presuming zero costs of production.

[2] Assume that not only are the buyers dispersed evenly along a line starting at the seller's location but that the negatively sloped linear demand curve forms an isosceles triangle with intercepts of the value of b. Accordingly, the quantity (x) taken by the buyer located at the first freight rate unit of distance (d) from the seller is $b - m - d$, where m stands for the net-mill (i.e. f.o.b. mill) price. The next buyer along the line must then purchase $b - m - 2d$, so together the two buyers will seek $2b - 2m - 3d$ units of the good. With three buyers, purchases become $3b - 3m - 6d$, and with four $4b - 4m - 10d$. Given 1000 buyers, we would obtain $1000b - 1000m - 500,500d$. If we replace d by K, that is the freight rate to the most

intersection would signify that the price would be raised by $(1/2)MC$. Continuing with the assumption of buyers distributed evenly along a line, and including marginal production and freight costs in the same diagram (i.e., raise BC to B'C' in Figure 13–1), indicates that price $\hat{P}$ on D takes the place of P (the nonspatial price that relates alone to marginal costs BC). We find that $\hat{P}$ is greater than P by one-half the freight rate BB' ($= k'$) to the halfway point in the market.[1]

Consider now from a position above the curves the convex shaped demand curve D' and the concave shaped demand curve D'', besides the linear demand curve. To make our situations fully commensurate, assume the true origin of the system to be at O' not O. That is to say, take O'b' as the vertical scale drawn at zero x; Ob ($=$ to $O'b' = O''b''$) thus appears simply as a device to show us that all demand curves in the figure have the same highest ordinate value. We are, in other words, here assuming that the concave upward demand curve D'' does not intersect the vertical scale nor does the linear curve, and, again, that each demand (D, D', D'') is subject to the same price (b) above which nothing will be purchased. Moreover, the three curves are assumed to be tangent at the nonspatial profit maximizing price P. It is immediately clear from the diagram (and the definition of elasticity that stands behind the revealed geometry) that the increase in price due to distances in the case of the convex demand curve (i.e. the increase from

distant buyer, the last relation reappears as $1000b - 1000m - 500.5K$. Now, $R = yx$, or in our case mill price m times quantity sold, i.e., mx. Assuming 1000 buyers in the market, we obtain $R = m(1000b - 1000m - 500.5K)$. Differentiating R with respect to m and setting the result equal to zero in order to obtain the profit maximizing price gives us for m the value $b/2 - K/3.996$, again this for the case of 1000 buyers distributed evenly along a line. It was originally shown, *Plant Location, op. cit.*, Appendix A, that the limiting value is $b/2 - K/4$, while if the buyers were distributed evenly over a plane, the net mill price would approach the limit of $b/2 - K/3$.

Observe further that if the net-mill price is $b/2 - K/4$, the delivered price to any point in the market is $b/2 - K/4 + k'$, where K is again the freight rate to the most distant buyer while k' is the freight rate to the location under consideration. Manifestly, at the halfway distant point $k' = K/2$, so by substituting $k'/2$ for $K/4$ the equation for the delivered price to the halfway point in the market becomes $b/2 + k'/2$. (Incidentally, the most distant market point must be (is) uniquely defined, *ibid.*) And, again, see the Appendix to Chapter 6 for details of the relations currently being described.

[1] Our geometry of dividing by "two" applies because of the assumption of a negatively sloping linear demand curve and the lemma that the marginal revenue curve falls at twice the rate of the linear demand. This condition further serves as the basis for our references to the halfway distant point. That is to say, consider the formula for the net-mill price, $b/2 - K/4$. By transforming it to $b/2 - k'/2$, where k' stands for the freight rate to the halfway point, the freight rate to the most distant point in the market is replaced by the freight rate to the halfway point in the market; thus a geometrical representation of net-mill price becomes possible. If the formula were $b/2 - K/3$ (as when buyers are evenly dispersed over a plane), the geometry would require that we add to marginal costs the freight rate to the two-thirds distant point along the line from the seller's plant rather than the freight rate to the halfway point in the market. Thus k' now assumes the cost to the two-thirds distant point rather than the halfway point in the market.

price P to price P') will be less than that for the instances of concave or negatively sloped linear demands.[1] Any firm contemplating sales over distances
would, therefore, be likely to visualize a greater potential sales radius (given
its spatial profit maximizing price) when the demand it faces is convex in
shape than it would under the other demand curve types discussed above.
Indeed, by regarding the concave demand curve, and noting that the curve
drawn marginally to it is shifted farther to the left than the other marginal
curves above price P, it is readily seen that the freight absorbed in price is
least under this type of demand. Price P'' obtains when demand is concave
upward. In general the spatial-delivered price charged any buyer under zero
costs of production is $b/2$ plus the difference between the freight absorbed in
deriving the seller's f.o.b. mill price and the freight rate to that buyer's location in the market.

Introduce now a potential competitor at the same time as our firm is
considering a location along a new "line". In other words, the market is
duopolistic. Our principal theorem follows that either firm is more likely to
locate at (or near) the market center under a convex demand curve than under
a concave upward or negatively sloping linear demand curve, *ceteris paribus*.

We are *not* proposing that profits are enhanced at central location; we
contend only that there is a greater likelihood of localization at the center of
the market when demand is convex. Our conclusion is reached because an
entrepreneur might suppose that his competitor would expect that his best
f.o.b. mill price will enable him to sell to peripheral points if he located at the
center of the market; hence the competitor might locate at the market center.
In contrast, if the demand were concave, the reasoning process could be
different. More specifically, an entrepreneur subject to convex demand might—
because of his experience in the business—realize that the impact of distance
on price is to raise price slightly. He therefore feels less compelled to economize on distance than he would if his firm and industry were subject to concave

---

[1] In Figure 13-1, we raised the marginal cost line by the freight rate to the halfway
distant point for each demand curve in order to *depict* relative impacts of demand curves
on prices over an economic space. However, the difference BB' technically applies only to
the case of even buyer dispersion along a line under conditions of *linear demand*. If we take a
concave demand of the form $p = \sqrt{aq+\beta}$ and a convex demand of the form $p = \partial q^2 + \delta$
and constrain them to the same b value as well as by requiring their tangency with a linear
demand curve at the nonspatial profit maximizing price $(b/2)$ under zero marginal production costs, the respective absorption rates are found to be least under concave demand
and most under convex demand. Varying our constraints (e.g. dropping the same b
constraint) would change the absorption rates but otherwise leave relationships unaltered.
Indeed, assuming other forms of concave or convex demand, e.g. increasing or constant
elasticity also changes the absorption rates. In fact, elsewhere this writer and Mr. Hiroshi
Ohta will show that negative or *excessive* freight absorption [respectively $dp/dD > 1$ and
$dp/dD < 0$] are also *a priori* (theoretic) possibilities. However, for the purposes of this book,
only the empirically likely situations require recording, and equally importantly, only the
ordinal relationships of freight absorption are required. These relationships are properly
indicated in Figure 13-1.

demand. Location of his rival at the center appears more likely to him and he, accordingly, tends to accept the central site as the most advantageous. Obviously, if he alone located away from the center, his rival would control more than half of the market.

It is the uncertainty of a rival's behavior, and more fundamentally the greater uncertainty of his desire to economize on distances which leads duopolists to localize when demand is convex. Thus, although quartile locations would always be best under the conditions of cost and demand assumed herein,[1] this distribution does not result because if the rival locates at or near the market center, the other firm would be in an unenviable position if it had arranged to locate away from that point. To sum up, if space does produce duopolistic relations in the short-run between sellers, the history of the industry's location practice will be influenced to some extent by the demand curve, with the convex demand curve inducing greater localization of homogeneous firms and the concave curve a greater dispersion of these firms.[2] We shall analyze in Section II what happens when numbers increase. For the moment, let us add the further thought that if firms do concentrate, in the short run, they could develop certain economies for the industry via their agglomeration at or near the market center which, in time, may endow such location with advantages over other sites.

Cost Curves and Locational Interdependence

The shape of the marginal cost curves may also be shown to influence the location of industry. To comply with tradition as much as possible, although still developing our main theme, let us consider the case of short-run rising marginal costs and compare the results with the case of short-run constant marginal costs.

It is readily evident in Figure 13-2 that an increase in the upward sloping MC by the amount EF (= BB′) will cause its intersection with MR to lie at a point to the right of that where the constant marginal costs with freight curve (B′C′) intersects MR. The delivered price to the point in the market specified by freight cost EF will, accordingly, be less under rising marginal costs than under constant marginal costs. That is to say, prices will be comparatively low at all points in the market under this marginal cost function. The tendency to disperse will, therefore, be less under upward sloping than constant marginal

---

[1] That quartile locations would be best, *ceteris paribus*, may easily be seen by recalling the formula $(b/2) - (K'/4)$ and noting that if rivals located at the opposite quartiles along the line and priced f.o.b. mill, the most distant buying point for either seller would be half that which would apply to a central location. The rise in the cost curve because of freight costs would, accordingly, be less. And see Chapter 6 for the opposite technique of subtracting distance from demand curves instead of adding the function of distance to the production cost curve when showing prices in a space economy.

[2] M. L. Greenhut, *Microeconomics and the Space Economy* (Chicago: Scott, Foresman 1963), Chapters 3, 5, and 6, and *Plant Location, op. cit.* Chapter VI.

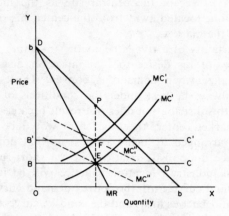

Figure 13–2: Marginal Costs and Freight Absorption

costs, as any seller may expect his rival to be more likely to locate at the midpoint of the market. This follows because the seller, under the defined conditions, may still be able to maintain sales to distant buyers as opposed to the possibilities under constant marginal costs. Again, if we could be sure that the rival would locate—as he should—at the other quartile point, the remaining firm would be more likely to take options for a location at the quartile point. But should a firm go to the quartile while the rival locates at the center, the results will be disastrous and the locational choice revealed as an error.

If we postulate a long-run decline in costs for any level of output and size of plant and firm, the opposite effect to upward sloping marginal costs is suggested, *ceteris paribus*. A tendency towards dispersion, especially in the newly developing market areas of the economy, may well be expected.

To ignore the short-run slopes of marginal costs, and to overlook the pattern of costs over time, amount to disregarding important forces in the selection of plant sites. Surely, theoreticians (and for that matter empiricists) should not confine their attention to elementary evaluations of taxes, transport weights and rates, *etc.* in their attempts to analyze location patterns in free enterprise systems; rather, they must go beyond these data to include a study of the forces which influence the conjectures of company officials as to what the behavior and location of their competitor(s) will be.

Freight Rates and Locational Interdependence

Apart from the shapes of the demand and cost curves, the freight rate on a finished product tends to determine the extent to which firms disperse so as to lessen the impact of distance on their economic activity. Thus we find that some freight rates promote localization while others lead to the dispersion of homogeneous firms. To understand this, let us remember that the way one firm locates is partly the result of how the rival is expected to locate. How the rival is expected to locate is due, among other things, to the importance of the freight rate on the final product, for the freight rate is a prime variable in the location process when buyers are dispersed over space rather than located at one consuming point (city). The greater the rate, the greater is the likelihood that the rival will tend to economize on distance and therefore the firms will tend to disperse; and *vice versa*. If the carrier uses basing points or basing lines (or zones), localization is induced. Similarly, commodity rates favoring shipment in certain directions will lead to greater localization, *etc.*, as we saw in Chapter 11.

Spatial Cost Differences and Locational Interdependence

Cost differentials over space increase the uncertainty of the rival's locational pattern, especially if costs are lowest at the center of the market area. Indeed, because of the likely location of a rival industry or a supplying industry at some central point in the economy, agglomerating advantages may exist there. In particular, the possibility of substitution among products would stimulate any given seller to price his product as low as possible at that market center. Because the production cost advantages at designated points (or more generally at certain points) compensate somewhat for freight cost advantages prevailing at other points in the economy, any likelihood of dispersion becomes less certain. Unevenness of production costs over space can be added to other uncertainties in the computation process, thereby increasing the uncertainty as to what the rival might do. When cost of production is variable over the economic landscape, the best course of action might *appear* to be to locate near the market center, especially if it offers some production cost savings.

Industrial Homogeneities—Heterogeneities and Locational Interdependence

It was noted in Chapter 12 that the homogeneity or heterogeneity of products within the industry, and the extent of substitution between the products of the subject industry and a rival industry both play a role along with cost differences over space (e.g., taxes, labor, *etc.*) and the price systems over space[1] in influencing uncertainty. They all determine the extent to which firms tend to localize or disperse in given market areas, and they must be considered by

---

[1] Recall, for example, that locations under a basing-point system would differ from those under an f.o.b. mill price system. And see Greenhut, *Plant Location, op. cit.*, pp. 57–91 and 140–162.

theorists and researchers if valid explanations of why industry has located (and locates) are to be given.

We have now established the point needed for the following sections of this chapter. There remains initially the proof that when there are more than two firms the tendency for dispersion is greater than in the duopoly-line case.[1] At the same time, the question will be resolved whether Lösch ignored locational interdependence because he deduced a perfect dispersion in the locations of firms belonging to a given industry.

II. LÖSCH'S SYSTEM AND LOCATIONAL INTERDEPENDENCE

The "rational" system of industrial locations proposed by August Lösch[2] seems to ignore locational interdependence, for, as noted previously, he conceived of an ideal intra-industry dispersion, and we have just seen that if—among other forces—demand curves are convex from above, and if marginal costs are increasing and freight costs are low, an intra-industry concentration of firms may often be expected to result. Even Lösch's fortuitous assumption of a homogeneous plain was shown to lead eventually to cost differentials over space.[3] The added uncertainty given by this spatial heterogeneity would further serve to cause intra-industry concentration.[4] The critique of Lösch's theory which follows will appear to uncover a logical inconsistency in his theory. It centers on the cost differentials and uncertainty which tend to arise even though the plain may have originally been homogeneously endowed.

A Critique of Lösch's Theory

Lösch recognized that the minimum size trading areas would differ for different products and industries. As a consequence, he realized that notwithstanding the homogeneous spread of Mother Nature's gifts, some cities would arise which are large in size (i.e., the trading areas for many products might happen to be centered at the same point), while other cities would be small, in fact be towns or hamlets. What Lösch failed to recognize was that *the agglomerating cost differences which would arise would induce, via locational interdependence, some intra-industry concentration*, as described earlier in this chapter. In effect, his rational system seemed to hold for a planned rather than a market economy, for surely the planned economy could require intra-

---

[1] A. Lerner, and H. Singer, "Some Notes on Duopoly and Spatial Competition," *Journal of Political Economy*, XLV (1939), pp. 145–186. E. H. Chamberlin, "The Product as an Economic Variable," *Quarterly Journal of Economics*, LXVII (1953), pp. 1–29.

[2] *Op. cit.*

[3] M. L. Greenhut, *Plant Location, op. cit.*, pp. 270–271.

[4] *Ibid.*, pp. 152–155.

industry dispersion while at the same moment permitting and even seeking inter-industry concentration.

Refutation of the Critique

My own desire[1] (or was it intuition?) led me years ago to the thought that a rather special set of conditions must hold for excessive concentration to occur in a competitive market economy. Consider, accordingly, the following:

Demand and Cost Conditions may be Expected to Encourage Dispersion. Suppose demand is not infinitely inelastic or even convex from above; suppose instead it is concave upwards, or even straight lined of negative slope. Then the non-constant sum aspects of the location game, as it would be played by tradesmen, must surely tend to induce industrial dispersion over time. On *a priori* grounds, one might expect that demand conditions would encourage dispersion. (We will have a great deal more to say about this thesis later on.)

Consider next the likelihood that as an industry matures it would tend to experience technological breakthroughs which improve its competitive position. This development means that cost levels should decline up to a point. During the specified growth period, the advantage of dispersion would be manifest in the industry. In turn, the practice of dispersion evinced during this period should also prevail in the long run. Surely this conclusion might be expected to hold even if over still longer periods of time costs ultimately do rise. In sum, the good habit of dispersing, as evidenced by the extra profit derived from being dispersed over space, should have permeated the system in full during the years over which costs declined.

With respect to freight costs and their localizing effect, what is the sense of discussing space if freight costs are assumed to be very low? To say the least, high freight cost should be assumed to hold, and such cost also leads to dispersion. And, if basing lines, zones, etc. prevail in the short run, may we not expect a developing public clamor against the discrimination that would be claimed to exist under such freight-rate practices? The situations of long-run intra-industry concentration because of freight costs would, accordingly, appear to be rare and unimportant.

Still one final *coup de grâce* may be levied against the possible charge of inefficient locations: we have in mind the existence of unequal costs and their localizing effects. Why should we assume the existence of lowest costs at some industrial center, with the further premise that substitutable product industries must be found at that center? Why not conceive of new industries and new resources and, in the process, assume the opposite cost distribution over space? The conception of a full set of alternative lowest production cost

---

[1] *Positive Economics and Policy Objectives* (London: George Allen and Unwin, Ltd., 1964), p. 117. "As regards subjectivity and possible bias, this operates in the scientific process . . . by influencing the selection of 'positive' theories, explanations or predications. . . . "

locations at many points in economic space would induce the dispersion of a given industry to some of these points. Locational efficiency (dispersion) could therefore be expected *even in the presence of unequal costs*, at least whenever newly considered resource advantages are found in a random pattern over the landscape of a developing economy.

Oligopolists Disperse even under Conditions where Duopolists Localize. As was mentioned in Chapter 12, Lerner and Singer[1] in their celebrated paper on location ventured the thesis that if three firms prevailed in the market, the one in the center of the line would tend to move outward. A constant tendency to break away from the others, they said, would exist over time. It is much the same as if a filling station happens to be in between two other stations along a highway. Such a station is disadvantageously located, because fast-driving tourists typically first begin to slow down when in sight of the first station and stop at the last station. Those motorists who are running out of gas tend to slow down long before reaching the stations, for they want to stop at the very first station lest their vehicles run out of gas. Depending upon the direction of travel, the one type of motorist favors the third station along the line (or the fourth or fifth if higher numbers are to be imagined), and the others the first. So Lerner and Singer in effect said, the fellow(s) in between had best move outward.

Chamberlin, working with a negatively sloped linear demand provided rather forceful support to the premise that industry generally tends to disperse over time.[2] We might, in fact, go beyond his thought by suggesting that even if demand is finitely limited, increasing returns prevail up to the optimal price, and this signifies that the firms are engaged in a nonconstant sum game.[3] The play in such game *among competitors* would not involve maximin-minimax results; a "spatial" saddle point holds only with respect to security-minded price-location followers not competitive duopolists or oligopolists. And so it was that Chamberlin, in effect, depicted a clustering form of dispersion as numbers beyond two were assumed to arise in the market, but still a dispersion rather than a concentration. However, let us probe more deeply into the game aspects of location when three or more firms exist.

Game Theory and Plant Location. We have already suggested that a

[1] *Op. cit.*

[2] See his *Theory of Monopolistic Competition*, 5th edition (Cambridge: Harvard University Press, 1946), Appendix C, and also see E. H. Chamberlin, "The Product as an Economic Variable," *op. cit.*, for the idea that over time, or given a location on a circular street or over a circular market area, there exists a stronger tendency to disperse fully. If a fourth, fifth, and still more firms locate after the leaders are already in the market, the dispersion, Chamberlin suggested, may either be complete or else a clustering form of dispersion occurs, depending upon the pattern prevailing before the entry of the later firms.

[3] M. L. Greenhut, "Games, Capitalism and General Location Theory," *The Manchester School*, XXV (1957), pp. 61–88, 86–88.

tendency to disperse arises in the case of three (or more) firms, even under conditions of infinitely inelastic demand. When finite limits are set to demand, the theories stress a still greater likelihood of the dispersal process. Typically, it is said, the "game-like" relations which might induce two firms to locate at the market center carry less weight when there are more than two firms in the industry. To see the whole process, consider the following:

The *maximin-minimax* principle suggests that, if there are three rivals, they might well select a central location. For example, one entrepreneur might reason that any rival, if he is forced to take out options or leases, or to purchase the land outright, would tend to behave similarly as he would. Thus each rival might consider two basic types of location: a location at the first or third quartile point, or one at the mid-point of the market. The one entrepreneur would then conjecture that there are four ways for his two rivals to locate at the quartiles as opposed to one distinct way for them to locate at the center of the market. In other words, one rival could locate at the first quartile and the other at the third quartile or vice-versa, or both could be together at either quartile; fifthly, each might locate in the center of the market. If the two rivals happen to locate at opposite quartiles, the marketcenter location would be as desirable for the third firm as the one at either quartile. If the two rival firms are both locating at either the first quartile or the third quartile, the central location is better for the third firm than one at the opposite quartile. Indeed, it is only when there are two rivals at the center that planned location by the third firm at one of the distant sites would be advantageous. The probabilities thus suggest that if the locator is a maximining type of person, his firm should be located at the center of the market. But note, if similar reasoning is attributed to rivals, a tendency to move off-center will be likely, especially should buyers be distributed over a plain rather than along a line.

Localization is not, we suggest, the way the locations of plants in viable industries are ultimately resolved. The game of plant location is not a constant sum. A type of maximax (dispersion) practice (not the previously described maximin location) will actually arise in the viable industries, even among decision-makers who are basically conservative about most selections they make in life. This dispersal tendency results because the uncertainty involved in plant location tends to dissipate over time, being based on the behavior of business rivals who are usually members of the same culture and who have the same economic objective of maximizing profits. Thus, though the *overall* decision processes of a man include, among other uncertainties, such matters as that of politics, and though they relate to people of different backgrounds, a person who may maximin in most decisions throughout his life could well adopt a maximax criterion about his and his rivals' locations. This tendency to maximax is not necessarily applicable to all the decisions made by the firm. It could well apply only to *location decisions* of the firm, for these decisions involve a more fundamental computation, including expectations such as that of declining marginal costs with developing technology. The otherwise conservative decision-maker may well locate away from rivals and expect them to do the same, even though on other matters he follows a more conservative approach.

The Maximax Force in Plant Location: the "Integer" Program. To support our contention that plant location decision making under uncertainty differs from overall decision making, let us again stress the condition that location decisions do not involve constant sums, because the greater the dispersion, *ceteris paribus*, the greater are the individual and total profits in the market. By realizing that a simple two person game tableau may be converted into a multiple firm "integer" program, the general tendency for optimality that underlies the location process is highlighted. For example, consider a tableau in which the alternative location combinations of rival firms are arranged by rows. Then let each different column entry depict "a" location of the subject firm given the alternative locations of rivals. Because the game is not a constant sum, the *mathematical solution* will not be the maximin-minimax solution; rather, the optimal obtained will be of the order of a maximax result. The firms will tend to disperse. Shall we say that among three firms any one might opt for a quartile or even better a sextile location instead of the maximin center location because it expects that its rivals will also want to disperse. Indeed, a little noise in indicating where options are to be taken in order to avoid a "surprise" accidental localizing at the same site is alone required for the dispersal result (certainly a form of legitimate collusion in practically any system of laws). The fear of being hemmed in and the fact that distant locations are obviously more profitable when several other plants are at a given center combine to point to the likelihood that in industries with 3 *or more firms*, locational dispersion is promoted.

Competition and Demand Over Time. It was specified earlier that convex demand encourages localization and concave demand promotes dispersion. But these conclusions were predicated on the spatial prices P″, $\hat{P}$, or P′ in Figure 13–1 (i.e. the delivered price to the buyer located at the average distance from the seller) being greater than the nonspatial monopoly price P. Over time, however, competition from other industries alone will tend to force prices in the subject industry to levels lower than the nonspatial monopoly price, and reverse effects will be realized as the demand curves are shifted leftward and lower prices result. Thus, opposite impacts apply in time to concave and convex demands even apart from an increasing number of firms in the subject industry. The localizing force of uncertainty disappears as the advantages of dispersing branch plants in new market areas and relocating old plants are learned, sooner or later, regardless of the shape of the demand curve.

Effective Dispersion "And" Localization

It appears, therefore, that the free enterprise system leans towards an approximation of Lösch's rational system. And when one adds shopping good items to the list of consumable items (e.g., women's dress shops which are justifiably placed side by side), one begins to visualize enough advantages for the locations that free enterprise societies obtain to rest comfortably in the thought of efficient capitalism. Intra-industry dispersion is promoted when economically sound; localization is promoted when consumers prefer and/or cost conditions warrant. However, even if our conclusion is that firms localize and disperse in efficient reflection of the spatial distribution of costs and wants, we would not have proven enough. Such finding is tantamount to saying that our resource allocations of nonspatial costs are efficient and so too are transportation costs apparently economized; but, it is another matter to say that each firm sells over the most efficient size and shape of market area. It could, in other words, be the case that firms disperse in accordance with the spatial distribution of cost and demand, but they sell over "wrong sized" and "improperly shaped" market areas. They would then be wasting transport facilities and failing to maximize consumer satisfactions. This problem is examined in section 3 of this chapter, after which we shall return to the question of dispersion over space by investigating the possibility of short-run mistake in locating an industry or city, i.e., wrong start . . . wrong (?) finish?

III. THE CHALLENGE OF MILLS AND LAV: ALTERNATIVE SHAPES OF THE MARKET AREA[1]

Mills and Lav derived certain comparisons between the circle and selected polygons. As is indicated in the part of their table reprinted below, the circle is more profitable than the hexagon which, in turn, is more profitable than the square, while the latter is more profitable than the triangle. The circle's profit maximizing size is also the largest, etc.

Basic Findings of Mills and Lav

Mills and Lav noted for certain identical size U's (defined in table 13-1) that

---

[1] E. Mills and R. Lav "A Model of Market Areas with Free Entry," *Journal of Political Economy*, 1964, pp. 278–288. The authors contend that industry equilibrium could result without space-filling polygons. But we shall assert that they overlooked the classic short- vs. long-run distinction, as their examples of nonspace-filling equilibria involved the monopoly type of industry, rather than competitive returns. Let us at this point further observe that they integrated demand curves over space in terms of polar coordinates, and then derived profit-maximizing sizes for the circle and for regular polygons such as the triangle, square, and hexagon. Correspondingly, they derived profit-maximizing prices which like M. Beckmann's [*Location Theory* (N.Y.: Random House, 1968), pp. 50–52] are counterpart to those referenced in previous footnotes in this chapter.

$$\text{TABLE } 13\text{–}1^*$$

	Triangle	Square	Hexagon	Circle
Profit Maximizing U	$-0.5434\left(\frac{c_3}{c_4}\right)$	$-0.6534\left(\frac{c_3}{c_4}\right)$	$-0.7121\left(\frac{c_3}{c_4}\right)$	$-0.7501\left(\frac{c_3}{c_4}\right)$
Maximum Profit	$0.0959\left(\frac{c_2^2}{c_4}\right)D - A$	$0.1067\left(\frac{c_2^2}{c_4}\right)D - A$	$0.1098\left(\frac{c_2^2}{c_4}\right)D - A$	$0.1104\left(\frac{c_2^2}{c_5}\right)D - A$

SOURCE: Reprinted from E. Mills and M. Lav, "A Model of Market Areas with Free Entry," *Journal of Political Economy*, 1964, p. 282.

* The mathematical developments supporting this table are recorded in detail in the appendix to this chapter. For the present we must only note that the symbols c_2, c_3, c_4 relate to complicated expressions which need not be explained at this point, except to say that c_3 is negative; D in the table stands for density; A stands for fixed cost, and U is the *shortest distance* from the seller's location to a perimeter point of his market area.

an inscribed circle would be more profitable than its related-superscribed hexagon, but that at still smaller sizes the superscribed hexagon would prevail. Specifically, they found that between the sizes -0.7075 c_3/c_4 and -0.7121 c_3/c_4, and in fact for sizes running up to irrelevant size -1.4624 c_3/c_4, the inscribed circle was more profitable than its related-superscribed hexagon. Shrinkage below size -0.7075 c_3/c_4 (with, to repeat, identical minimum size distance (U) being used to compare the several shapes) would yield, however, an inscribed circle of lower profitability than its related hexagon. Over these smaller sizes, the superscribed hexagon completely replaces the circle. Comparably, we could find very small sizes where a superscribed square (and triangle) would prove to be more profitable than a related inscribed hexagon (and square). But a trap exists, as we shortly shall see.

Good Mathematics, Limited Economics

There is advantage in presenting the main findings of Mills and Lav in diagrammatic form. In this connection, recall that basic to their results is the finding that the hexagon is more profitable than an inscribed circle on sizes ranging from zero to -0.7075 (c_3/c_4). For our purposes, to repeat, we need not concern outselves at present with the meaning of c_3/c_4 except to remember that c_3 is negative in sign; in fact, we will drop c_3/c_4 and related references in immediately forthcoming materials, though for readers preferring detail, we suggest they should turn to the appendix to this chapter before proceeding further.

Revenues less variable costs (henceforth simply revenues) for circles and hexagons are shown in Figure 13–3, in accordance with Mills and Lav, by the curves OC and OH respectively. We find that the revenue break-even points exist at sizes zero and 0.7075; one larger size break-even point, at 1.4624, is not included in the diagram. Fixed costs (henceforth simply costs) are shown on the vertical scale in Figure 13–3. Three alternative costs OA, OA', and OB' are recorded in the figure. Two main alternatives may be "viewed" via Figure 13–3: sizes less than and sizes greater than 0.7075.

(1) Mills and Lav asserted there are competitive equilibrium possibilities which will involve circular market areas. Such equilibrium result would arise in the event that costs lie above the ordinate value OA in the diagram. For example, if competition just happens to compress the circle (or, say, the hexagon) to the size 0.7121, with costs being slightly above OA', firms possessed of hexagonal market areas would suffer a net loss while those in control of a circular area (inscribed within the hexagon) might reap zero profits and survive. Why would the superscribed hexagon be less profitable? We would suppose, as noted in Part II of our text, that it is less profitable because each increase in the size of a market area brings into the seller's trading radius a set of buyers whose demand is weaker than that of buyers located more proximate to the seller, and this is particularly true of large size hexagons. In

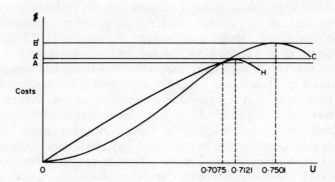

Figure 13–3: Selected Area Size

other words, behind Mills' and Lav's findings for sizes greater than 0.7121 is apparently the condition that any increase in distance from one hexagon and its inscribed circle to a larger hexagon and inscribed circle involves a revenue addition which is *relatively* greater for the circle than the hexagon. In fact, the net increment in the case of the circle is positive while that of the hexagon for sizes slightly greater than 0.7151 is negative. It would, accordingly, follow from Mills and Lav that some competitive equilibria possibilities will be marked by circular market areas. But, *we shall argue* this never occurs. To try first to support their claim, we must review selected findings on spatial markets.

It was shown years ago in the writer's *Plant Location* book (some requisite conclusions of which were presented in Chapter 6 and its appendix, and repeated earlier in the present chapter) that the freight absorption rate when

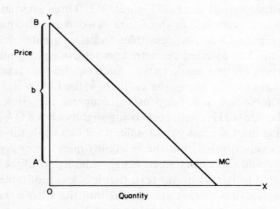

Figure 13–4: A Selected Demand, Cost Possibility

buyers are distributed evenly along a line approaches $K/4$ whereas, if the buyers are distributed over a plain, the rate approaches $K/3$. In terms of Figure 13–4, the profit maximizing f.o.b. mill price would equal $b'/2 + O\bar{A} - K/3$ (or $K/4$ as the case be), where b' is equal to $\bar{A}B$. It was also demonstrated that the f.o.b. mill price of the seller falls as each market area is extended, with the profit maximizing distance being greater and the profit maximizing f.o.b. mill price being lower in the case of buyer·dispersion over the plain compared to a line. (These findings on price relate, in turn, not only to the greater distance of the furthermost buyer but the greater freight absorption rate in the case of the plain compared to the line.) Along with similar findings of Mills and Lav—where they used identical distances (U) in comparing circles and hexagons, etc., rather than *the freight rate variable K used by this writer*—we are led to the following specification which (we shall shortly see) would help support their results: Given any size market area, the amount of freight absorption applicable to buyers contained within a circle is less than that applicable to a hexagonal market area which *superscribes* the circle. This result follows if the seller conceives of identical gross demands for all his buyers (in or beyond the circle) since, then, he would lower his f.o.b. mill price when selling over the extra n miles of the hexagon compared to its inscribed circle.

With these relations in mind, suppose a hexagon is extended from the size 0.7075 to one of greater size. We know from the findings of Mills and Lav that a net increment obtains in revenues. (Observe that the slope of OH in Figure 13–3 is positive at 0.7075.) And we further know that a comparable addition to the size of the circle adds even a larger relative increment for this particular market shape area. Once the size 0.7121 is reached, however, any continued addition to the hexagon under the Mills–Lav formulation involves deviation from their profit maximizing results. One might infer that if a seller tries further to increase his trading radius [the U in Mills and Lav's presentation, the limit to K ($\equiv k$) in the Appendix to Chapter 6], he must reduce his f.o.b. mill price by absorbing more freight than he should under the prevailing conditions of cost. In other words, *one might infer* from the Mills–Lav paper that at the profit maximizing prices and sales radius (U) which they derived, the maximum profit hexagon is *inscribed* in the maximum profit circle; hence, any attempt to go beyond this profit maximizing size 0.7121 would require a greater amount of freight absorption and a lower non-discriminatory f.o.b. (net-mill) price than that which is optimally ordered. (Later on, we shall demonstrate the error in this inference, and point out the correct formulations and results. For the time being, however, we shall continue with the Mills–Lav formulation under the assumption their findings are correct, and in the process provide the most favorable interpretation we could conceive of for the results they obtained.) Note, accordingly, that when U is 0.7501, the circle is of maximum size and sales beyond that size would appear to require similar deviations from the profit maximizing rules for the circle.

(2) Pursuant to the above, Mills and Lav noted that in certain situations the number of independent existences would be maximized by market areas circular in form. This result applies when profits are zero for the hexagon above size 0.7075, such as would hold if costs were less than OA′ but greater than OA in Figure 13–3. At such level of costs, a hexagon of maximum profit size would be less profitable than its own inscribed circle. One might infer here that if a seller tried to increase his hexagonal (or circular) market areas, relatively more buyers are added in the circular case *vis-à-vis* the hexagon so that decreases in price via freight absorption toward the profit maximizing prices would yield a greater increase in profits in the case of the circle than the hexagon. But then, if profits are noticeably positive for the circular market area, new competitors may enter and this entry would compress the inscribed circle to smaller and smaller size until the then relevant cost level equals the revenues of the circle. Since we must still be talking of a market area size greater than 0.7075, the number of independent existences under the circular trading area is therefore greater than if the hexagon prevailed.

The above specializations of the Mills and Lav theory assume, let us repeat, a cost level at least equal to or greater than OA in Figure 13–3 which, in turn, require a circle or hexagon of size 0.7075 or larger. But suppose the cost level is lower than this; that is to say, suppose cost is less than OA. We would then evaluate circular and hexagonal areas of size less than 0.7075. In such cases, the hexagon would prevail and Lösch's theory would prove applicable. If one accepts the Mills–Lav model and results, the real problem is simply to determine whether market areas will be of size 0.7075 or greater.

Market Area Sizes Under Competition. It was indicated in the *Plant Location* book (pp. 295–298) and the Appendix to Chapter 6 of this book, equation 19, that the greatest length of a circle arises when transport costs are 3/4ths of the price intercept *value above the allocable costs of production* per unit of output. In other words, let marginal cost of production at the profit maximizing quantity and sales radius be OĀ in Figure 13–4, let ĀB equal b', where OB $(= b)$ is the maximum price possible. So, OĀ + ĀB = OB; Let the transport rate t over maximum distance u (i.e., tu) be K. And, let K be at the maximum distance possible, 3/4ths b'. F.o.b. mill price *above production costs*, we know, is $(b'/2)$–$(K/3)$, hence $b'/4$ in case of the circle. [In terms of Figure 13–4, it equals $(b'/4)$ + OĀ.] Observe now that b' corresponds to Mills' and Lav's $-(a/b)-k$, as derived in the appendix to this chapter; and also observe there (immediately, following equation 9) that $c_3/c_4 = -[(a/b)-k] (1/t)$; then taking 0.7501 = 3/4, it follows that U $= -0.7501 (c_3/c_4)$—in the Mills, Lav example—is equivalent to our K $= (3/4) b'$, since we have U $= (3/4) b' (1/t)$ or tU $= (3/4) b' =$ K. Thus at the critical point of the Mills–Lav theory, i.e. U $= -0.7075 (c_3/c_4)$, the freight costs are approximately seventy percent of the difference between costs OĀ and the maximum price the firm can charge.

Suppose we assume marginal production costs are of comparatively great magnitude, such as, for example, that they are 1/2 of the highest price a buyer will pay for a single unit of the good.[1] The freight cost to the boundary point of 3/4ths of the resulting rather small b'—i.e. for the area 0.7501— would still be substantial, in this case being 3/8ths of the highest price the buyer would pay. In terms of a $5600 automobile, the maximum profit trading area of a manufacturer would run as far out as $2100 of freight cost.

Then for the minimum size sales area in which the circle is still the most profitable market area shape (namely size 0.7075, which is roughly 95 percent that of 0.7501), the freight costs to its most distant buyer would be roughly 36/100ths of the highest price the buyer would pay for the good. When marginal costs are (1/2) b, freight costs over the competitive sizes of market areas in which the circle could exist would lie approximately between 3/8.5 and 3/8ths of the highest price the most distant buyer would pay for the good. We suggest that market extensions of this size would be extremely great; indeed, for a firm to have this size market area and yet to record zero economic profits would be even more surprising.

It requires final consideration that the Appendix to Chapter 6 indicated that when buyers are evenly dispersed over a plain, the buyer who is located at the *average* distance from the seller is at a freight rate distance 2/3rds that of the most distant buyer. Freight cost *to this location*, or more generally the freight cost which one finds typically recorded by research teams, namely the average ratio of freight cost to product price *per buyer*, would be approximately 25 percent of the b intercept value under the conditions specified above. This ratio is also much too great.[2]

(3) What the circle-hexagon case boils down to is this: Starting with an extremely small circle, we would find that market area extensions via a *superscribed* hexagon, or a still larger *superscribed* square, or an even larger

---

[1] It can be shown that elasticities may be converted to the ratio MC/b via $e-1/e+1$. From estimates of elasticity by Adelman and Leontief [e.g. see M. A. Adelman, *A & P! A Study in Price-Cost Behavior and Public Policy* (Cambridge, Mass: Harvard University Press, 1959), pp. 472–473 and W. Leontief "Elasticity of Demand and Cost Data", *American Economic Review*, Dec., 1940, p. 815], one would conclude that $MC/b = 1/2$ would constitute rather substantial costs of production and typically be much less.

[2] A recent study of the Bureau of Transport Economics and Statistics of the Interstate Commerce Commission, *Freight Revenue and Wholesale Value at Destination of Commodities Transported by Class I Line-Haul Railroads*, Washington, 1959, p. 20 indicates that freight costs typically range between 1 and 5 percent the price charged to the "average" buyer. The freight costs required by the Mills-Lav theory, based on the b intercept value, occurred in one of fifty-three cases, and possibly one other depending upon the number of significant digits we would use. But even in the one or two cases, only a necessary condition for a circular market area would be on hand: the firm whose freight costs were so substantial could be one subject to small production costs and hence still be selling over a rather restricted hexagonal market notwithstanding its comparatively great freight costs; or, the firm could be a spatial monopolist. Even the one or two possibilities indicated here thus fail to provide a "sufficient" condition for the existence of a circular market area in the presence of competition; in contrast, all of the other commodities reject the "necessary" condition for the possible existence of competitively determined circular markets in practice.

superscribed triangle would increase profits up to the point of a maximum profit size triangle; then the limit is reached for the maximum profit size square, next the maximum profit size hexagon, and ultimately the circle. But though the mathematics appears to be interpretable, the related economics appears to be faulty. We should, in the event of spatial competition, not have to choose between maximum size U's but rather very small size U's. Then it would follow that if we have a *very small* hexagon which yields negative profits and we can superscribe a "break-even" square, chances are that except for special topographical and national boundary cases, our alternative would have been not only the given superscribed square but a *larger* hexagon with an equal total of sales. What the square of a given area can do, the hexagon can do better. So, only in special cases would the "outline" of a triangle or square prevail. Why not the circle in place of the hexagon? Here our answer assumes Löschian form. Empty pockets of demand indicate an opportunity exists to expand to hexagons superscribed over circles, albeit enlargement of the circles themselves as circles may not be possible. The choice, we contend, proves to be one where we may superscribe one shape (regular or irregular polygons, depending upon topography, etc.) over the "rounder" shape, with an increase in furthermost distance U being the case. We cannot continue to superimpose a round or rounder shape. At the same moment, we expect pragmatically to be at sizes smaller than the spatial monopoly size of 0.7075. The conclusion—even if we accept Mills' and Lav's derivations—is that the market area shape which predominates in the long run is the hexagon. But let us now present another (more vital) side of our objection to their theory.

Another Objection, No Constraint Placed on Demand. According to Mills and Lav, the profit maximizing U for the triangle, i.e. the shortest distance from the seller to the perimeter, is 0.5434. (See Table 13–1.) But note, within the *triangle* there exists a small triangle formed by connecting the seller at the center by direct line to any vertex point (i.e. u) *and* then by shortest distance (U) to the closest perimeter point that is near that vertex point; this small triangle has angles of 30°, 60°, and 90°, and from elementary trigonometry we, therefore, know that the length u is twice U. In other words, the distance u is 1.0868 (i.e. 2×0.5434), as shown in Table 13–2. Correspondingly, the longest distance (u) from a firm at the market center to a vertex point of a *square* market area is $\sqrt{2}$ times the shortest distance. This multiplier $\sqrt{2}$ stems from the Pythagorean theorem. Specifically, for the triangle contained within the square which connects the seller to the perimeter by shortest and longest distance, we know that $AB^2 + BC^2 = OC^2$. Because AB, equal to the shortest distance (U), is also equal to BC (along the perimeter), it follows that the longest distance (u) is $\sqrt{2}$ times the shortest distance. (See Appendix Figure 13A–1 for visual reference to a triangle within the square.) The multiplier of U in the case of the hexagon is $(2/\sqrt{3})$, also via the Pythagorean theorem, where BC is now 1/2 (OC). [And see Appendix A for visual reference to a triangle within the hexagon.] But Mills and Lav also derived as the profit maximizing f.o.b. mill price for the triangle, square, hexagon, and circle the value 0.25 of the highest price the buyer will pay for the good (see equations 8ff. in the appendix to this chapter for further details). But the u's are, of course, distances which are also expressed directly in terms of the highest price a buyer will pay for the good, and it follows that in each market area type other than the circle, the coefficient of the net-mill price, 0.25, plus that of the cost of distance ($0.75 < x < 1.0868$) exceeds the maximum price coefficient (unity) that buyers will pay for the good. See Table 13–2 for all u's. Negative demand is, thus, included in the mathematics of Mills and Lav. Rather than derive polygons inscribed in the circle of profit maximizing size, they presented polygons which extended beyond the maximum possible economic distance u. This explains (not lower mill prices or different ring increments) why some increases in U's <0.75 yielded smaller profits for superscribed hexagons.

TABLE 13–2

	Triangle	Square	Hexagon	Circle
The Mills and Lav U	0.5434	0.6534	0.7121	0.75
The Required u	1.0868	0.9240	0.8203	0.75

Much smaller U's can be shown to be required under non-negative demand constraints than those computed by Mills and Lav. At the same time, the properly constrained profit curve for the hexagon (see Figure 13–3) shifts to the left and intersects the profit curve for the circle at a downward sloping portion of the curve. But then, proper comparison is not between identical U's; rather, circle size U and hexagon size u's should be compared. Research completed too recently for detailing here appears to indicate conclusively that the circle prevails only under simple monopoly conditions in economic space and that a superscribed hexagon replaces *any* circle under conditions of competition.[1]

[1] It should be emphasized that the assertion entered above is broader than any proofs entered there as, to repeat, it is suggested by research that was only in progress by the author and Mr. Hiroshi Ohta when the text material was galley proofed. Our computer runs under constrained optimization conditions were, in other words, not completed as of the last feasible date for recording additional specifics ré market areas in this book. It is believed, however, that even without these data, the spatial equilibrium properties of the hexagon have been substantiated and the circle put to rest. We offer below some further (intuitive) explanation of the last statement in the text above for the situation where nonnegativity conditions hold and selected price constraining parameters apply which reflect the condition of very slight competition from very distant points. The statements below—in conjuction with text materials above—are believed to explain clearly why the hexagon *must* prevail whenever an organized oligopoly or spatial monopoly(ies) market has been replaced by unorganized oligopolists in competition in economic space.

Assume the following: (1) A monopoly market initially prevails over an economic space; (2) subsequently, very distant "competitive" entry causes the circle to be compressed

Conclusions and Summary of the Mills–Lav Theory

As Cournot pointed out (or as Grossack[1] deduced under very different assumptions), entry by competitive oligopolists increases supply and yields a demand (market area size) of smaller magnitude for a given firm than previously prevailed. Although competitive entry will not reduce the size of the circle or regular polygon according to the geometrical series of Cournot—since we must initially expect some empty space filling possibilities for the new entrant besides some inflexible pricing—a shrinkage nonetheless must in time result after enough entry. With sufficient competition over the landscape, market areas will shrink below the profit maximizing circle size and the circle will therefore be replaced by the hexagon. It follows that only if we assume the pure spatial monopoly type, or fortuitously enough accept a full set of non-overlapping spatial monopolists who happen only to be covering their opportunity costs, do we accept the circle as the viable market form. Given profits and competitive entry the hexagon replaces the circle.

There is, let us re-observe, no reason for the square to replace the hexagon, or the triangle to replace the square. The corollaries just do not obtain. We simply cannot superscribe a larger square (or triangle) over a hexagon (or square) since—unlike the circle and hexagon case—the entire economic space is already filled once the hexagon has replaced the circle. It is, therefore, in the pure sense quite illegitimate to inquire into very small size areas where a superscribed square (or triangle) would be more profitable than its inscribed hexagon (or square). Only equal area sizes (not superscribed

a little. Now, by definition, "competitive entry" means the original seller (i.e. the former monopolist) conceives of a leftward shifted AR curve. The profit curve for the circle (e.g. Figure 13–3) is shifted leftward and downward. But circular market areas are tangent at best. There exist, accordingly, would-be buyers located outside of the seller's shrunken market area. Though under monopoly conditions the profit maximizing f.o.b. mill price is greater for a smaller circle than a larger one, much lower mill prices (which in a zero profit equilibrium are greater for hexagons than circles) can be shown to exist when competition accounts for the smaller market area. (These particular results will be presented by this writer, H. Ohta, and M. Proctor at the 2nd World Congress, Econometric Society, Cambridge, England, Sept., 1970, under the title "The Stability of Alternative Market Area Shapes and Sizes Under Conditions of Competition in Economic Space.") The sum of this lower price and the cost of the greatest relevant distance is less than the maximum price which distant buyers (still within the monopoly circle limits) would pay for the good. Hence an irregular polygon may be superscribed over the shrunken circle. Unlike the Mills-Lav case, such polygons come within the maximum u possible. (Obviously, no negative demand must apply when a sales radius is extended by superscribing an irregular polygon over a circle whose size is <0.75.) The profits of the polygon (because of larger demand and sales) are greater than those of the shrunken circle. They induce further entry, shrinking in turn the sizes of the polygons and increasing the number of sellers in the market. Given competitive impacts, networks of regular hexagons ultimately replace the circles and irregular polygons.

[1] I. Grossack, "Duopoly, Defensive Strategies, and the Kinked Demand Curve," *Southern Economic Journal* (April 1966), pp. 406–416.

areas) should be compared. (See Appendix A.) In contradiction of Mills and Lav, the hexagon alone is thereby revealed as the competitive stable *equilibrium* market area shape.

We are able to accept non-hexagonal forms in only a general sense, and this if and only if net revenues via profit making sales would be greater for some irregular form than the inscribed regular polygon. Such greater area, in turn, obtains if and only if an uneven distribution of population and/or land surface or its like prevails. We know, of course, that such condition will arise to some extent, even under Lösch's initial conception of a homogeneous plain. Because of discontinuities and peninsular like extensions, the rational land-scape that is reflective of a competitive equilibria may prove to be one marked roughly by triangles, squares, hexagons, besides shared market shapes by two or more firms. At the base remains, however, the hexagon as the ideal form. We shall have more to say about this point in Section IV.

IV. THE SPATIAL PROPERTIES OF THE LONG-RUN EQUILIBRIUM OF THE FIRM AND CITY

Now think of an industry which has very advanced technology and is subject to high costs of transport and hence a "comparatively limited demand." Assume for the sake of simplicity that the demand is linear in form and negatively sloped. Insert, then, the first firm in the market. *The maximum profits principle requires* that the firm select that number of plants which permits it to divide the demand among each of its plants so that *each plant is of optimum size and produces at lowest cost.*[1] If the optimal number of plants possible for the firm is of such order that rather than derive economies from centralized accounting, finance, research, buying, and selling operations, diseconomies quickly arise from unwieldy business structure and faulty communications, there should be room for many rivals, firms and plants, *ceteris paribus.* But each firm, if a maximizer, will rationalize its operations *in any case* to attain the right size.

Monopoly Situations

Suppose there appears to be room for only one firm. Then, a monopoly-profit situation exists, unless we stipulate that rival firms can locate in a distant market and by so doing will cause the market area of the subject firm to be compressed to the point where no windfalls persist. If, by assumption, we do not permit enough firms to enter so that market areas overlap and are compressed, we are, in fact, conceiving of a maximum-profit spatial monopolist, and, of

[1] M. L. Greenhut, *Microeconomics, op. cit.*, Chapter 8. Also see D. Dewey, "Imperfect Competition No Bar to Efficient Production," *Journal of Political Economy*, LXVI (1958), pp. 24–33. Still earlier, see Don Patinkin, "Multiple-Plant Firms, Cartels, and Imperfect Competition," *Quarterly Journal of Economics*, LXI, 1947, p. 203.

course, the trading area will be circular over a homogeneous plain. A natural monopoly (or entry-limiting cartel) then exists, and it may have to be broken up. But a natural monopoly situation would be very unusual in our day and age of advertising and expanding demand, to say nothing of competition from firms and plants located together as well as at a distance.

Duopoly Situations

Suppose there is substantial indivisibility in the market such that, for example, if one or two firms established one, two, or a few plants of optimum size, there would be a small unsatisfied portion of the total demand left over. Perhaps there would be room for two rather than three larger than optimum size firms if MR is to be equated with MC. In this case, excessive profits would occur. If competition from a distance or even from rival industries does not arise to reduce the demand curve (that is, cause it to shift to the left, leading to the establishing of optimum size plants without economic windfalls), monopoly profit returns would surely prevail. Again, this situation would be very unusual, except in the short run. In the long run, one must expect a decrease of indivisibilities and the formation of similar industries and of new market areas dotted by the new plants of rival firms. The long-run situation is not characterized by substantial indivisibilities, for continuities develop over time.

Our present case thus suggests that enough competition arises in duopoly markets, even if the market areas of the firms only intrude on each other slightly. When this happens, the hexagon completely replaces the circle. And, if circles still prevailed for a while, unfilled demand would leave room for further entry (e.g. by new branch plants) so that sooner or later hexagons would arise.

Oligopoly Situations

In maximizing profits over continuous systems, where total demand relative to technology is comparatively large, firms will organize the number and size of plant which yield them the lowest possible average cost. Again, no non-optimum, inefficient production point eventuates, for the AR curve lies above AC. If there is room in the market for a limited number of truly optimum size firms and plants, and should there be firms in the market with plants of optimum size but not with their own optimum *number of plants*, a differential loss would obtain for such firms. New managers or firms will sooner or later enter causing uneconomic size firms to leave the market, or else attain proper size. Correspondingly, the size of the market area must reach the equilibrium (minimum) size where economic returns cover all opportunity costs.

Suppose profits in an industry are excessive, so that some profit maximizing firms with more than their optimum set of plants and size of plants earn extra large profits. Then what?

We have claimed that profits up to a certain specified extent is the return for uncertainty. So, if profits are excessive compared to the degree of uncertainty which prevails in a given activity, a windfall, a surplus, or bonanza, if you prefer, obtains. But we have long learned from competitive economic theory that if a windfall obtains and entry is open new firms and plants will invade the market, the demand curve will shift to the left and price will be reduced accordingly. Open entry in a continuous system marked by unorganized oligopoly—where, by definition, collusion is ruled out and entry does occur—must yield in time a set of returns and market area size perfectly commensurate with uncertainty. Competition with open entry among oligopolists accomplishes this result, just as would the purely competitive economy yield a set of differential rents perfectly commensurate with its set of differences in abilities and risks.

This thesis indicates that the location of firms and their plants must be so arranged in space that there is an optimal distribution. This follows because if in the economy only one firm and its plant(s) is optimal in size and location, the basic, proper rate of return is thereby established for the uncertainty to which the industry is subject. Any out-of-lineness among other plants and firms, and, of course, other industries, must lead to a pattern of entry or exit. Those enterprises which enjoy excessive returns will find that new entries are induced and relocations of plants are brought about. Those enterprises and industries which have insufficient returns must expect an exodus from the industry and a shifting to the point where proper rewards ultimately take hold.[1]

Localization may be Economic. In industries characterized by sharply divergent costs from place to place, a concentration of firms and plants may properly arise and, because costs are more variable than demand, the advantages of dispersion [except possibly for a small plant(s) or firm] would not apply. If costs, however, are not greatly divergent in space, a Löschian dispersion ensues more readily, unless inadequate or excessive returns are accepted as a norm—and this is contradictory to the rational man assumption that marks all of classical economic thought. Finally, where demand is heterogeneous over space, an intra-industry localization may, of course, occur.

Entry and Exit and Dispersion. The competition from plants located within a market area and in adjacent market areas leads then to the necessary entry-relocation-exit process that holds in a continuous system where demand is sufficiently large to be divided among many plants belonging to either a

[1] M. L. Greenhut, "The Decision Process and Entrepreneurial Returns," *The Manchester School* (September 1966), pp. 247–267.

large or small number of firms. The entry-relocation-exit process leads to a set of optimum size firms, with a profits hierarchy for activities subject to different constraints. Lösch's rational system of minimum size hexagons, therefore, holds in the free enterprise system. It holds in the modified sense noted previously in this and the preceding section of Chapter 13, but in much the same way that an omniscient manager of a system of regulated enterprise would direct. The conclusion of the theory of locational interdependence that in certain cases firms localize, such as where demand is convex and marginal costs of production are rising, proves to be a short-run finding. In the long run, we must gain that shuffling of plant sizes, production and freight costs, and more generally investment and location which elicit (and enable) returns for economic activity commensurate with the uncertainties of doing business. Moreover, the market area surrounding the competitive plant (and firm) is typically hexagonal in the long run.

Our theory thus supports in a broad way the rational network presumed by Lösch. His conception relates, of course, essentially to societies that would not be marked by irregularities, discontinuities, shopping good frills, or, more generally, capitalistic uncertainties. But what about the possibility that short-run error may have led, for example, to excessive concentration of firms and the establishment of a large city, which firms and city ultimately survive because agglomerating advantages make them efficient? Could it not be the case that a different city (and firms) should (and would) have arisen, possibly nearby or at a great distance, which would have been much more efficient? Would it not also be the case that the historical accident signifies least-cost production on "a" LRAC curve but not on the lowest LRAC curve that could have obtained?

The City (Industry) which Originally was Improperly Located. There is a correspondence between the present problem and the dynamic possibility of taste and technological change which, if known in prospect rather than retrospect, would not only have elicited a very different beginning and a significantly different growth path, but conceivably a different (better) final position. Just how similar (or possibly analogous) are the situations?

Suppose we assume the automobile industry began in Detroit, Michigan simply because a few men lived there who created an atmosphere which attracted more men of the same kind.[1] Further suppose that Granite City, Illinois really had the natural resource advantages for this industry. Alternatively, suppose the beer industry began in Milwaukee, Wisconsin because certain men happened to live there but that, at the same time, the city possessed natural resource advantages for this industry. May it be the case that the automobile industry survived in Detroit because the firms (and hence the

[1] See W. R. Thompson, *A Preface to Urban Economics* (Baltimore, The Johns Hopkins Press, 1965), p. 45, who notes that the bar-room in the old Pontchatrain Hotel had reportedly been a center of early automotive technology.

city) originally were monopolistic in power, which dominance produced in time such economic advantages that, today, no other location is feasible at the beginning. Indeed, it may be recognized that the Granite City development would have been even more glamorous than that of Detroit.

One final assumption would be helpful. Let us assume that the automotive and beer industries are identical in risk and uncertainty. In fact, for present purposes let us select the more precise definition of industry which we proposed in Chapter IV, namely that the risk component as well as the uncertainty component are identical for each industry; so too is, of course, the aggregate index value of risk and uncertainty in the manufacturing and selling of automobiles and the brewing and selling of beer. If everything else is equal, including the fact that the marginal firms in each industry are located elsewhere (perhaps in another country), and that such firms produce at identical efficiencies, it is manifest that the profits for uncertainty would be greater in the manufacture and distribution of beer than in the manufacture and distribution of automobiles.

One might surmise that some exit and entry would proceed from the automobile industry to the beer industry, directly or indirectly. Alternatively, one might expect to find a tendency on the part of some enterprisers (and their capital) not to leave the industry, but, in effect, to relocate over a long period of time. Indeed, if we propose that there are relatively many industries experiencing returns fully commensurate with those in the beer industry compared with the automotive industry's rate of return, and we recognize the transcendental importance of entrepreneurship over investment capital (by which we mean capital follows men), we might anticipate that given sufficient time the firm and the industry would relocate while the city either disintegrates or acquires new character. We do not, however, propose this thesis as an inviolate rule, in light of the possibly analogous situation we cited in the paragraph which introduced our present discussion. That situation must be considered now.

Suppose it is possible for foresight to be as good as hindsight. The person, the firm, the industry, and the economy would obviously have to be better off than otherwise, *ceteris paribus*. But suppose a difference exists between foresight and hindsight and mistakes are made. Some exit from some industries, such as the automotive industry, and some entry in some industries, such as the beer industry would arise as soon as out-of-linenesses develop. The change in numbers of firms would bring about a degree of regularity and conformability among industries, via which profits would be balanced with uncertainty. In fact, full conformity of profits to a given uncertainty would be tend to arise but only within an uncertainty category. *This particular thesis is justifiable* even though, in a different (but largely similar) context, we in effect proposed the story of the bears and the porridge to support the concept of lowest-least cost production by *all viable firms* with no blending taking place so that only optimal cost production takes place. *This thesis is justified in the present context* because the profit returns for different uncertainty indexes—as we mentioned in Chapter 2—need only be monotonic; as such, they may well be somewhat discontinuous, especially at levels of great (and greater) uncertainty where firms and industries are few and norms are not easily identified. This discontinuity means that one cannot seek, on a priori grounds, a given rate of return on investment for a particular uncertainty which is greater than that applicable to the next lower order of uncertainty by exactly the amount that the rate for the still lower order is greater than that applicable to the still smaller uncertainty, *etc.* All we may be sure of is that a monotonicity of returns applies to increasing levels of uncertainty. Firms may, accordingly, shift between industries rather than relocate to new cities when a mistake in the past has been made.

V. CONCLUSIONS AND SUMMARY

The theory and approach of this chapter recognizes, without *a priori* identification of the industries concerned, that some industries may only appear to fit the Löschian pattern exactly, while most will do so very inexactly. In the limit, the perfectly rational landscape would hold, even though viewed from the practical-real world in which we live, this pattern stands only in the modified form which reflects the spatial irregularities that arise. Forces traceable to geography, politics, demand, technology, and law may establish very uneven polygons; and some uneconomic intra-industry concentrations may arise. In any and all cases, however, there is a tendency for historical mistakes to disappear in time, although past errors can never be fully overcome. A rational market area network made up essentially of hexagons and efficient firms thus develops over time under competition. But, there is no need to presume that anyone person or group causes this to be brought about *ex ante*, or that anyone can identify it empirically *ex post*.

Appendix to Chapter 13

On Lösch's Hexagon *vis-à-vis* Mills' and Lav's Circle and Selected Polygons

We presented in Chapter 13 a theory which reconsidered Lösch's statement on the hexagon, and reinterpreted the Mills and Lav modification in such way that a new composite view of the spatial equilibrium was obtained. We accepted Lösch's theory,[1] but not that of Mills and Lav.[2] Because a rather full understanding of the Mills and Lav system is fundamental to the several disclaimers recorded in Chapter

[1] *Die räumliche Ordnung der Wirtschaft* (Jena: Gustav Fischer, 1943).
[2] "A Model of Market Areas with Free Entry" *Journal of Political Economy* (1964), pp. 278–288.

13, we shall present a fairly complete view of the basis of their mathematical development.

I. BACKGROUND

Lösch derived the theory that under certain assumptions firms would sell in hexagon-shaped, space-filling market areas, with each firm located at the center of its particular market area. His critical assumptions are that firms maximize profits, that there is free entry in all industries, that there is a homogeneous distribution of resources over space, *and* that in order for industry equilibrium to exist market areas of firms must completely cover the space.

Recently, Edwin S. Mills and Michael R. Lav claimed that the last of Lösch's assumptions should be a theorem, and that, as a theorem, it is not correct. They agree with Lösch that industry equilibrium is achieved by firms continuing to enter (leave) the industry as long as more than (or less than) normal profits prevail. Moreover, as firms enter (or leave) an industry, market areas will tend to change so as to maximize profits. Further they note that two conditions characterize the long-run industry equilibrium. First, all firms will be making zero economic profits; and second, no additional firms can enter the industry without causing profits to become negative. And they conclude that the market areas are such that there exists over the space the maximum number of firms possible per square mile.

To disprove the theorem, Mills and Lav consider a special model which satisfies the assumptions of the theorem and, in addition, include six simplifying assumptions.

    I. There is a single commodity which can be conceived as produced at any point in a two-dimensional space under the same cost function.

    II. At any point in the space, the total cost function for producing x units of output is one of constant MC and decreasing AC, a good function considering our theory of profits for uncertainty with tangency resulting between a negatively sloping AR and an adjusted AC curve. They define cost as

(1) $$A + kx.$$

    III. Transportation cost per unit per mile is the same everywhere; thus, the cost of shipping one unit of output u miles is

(2) $$t\mathbf{u}.$$

    IV. Each firm sets its f.o.b. price and sells to anyone who wishes to buy at that price.

    V. All consumers are distributed over the economic landscape with a uniform density of D per square mile.

    VI. Each consumer has the same demand curve which is linear in price. By price is meant net price before transportation charges. Thus the demand curve is represented by

(3) $$x_f = a - b(p + t\mathbf{u}),$$

where x_f is quantity demanded per consumer, p is the f.o.b. mill price set by the firm, and $p + t\mathbf{u}$ is the price per unit of output that the consumer must pay.

318   SPATIAL DISTRIBUTION

Given these assumptions, Mills and Lav are able to derive selected preliminary results. The first of these is that the consumer will buy from the firm closest to him if the f.o.b. price set by all firms is the same. That this is true follows from the fact that $p + t\mathbf{u}$ will be the smallest for the lowest value of u, that is $p^0 + tu^0 \leqslant p^0 + t\mathbf{u}$ if and only if $u^0 \leqslant \mathbf{u}$.

The second readily evident result is that the total sales of the firm can be found by integrating the demand equation over its market area and multiplying by D. If we integrate the demand curve over the market area, we obtain the average sales per consumer over the market area and, by multiplying by D, we derive the total sales for the market area.

The third obvious result is that the firm will sell only in regular shaped market areas with the firm located in the center. By regular shaped market areas we mean circles and regular polygons, such as triangles, squares, and hexagons. In deference to the assumption of homogeneous space and the definition of industry equilibrium, irregular shaped market areas are eliminated because an irregular shaped market area could be replaced by a slightly smaller regular shaped market area with the same profitability. Moreover more firms will operate over a landscape marked by regular shaped market areas.

II. THE MATHEMATICS OF MILLS AND LAV

Mills and Lav used polar coordinates in integrating the demand function over a given area. Thus in integration over a circle, the variables of integration ($\mathbf{u}$ and θ respectively) will be measured from O to U (the radius length of the circle), and from 0 to 2π since a circle involves 2π radians.[1] In integrating over a regular polygon (e.g. Figure 13A–1), $\mathbf{u}$ (any distance from the center up any perimeter point) will vary from O to $U/\cos\theta$, and θ will vary from O to π/s. We shall see that these limits, in conjunction with D, provide $(1/2)s$ of the total sales; multiplying the integral by $2sD$ will therefore yield total sales. In order to appreciate these relations consider the following:

Figure 13A–1 represents a square market area; thus $s = 4$. We are integrating over the area ABC and multiplying the result by $2sD = 8D$ to obtain total sales over the entire square, as there are 8 triangles of size ABC in the square. Using polar coordinates, let $\mathbf{u}$ vary from the origin A $= (0, 0)$ to some point on the line BC, that point depending on the angle θ. Angle θ is the relation between the point C on BC and the distance U; it is measurable as $\cos\theta = U/u$ where $u = \sqrt{x_0^2 + y_0^2}$, with x_0 and y_0 being a coordinate on BC and $(x, y) = (0, 0)$ at A. For example, if $\theta = \pi/4$, then $u = $ AC and U $= $ AB and $\cos \pi/4 = $ AB/AC by definition. Thus $u = U/\cos\theta$ is the upper limit for $\mathbf{u}$ and $\pi/4$ is the upper limit for θ.

From the above discussion, the total sales x of a firm with the shortest distance U to its perimeter is obtained by a double integral for the polygon or circle case (as in Figure 13A–2).[2] For a regular s-sides polygonal market area, we find—

[1] When Mills and Lav put limits on the integrals, they assign to U the shortest distance to the perimeter.
[2] When we write $\int\{\int f(\mathbf{u})d\mathbf{u}\}d\theta$, we mean to integrate $f(\mathbf{u})$ first with respect to u holding θ constant. Then we obtain $\int F(\theta)\, d\theta$ and we integrate it with respect to θ. A double integral is used since we are estimating the volume of a conic figure. Using a circle as an example, we first integrate with respect to $\mathbf{u}$ which gives us the area under the line AB in Figure 13–A2.

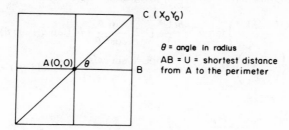

Figure 13A–1: Integrating Demand over a Square Market Area

$$(4) \quad x = 2s\mathrm{D}\int_0^{\pi/s}\int_0^{U/\cos\theta}[a-b(p+t\mathbf{u})]\,\mathbf{u}du\,d\theta$$

And, for a circular market area, we have—

$$(5) \quad x = \mathrm{D}\int_0^{2\pi}\int_0^{\mathrm{U}}[a-b(p+t\mathbf{u})]\,\mathbf{u}du\,d\theta$$

Note that the demand function is multiplied by $\mathbf{u}$ in both cases because of the transformation from cartesian to polar coordinates. Equation (4) yields (4′). Thus

$$x = 2s\mathrm{D}\int_0^{\pi/s}\left\{\frac{a\mathbf{u}^2}{2}-\frac{bp\mathbf{u}^2}{2}-\frac{bt\mathbf{u}^3}{3}\,\bigg|_0^{U/\cos\theta}\right\}d\theta$$

$$x = 2s\mathrm{D}\int_0^{\pi/s}\left\{\frac{a\mathrm{U}^2}{2\cos^2\theta}-\frac{bp\mathrm{U}^2}{2\cos^2\theta}-\frac{bt\mathrm{U}^3}{3\cos^3\theta}\right\}d\theta$$

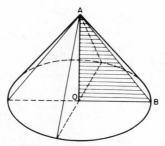

Figure 13A–2: Production Requirement, $a-bk>0$

Then integrate with respect to θ, which is taking the area of OAB and adding it up for every angle θ up to 2π. Thus, just as we estimate the volume of a cube by finding the area of the base and multiplying by the height, we find the area of the triangle OAB and multiply it by the number of radians in a circle (2π).

Making appropriate substitutions on integrating[1] we obtain

$$x = 2sD\left\{\left(\frac{aU^2 - bpU^2}{2}\right)\tan\theta - \frac{bt\,U^3}{3}\left[1/2\left(\frac{\sin\theta}{\cos^2\theta} + ln\,(\tan\theta + \sec\theta)\right)\right\}\right\}\Bigg|_0^{\pi/s}$$

$$(4')\quad x = 2sD\left\{\left(\frac{a - pb}{2}\right)U^2\tan(\pi/s) - \frac{bt\,U^3}{6}\left[\frac{\sin(\pi/s)}{\cos^2(\pi/s)} + ln\,(\tan(\pi/s) + \sec(\pi/s))\right]\right\}$$

Equation (5) yields

$$x = D\int_0^{2\pi}\left\{\frac{au^2}{2} - \frac{bpu^2}{2} - \frac{btu^3}{3}\Bigg|_0^U\right\}d\theta$$

$$x = D\int_0^{2\pi}\left\{\left(\frac{a - bp}{2}\right)U^2 - \frac{bt\,U^3}{3}\right\}d\theta$$

$$x = D\left\{\left(\frac{a - bp}{2}\right)U^2 - \frac{bt\,U^3}{3}\theta\Bigg|_0^{2\pi}\right\}$$

$$(5')\quad x = 2\pi DU^2\left(\frac{a - bp}{2} - \frac{bt\,U}{3}\right)$$

The firms total profits are

(6) $Y = px - A - kx$

We then substitute the appropriate values for the trigonometric relations[2] in (4'), doing this respectively for the triangular, square, and then hexagonal market areas;

[1] From a table of integrals we obtain

$$\int\frac{d\theta}{\cos\theta} = ln\,(\tan\theta + \sec\theta),$$

$$\int\frac{d\theta}{\cos^2\theta} = \tan\theta, \text{ and}$$

$$\int\frac{d\theta}{\cos^n\theta} = \frac{1}{n-1}\left(\frac{\sin\theta}{\cos^2\theta}\right) + \left(\frac{n-2}{n-1}\right)\frac{d\theta}{\cos^{n-2}\theta}$$

Thus

$$\int\frac{d\theta}{\cos^3\theta} = \frac{1}{2}\left[\frac{\sin\theta}{\cos^2\theta} + \int\frac{d\theta}{\cos\theta}\right] = \frac{1}{2}\left[\frac{\sin\theta}{\cos^2\theta} + ln(\tan\theta + \sec\theta)\right]$$

[2] For the triangular market area, $s = 3$; thus $\sin\pi/3 = \sqrt{3}/2$, $\tan\pi/3, = \sqrt{3}$, $\cos\pi/3 = 1/2$, and $\sec\pi/3 = 2$. Substituting these values in (4') yields:

$$x = 2sD\left\{\left(\frac{a - pb}{2}\right)U^2\sqrt{3} - \frac{bt\,U^3}{6}\,[3.4641 + 1.311641]\right\}$$

$$x = 2sD\left\{\left(\frac{a - pb}{2}\right)U^2\sqrt{3} - bt\,U^3\left[\frac{4.775741}{6}\right]\right\}$$

$$x = 2sD\left\{\left(\frac{a - pb}{2}\right)U^2\sqrt{3} - 0.7969bt\,U^3\right\}; \text{ and similarly for the square, hexagon, and}$$

circle.

and similarly with (5′) for the circular area. Then we substitute (4′) and (5′) into (6) for all market areas to establish the relations (7)

(7T) $\quad Y_T = 6DU^2\left[\left(\dfrac{a-bp}{2}\right)\sqrt{3}-0.7969bt\,U\right](p-k)-A$

(7S) $\quad Y_s = 8DU^2\left[\left(\dfrac{a-bp}{2}\right)-0.3848bt\,U\right](p-k)-A$

(7H) $\quad Y_H = 12DU^2\left[\dfrac{a-bp}{2\sqrt{3}}-0.2027bt\,U\right](p-k)-A$

(7C) $\quad Y_c = 2\pi DU^2\left[\dfrac{a-bp}{2}-\dfrac{bt\,U}{3}\right](p-k)-A$

Since it is assumed that the firm sets the best price possible and sells to all who wish to buy, it will be useful to find the profit-maximizing price. This may be done either by taking the partial derivative of Y with respect to price and setting it equal to zero or by using the equal marginal principle, MR = MC. We work with the former. Thus, substituting in equations (7) the partials of Y with respect to p yields[1]

$$\frac{\partial Y}{\partial p_T} = 6DU^2\left(\frac{a\sqrt{3}}{2}-\frac{bp_T}{2}\sqrt{3}-0.7969\,bt\,U\right)-6DU^2(p_T-k)\frac{b\sqrt{3}}{2} = 0, \text{ and, by}$$

elementary manipulation, we obtain

(8T) $\quad p_T = \dfrac{a}{2b}+\dfrac{k}{2}-0.4601t\,U,$

$$\frac{\partial Y}{\partial p_s} = 8DU^2\left(\frac{a}{2}-\frac{bp_s}{2}-0.3848bt\,U\right)-8DU^2(p_s-k)\frac{b}{2} = 0 \text{ and, in turn}$$

(8S) $\quad p_s = \dfrac{a}{2b}+\dfrac{k}{2}-0.3826t\,U,$

$$\frac{\partial Y}{\partial p_H} = 12DU^2\left(\frac{a}{2\sqrt{3}}-\frac{bp_H}{2\sqrt{3}}-0.2727\,bt\,U\right)-12DU^2\,(p_H-k)\frac{b}{2\sqrt{3}} = 0 \text{ and, in turn}$$

(8H) $\quad p_H = \dfrac{a}{2b}+\dfrac{k}{2}-0.3509t\,U,$

[1] For example, setting the partial derivative of Y_T with respect to p equal to zero, we obtain

$$\frac{\partial Y_T}{\partial p} = 6DU^2\left(\frac{a\sqrt{3}}{2}-\frac{bp\sqrt{3}}{2}-0.7969btU\right)-6DU^2\,(p_T-k)\frac{b\sqrt{3}}{2} = 0, \text{ or}$$

$$6DU^2\left[\frac{a\sqrt{3}}{2}-0.7969btU-p_T\left(\frac{b\sqrt{3}}{2}+\frac{b\sqrt{3}}{2}\right)+k\frac{b\sqrt{3}}{2}\right] = 0. \text{ Thus}$$

$$-p_T\,(b\sqrt{3}) = \frac{-a\sqrt{3}}{2}-\frac{kb\sqrt{3}}{2}+0.7969btU$$

$$p_T = \frac{a}{2b}+\frac{k}{2}-\frac{0.7969}{\sqrt{3}}tU; \text{ or, } p_T = \frac{a}{2b}+\frac{k}{2}-0.4601tU$$

$$\frac{\partial Y}{\partial p_C} = 2\pi DU^2\left(\frac{a}{2} - \frac{bp_C}{2} - \frac{btU}{3}\right) - 2\pi DU^2\,(p_C - k)\frac{b}{2} = 0, \text{ and in turn}$$

(8C) $p_C = \dfrac{a}{2b} + \dfrac{k}{2} - 0.3333t\,U,$

where the coefficients of tU denote the freight absorption rates for the given market shapes.[1] From the profit maximizing U, as derived later via equations (10), it can be shown that the profit maximizing (nondiscriminatory) f.o.b. mill price is the same for the triangle, square, hexagon, and circle, equal to $-.25$ (C3/C4).

Substituting the values of (8) back into the equations (7) gives us

(9T) $Y_T(U) = 1.1004\,Dc_4U^4 + 2.3910\,Dc_3U^3 + 1.2990\,Dc_2U^2 - A,$

(9S) $Y_S(U) = 0.5855Dc_4U^4 + 1.5304\,Dc_3U^3 + Dc_2U^2 - A,$

(9H) $Y_H(U) = 0.4269\,Dc_4U^4 + 1.2160\,Dc_3U^3 + 0.8600Dc_2U^2 - A,$

(9C) $Y_C(U) = 0.3491Dc_4U^4 + 1.0472Dc_3U^3 + 0.7854Dc_2U^2 - A.$

where $c_4 = bt^2$, $c_3 = -t(a - bk)$, $c_2 = (a - bk)^2/b$, $c_4 > 0$, $c_3 < 0$, $c_2 > 0$, and $c_2c_4 = c_3^2$. Notice $a - bk$ is the point demand for output of the firm, if price equals marginal cost. If $a - bk$ is not positive, no output is produced. See Figure 13A–3.[2]

By taking the derivative of Y with respect to U and setting it equal to zero, equations 10 are obtained—

(10T) $(4.4016Dc_4U^2 + 7.1730Dc_3U + 2.5980Dc_2)U = 0,$

(10S) $(2.3420Dc_4U^2 + 4.5912Dc_3U + 2Dc_2)U = 0,$

[1] To relate Mills' & Lav's system more closely to our own, remember that in M. L. Greenhut, *Plant Location in Theory and Practice* (Chapel Hill, University of North Carolina Press, 1956, 61, 67), Chapter VI and Appendix A, it was first established that if buyers are distributed uniformly over a plain, net-mill price would, in the case where Mills' and Lav's b is unity, equal $\dfrac{a}{2} + \dfrac{MC}{2} - \dfrac{tu}{3}$, where we use MC in place of their k and tu in place of our K. Where buyers are distributed evenly over a line, it was shown that the profit-maximizing net-mill price is equal to $\dfrac{a}{2} + \dfrac{MC}{2} - \dfrac{tu}{4}$. Note, the freight absorption rate tu/3 is greater when buyers are distributed over a plain than when they are dispersed over a line tu/4. However, in the system derived in *Plant Location*, the greatest distance (u), not the shortest (U) was used. It was also found that the distance along any line was greater when buyers were distributed over a plain and not only on one line. The combination of lower absorption rate (line vs. plain) and shorter distance (line vs. plain) worked in favor of a higher net-mill price (i.e., smaller freight absorption) in the case of the line. Each extension in the line case does not add as much to the firm's profits as it does in the case of a distribution over a plain, and the market length u is therefore less. Similarly, note the prices in (8) where, in contrast, we find that in order to have the same "minimum" distance, the net-mill price must be least in the triangle, etc.; in other words, the circle, being *inscribed* within any of the regular polygons, can take advantage of its shape with the highest f.o.b. monopoly price. See the Appendix to Chapter 6 of this book for other aspects of spatial pricing and freight absorption.

[2] Mills and Lav are not claiming that the firm would set price equal to marginal cost. They are ruling out the case represented in Figure 13A–3. That is, when $\mathbf{u} = 0$ (the firm is selling at a point), the demand function is $x = a - bp$ and if $p = k$, then $x = 0$. In this case, costs are such that production would never take place. If $a - bk > 0$, the firm is selling to some point(s) in space ($\mathbf{u} \neq 0$), and would maximise profits by setting $MR = MC$.

TABLE 13A-1

	Triangle	Square	Hexagon	Circle
Profit-Maximizing U	$-0.5434(\frac{c_3}{c_4})$	$-0.6534(\frac{c_3}{c_4})$	$0.7121(\frac{c_3}{c_4})$	$0.7501(\frac{c_3}{c_4})$
Maximum Profit	$[0.0959(c_2^2/c_4)D]-A$	$[0.1067(c_2^2/c_4)D]-A$	$[0.1091(c_2^2/c_4)D]-A$	$[0.1104(c_2^2/c_4)D]-A$

Reprinted from E. Mills and M. Lav, "A Model of Market Areas with Free Entry," *Journal of Political Economy*, 1964, p. 282.

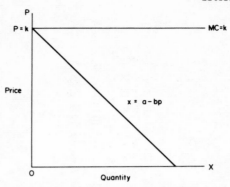

Figure 13A–3: Integrating Demand over Economic Space

(10H) $(1.7076Dc_4U^2 + 3.6480Dc_3U + 1.7200Dc_2)U = 0$,
(10C) $(1.3964Dc_4U^2 + 3.1416Dc_3U + 1.5708Dc_2)U = 0$.

One solution for all four equations is $U = 0$, but this yields a minimum profit of $-A$. Two other solutions are possible with the quadratic form. Both solutions will be positive; and, the smallest of the two must yield the value of U which maximizes profits. To illustrate, consider equation (10S), where the relevant coefficients are repeated below.

$2.3420c_4U^2 + 4.5912c_3U + 2c_2 = 0$.

Thus

$$U = \frac{-4.5912c_3 \pm \sqrt{(4.5912)^2c_3{}^2 - 4(2.3420)(2)c_2c_4}}{(2)(2.3420)c_4}$$

Since $c_2c_4 = c_3^2$ we have

(11) $U = -\dfrac{c_3}{c_4}\left[\dfrac{(4.5912) \pm \sqrt{(4.5912)^2 - 8(2.3420)}}{4.6840}\right]$

By solving equation 11 and similar equations for the triangle, hexagon, and circle, we obtain the value of U that will, in each case, maximize profits. By putting these values back into equations 10, we derive the level of maximum profits. Table 13A–1, p. 323, provides these values.

To show that there are values of U for which profits in circular market shapes, Y_C, are greater than profits in hexagonal market shapes, Y_H, set equation 9H equal to equation 9C and solve for values of U where $Y_C = Y_H$. The derived values of U are 0, -0.7075 (c_3/c_4), and -1.4624 (c_3/c_4).[1] In other words, the basis for our

[1] Setting 9H equal to 9C we have
$0.4269\,Dc_4U^4 + 1.2160\,Dc_3U^3 + .8600\,Dc_2U^2 - A =$
$0.3491\,Dc_4U^4 + 1.0472\,Dc_3U^3 + 0.7854\,Dc_2U^2 - A$
or $(0.4269 - 0.3491)c_4U^4 + (1.2160 - 1.0472)c_3U^3 + (0.8600 - 0.7854)c_2U^2 = 0$
or $U^2(.0778c_4U^2 + .1688c_3U + .0746c_2) = 0$
Thus

$$U = 0 \text{ or } U = \frac{-.1688c_3 \pm \sqrt{(.1688)^2c_3^2\,2 - 4(.0778)(.0746)c_2c_4}}{2(.0778)c_4}$$

Figure 13–3 is founded in the relations between 0 and -0.7075 (c_3/c_4), $Y_H > Y_C$, and between -0.7075 (c_3/c_4) and -1.4624 (c_3/c_4), $Y_H < Y_C$. Since -0.7075 $(c_3/c_4) < -0.7121$ $(c_3/c_4) < -1.4624$ (c_3/c_4), there are values of U according to Mills and Lav for which profits in the hexagonal market shapes are increasing, but for the same values the profits in the circular market shapes are larger.

$$= -\frac{c_3}{c_4}\left[\frac{(.1688 \pm \sqrt{(.1688)^2 - 4(.0778)(.0746)}}{.1556} \right]$$
$$= -0.7075 \ (c_3/c)_4$$
$$\quad\ -1.4624 \ (c_3/c)_4.$$

PART FOUR

GENERAL EQUILIBRIUM, WELFARE, AND SOCIAL POLICY

14

General Equilibrium, Welfare, and Economic Space

WE AIM NOW TO SHOW that a spatial unorganized oligopolistic economy in long-run equilibrium possesses general equilibrium properties and welfare characteristics substantially similar to those of pure competition. We shall also indicate where unorganized oligopoly differs from the purely competitive system.

I. THE WALRAS MODEL AND ECONOMIC SPACE

The Walras model of general equilibrium may be used to stress selected details of our theory. While applying his model, we will also be able to examine the impacts of space on economic thought.

(1). Throughout this book the tendency of particular segments of the market to reach equilibrium has been indicated. Thus we know that the individual consumer seeks to allocate his funds so that his MRSxy (i.e., his ratio of satisfactions per last unit of x for a last unit of y) equals Px/Py. This means that the last unit of expenditure for any one good yields the same relative satisfaction for the consumer as was obtained from the last unit of expenditure for any other good. Accordingly, a reallocation of expenditures would involve a decrease in relative satisfactions.

(2). It has also been a vital part of our analysis that business firms allocate hired resources so that their MRTSyx = Px/Py, where in this section I of Chapter 14, to distinguish factor from commodity substitutions, we follow the tradition of reversing the order of the subscripts from that followed in utility theory, and where we further distinguish producer from consumer substitution by using the reference marginal rate of technical substitution in place of marginal rate of substitution. More generally, the subject condition states that business firms allocate hired resources so that the MRRSyx = MEx/MEy.[1]

---

[1] This equation requires that, in the equilibrium, the marginal physical product *per unit worth of increased expenditure* for one factor equals the marginal physical product *per unit worth of increased expenditure* for all other hired factors. In addition, it stipulates that the marginal revenue product derived from the marginal physical product cannot be greater than or less than the increased expenditure, but must be the same. For details see Chapter 9.

In other words, the net increase in revenue added by the last unit of every factor employed must equal the net increase in cost resulting from its employment. Given this equality, the firm will be using both the least cost and the maximum profit combination of production factors.[1] As long as the given conditions remain unchanged, reallocation of resources in any direction must cause lower net returns for any firm. Moreover, it would also decrease the total output value. (We assume that prices are not already distorted by different degrees of monopoly, or monopsony, or by government fiat etc. so that no offsetting changes are possible.) Not only would the valuation of total output then be maximized *under existing scales of preference and cost*, but if SRAC = LRAC = SRMC = LRMC = MR and there is no monopsony, technical efficiency would also be at its greatest. Monopsonistic distortions and uneconomic size plants would thereby be ruled out—the former by assumption and the latter by the designated equality conditions.[2] These particular relations, however, suggest a distinction between what may be called the basic and the desired conditions of general equilibrium. What is required to obtain equilibrium and what is desired may not be the same. For the present, we are interested chiefly in the basic conditions.

In order to assure stability, two other requirements must be met *in addition to* the two conditions already given in the equations between MRSxy and Px/Py (condition 1) and between MRRSyx and MEx/MEy (condition 2). Before defining these additional "basic" requirements, however, let us note certain vital elements that are inherent to condition (2) above given our conception of unorganized oligopoly in general equilibrium.

Under the system of general equilibrium the rates of pay for homogeneous factors are identical, a datum intrinsic to the full meaning of MRRSyx = MEx/MEy. Nonfulfillment of this condition would signify that some employers could replace a factor with an identical one which would be more cheaply employed elsewhere. The economy would, therefore, be unstable.[3] Seen from another standpoint, if any firm is monopsonistic, all other firms employing the same factor must be identically monopsonistic. Otherwise, the strangest assortment of improbably offsetting conditions would be necessary to provide an efficient stability. But let us dwell on this vital point for a moment or two longer:

[1] There are as many least-cost combinations as there are different outputs. In the short run, the right least-cost combination is shown by its ability to yield the best net return.

[2] Recall that monopsonistic conditions create a series of SRAC curves and an associated LRAC curve on a higher level than under purely competitive buying. Any exception to this would require factor willingness to work at a discount for small monopsonies—which is a quite improbable situation. Accordingly, superimposing the optimum-sized plant under monopsony on the competitive LRAC will make the best monopsonistic SRAC greater in cost than the best competitive SRAC, besides being a smaller plant.

[3] The economy might then also be called monopolistic. See M. W. Reder, "Monopolistic Competition and the Stability Conditions," *Review of Economic Studies*, VIII (1941), pp. 122–125.

We are recognizing and accepting what might at first blush appear to be asymmetry in our theory. That is to say, one might believe we are distinguishing arbitrarily between the properties of the negatively sloping marginal revenue function, and the positively sloping marginal expenditure curve, accepting the former but condemning the latter. The negative slope of the revenue function, we would appear to be saying, reflects a return for uncertainty which is integrally proper for a free enterprise system; at the same time we would be claiming that monopsony contains an undesirable arbitrariness. This, in fact, *is* our view, at least to the extent that we are considering that facet of monopsony which complements pure monopoly, not oligopoly; another component of monopsony, we shall note, is rooted in acceptable phenomenon.

Consider monopsonistic power where there is only one buyer in a given economic space; let this buyer be able to acquire initial factor inputs at low prices and additional inputs at rising prices due to the different reservation prices of suppliers. This advantage, let us hasten to add, relates essentially to the absence of competition. No justification therefore exists for the controlled level of factor's prices. To the extent, however, that the purchase of initial inputs at lower prices is not imposed on suppliers because of less than full employment hiring policies but rather reflects preferences among some suppliers for use (or employment) by "selected" buyers (e.g. spatial preferences for work), the upward sloping average and marginal expenditure curve is acceptable. When founded on this basis, any existing unorganized "opsony" would be an approved counterpart of unorganized oligopoly. In fact, the cost level of the firm would not necessarily be higher than that of the purely competitive buyer. The monopsonistic buying which we derogate in this book is, therefore, that which is counterpart to monopoly, not that which is the counterpart to an unorganized oligopoly.[1]

(3). The third basic requirement for general equilibrium is that AR = LRAC = SRMC = LRMC in those markets which have no uncertainty-restricted entry. If this condition does not hold, losses or profits would (or could) exist, and instability would result.[2]

(4). The fourth basic requirement for general equilibrium is that SRMC = LRMC = MR in those markets having some uncertainty restricted entry. Moreover, AR would have to be greater than LRAC (not adjusted LRAC), with no further exit being indicated and with further entry being

---

[1] We are, in effect, conceiving of supplier preferences for particular buyers to be similar to entrepreneurial preferences for different uncertainty. Thus, the extra cost to society in the form of smaller output by the industry in question, *ceteris paribus*, reflects greater satisfaction (job preference) on the one hand and necessary income (for uncertainty) on the other hand.

[2] When condition 3 holds, the entrepreneur—as well as the hired factors—receives his marginal product contribution. Relatedly, if constant returns to scale exist, the marginal product contribution of each factor times the quantity of each factor employed will be equal to the total product.

restrained by uncertainty.[1] Implicitly, all opportunity costs are received in full.

Basic and Desired Conditions

In any *mixed economy* which fulfills only conditions (1) and (2), consumer satisfactions would not be maximized, nor would resource allocation be most efficient. These two *basic* (necessary) conditions would be met, but not, let us say, *all basic* (sufficient) ones as well.

To see this, note that the fixed resources (namely, the entrepreneur's fixed capital) would be receiving higher returns in the complex markets than in the other markets. This is because fulfillment of condition (2) only helps establish the general equilibrium; without conditions (3) and (4) governing the size of plant and the degrees of monopoly, there is no guaranty that the general distribution of income would be the proper one.

What are the implicit conditions required for the efficient general equilibrium of a mixed economy? They are as noted above: (I) the absence of monopsonistic forces which do not relate to supplier preference so that adjusted or unadjusted SRAC = LRAC = SRMC = LRMC = MR, as the case be, with the most efficient size of plant(s) being in use under the given structure of wants. And (II) properly arranged average revenue functions under simple or complex conditions so that the equality between MRRSyx and MEx/MEy also provides AR greater than MC proportions everywhere by the appropriate rates R; only then are consumer satisfactions maximized and incomes fully earned.

Implicit to condition (2) is, let us repeat, the nonexistence of monopsonistic forces unrelated to supplier preferences, and implicit to conditions (3) and (4) is the long-run receipt of full opportunity costs. We shall refer to these two required (implicit) properties of our system as desired conditions. It is in this context that we set forth the proposition that when the basic and desired conditions apply, the resource allocation is the most efficient possible given society's wants.[2]

[1] Compare with M. Reder, *op. cit.*, and R. Triffin, *Monopolistic Competition and General Equilibrium Theory* (Cambridge: Harvard University Press, 1940), especially pp. 8, 9, 54, 67. Note that conditions 3 and 4 are what have long prompted such general thoughts as that by R. Dorfman, P. Samuelson, and R. Solow, *Linear Programming and Economic Analysis* (New York: McGraw-Hill, 1958) . . . that one cannot readily see that the ever-changing, imperfect, oligopolistic world has a statically timeless, frictionless, perfectly competitive equilibrium.

[2] It is probably self-evident that a general equilibrium for a complex market economy hinges on the proverbial thread. For example, after stability has been reached, any minute tilt or movement of the average revenue curve of any firm will induce widespread repercussions. Observe also that, under the desired conditions, the relatively small firm with a *very large* plant in a given community possesses a graver monopsonistic threat to economic efficiency than does the large firm with *many scattered* small plants. A complex economy in space presents different minutiae than the noncomplex simple economy. It is in this spirit

Purely Competitive and Oligopolistic Equilibria

It is well established in economics that competitive equilibrium will involve maximization of the total value of all finished commodities produced in the economy. The reasoning here is that if there is any opportunity to increase profits, businessmen will increase some output at the expense of another. In our terminology, they do this by equating the MRRSyx with MEx/MEy. Moreover, if the competitive equilibrium is to be unique, society's revealed preference must hold. Thus, if at one set of prices A is shown to be preferred to B (i.e., A is equal or higher in price than B, yet people buy more of A than B), there is no other income total and distribution for the given society which would reveal B as preferred to A under a different set of prices (i.e., where the price of B equals or exceeds that of A and yet people buy more of B than A). In cases where revealed preference does not hold, the outcome is multiple equilibria rather than a unique equilibrium.

Theory has long accepted that the production frontier or transformation locus is convex upward. Better yet, we may say that a nation's production possibilities form a convex set. Baumol uses this relation to note that fixed prices (costs) can be so arranged as to form a tangent to some point on the frontier of the convex set.[1] And, since any frontier point on the convex set yields greater output for any cost combination than does any interior point, it is also technologically efficient. In the process of equating MRTSyx with Px/Py, we move to the frontier. In light of different size establishments, we also have SRAC = LRAC = SRMC, hence = LRMC, for each viable (surviving) firm. If, finally, we consider the set of indifference curves (and thus the set of prices) prevailing at a given moment—one curve tangent to, others overlapping, and still others far from the convex set—then for *the particular society* there is a fixed point which would yield the competitive equilibrium. Significantly, this equilibrium point would be technologically efficient under conditions of pure competition.

What about the particular case of unorganized oligopoly? Do the results noted above hold without modification of words? Of course, we know that in oligopoly, MRRSyx = MEx/MEy, and this condition places the representative firm at the least cost combination for the given output. But, what are the forces which determine the make-up of the industry, of all industries, and hence the outputs applicable to the frontier?

At the true optimum point for an industry, the relevant industry output level has been partly determined by some indifference curve applicable to society in general at that "long-run" moment. In other words there are forces in unorganized oligopoly which move firms to the optimum cost point

that Isard objects to modern general equilibrium theory and its customary abstraction from space; see W. Isard, *Location and Space Economy* (New York: John Wiley & Sons, Inc., 1956), p. 25.

[1] W. J. Baumol, "Activity Analysis," *American Economic Review*, XLVIII (1958).

appropriate for the particular society. With these thoughts in mind, we may rephrase our question as follows: do forces exist in this market such that given the indifference curve set and all least cost curves, producers move toward optimum cost points? Do they move towards the unique ultimate tangency point between the convex set and *an* indifference curve?

One answer might be that mathematical exactness does not hold for unorganized oligopoly in the same "inimically stable" way as it does for pure competition. There is no tangency of a horizontal AR curve to an unadjusted AC curve. So it would seem in oligopoly, especially assuming a "wrong" start somewhere in the economic space by some industries, that we lack the "fine" assurance of entry or exit taking place *perfectly*. Instead of an AR, AC identity at an easily graphed minimum point, we must support our diagrams with qualitative statements. Thus if returns from one industry are out of line with those of other industries, a bonus or relative loss will envelope the market, and this bonus or loss encourages shifting of locations, market areas, product types (i.e., differentiations), and the like. The economy moves toward a series of differentials in net returns which tie up perfectly with the existing uncertainty (including, let us repeat, indivisibility). This lends stability to the system. In fact, as found in Chapter 8, an irrepressible tendency exists under free entry for oligopolistic firms to produce and price in such way that a proper AR, MC proportion holds within a given industry. As a consequence, we must also realize that the semantic *uncertainty-profits* might just as well have been *uncertainty-cost*. Any greater uncertainty of a return in one occupation compared to another is, in other words, as much a drain on (or loss to) the individual as is the pay he would surrender under perfect knowledge if he refused the alternative employment. Moreover, when economic relations are viewed in real terms, the AR > MC proportion will be seen to hold among industries just as it does within an industry. Manifestly, the AR > MC proportion yields the tangency between the appropriate indifference curve and a point on the frontier of the convex set, provided that "right" AR > MC differentials prevail coterminously with the "right" set of returns for all firms.

To sum up, the division of output among firms and industries is determined by the structure of wants and the costs (including uncertainty) of satisfying the wants. In the complex space economy, the costs of satisfying wants are to no small extent dependent on the availability of entrepreneurs (and of skills) to a particular industry, hence to all industries. The general equilibrium output thus ties up with the availability of entrepreneurs just as the basic natural resources of the economy help to determine its total output.

II. PARETO OPTIMALITY IN THE UNORGANIZED OLIGOPOLISTICALLY COMPETITIVE ECONOMY

We may illustrate the equilibrium process in diagrammatic form. In doing so, we shall reuse, with permission, a set of diagrams presented by Ferguson[1] although we shall not be dealing with perfect competition. Only a few explanatory words for each diagram are necessary at this point in the development of our theory.

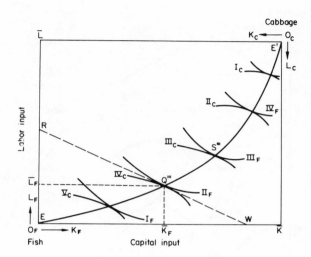

Figure 14–1: Production Map in Input Space: Optimum Conditions of Factor Substitution

Let capital and labor inputs be shown respectively on the horizontal and vertical scales of Figure 14–1, and observe that there are two commodity alternatives (Fish and Cabbage) under consideration. Figure 14–1 is in the form of an Edgeworth box. At any point not on the contract curve EE′, inadequate production prevails. For example, consider a point to the left of S‴ on III$_F$ and imagine another isoquant curve, say a curve II$_{C'}$ between II$_C$ and III$_C$ which intersects III$_F$ at that point. The slopes of the curves would differ, indicating that for the flatter curve there exists at that point the ability to release a large quantity of K for a small quantity of L while still maintaining output. And conversely for the steeply sloped isoquant, where a large quantity of L may be made available in exchange for a small quantity of K. The total effect is that more resources are available for producing greater quantities of fish (F) or cabbage (C), or both. Only points on the contract curve represent optimal output alternatives. And most significantly from the standpoint of any producer, prices for homogeneous factor *inputs* are the same regardless of

[1] C. E. Ferguson, *Microeconomic Theory* (Chicago, Irwin and Company, 1966), pp. 379–384. We have made a slight change in Ferguson's Figure 16.2.4, recast as our Figure 14–4.

final product-selling conditions. The common capital, labor input-price ratio (such as RW) must be equated with the marginal rate of technical substitution (MRTS). Production will stabilize at some point along the contract curve EE' of Figure 14–1.

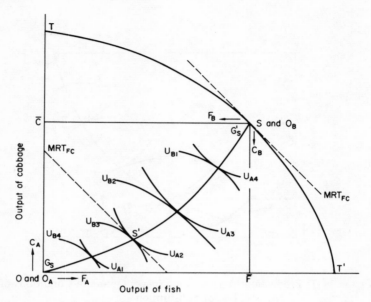

Figure 14–2: Production-Possibility Frontier in Output Space: Optimum Conditions of Exchange

In Figure 14–2 the mapping from input space (MRTS) for K and L is made over to output space, and the marginal rate of transformation (MRT_{FC}) curve is set forth. Any point on the contract curve EE' of Figure 14–1 represents an output of F and C which belongs somewhere on the frontier of Figure 14–2. So we let the tangency point S in Figure 14–2 be the transform of S''' in Figure 14–1. It further follows that this total output S of F and C is allocable to consumers A and B according to their respective bargaining ability, as found along the contract curve $G_sG'_s$. No point off the curve is admissible since either or both consumers would be better off (with no one less well off) at some point along $G_sG'_s$ compared to any point off the curve. As with the MRT, the marginal rate of consumer substitution MRS requires equality between the final product price ratio and the consumer's indifference curve. We shall shortly see that *if* output *S is given*, and assumed to be an equilibrium result, a unique consumer acquisition level, S', applies which must conform to the conditions of production (MRT). Thus, if the output S applies, $MRS_{FC} = MRT_{FC}$. But first, let us turn to Figure 14–3.

Three utility-possibility frontiers are shown in Figure 14–3, two of which, the $G_sG'_s$ of Figure 14–2 and a $G_RG'_R$ curve not drawn elsewhere, apply to specific outputs on the MRT such as point S; the third frontier, VV', also relates to a point on the MRT; but this one is special in the sense of depicting the highest points for all utility possibilities such as $G_sG'_s$, and $G_RG'_R$ over all production alternatives of F and C. VV', in short, reflects the optimum points such as S' which is repeated as S'' in Figure 14–3. There is an infinity of equilibrium possibilities suggested in Figure 14–2 which is reducible by one dimension to yield VV'. We shall demonstrate this condition with specific reference to our theory of unorganized oligopoly, and we shall subsequently identify the optimal equilibrium output for the system.

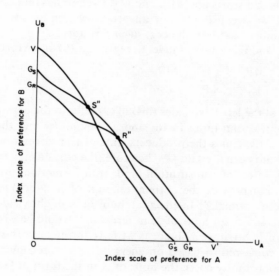

Figure 14–3: Utility-Possibility Frontier: From Output to Utility Space

The MRS principle requires equality of prices with consumers preferences between commodities. Recasting relation (1) in section I to the specific terms of fish and cabbage, we obtain—

(5) $MRS_{FC} = \dfrac{P_F}{P_C}$

In unorganized oligopoly—

(6) $P_F = \dfrac{t(R_F)}{MP_F} = MC_F$ and $P_C = \dfrac{t(R_C)}{MP_C} = MC_C$

where R refers to the multiplying extra required for uncertainty and t is the basic required "certainty" return for "a" generalized factor of production.

Significantly the MC_F and MC_C in (6) are our adjusted costs.[1] In the long-run sense, equation (6) also involves the equality of price with the adjusted AC curve.[2]

But—

$$(7)\qquad \frac{P_F}{P_C} = \frac{MC_F \text{ (marginal cost of } F \text{ in terms of a factor X)}}{MC_C \text{ (marginal cost of } C \text{ in terms of a factor X)}} = MRT_{FC}$$

Hence—

$$(8)\qquad MRS_{FC} = MRT_{FC}$$

Perhaps we should repeat at this stage that any claim which states that a multiple such as R distorts the MRS and MRT relation is inapplicable. This is because the R we are using is not an arbitrary number. It is a precisely determined number based on the cost of uncertainty.

To understand this vital point, let us rearrange (6) in the form (9) below—

$$(9)\qquad \frac{t}{P_F} = \frac{MP_F}{R_F} \text{ and } \frac{t}{P_C} = \frac{MP_C}{R_C}$$

Then we see that the left-hand sides (lhs) of (9) refer to the consumer's rate of substitution between an input factor and a commodity and the right-hand-sides (rhs) are $(1/R)$ times the producers' rate of transformation. Because of the multiple R, it is usually said—"Therefore, the consumers' and producers' corresponding rates of substitution and transformation are not equal. Consumers do not provide the optimal amount of X (labor) and allocation cannot be Pareto optimal."[3] In effect, an hour of X might yield, say a MP of 6F, while if $R_F = 1.5$, an hour of X in terms of t would be worth 4F, whatever the price of F. So, if we assume, as we have throughout this book, that R refers to an income return based on energy expenditures under uncertainty (i.e., R is an opportunity cost), the hour of X in the form of factor pay must be worth 6F, otherwise the return for it is out of line. R, in other words, is not separable from t and equation (6) above should appear as in (10)—

$$(10)\qquad P_F = \frac{(t \cdot R_F)}{MP_F} = MC_F \text{ and } P_C = \frac{(t \cdot R_C)}{MP_C} = MC_C$$

The transformation from perfect or pure competition theory to un-

---

[1] The multipliers R_F and R_C in (6) do not have to be the same.

[2] We observed in the Appendix to Chapter 5 and in Chapter 8 that if uncertainty is treated as a variable cost related to the actual energy "utils" expended by the factor, the marginal cost curve would be affected accordingly. Our reference above to the adjusted MC as well as AC curves is in this key. Details of the variable cost adjustment process are provided in the Appendix to Chapter 5.

[3] J. Henderson and R. Quandt, *Microeconomic Theory* (New York: McGraw-Hill, 1958), p. 207.

organized oligopoly theory ultimately establishes returns that are isomorphic to those in perfect competition; this transformation must involve non-arbitrary R's. And if these R's are looked at from this angle, the equality between MRS and MRT, as in (8), follows accordingly.

Thus we see in Figure 14–2 that because $MRS_{FC} = MRT_{FC}$ in equilibrium, the bargaining between consumer A and consumer B must eventuate at point S'. In turn the transform of S' in Figure 14–3, namely S'', must hold if output S along production frontier TT' in Figure 14–2 is assumed to apply; and correspondingly for R'' related to a point R' related in turn to an output R.

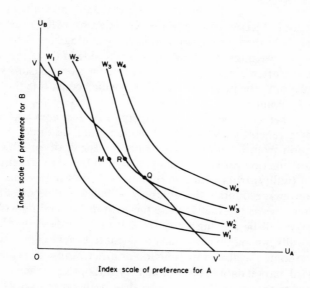

Figure 14–4: Maximization of Social Welfare: From Utility Possibilities to "Constrained Bliss"

If next we assume a known set of social welfare functions, as in Figure 14–4, a point such as Q can be identified. Manifestly, any point other than Q on the utility-possibility frontier VV' is less desirable. Only Q is on the contract curve and also offers greatest social welfare. It is therefore preferred to any other point.

May point Q ever be reached by any society? To answer this question, suppose we consider a voter "B" who recognizes that if there is equilibrium at P, he is better off *vis-à-vis* voter "A" than he would be at any ordinate values less than P. However, let us provide voter "B" with a true love for his fellow man, or, if you prefer, let us have him accept a social benefit (welfare) function in place of his own purely personal interests. Imbue him with a social responsibility such that if smog prevails at P—and smog he knows affects his fellow man even though he himself is undisturbed by it—he accepts as a complement to his independently formed preferences a social welfare such as $W_3W'_3$. By taxation, he would have his economy move toward Q. In effect, whether or not the social welfare curves in Figure 14–4 reflect objective data that cause the consumer to vote in the best interest of society (e.g. though he dearly loves butter, he votes less butter for himself and more guns for society because of his fear of invasion from foreign people), or whether it reflects a love for his fellow man, a unique blissful equilibrium *is* identifiable and attainable. Significantly, the unique blissful equilibrium is marked by all the fundamental objective market data stipulated by MRS = MRT. Rather than making short shrift of economic theory by apologizing for not including externalities *etc.*, we ought to stress the opposite side of the coin.[1] Identifiable externalities are often considered by voters, for the same reasons which cause them to conform to the principles and forces which constitute the "bed-rock" of classical economics.

In sum, whether we speak of oligopoly or perfect competition, whether we speak of a general social welfare function entailing direct personal gain (e.g. protection from invasion), or whether we speak of an ethically rooted social welfare function providing personal gain in the indirect sense [personal gratification (utility) from acting in interests of one's fellow man], the basic principles of microeconomic theory apply. What we alone must surrender *a priori* is knowledge as to exactly where the economy is tending with respect to VV'. We may well be moving away from P or an oppositely placed point; more specifically, we may expect at any moment to be tending to move towards a point Q via some social welfare function or other. Consumers and producers usually regard market data as given; and they will optimize their own positions in conformance therewith. Most vitally, they both cause to arise and accept new data via a social welfare function (e.g., the general willingness to be taxed at higher rates such as was shown in 1968 in the United States) which conceivably will move all towards a unique optimal point.

III. FINAL NOTES

We have not entered in great detail into such matters as social cost vs. private costs, or the "uniqueness" of the unorganized oligopolistic equilibrium because these subjects are integral to the whole of microeconomic theory and therefore not of unique importance in this book. We should, however, never-

[1] See H. Demsetz, "Towards a Theory of Property Rights," *American Economic Review*, 1968, pp. 347–359.

theless deal with two matters that are peculiarly fundamental to this book and which, in turn, are vitally related to the relationships (1) through (10) presented above.

(I) We found earlier that a set of LRAC curves obtains for any given firm in the economy. But then, the final equilibrium, based as it is on different cost and demand conditions at different sites, might render what otherwise would have appeared to be a low cost site an impossible point of production; in other words, after rental bids are entered for all lands, and after returns for uncertainty commensurate with foregone alternatives are also applied, and after dynamic changes occur, an otherwise appearing least-cost site might prove to have been completely inadequate. In the same connection, recall that R in (6) or (10) is related to the energy utils of a given producer, and that each producer operates under his *own set* of applicable uncertainties and alternatives; thus a deviation in society's final selection of the truly viable firms may sometimes appear to occur. More specifically, if sharp restraints to entry exist in the market, the possibility that more than one technologically non-optimum size firm will prevail in the long run appears to be feasible. What is optimal, let us note, actually depends upon the set of alternatives open to the managers of the firm. And the advantage that the optimal-optimorum firm possesses is simply a greater ability to wage and win a price war. This means that the inclusion of R guarantees us only that some optimal, representative firm(s) will survive in the long run: at best we possess only a high probability (not a certainty) that the optimal-optimorum firm will be among the survivors in any given industry.

To conclude: We may expect that each firm will produce at the optimal cost point of its own optimal LRAC curve, and that the firms which survive in the market will *tend to be* of the following order: (a) the basic surviving member(s) of the industry will *tend to be* the optimal-optimorum firm(s), and (b) the firm(s) closest to the optimal-optimorum will *tend to be next* found in the long run of the market. This last condition recognizes the discreteness in demand over economic space and in technological changes over the space. The combination of the two, together with the existence of only a limited number of most efficient managers for all industries, may then require a sudden jump from large to much smaller units. We are therefore speaking strictly in terms of likelihoods. And we are stipulating that in each industry we should "expect to find" some optimal-optimorum units as well as some less efficient firms in the sense that the skills and capacities, and hence the opportunities of its managers are not of the same kind as that of the best managers in the field.

(II) The outlines of the hexagons that prevail will vary in size over the landscape. These variations will reflect inter- and intra-industry difference, the varying degrees of localization that may occur, the inequalities in costs over space, the divergent densities of population and demand that must arise over the space, and related conditions. It is also implicit to our theory that the

TABLE 14–1: COEFFICIENT OF LOCALIZATION, SELECTED GROUPINGS OF MANUFACTURING INDUSTRIES, UNITED STATES, 1962

Industry	United States ($1,000,000)	Region (percentage distribution)									Coefficient of localization
		New England	Middle Atlantic	East North Central	West North Central	South Atlantic	East South Central	West South Central	Mountain	Pacific	
Personal income	439,661	6.5	21.8	21.1	8.0	12.4	4.5	7.6	3.7	14.4	.11
All manufacturing (value added)	179,256	7.5	23.3	29.2	6.2	10.7	4.5	5.4	1.8	11.4	.08
Food and kindred products	20,856	3.9	20.0	24.8	12.3	10.0	4.9	7.1	3.0	14.4	.72
Tobacco products	1,645	—	7.5	—	—	71.6	17.2	1.0	—	—	.52
Textile mill products	6,098	14.0	19.4	9.2	3.6	53.6	7.4	1.0	—	1.6	.33
Apparel and related products	7,151	6.4	51.4	10.6	4.1	11.6	7.6	3.5	—	6.5	.30
Lumber and wood products	3,606	4.7	6.9	25.9	3.6	13.3	8.1	7.7	5.0	38.2	.16
Furniture and fixtures	2,838	5.0	18.6	24.6	5.3	22.4	6.0	5.0	.7	11.2	.12
Paper and allied products	7,044	10.9	19.9	24.4	7.3	15.0	6.2	6.0	1.8	11.3	.17
Printing and publishing	9,996	6.6	35.1	20.8	5.3	7.8	2.6	4.0	1.0	9.6	.17
Chemicals and allied products	16,062	3.0	26.3	19.1	5.4	17.2	8.2	12.0	3.6	6.0	.30
Petroleum and coal products	3,439	—	13.4	17.6	4.7	3.6	1.7	37.0	—	14.7	.26
Rubber and plastics	4,316	15.4	18.6	37.6	10.2	5.5	5.4	3.3	1.0	—	.31
Leather and leather products	2,102	29.4	25.8	17.6	7.9	4.1	6.0	—	2.5	11.2	.06
Stone, clay, and glass products	6,605	4.8	21.5	26.5	2.4	12.4	5.2	7.2	3.0	6.3	.26
Primary metal industries	13,744	4.4	26.4	42.2	5.4	7.2	5.1	3.6	.9	10.5	.20
Fabricated metal products	11,119	8.8	22.3	38.2	7.0	5.8	3.8	4.0	1.0	7.8	.27
Machinery, except electrical	16,068	10.6	20.5	44.3	4.5	3.8	2.2	4.0	1.0	12.3	.21
Electrical machinery	15,594	10.6	27.7	32.4	7.6	5.6	3.6	2.3	—	18.3	.26
Transport equipment	20,946	5.4	11.8	43.7	6.2	5.8	—	3.2	—	18.3	.30
Instruments and related products	4,303	12.7	45.2	19.3	—	—	—	1.6	—	18.3	

SOURCE: Calculated from data in U.S. Bureau of the Census. *Annual Survey of Manufacturers* (1962); and U.S. Bureau of the Census. "Personal Incomes by States." *Statistical Abstract of the United States* (1965) p. 334. Reprinted from H. Nourse, *Regional Economics* (New York: McGraw-Hill, 1968) p. 65.

market area shape of the firm(s) must comply in the long run with the statements in Chapter 13. The development of large and small cities over the space then reflects not only existing differences in resources, climate, topography, and their like, but all the forces that are inherent to individual differences and man's wants.

(III) It is not surprising that on empirical grounds we can point to industries (such as those recorded in Table 14–1) which, for example, in spite of their high coefficients of localization, are nevertheless not perfectly oriented to markets. At the same moment, those firms which exhibit much lower coefficients of localization are never found to be scattered in perfect correspondence with what the location quotient and its related theory seem to require. The claim made by so many that practice and theory differ simply reflects the incompleteness of prevailing theories. With a more realistic theory, we not only would be better able to *understand* the lives we lead and weigh more accurately the intricate world in which we live, but, as Chapter 15 endeavors to show, our applications of theory and the direction and guidance we give to human affairs would be changed and, we believe, vastly improved. This is assuredly the hope of anyone who speculates about economic matters.

Appendix to Chapter 14

Further Statement on Pareto Optimality in the Unorganized Oligopolistically Competitive Economy

We have established the efficiency-equilibrium conditions of the unorganized oligopoly economy. In this appendix we shall specify in detail some consumer-based relations which were assumed to be understood by the reader in Chapter 14.

I. CONSUMER UTILITY MAXIMIZED

We know that consumers maximize their satisfaction when their marginal rate of substitution for commodities is equal to the price ratios of the goods. Rewrite $\text{MRS}_{xy} = P_x/P_y$ as—

(1) $-\dfrac{\partial q_j}{\partial q_k} = \dfrac{p_k}{p_j}$,

where we assume the second order conditions (i.e., the maximizing conditions) are met.

Pareto optimality in a general sense involves a given level of satisfaction for i consumers. In other words, satisfactions $S_i{}^0$ are constant, where $i = 1, \ldots, n$. Then the maximizing of the kth consumer's satisfactions, S_k, over m goods in the system, assumes Lagrangian form—

(2) $S_k = S_k (q_{k1}, q_{k2}, \ldots, q_{km}) + \lambda[S_i (q_1 - q_{k1}, q_2 - q_{k2}, \ldots, q_m - q_{km}) - S_i{}^0]$

Setting the partials to zero yields identity in the ratio of commodity substitution for all m goods and all consumers. Each consumer adjusts his marginal rate of substitution for commodities so that it balances with the prevailing objective market data, i.e., the prices in the market.

The producing sector operates similarly—in an unorganized oligopolistic economy. Profit maximization for a firm t involves—

$$(3) \quad -\frac{\partial q_{tr}}{\partial q_{ts}} = \frac{p_s}{p_r} + R'$$

That is to say, under purely competitive buying and oligopolistic selling, the partial derivative $\dfrac{\partial q_r}{\partial q_s}$ is inversely related to the negative of the factor prices plus a given quantity, where the quantity R' is positive and relates to the relevant uncertainty. Viewed from another direction, specifically where the term p_s/p_r refers to output prices, the price ratio line is seen to involve tangency with a diminished (by $-R'$) production frontier. Proceeding exactly as in (2) yields a relation—in equivalent form to (2) − such that with each of i firms maximizing and producing its optimum output, the product substitution of all firms (similar to consumers) would conform to the prevailing ratio of costs. Any reallocation of inputs to raise the output level of any firm must entail a smaller output for another firm. In other words, by realizing that the *individual* income "util" R of all producers has no effect on the output of the surviving firms (though the number in the market is, of course, affected), we would have on display the Paretian optimality (and stability) conditions of the individual members of the unorganized oligopolistic economy; in turn via (3), we would have the reduction in total output attributable to the cost of uncertainty. Through this specification of the R's, we readily appreciate the fact that uncertainty cuts into the industry's output and, in the process, yields a transformation curve for the entire economy of smaller magnitude and slightly altered shape.[1]

[1] As T. Rader has shown, the production and exchange economies are isomorphic to each other. In turn, the separate systems described by (2) and (3) are completely specifiable by either (2) or (3). See his "Edgeworth Exchange and General Economic Equilibrium," *Yale Economic Essays*, 1965, pp. 133–180.

15

The Theory of the Firm in Economic Space and Social Policy

The impact of space on the theory of the firm and in turn on social policy is an exhaustive subject in its own right. Elsewhere, this writer has examined the impacts of economic space on the regulation of public utilities,[1] and in another place he has surveyed its implications with respect to trade union theory.[2] Selected facets of the impacts of economic space on excise tax theory may also be viewed. And in fact, the author has elsewhere related space to the theory of economic development.[3] The present subject, we might add, also has potential effects on such models as the input-output model. Our objective here will, however, be to demonstrate what seems to be the most general of all possible impacts of our theory of economic space on social policy: namely, the interpretation of the anti-trust laws of the United States. To accomplish this, we shall first review some of the vital relations in a space economy which tie-up closely with our present subject; we shall then outline those elements of our model that are directly applicable to the anti-trust laws, and present the errors in anti-trust policy which stem from the application of classical economic theory. When these preliminaries are done, we shall apply the standards derived from our theory to see whether perspective and policy would be significantly changed.

I. REVIEW AND SUMMARY ILLUSTRATIONS OF A SPACE ECONOMY

Assume an economy in which resources are not evenly distributed—a likely enough starting point given the geographic, geological, social, and economic patterns we find over economic space. It would then be reasonable

[1] "On the Question of Realism in Economic Theory and the Regulation of Public Utilities," *Land Economics*, XLII, 1966, pp. 260–267.

[2] *Microeconomics and the Space Economy* (Chicago: Scott, Foresman 1963), Appendix B.

[3] "Needed, A Return to the Classics in Regional Economic Development Theory," *Kyklos*, XIX, 1966, pp. 461–480.

to expect people to aggregate at points of most favorable resource combinations (transportation, mineral, agricultural, etc.), though, in time, a few nongregarious or unusually adventuresome individuals will move away from the areas of concentration to the peripheral points of a market. From these new sites they may retain contact with their place of origin and also establish new social and economic relations. The market areas of traders then begin to take the form of circles, and we may dismiss at once the case of *all* buyers and sellers at a point.

Buyers at a Point—Sellers Distributed over an Area

As population grows and continues to disperse and as economic activity becomes increasingly complex, a variety of market areas (and sales radii) appear. In some lines of activity, such as extractive enterprise—mining, fishing, agriculture—it appears likely that production sites will be geographically dispersed while consumption will be found largely at a point. (Recall that this is the second nonspatial market pattern that was described in Chapter 4.) Pure competition and the Walras general equilibrium system, as modified by the distance-rental factor, remain theoretically possible. This would hold broadly true even though several—rather than one—consumption points may exist for any one supplier. Indeed, this characterization fits the heavy type of extractive enterprises. These activities modify traditional economic theory by making the distance-rental factor quite important, and they tend not to fit the scheme of point formed consumption as well as do other activities in the primary stage of production.

We hold that a purely competitive agricultural market could best be conceived when sellers are small, many, and distributed around consumption centers. But when sellers are large, as in the petroleum-extracting industry, they tend to sell to several point-formed consumption centers and the locational oligopolistic market would then arise.[1] The agricultural industry appears to provide the best empirical possibilities for the market types of traditional economic analysis.

Sellers at a Point—Buyers Distributed over an Area

As population grows, and technical innovations are instituted, manufacturing activities become more widespread. Some activities locate at the most favorable resource points,[2] with their buyers being distributed at varying distances

---

[1] In essence, T. Palander was quite concerned with the monopolistic type of market area in his otherwise cost system of location theory. See his *Beiträge zur Standortstheorie* (Uppsala: Almqvist och Wiksells Boktryckeri, a.b., 1935), pp. 143–162. For a monopolistically competitive solution, see S. Enke, "Space and Value," *Quarterly Journal of Economics*, LVI (1942), pp. 627–637.

[2] See A. Weber, *Theory of the Location of Industries*, trans. by C. J. Friedrich (Chicago:

around the production center. This structural pattern permits the conception of any of the traditional spaceless market types. (In particular, we have the third nonspatial market type described in Chapter 4.) When sellers are located at a point, freight cost on raw materials is typically greater than on finished products. However, even if the relative differential is extremely great, so that a substantial concentration of industry may be expected, the limited number of sites at a given center suggests that a spaceless type of oligopoly is more likely under the defined spatial distribution than a market characterized by perfect or monopolistic competition. Let us examine this assertion in greater detail.

Suppose initially that significant economies of scale apply to a given activity. After the short-run equilibrium position has been reached (MR equals MC), it will pay each of the manufacturing firms to continue to adjust production by rationalizing their plants to optimal size. But, of course, a zero profit tangency between long-run average costs and average revenue is not attainable here as it is in the other market types, partly because of the large plant size and investment required and partly because of the small number of firms originally in the industry at the given production point. Entry by other rivals, at this stage of development, is already made difficult by oligopolistic uncertainties and a limited number of available sites. Indeed, indivisibilities are likely to be numerous and the additional entry constraining factors which may have arisen, such as sales promotion expense, product differentiation, habit, custom, trade agreements, control of raw material supply, price warfare, business espionage practices, and the like, all create further problems that tend to make substantial new entry almost impossible.[1] The relatively few firms at any given center leads, in short, to a policy of mutual awareness. Because firms are linked together in chainlike fashion, and because there exists some slight contact advantage between certain sellers and selected buyers, the firms are confronted with the ingredients of price leadership or other kinds of oligopolistic pricing. The classical tendency for long-run average costs to be equated with average revenue cannot logically be expected for this case of seller concentration with buyer separation. Zero economic profits for even this market appear as an unattainable possibility rather than as an inevitable underlying tendency.[2]

Chicago University Press, 1926); and E. M. Hoover, *The Location of Economic Activity*, 1st ed. (New York: McGraw-Hill Book Co., 1948).

[1] For the problem of entry in the complex markets, see H. H. Hines, "Effectiveness of Entry by Already Established Firms," *Quarterly Journal of Economics*, LXXI (1951), pp. 132–150. Also see G. W. Stocking and M. W. Watkins, *Monopoly and Free Enterprise* (New York: The Twentieth Century Fund, 1951), pp. 117ff.

[2] See A. Sherrard, "Advertising, Product Variation, and the Limits of Economics," *Journal of Political Economy*, LIX (1951), pp. 126–142. He objects to monopolistic competition as an appeal to raw reality because, he claims, it does not provide a standard by which the existing pattern of allocation can be judged. Similarly, G. Stigler, *5 Lectures on Economic Problems* (London: Longmans Green & Co., Ltd., 1945), pp. 18–19, says monopolistic competition is a definition of equilibrium and not a theory of the "conditions" of an equilibrium against which economic events can be analyzed.

Sellers and Buyers Distributed over an Area

In time, the nonspatial manufacturing oligopolistic type described above will shade into a wholly spatial type of oligopoly. Additional points of seller concentration may be expected to appear, and space becomes a factor on both sides of the exchange. In our terms, a fully spatial economy emerges. The following discussion not only illustrates this condition but, even more broadly, suggests other origins for spatial oligopoly.

Visualize one seller or a group of sellers located at a point and selling over an area surrounding the production site, as described above. The market area tends to take the shape of a hexagon, with the size of the area being limited by the freight rate and consumer demand.[1] The number of sellers is small, and this causes the seller or sellers within any market area to become subject to a cross-interdependence with the seller or sellers near the center of adjacent market areas. However, because resources and population tend to be heterogeneously distributed over an area, the market area of a firm (or firms) does not form a perfect hexagon. It forms instead a somewhat irregular polygon of, at best, a hexagonic nature.[2] In this situation, competition from other market centers will not by itself bring profits down to the value of uncertainty in the industry. Furthermore, because there is a sharp limit to the number of firms in any one industry which can locate at the production center, and because the population is unevenly scattered, prices will not necessarily be forced down to the requisite profit equilibrium. For this to happen, entry, both proximate and distant, will usually be needed.

All these considerations suggest that any level of profits may exist in the short run. They also indicate that once markets draw together (i.e., overlap or become tangential in space), without leaving open areas between them, seller as well as buyer dispersion has replaced the isolated market of seller concentration and buyer separation. Market centers, in effect, will have rapidly become aware of each other. Because price cuts at a distance will lead to price wars as the reaction spreads from one market to another, we find, over time, that varying degrees of warlike oligopoly will tend toward a less and less hyper-competitive system between a production point and other central places.

Sellers and Buyers Distributed over an Area—Free Entry from Without

Imagine a bell-shaped average cost curve and a negatively sloping average

[1] See W. Arthur Lewis, "Competition in Retail Trade," *Economica*, II (1945), pp. 202–234; and A. Lösch, *Die räumliche Ordnung der Wirtschaft* (Jena: Gustav Fischer, 1944).

[2] See Lösch, *op. cit.*, Chapter 10, footnote 1; and M. L. Greenhut, *Plant Location in Theory and in Practice* (Chapel Hill: University of North Carolina Press, 1956), pp. 269–271. Also see W. Isard, *Location and Space Economy* (New York: John Wiley & Sons, Inc., 1956), p. 274, footnote 17.

revenue function—the latter reflecting the small numbers of firms comprising an industry in a particular area. Imagine further an intersection between the curves, with profit surpluses existing and the sales area extended as far as practical. Now consider the appearance of competition at distant points, followed by the contraction of sales radii as the more distant buyers are attracted to a new seller nearer to them. The average revenue curve for the original seller tends to shift to the left, and his market area shrinks on all sides.

The shrinkage is not perfectly uniform because the polygon may be pushed out on one side or another. This imperfect shape of the sales area is conditioned by heterogeneity of product and discontinuity of resources and land surfaces (e.g., a mountain range as a transport shield). There is, furthermore, no inherent reason why competition from other market centers will cause the curve of average revenue to be tangent to the average cost curve. Rather, as a result of location-price principles and the relatively small number of sellers sharing a given market area, the tendency will be for the firms at the respective market centers to abstain from rigorous price competition and thereby to help maintain their original profit positions.[1]

Sellers and Buyers Distributed over an Area—Free Entry from Within

Imagine that the existence of profits causes new sellers to locate at the profit-making production center. As before, marginal revenues are equated with the relevant marginal costs in both the short run and the long run, but there is still no inherent tendency for a zero profit tangency to arise between the average revenue curve and long-run average cost curve. The number of similar firms is limited by the existing indivisibilities in machines, equipment, research, etc., and by the spatial discontinuities—or, shall we say, the spatial indivisibilities—at any given production center.[2] We further find that contact advantages with buyers will differ, and mutual awareness with reciprocal action will tend to develop.

A priori reasoning suggests that the market described by a spatial scattering of consumers allows relatively few sellers to locate in any given market area. Each seller then takes the expected action of others into consideration in planning his own policies. Linkage of one firm with another leads to an oligopolistic behavior pattern, even though there may be many firms in the entire economy. Long-run profits are possible with some competition from outside as well as inside the market area. As noted elsewhere,

[1] For more on this expectation, see originally M. L. Greenhut, *Plant Location in Theory and in Practice*, Chapter II, section 3.

[2] See E. H. Chamberlin, *The Theory of Monopolistic Competition*, 5th ed. (Cambridge: Harvard University Press, 1946), pp. 239–241; and F. Machlup, *The Economics of Sellers' Competition* (Baltimore: The Johns Hopkins Press, 1952), pp. 233–236, 240–241.

spatial indivisibility adds to uncertainty and other indivisibilities in denying the extent of free entry necessary for the classical competitive equilibrium. However, the combination of entry of a sufficient number of firms (plants) at a distance and, in particular, at a proximate point leads ultimately to some shading of price to a level commensurate with prevailing uncertainties.

The Field of Wholesaling

The expansion of a capitalistic economy is reflected not only in the tendency toward a spatial oligopoly in manufacturing but also in similar tendencies in wholesaling and retailing. Generally speaking, outside the fields of agriculture, wholesalers form a spatial market for manufacturers, as, in turn, retailers do for wholesalers. Thus, the spatial distribution of wholesalers helps establish a spatial oligopolistic market among manufacturers; at the same time, these wholesalers are spatial oligopolists themselves. Under conditions of uncontrolled resale pricing, the wholesaler watches the discount prices not only of nearby rival wholesalers who are seeking to attract his customers from him but also of competitors at the fringes of his market area. At a particular location, he has contact advantages with buyers which enable the substitution, of, say, more efficient service for competition in price from time to time.

The Field of Retailing

Fairly comparable results hold true in the retailing fields where consumers may be expected to be located in a hexagonal area around the individual retailing shops. The limit to the retailer's sales radius is not so much the dollar-and-cent freight cost as the transport burden (mainly time-convenience) to the consumer. Accordingly, the encroachment by one more retailer on the market area of another through competitive price practice is often sporadic. This indeed is the relationship normally observed at any moment in time among the shops of a heterogeneous type of oligopoly in which a live-and-let-live price system generally prevails. The market is spatial and does not conform strictly to the requirements of the nonspatial market types stressed in traditional economics. Chainlike price policy or zone-based delivery of goods is also promoted by economic space.

Agricultural Activities

Even though the agricultural industry is often cited as an example of an industry of purely competitive order and, in fact, often contains point-formed consuming centers for the farmers scattered around these centers, it is interesting to observe that many who analyze particular markets conclude by stressing the monopolistic aspects of the agricultural economic space.[1] Indeed,

[1] D. C. Norvel & M. K. Thompson, "Higglering in Jamaica & the Mystique of Pure Competition," *Social and Economic Studies*, vol. 17, No. 4, Dec. 1968, pp. 407–416.

note that even in what was described in Chapter 3 as a classical type of market (i.e. point formed buying), the "possibility" of a zero sloped average revenue function is often ruled out by assumption and stress placed instead on the more likely situation of relatively significant sellers existing in the space who are mindful of each other. This mindfulness—or more generally the monopolistic character of the economic space *even under the condition of point-formed demand*—is perhaps no better illustrated than by a recent inquiry of Professor Stevens into the properties of the von Thünen ring.[1] The investigator *assumed* a negatively sloping demand curve, perhaps because of the thought that alternative land uses prevail from ring to ring and within each ring, and accordingly that a less than infinite (or even less than very large) number of sellers would probably pack the economic space (ring). Some kind of monopolistic return would thereby result. Given a negatively sloping AR function, Professor Stevens then formulated a quadratic programming model. His model brings out sharply the significance of our thought framework, both from the standpoint of pure theory and its application; though conceived in terms of agricultural economic space, the model also has rather obvious extensions to other industries.

Consider both the demand function $y_i = \dfrac{a_i - P_i}{b_i}$, where y_i is the quantity of the good, and the objective function in (1) below, which was designed to determine the (distributive) returns to productive factors within a given von Thünen ring.

$$(1) \quad \text{Max } z = \sum_i a_i y_i - \sum_i b_i y_i^2 - \sum_i \sum_j x_{ij} A_j E_i (r_i t_i + C_i)$$

The first two terms on the right-hand side of the equality yield total revenues while the remaining expression aggregates the cost of operations. The programmed solution involves, as one would expect, the classical equality of marginal cost and marginal revenue. Note that price P_i is equal to $a_i - b_i y_i$ and that the derivative of total revenues with respect to y_i is $a_i - 2b_i y_i$. (Manifestly, it should not be surprising that one who works with economic space may formulate an AR greater than MR = MC, even when stress is placed on agricultural pursuits.)

Stevens is concerned with the question whether the landowner may extract an extra rent at the expense of monopoly profits. His answer is "no," as he asserts that attempts to do so would generate nonprofit-maximizing pricing and so fail. It would, in fact, seem that if the activity is of the kind that landowners could pursue, they would extract for themselves the underlying land rents as well as the monopoly profits. Then, a classical "noncost outlay" case would exist, since one might attribute to the land its opportunity rental cost plus the surplus (i.e. monopoly rents) over and above the value of

[1] B. Stevens "Location Theory and Programming Models: The von Thünen Case" *Regional Science Research Institute Discussion Papers Series*, No. 19, Nov. 1967, pp. 1–32.

the lost alternatives. If, however, we do not look only at the use of agricultural land by the landowner himself but consider more generally any industry and any point formed buying center, we would tend to consider the "firm" as an entity distinct from the landowner. The surplus (monopoly rents) could then be appropriated by the landowner if, and only if, by adroit bargaining he and other absentee landowners who own property in the ring happened to collaborate to extract the windfall from any and all potential monopolists. It is clear that this is a rather doubtful outcome. In fact, consider the following basic result.

By amending the Stevens' framework and assuming a system of oligopolies (and related uncertainties), what Stevens refers to as monopoly rents (P > MC) reappears as a "rental type" payment necessary to warrant engaging in the activity in question. In no way at all would the landowner be able to appropriate any part of the residual left to the firm unless he himself is the firm. Given a demand function $P_i = a_i - b_i y_i$ and a marginal revenue $a_i - 2b_i y_i$, we find that the inextricable mix of uncertainty, oligopoly, and economic space provides a natural divisor of "2" to the term $b_i y_i^2$; that is, a curve drawn marginally to a negatively sloping linear curve is (1/2) the value of the other at a given point. The divisor "2", if applied to $b_i y_i^2$ in the objective function, would yield a P = MR adjusted = MC adjusted. In effect, it is a numerical expression of the "R" variable cost (and revenue) adjustment that we made in Chapter 5, with the absolute difference between P and MC classical being a function of the relevant point elasticity of demand. The efficiency and other properties of our system would, therefore, hold whether or not we are considering a point formed business or consumer buying center or a set of spatial buying activities involving consumers or wholesalers, retailers, manufacturers, or farmers. It is also significant to remember that even if a purely competitive seller did exist over the given economic space, our theory need not be changed nor adulterated. On the contrary, as we have already suggested, if pure competition is admitted, the continuously divisible system cited in Chapter 5 applies. This signifies, in turn, that uncertainty is either nonexistent or at the most nonsequitur for the purely competitive economy. Our framework of thought, to repeat, is fully general, and any economic policy which conforms to its basic conclusions and is applied to an economy conforming to its model would thus tend to be practical.

Conclusions and Summary of Section I. To conclude this section: (1) Traditional economics has not been concerned in its analyses with the wholesaling and retailing trades or with relatively large economic units as such but has concentrated chiefly on the economics of small size agricultural and manufacturing enterprises. The general disregard of wholesalers, retailers, and large size establishments appears as too broad an abstraction. Economic theory requires an investigation of all forms of product and factor pricing, with the input-output functions of the retailer and wholesaler, and those of the relatively large farmer and manufacturer being as vital to theory as those of the small firm. Significantly, each field of activity seems to display the characteristics of spatial oligopoly, though more empirical evidence and specialized analysis will, of course, be needed before complete faith can be placed in this proposition. (2) It is essentially only when all buyers are located at, or in the environs of a point (e.g., the wholesale agricultural market), that the purely competitive or monopolistically competitive equilibrium can be conceived as practical. It is unlikely that the other possible types of structural alignments would (or could) yield these market types. We further claim that the situation in which all producers and consumers are at a point (as implicitly conceived of in the classical and Chamberlinean formulation) is improbable, as is the situation in which all (or at least very many) sellers are at a point. Therefore, these economic markets appear to be practical possibilities only where sellers are scattered over an area while buyers are heavily concentrated at one or a few points (e.g., the markets for some foodstuffs, or for textiles among clothing manufacturers). But even this possibility lies outside the customary economic theory because (a) it imputes a distance-rental function to the equilibrium, as a detailed study of the Stevens' model would show, and (b) requires that one ignores the monopolistic advantages of better contact. Moreover, in the limit, the purely competitive and monopolistically competitive markets depict the unlikely situation of uncertainty approaching zero, or at any rate being evaluated in an identical way by all firms in all industries.

II. THE ELEMENTS OF OUR MODEL RELEVANT TO ANTI-TRUST POLICY

The normative social theory of a people differs sharply from their *de facto* social theory, for the latter relates to what exists whereas the former describes the ideal to which a given culture may point. The theory of pure competition has served for many decades in a normative role among Western nations. Unfortunately, one may argue, its contradiction of space realities limits its overall view of economic relations. By conceptualizing a competitive free entry oligopoly, we are able to set forth a counterpart formulation to the classical theories of pure competition. What *could be* is, of course, not necessarily the same as what is.

Oligopoly, not Monopolistic Competition

The market that is isomorphic to pure competition is not a spatial form of monopolistic competition. The Chamberlinean market type fails as a norm or as a *de facto* theory for several reasons.

(1) The system's long-run position is inefficient from the standpoint of (a) consumer satisfaction, since there are varying excesses of AR compared

to MC which are not based on the forces of scarcity, such as risk or uncertainty; there is, indeed, added inefficiency due to (b) the resource factor combination, as we find that the "claimed" underlying trend is toward less than the optimum rate of output.

(2) Monopolistic competition would fail to induce enough private investment because it is a high cost, zero profit system.

(3) Monopolistic competition is easily recognized as unnatural if we remember that the concept of space points to (a) a system of indivisible exclusions at any point, and (b) a substantial freight cost (i.e. transportation) burden. Each of these constraints sharply limit the number of firms in any market area.

(4) The ethic of the free enterprise system, which (a) reflects the belief that each person must find his own way. In turn, the business realities of the system establish as a basic property of the system, (b) a behavioral uncertainty among producers. These forces constrain entry.

(5) Following Stigler and the so-called Chicago School,[1] what really amounts to a set of different cost curves, demand curves, and tangency points in monopolistic competition theory simply defines a market without any normative content at all. A system of monopolistic competition is just not compatible with economic space;[2] rather, we propose that a system of oligopolies, generally heterogeneous in nature because of space, product type, and other capitalistic forces, marks the economy.

The identification of spatial oligopoly as the market type which is isomorphic to pure competition does not establish it *per se* as a normative social economic goal. On the contrary, *de facto* society is clearly distinguishable from the normative state. *De facto* spatial oligopoly may result in excessive profits and steeply drawn marginal revenue curves which, under laws of probability, suggest that production will take place at levels less than or greater than the optimum cost combination; in turn, a *normative* spatial oligopoly theory will tend to center attention on productive efficiency of the kind which underscores firms in pure competition.

Technological efficiency requires that the average and marginal revenue curves be tilted only slightly so that they naturally reflect the spatial and product differentiation that prevails in the system. Within the verbal restriction of the word *naturally* lies the fundamental meaning of the term economic

---

[1] E. H. Chamberlin, in his chapter on the "Chicago School," *Towards a More General Theory of Value* (New York: Oxford University Press, Inc., 1957), cites M. Bronfenbrenner as the originator of this term.

[2] The claim that Lösch, Isard, and others have related location economics to monopolistic competition is much in doubt, especially considering the uneven spatial distribution of people. For example, see sources in note 2, p. 348. Also see D. Dewey, "Imperfect Competition No Bar to Efficient Production," *Journal of Political Economy*, LXVI (1958), pp. 24–33. Dewey contends that (p. 32): "It also follows, contrary to the conclusion advanced in most treatments of spatial competition, that free entry cannot eliminate all monopoly profit when a transport cost is the source of market imperfection."

efficiency, for if only earned profits prevailed in the long run, an AR greater than both MR and AC *could be* economic. In fact, it does not matter that the uncertainties and indivisibilities between industries in the same market area may differ and that AR greater than MC discrepancies arise; this is so because what appears to be an output restriction in one industry compared to another would not be due to any capricious reason (as is the case in space-less monopoly theory). The discrepancies would instead reflect consumer differences in choice, and the volatile changes of want satisfaction which find economic expression in the form of (a) greater uncertainty, (b) the need for higher profits, and thus (c) an AR, MC difference in one activity unequal to the AR, MC difference in another activity. In this kind of market no arbitrary premium is exacted from consumers, provided, of course, that entry is open and there is no collusion. In a supporting manner, the finance, research, technology, and spatial indivisibilities which vary from industry to industry may be understood to restrict numbers and outputs differently; in this way, they reflect the true cost of economic activity. When seen in this light, an underlying identity between all firms and industries is easily visualized in the equilibrium.

Gently sloping AR and MR functions increase the probability of production at or near the optimum cost point, since the marginal revenue curve must remain close to the long-run average cost function for a range of output rather than passing it by randomly and quickly. Since competition between firms stimulates operational efficiency, policies of social control require the maintenance of competition. Production at the optimum cost point is the normative goal, and attainment of this objective is most probable if long-run profits are permitted. At the same time, the extent of profits and the market control of individual business firms must be limited by allowing substitute products to be introduced.

Pure Competition in a New Form

A vital aspect of space economics, at least insofar as the theoretician is concerned, relates to the question of whether a spatial conception of economic relations should replace the other models formulated to explain our economy. Is it true that a "revolution in analysis is called for—a new set of questions, a new philosophical foundation?"[1]

We believe that neither a revolution nor a full replacement is indicated. However, because it is impossible to conceive all the purposes to which economic theory "can be applied," we can only say intuitively that the traditional theory of pure competition and/or its transform, our theory of unorganized oligopoly, would be effective for most purposes.

When set forth as a norm, the unorganized oligopoly market requires gently sloping average revenue and marginal revenue curves. This requirement,

[1] Sherrard, *op. cit.*, p. 142.

more likely than not, insures effective resource allocation and an efficiency level complying closely with the needs of a consumer-centered economy. We grant that consumer wants are not autonomous, as perhaps was the case in Marshall's world; we also grant that these wants are influenced and shifted by advertising. Whatever consumer wants may be, regardless of their cause, they can, however, be taken as data in certain uses of economic theory. The problem of the economy, in any case, is still to fulfill wants fully and precisely with the greatest efficiency. The fundamental situation to be analyzed by complex economic theory therefore remains essentially the same as that applicable to purely competitive economic theory.

A complex market norm demands free entry[1] and as much competition as possible. Collusion, cartels, conspiracies, restraints of trade, price leadership, fair trade laws, price cartels, agricultural subsidies, protective tariffs, and blocked exchanges, all go out the window just as quickly under space microeconomics as under the theory of pure competition. Indeed, the conclusions of pure competition so nearly duplicate those of normative oligopoly that the former, rather than the latter, system of thought should and can be used in numerous instances. Unfortunately, as we shall see next, it has misled many economists, and we shall accordingly contend that the theory of unorganized oligopoly is usually the easier one to apply in practice.

III. INADEQUACIES OF CLASSICAL THEORY AS A GUIDE TO ANTI-TRUST POLICY

It has long been a source of amazement to the author how economists, steeped as they claim to be in a science of positivism, are able to advocate an "intent" or "market structure" test for resolving "anti-trust" cases. Under the doctrine of positivism the function of the scientist is said to be not to tell people what they should do, but to describe and explain the experiences of man, and to evaluate events on the basis of selected criteria. As formulated in the area of "positive anti-trust economics," one might well anticipate that the market performance of the firm would be the variable cited by economists as the proper basis for policy. Instead, American economists often claim that either the intent of the defendant, or the market structure of the industry must serve as the crucial factor of consideration.[2]

---

[1] Free entry is the basis for much of the writings on government and business. For example, see C. Wilcox, *Public Policies Toward Business* (Homewood, Ill.: Richard D. Irwin, Inc., 1955), p. 875; and A. Papandreau and J. T. Wheeler, *Competition and Its Regulation* (New York: Prentice-Hall, Inc., 1954), Chapter 12. Indeed, this idea of free entry being equal to efficiency is not novel, but is accepted in the more technical works in economic theory, such as J. Bain, *Price Theory* (New York: Henry Holt & Co., Inc., 1952). For example, Bain writes (p. 447) that: "Oligopoly can offer operational efficiency in scale of firms, and it may in the long run be forced to approximate it if entry is relatively easy, but it need not."

[2] See A. E. Kahn, "Standard for Anti-Trust Policy," *67 Harv. L. Rev. 28* (1953),

Intent and Classical Economics

We assert that the intent of corporate officials should be non-sequitur to any litigation involving an economic offense against the general public. This is not to say that intent would not be a critical consideration in private litigations or in non-economic offenses against society, including, of course, torts, felonies, and other offenses. But the benevolence or malevolence of the butcher, the baker, the candlestick-maker, it would seem, should be of no vital interest to economists.[1] We do not claim that voters and legislators should be oblivious to the need for safe-guarding the people's ethics, or effecting certain social results, and their like. But we do claim that matters of this kind are not for the economist to determine. The statutes designed to accomplish economic effects should be evaluated by economists solely in terms of their economic content. And this should hold true although the same statutes may also be evaluated (and applied) by others against the background of non-economic forces. Our objective is to find an economic yardstick for determining anti-trust violations but to do this using economic science alone. Such a yardstick must be readily understandable and applicable in the courts of our land. Consider, accordingly, the market structure test that has been advocated by many.

The Market Structure Test and Classical Economics

The market structure of an industry has been used by economists to resolve the right or wrong of a company's policies. But this is irrelevant in cases involving an economic offense against the public. Attempts to measure departures from atomistic competition, as with intent, should not lie in the hands of economists (nor others). Market structure tests supposedly relate to *degrees* of monopoly (or size). But measurements of the degree of monopoly,

reprinted in E. Mansfield's *Monopoly Power and Economic Performance* (New York: W. W. Norton, 1964), pp. 144–164.

Professor Kahn himself does not unambiguously endorse either the intent or market structure test. But he refers throughout his paper to statements by jurists and economists which emphasize the one or the other and, on his own part, appears to favor intent, especially in cases falling under Section 2 of the Sherman Act: "The inescapable conclusion is that from a practical standpoint the criterion of intent alone 'fills the bill' for a sensible anti-trust policy in such cases," p. 161.

[1] If our sense of fair play and good ethics causes us to consider as a bad business practice not only an offense against another private individual, but an offense against society, then, of course, a statute, if needed, could be passed against such activity (e.g., the FTCA Act of 1914). Of course, the common law of unfair competition would also be available. In any case, nothing stated above should be construed to apply to statutes safeguarding the nation's ethics. It deserves mention here, though we shall stress the point later in the text, that we are only considering herein the statutes supposedly designed to effect selected economic ends. We are not concerned with ethical or social matters, or the ethical or social aspects of the laws to be referred to herein.

such as the one which compares the differential between selling price and marginal costs, are highly arbitrary—as may readily be seen in their disregard of uncertainty. Similarly, the estimate of the degree of monopoly based on the proportion of the total sales in an industry that happens to be made by the largest two, three, or four firms, as selected by the examining authority, is highly arbitrary. Measurements such as these reflect the engineering (and related) differences between industries more than they relate to what is in fact an acceptable or unacceptable concentration of economic activity.

It is significant that besides involving arbitrary measurements, the market structure test places the expert in the position of actually determining right and wrong on the basis of the postulates (or, let us say, beginning assumptions) which form a scientific model. Thus, in economic theory, ideal results are deduced from the assumption of an infinite number of microscopic firms, for such firms would—given specified additional conditions in the model of pure competition—produce efficiently and maximize consumer satisfaction in the process. The proper yardstick for evaluating a claimed anti-trust violation, we assert, cannot relate to the postulations in an economic model any more than may the assumptions in a theory of the physical universe serve as the basis among physicists for their prescriptions as to how best to conquer space. Assumptions as to the kind, size, and number of firms should be left where they are, simply as the beginning points in constructing a theory. Assumptions should not be confused with the deductions of a theory and applied as if they themselves provide the goal to be attained.

The Proper Guideline

It is with the consequences of economic theory that we gain the requisite material for designating and measuring the economically effective and ineffective, or the economic good or bad, in anti-trust cases. The standard we now suggest is entirely unconcerned with intent, size of firms, number of firms, tilt of demand (i.e., average revenue) curves, and the like. Only the results in the market serve as the proper *economic* bench-mark for evaluating the *economic* activity of a firm under an anti-trust attack. With this said, let us proceed with our recommended interpretation of the anti-trust laws.

IV. OUR STANDARD AND SOME ILLUSTRATIVE APPLICATIONS

Effective economic regulation of business, as gleaned from our more realistic theory, has certain basic referential points. They are as follows: encourage free entry, tolerate natural restraints, permit institutional restraints only where clearly necessary to arouse other desirable actions, and attack with force all other restrictions on competition of institutional origin. Against these, specific fact situations may be measured. Wherever an enterpriser's acts artificially limit the development of alternative sources of supply, they are monopolizing acts, and are accordingly bad. This highly elementary standard for social policy arises clearly from classical theory as well as our own. Unfortunately, the fact that economic theory deals only with an abstract world has caused many economists to overlook its true meaning and to stress intent or market structure. In any case, our discussion will now show that (1) no other standards are necessary, and that (2) vital cases may be measured consistently on this basis. We shall use footnotes to sketch the details of *particular* cases where readers may not be familiar with them, and we suggest a careful reading of these notes.[1]

(A) *Section 2—The Sherman Anti-Trust Act.* Let us select the U.S. Steel Company Case of 1920,[2] the Alcoa Case of 1945,[3] the Columbia Steel Case of 1948,[4] the United Shoe Machinery Case of 1953,[5] and the duPont Cellophane Case of 1953[6] as the basis for examining the meaning of section 2 of the Sherman Act. This section holds that monopoly or the act of monopolizing is illegal. Under it, the question whether size itself is an offense has been faced by the courts. Lengthy discourses have resulted which inquired into the intent of the large size firm, the extent to which it dominated the industry, the meaning of the term industry, the ascertainment of commodities competing with the subject company's product, and the appraisal of all practices pursued by the firm over the years in question. What a task for a team of lawyers, especially since economists themselves could not and cannot yet answer many of the questions about industry and products asked by the courts!

[1] Economists who wish to be reminded of the cases described in the following footnotes, but who do not have the time nor inclination to study the actual decision rendered by the court will find a good review in Chapters IV through VII of C. Wilcox's *Public Policy Toward Business, op. cit.*

[2] 271 U.S. 417 . . . Bad practices such as the Gary dinners where prices and related matters were discussed had been discontinued before the action was brought. The issue was thus whether size alone violated section 2 of the Sherman Act. Held "no."

[3] 148 F. 2d 416 . . . No bad practices worthy of note were proven, but the company expanded to meet each new opportunity. It was held that such expansion, though natural and proper on the part of the directors, was bad because the company was so large. Vital to this decision was the measurement of market control by the firm.

[4] 334 U.S. 495 . . . Existing capacity in the West Coast areas was purchased by a subsidiary of U.S. Steel. This enabled the company to have a fairly large part of the West Coast market, as elsewhere in the United States. Held, approximately 25 percent control of a market is reasonable and expansion to this size is legitimate.

[5] 110 F. Supp. 295 . . . Practices in leasing equipment favored those who used United Shoe Machinery and not that of rivals. Held, practices which could be pursued by small firms without being condemned were bad in the hands of large firms.

[6] 118 F. Supp. 41 . . . DuPont produced approximately 80 percent of the total output of cellophane in the United States. The Sylvania Co. produced the rest. Cellophane is used largely in food packing and constituted as much as 46 percent of the transparent films used to package fresh produce. Held, cellophane competes with many other products.

The common thread that should govern these cases is not the degree of market control, the definition of a product or an industry, the question of intent, or related matters, but the issue of practices. And by practices we do not confine ourselves to predatory acts and side-room bargains; we simply mean practices which harmfully restrain entry and which are otherwise not approved.[1]

That the U.S. Steel discontinued its pools, its trade meetings, and other objectionable activities, before a suit was instituted, that Columbia Steel would control less than 50 percent of West Coast capacity, that cellophane is in competition with other flexible wrapping materials, would all be irrelevant matters. What would count would merely be whether entry is restrained through man-made institutions without any *clear* offsetting advantage. The standards of Learned Hand in the Alcoa Case come close to those that are integral parts of economic theory . . . but only close.[2] An industrial giant must have the right to enter new markets, even to anticipate new markets, otherwise the giant loses its incentive to innovate and progress. Entry may be kept open by compulsory licensing and other arrangements, and this is the way economic ends should be gained. Of course, if the industry proves to be such that a firm reaps substantial economies of size which, when compared to the magnitude of demand, permits no other firm's existence, the natural monopoly market exists and a special kind of regulation is, accordingly, in order. Generally, however, demand is not so limited relative to economies of size. So, other firms may be induced to enter by required patent licensing, by imparting technical know-how, and the like.

In our view, then, giant firms should be limited in their actions only in the sense, for example, of not having the right to buy up existing capacity *if* this limits significant entry by others (Columbia Steel), or not having the right to use the technique of leasing so that entry is inhibited into particular markets (United Shoe), or, for further example, not having the right to engage in cross-licensing agreements which are not open to other enterprises on proportionately equivalent terms (duPont and Sylvania). And by industrial giant we mean not only the national concern, but any enterprise which, by its practices, effectively limits the number of alternative sources available to buyers in and outside of its market area. As is explained in the note below, there may be a rule of reason.[3] What is reasonable under our standard would

---

[1] A more complicated search into, say, harmful effects is not fundamentally necessary to the free-entry standard. It suffices under our standard to demonstrate that entry is restrained without *clear* offsetting advantages to the public, such as society may claim for the patent.

In, however, the harmful "effects" key, see S. C. Oppenheim, "Guides for a Revised Anti-Trust Policy," 50 *Michigan Law Review*, 1139, 1952.

[2] Mere size without practices that forcefully restrain do not violate our standards. But see E. Rostow, "The New Sherman Act," 14 *University of Chicago Law Review* 567, 1957, for a full preference for the Alcoa view in accordance with the theory of pure competition.

[3] Notice that a rule of reason stipulation is a natural part of our standard . . . though

usually be judged in the light of whether or not entry into the market remains possible and likely, or can be made possible and likely.

(B) *Section 1—The Sherman Anti-Trust Act.* Collusion between firms as in price leadership (American Tobacco, 1945),[1] price fixing (Trenton Potteries,[2] Socony Vacuum[3]), through trade associations which designate what members are to do (The Sugar Institute[4]), through rebates (Standard Oil[5]) and intended parallelism of action (Interstate Circuit Co.[6]) would be illegal per se, for section 1 of the Sherman Act asserts that contracts, combinations, or conspiracies in restraint of trade are illegal. In turn, artificial price hikes and monopolistic restraints violate our standard. These restraints, we might note further, have the effect of cartelizing an industry, so that even if open entry exists society does not gain; only the abscissa values change as a result of new entry, not the ordinate values as well. Conscious parallelism of action —when in the form of a systematically followed price practice over space —would similarly be condemned. What is a competitive oligopolistic pricing system compared to an organized oligopoly pricing system is more easily determined in a space economy than in a world of zero freight costs.

(C) *Sections 7 and 8—The Clayton Anti-Trust Act.* Standards under sections 7 and 8 of the Clayton Act are similarly derived. These sections, let us recall, object to intercorporate stockholding (Section 7) and interlocking directorates (Section 8), where the effect is substantially to lessen competition (7) or to violate some other anti-trust provision (8). We need not bog ourselves down with such problems as whether—in estimating the extent of market control possessed by a firm—the market for Duco should include or exclude

in a slightly different way than has been the interpretation in our courts. Under our standard, we would inquire into the reasonableness of the defendant's acts only in so far as the gains by society (e.g., lower costs, innovations as under patent policy and patent laws) outweigh unmistakably the restraints on entry that are embodied in the practice. What is reasonable about the practice(s) must be judged in light of society's view of the restraint. For example, though the restraint of free entry may be reasonable in so far as the competitive firms are concerned, it must also be reasonable from the standpoint of providing clear benefits to society, and this will usually mean reasonable from the standpoint that entry into the market remains possible and likely. Our approach, therefore, limits the possible range of the rule of reason.

And see C. Wilcox, "The Verdict on Anti-Trust and its Significance," *Papers and Proceedings, American Economic Review,* XLVI, May 1956, pp. 490–495. He notes that the Business Advisory Council (in its report on *Effective Competition,* submitted to the Secretary of Commerce in late 1952) favored an extension of the rule of reason approach whereas the *Report* of the Attorney General's National Committee did not urge any extension of the rule of reason. Under existing interpretation, the controversy is widespread and, we suggest, unnecessary. Also see J. S. McGee's comments on reasonableness in "Predatory Price Cutting: The Standard Oil (N. J.) Case," *The Journal of Law and Economics,* I, 1958, pp. 137–143.

[1] 328 U.S. 781.   [2] 273 U.S. 392.   [3] 310 U.S. 150.
[4] 15 F. Supp. 817; 29 U.S. 553.   [5] 221 U.S. 1.   [6] 306 U.S. 208.

nonautomotive uses, nor need we stress whether 23 percent ownership of another company is sufficient to establish dominance and hence lessen competition (duPont and G.M.[1]). Our standard refers simply to the question whether entry is still open after the practice. If it is and collusion between firms on the same level is not permitted, we reason that the market performance of a given firm will be good.

(D) *The Celler Act.* The Celler Act extends the provisions of Section 7 of the Clayton Act to cover not only the acquisition of stock but its use to effect a merger. This act may be evaluated and applied in the same way as Sections 7 and 8 of the Clayton Act. Thus, the purchase of one company's assets by another is objectionable whenever the existence of one firm in place of two has the effect of restraining other entry (Pillsbury Mills[2]). Indeed, the act of purchasing existing facilities should be treated more harshly than other expansions. Thus, cost advantages gained from the merger should not offset the development of restraints against entry. The large firm that desires to expand further should be permitted this development, but generally not by acquiring existing facilities (as was permitted in Columbia Steel). The avenues open to new entrants should be kept as free as possible.

The Celler anti-merger Act portends a much larger story than that which is possible to recount here. Indeed, the sets of recent interpretations of this act have imparted a flavor to the Cellar Act similar to that of Robinson-Patman, and only detailed references (and quotations) could fully manifest this development. Suffice it to point out that mergers of any kind, even those which would have tended to have the effect of lessening competition if one of the two firms would have decided *at some future time* to produce the same product as that produced by the other firm, have been ruled bad under the act. This extreme holding applies even though substantial competition continues from other firms in the market. Thus, in the celebrated Brown (Kinney) Shoe Case,[3] where the Brown and Kinney outlets marketed 57.5 percent of the sales of women's shoes in Dodge City, Kansas, the law was held to have been violated. In fact, the perspective of the Court in favor of atomism was well reflected by its conviction that sales by the combined store in excess of 5 percent of the total sold of at least one product line (men's, women's, or

---

[1] 353 U.S. 586 . . . DuPont interests held 23 percent of voting stock of G.M. Only in sales of Duco lacquers was there a clear chance that the influence of stock ownership may have governed GM's buying policy. Held, 23 percent ownership against the background of overwhelming sales of Duco lacquers to the Chevrolet division of GM involves substantial lessening of competition within the meaning of section 7 of the Clayton Act. And see R. W. Harbeson, "The Clayton Act: Sleeping Giant of Antitrust?" *American Economic Review*, XLVIII, 1958, pp. 92–104.

[2] Docket No. 6000 *F.T.C.*, *Remand*, Dec. 28, 1953. And see D. Dewey, "Mergers and Contents: Some Reservations about Policy," *The American Economic Review* LI, 1961, pp. 255–262, also H. A. Einhorn & W. P. Smith, *Economic Aspects of Anti-Trust* (N. Y. Random House, 1968), pp. 201–212.   [3] 370 U.S. 294 (1962).

children's shoes) in 118 cities alone was *sufficiently* bad in the sense of indicating a *possible* trend which must be stopped.[1] While in our view, the burden of
proof that a merger *is* economically desirable might well be placed on the
merging firms, whereas the burden of proof that other practices actually fall
outside our concept of unorganized oligopoly might well be placed on the
Department of Justice or the Federal Trade Commission, the recent interpretations of mergers have completely lacked this perspective. The theory of
oligopoly presented in this book contends that organized oligopoly is bad
per se. Thus, any merger leading to (or portending a state of) monopoly or
organized oligopoly is also bad per se.[2] Correspondingly, a merger which
would constrain future entry is similarly bad. But the mere revision of market
shares via a merger which does not otherwise amount to a per se violation
should be outlawed only if no economic benefits at all may be projected and
the possibility is substantial that the merger will bring about a state of

[1] And see D. D. Martin, "The Brown Shoe Case and the New Antimerger Policy",
American Economic Review, LIII, 1963, pp. 340–358, where the writer observes that the
lines of commerce selected by the Court (men's, women's, and children's shoes) were neither
broad as in the duPont cellophane case nor narrow as in the duPont-GM case. Correspondingly, section of the country was given meaning in light of the fact situation in the
subject case, in particular determined by the cities where the combined firm had outlets.
Most importantly perhaps, the trend toward *oligopoly* (whatever the Court meant by that)
and the similarity of mergers to tying clause cases (in so far as concerns their market impact)
appeared to justify a stricter holding under the Celler Act than that under the Sherman Act.
(To be sure, tying contracts impose a substantial barrier to entry and in this respect, like the
merger, deserve stricter review—see J. W. McKie, "The Decline of Monopoly in the Metal-
Container Industry," *American Economic Review*, XLV, Proceedings May 1955, pp. 499–
508.) As Professor Martin observes, market share statistics have been relegated to a subsidiary role under this statute as mergers are being held bad even though market shares are
small.

[2] The reader may wonder how a state of organized oligopoly would be identified?
This question, of course, is subject matter for a full paper (or chapter, or probably a book)
directed exclusively to the subject. We shall, nevertheless, attempt to outline in this note
certain inter-company relationships that might be evaluated in the courts as a matter of
evidence which helps determine the character of the market. For example, as suggested
elsewhere in the book, any spatial pricing system of the basing point variety (where phantom
freight applies) would point to organized oligopoly and thus be bad. Also, dominant firm
price leadership would be indicative of what we mean by organized oligopoly. In this
connection, we do not have in mind the dominance which one firm may exercise in the early
(formative) days of an industry, but the continuing dominance of the firm. (See J. W. Markham, "The Nature and Significance of Price Leadership," *American Economic Review*,
XLI, 1951, pp. 891–905). Other forms of price leadership [(K. E. Boulding, *Economic
Analysis*) rev. ed. (New York, Harper & Press, 1948) pp. 58, ff.; also see, R. Leftwich, *The
Price System and Resource Allocation* (New York Rinehart & Co., 1956), pp. 241–244], in
particular so-called barometric price leadership, would not be a *per se* indication of organized oligopoly, for as noted by Markham in his discussion of the tobacco case (*op. cit.*), this
type of organization tends to break down in certain periods of stress and maturation of the
industry. But, of course, let us reobserve that the state of organized (collusive) oligopoly may
take diverse forms, and only the weight of evidence that is presented may indicate its
existence or nonexistence.

organized oligopoly. Such decision as that in the Bethlehem-Youngstown merger,[1] where according to the Court the firms were too large in that they sold as much as 48 percent of the total sales in four important states (Michigan, Ohio, Pennsylvania, and New York), manifests a present day equivalence in belief in our courts that merger of large size firms amounts to a state of organized oligopoly.[2] Indeed, close reading of the Pabst-Blatz case[3] points to the thought that if the sales of firms in certain markets are relatively large (e.g. 24 percent of the sales made in Wisconsin are attributed to the merged firm) while they compete as a comparatively small firm (say 4 percent of total sales) at market points lying outside of the area in which they are significant, the merger is still bad because the one section of the county (e.g. Wisconsin) *could be* subject to (some sort of?) monopolistic controls.

The Pabst-Blatz (type of) ruling ignores the competitive impact of distant sellers (and markets) on a given seller. Just what consumers in Wisconsin lose—provided we assume unorganized oligopoly throughout the country and provided we have other laws which protect them from *undue* price discrimination by Pabst and Blatz within the state—should be determined rather than simply assumed to exist.[4] Nor is it satisfactory in any way at all—according to the theory of this book—for Courts to propose, as did the Supreme Court in the El Paso case,[5] that indirect competition (not even direct competition, please note) from one of the firms moves the merger outside

---

[1] 168 Fed. Supp. 576 (1958).

[2] Under the theory presented chiefly in Chapters 5, 8, & 13 of this book, size alone is not an offense and even a duopoly market may be competitively efficient. And see L. S. Keyes, "The Bethlehem-Youngstown Case and the Market-share Criterion," *American Economic Review*, LI (1961), pp. 643–657, where the author expresses concern that a market shares standard will be accepted contending instead that the *competitiveness* of the firms should be determined. In contrast, see C. Kaysen & D. F. Turner, *Anti-trust Policy: An Economic and Legal Analysis* (Cambridge: Harvard University Press, 1959), esp. 148 ff.

[3] 384 U.S. 546 (1966).

[4] We used the term *undue* price discrimination in the text so as to exclude a system of spatial discrimination in which the seller systematically absorbs some freight by charging distant buyers a delivered price higher than the price paid by more proximate buyers by slightly less than the full amount of freight. This type of spatial price discrimination will be shown in another writing to increase profits and outputs, and in the long run effectuate a lower *schedule* of prices over the space; it will also be shown to be a natural form of pricing over economic space. In contrast, a system of spatial pricing in which distant buyers pay a lower delivered price for reasons related to attempts to meet the price of distant competitors in the market or to capture sales which otherwise could not be made because of "b" intercept price values, competition from substitutable goods, etc., *could be* arbitrary. Though many judges, and for that matter economists who do not have a "space economy" perspective believe that so-called "good faith" price discrimination provides consumers with alternative sources of supply, and that this means greater competition, which is good for the consumer, we repeat the charge of possible arbitrariness. This type of price discrimination can lead to the systematizing of prices over economic space. If long pursued in a consistent manner, it would portend a state of organized (not competitive) oligopoly. Even before then, nearer buyers are discriminated against rather sharply and unfairly.

[5] 376 U.S. 651 (1964).

of the law. The *possible* lessening of competition (as in the Penn-Olin case[1]), at least to the extent that one of the merging firms *could* enter a market (even though in all likelihood it would not so enter regardless of the occurrence or nonoccurrence of the merger) is a strange thesis. In particular, it is strange to imagine that such possible competition is a root of (or basic to) the well-being of our economic system. If extra profits exist, there *there will be entry* if entry is kept free.

Pure or perfect competition appears to stand in the wings as the market type sought by the Celler Act. Indeed, it has been essentially only in the Proctor Gamble-Clorox case[2] that we find any significant attention being given by the court to "barriers to entry", in this case barriers attributable to higher "expected" advertising costs. But even here, Proctor's mere presence "on the market fringe" was the key consideration in the final decision, not the question whether organized oligopoly prevailed or might prevail because of the merger, nor the question whether a significant barrier to entry would arise. This "fringe" presence, as in the other recent merger cases, was the potential competition needed in the economy according to our courts; without it, inefficiency and nonsatisfaction of consumer wants would follow since oligopoly per se now appears to be bad in the courts, not just organized oligopoly.

(E) *Trade Marks and Trade Names—A New Act to Replace the Lanham Act.* Through new entry the tendency is for efficient economic enterprise to take the place of inefficient plants and firms. But new enterprises are often confronted by an awesome array of existing marks and names.[3] This barrier is so formidable that oligopolistic markets tend to be open more to existing enterprises that are willing to expand to new lines than to completely new establishments. Limitations of this kind are not desirable. New firms should be encouraged to enter and to compete if a free enterprise economy is to prove efficient; and, one way of accomplishing this is to allow prospective rivals a rather close copy of existing marks and names, provided, of course, that sufficient safeguards are established to protect the original firms from an encroachment on reputation through inferior goods.[4] By permitting close copy of marks and names, subject only to the requirements that existing product reputations should not be damaged, a change in advertising standards would arise. Formulas and expressions coined by advertisers would not be effective at all. Close copy of mark and name requires that consumers must be convinced that their ability to distinguish between one brand and another

---

[1] 378 U.S. 158 (1964).   [2] 386 U.S. 568 (1967).

[3] M. L. Greenhut, "Free Entry and the Trade Mark-Trade Name Protection," *Southern Economic Journal*, XXIV, 1957, pp. 170–181.

[4] *Ibid.* The permission to copy (i.e. the degree of closeness permitted) involves the question of property rights. It may be that in this regard the standard required would be that the reasonably informed consumer should be able to distinguish the original product from the copy.

is of vital advantage. And this conviction involves informative advertising' not so-called persuasive advertising.

(F) *The Miller–Tydings and Robinson–Patman Acts.* Space does not permit detailed examination of the impact of our theory on interpreting (and applying) the Miller–Tydings and Robinson–Patman Acts among others. Suffice it to say with respect to the Miller–Tydings Act that traditional objections to the fair-trade provisions would stand. With respect to Robinson-Patman, our theory regards the larger enterprise in a much more gratuitous way than does the subject law. It follows that injury to competition rather than a competitor is clearly the desired standard. We are concerned with the overall system and not with each individual firm, as our space oligopoly theory does not extol the virtues of the small firm per se. Similarly, the FTC power to limit quantity discounts should be eliminated. If we must have them, it is desirable to have symmetrical rules governing brokerage and other services, as well as ways of estimating manufacturing cost differentials. However, this last point is not closely tied up to the thesis of this paper and we need only re-emphasize the conclusion that atomistic competition—in itself—is not an end supported by our theory.

Patents and Vertical Integration Under the Proposed Anti-Trust Standard. Under the free entry (no collusion) norm, such anti-trust problem fields as patent licensing and vertical integration fall readily into place. We suggest compulsory licensing of other firms after some years, though, of course, social choice may prefer institutional restraints on entry, in the belief that the innovations thereby gained offset entry limitations. We feel that licenses tendered to one should be tendered to all, both existing and future firms, although this practice itself points to the need for a further requirement. Proportionately equivalent terms . . . if restrictive as to price, output, and sales radius, i.e., market area . . . would have the effect of organizing the oligopoly. Restrictions under patents must therefore be limited and, accordingly, we suggest that the Lime Materials Case[1] comes closer to our theory than the General Electric Case of 1926.[2]

As firms build up and down in a vertically integrated form, the entry and competition of other firms tend to be restrained. Here as elsewhere what matters is not total size, national dominance, 40, 62, 83 percent market control, intent, and related matters. Impact on entry in the *affected market area* alone must shape our policy. This means that if the second stage is monopolized, so too will entry be restrained in the first stage (Yellow Cab).[3] But if the

[1] 333 U.S. 287 . . . A price-fixing arrangement between "cross-licensees" was held bad.

[2] 272 U.S. 476 . . . Held, a patentee can fix the prices to be charged by a licensee.

[3] 332 U.S. 218. Clearly, if the buyer of a product is a monopolist, for example, a taxi cab operator in a given city, and this buying company is owned by a manufacturer, the manufacturer in question excludes other producers from the sales area in question.

But note the sharp analysis of this case by G. Stocking and M. Watkins, *Monopoly and the Free Enterprise* (New York, 1951), pp. 296–299. They point out that if the local monopoly

second stage offers alternative sources of demand, alternative sources of supply should be possible.

V. CONCLUSION

No single standard for decision-making can be applied without strain to all situations that could arise. One can only say that the stresses and strains during a period may be such as to require a modified use of a standard. Moral principles, ethics, customs, and social values of people change. The courts in interpreting existing mores may modify a standard so severely that it looks quite different from its original form (Appalachian Coals[1]). In much the same way, we recognize that, even if business structures and policies are evaluated uniformly—for example, under the policy of keeping entry "as open as is possible under the existing forces of indivisibility and uncertainty"—we may nevertheless obtain contrasting applications. Doctrines and dogma are used in different frames of reference from person to person. It is, indeed, most unusual for any one person regularly to use a given measuring stick in a perfectly consistent way.

Economists, lawyers, and judges merely flirt with applications that are both logical and unvarying. In the social sciences particularly our decisions are likely to be far from impeccable taken from any standpoint. It is because of this—or at least because the author believes that this is so—that our policy standard is proposed. It is not claimed that all situations can be judged simply on the basis of our theory. It is suggested, however, that all fact situations can be and should be judged in as broad a context as possible, and we assert that our free entry, no collusion requirement fulfills these roles.[2]

Under pure competition theory, one would tend to extol the small firm and hence create such acts as Robinson–Patman. Moreover, injury to any competitor rather than to competition would, in general, be considered a bad practice. Correspondingly, protection to all small firms, with limits on lawful price differentials, would tend to arise.

itself is regulated, then the local authorities should not permit any abuse of the vertical integration. We may generalize as follows: If from one community to another there exist different users of the output of the earlier stages, such that in the trading area normally required for the erection of the earlier stage plant there are alternative buyers independent of the vertically integrated unit, entry *per se* will not have been restrained in violation of the law.

[1] 288 U.S. 344 . . . Though price fixing between firms has been customarily condemned, this policy was discarded during the depression years, as in the subject case.

[2] The standard does not require legitimate inference drawn only by economists, as was proposed by E. Mason several years ago. See his "Market Power and Business Conduct: Some Comments," *Papers and Proceedings, American Economic Review*, XLVI, May, 1965, pp. 471–484. The lawyer and judge are equally qualified to apply our standard while alternatively "some kind of an expert" is needed to determine whether 70 percent control of a market is monopolistic or whether cellophane is part of a broader product, etc.

A strict application of pure competition economics to the anti-trust field is even more disturbing when the theory's preference for small firms is applied under the Sherman Act, and then related to the twentieth-century American business scene. Especially is this true if the person who applies the law happens to be a lawyer or judge. How small is small? Does the economist really want atomistic units? Clearly, the difficulties involved in applying the postulates of abstract economic theory are manifold, and this condition has led to varying standards from case to case and judge to judge.

Thus we find, on the one hand, that size in itself has been held to be no offense. But on the other hand, we find that such view contradicts the assumptions of pure competition, so that a person steeped in this philosophy may object to size alone. In turn, we find one court inquiring into intent, so that if the company is large its practices combined with bad intent would constitute a violation of the Sherman Act. Yet another court might find something reasonable in the intent, even if it is a large firm. Its judge might conjecture that the economist does not really believe in nor want an economy of atomistically sized enterprises. What the economist believes, the court might feel, is that competition should be fair, workable, and *reasonable*. And indeed, for the judge who takes this view of the theory of pure competition, it is but a small step to maintaining that reasonableness requires reasonable behavior with respect to property rights and this even though society may regard the behavior as unreasonable to consumers. Manifestly, the courts have long accepted the responsibility of protecting business property rights and when this is accomplished and competition also appears reasonable and considerate, the public, it can be said, will have to benefit, sooner or later.

What happens under pure competition theory is, therefore, a great many contradictory applications by different judges and courts, largely because economics itself seems to be too abstract and inapplicable, without the "logical adjustment" to be made by the court. As a consequence, our experts at law are forced to examine questions that even economists cannot answer for themselves: such as whether 23 percent, 60 percent, or 80 percent control is a monopoly, or whether the maintenance of small competitors is absolutely essential or whether intent and reasonableness are proper and integral parts of the theory.

We have contended that our theory and standard reflects the business world sufficiently well for its main tenets to be adopted without excessive manipulation by jurists. We held that price fixing and collusion in general would lead to an ineffective economy while, in contrast, a reasonable approximation to the effectiveness of pure competition could be expected if entry into and exit from the market are kept open. It was, therefore, proposed that intent and reasonableness should be ignored except from the standpoint of special society approval (e.g., patent laws, and see note 1, p. 359). Size too, we held, should be considered irrelevant, and efficient firms should be permitted to reap their full rewards without price limits being imposed by trade commissions. "Free entry and no collusion permitted," we assert, is a standard that is comparatively easy to recognize. Of course, the determination of when it is being violated or not, as with other litigations, must be and will always remain a matter of evidence.

16

Theory of the Firm in Economic Space

We have asserted that a spatial oligopoly is likely to be established when firms and people are dispersed over space and transport costs are significant. If collusion is not permitted and free entry and exit is maintained, the system will be efficient and will maximize consumer satisfactions.

The efficiency and consumer maximization results of the space economy take place in the long run in industries within which competition of firms exists. However, during the early stages of an industry's development, the competitive spatial oligopoly that arises may well be characterized by different kinds of oligopolistic relation types than that stressed in this book. Thus, a Stackelberg disequilibrium, a "leader-follower" system, or even a "market-shares" industrial pattern may prevail. Typically, the substantial impact on price of a spatially differentiated firm lessens the likelihood that the "leader-leader" pricing practice inherent to a Stackelberg disequilibrium will prevail. We may generally expect a "leader-follower" or a "market-shares" relationship to arise as a consequence of spatial differentiation in the early days of an industry's development. (Of course, we are assuming that collusive oligopoly is ruled out by effective anti-trust regulation.)

Competition in economic space is thus of a slightly different order than nonspatial competition. We propose, furthermore, that a "leader-follower" or "market-shares" market type converges in time to the "follower-follower" market, *as entry continues over the space at distant and proximate points to any given seller, and as individual plants and firms become less and less important.* In other words, the maturing of the free entry—exit industry over an economic space yields what appears to be a range of "price independence" for a plant or firm. Thus the firms in the spatial variant of the Cournot "follower-follower" market, in effect, ignore their rivals by assuming a fixed supply and fixed price for their rivals, up to a point. The resulting range of price independence is particularly significant with respect to prospective lowering of prices as the whittling away of sales resulting from competitive entry, *and* the advantage in an indivisible system of some larger sizes of plant(s) and firm(s) *vis-à-vis* very small sizes of plant(s) and firm(s), lead to minimum prices. The space economy stabilizes at the point where opportunity costs are covered in full, without surplus or loss, and economic efficiency along with maximum consumer satisfactions prevails.

It is clear that a space economy is not fully described by reference only to production-cost curves, to final good f.o.b. prices, and to some undefined set of consumers. Delivered prices must be minimal and all consumers in the economy must be included in the analytical framework that is used. The market areas of the firms must be determined, and here we found that they take on the general appearance of a system of hexagons under conditions of competitive oligopoly. But note, not all of the hexagons will be of the same size, neither for firms belonging to different industries nor for those belonging to the same industry. In the different market areas, technology may vary a little, demands may be of contrasting order, and uncertainty conditions need not be identical. These forces (technology, demand, and uncertainty) combine to determine the extent of entry necessary to (and permitted in) each market area for equilibrium results. When combined with the uneven distribution of consumers which stems from the above conditions, we find that intra-industry market area shapes will not be identical in size nor even regular in "polygonic" form. Planners who seek to follow the theories of Burgess, Hoyt, Harris, and Ullman, or others are warned that no universally accepted plan is possible. Over each strip of earth at any given point in time, the concentric zone, sectoral, or multiple-nuclei format must be modified so that the plan conforms to the climate, industry, and resources that characterize the area under consideration.

Our theory is simply that a spatially-isomorphic counterpart to pure competition exists in the form of a competitive oligopoly in which individual plants and their firms earn the opportunity return imputable to them. The precision of the economic equilibrium does not reach the point of yielding identical geographic configurations over space, and accordingly we are not contending that a "universal" competitive oligopoly exists. We have stated instead that over time and over economic space there will be industries for which the friction of distance is insignificant; and there will be industries in which collusion prevails. It is possible that perfect competition or a monopoly of the simple monopoly or organized oligopoly type may prevail. But significantly, except when simple monopoly or organized oligopoly exists, the mix works out ideally. Our unorganized oligopoly requires a profit for uncertainty in addition to rents for risks, skills, fertilities, *etc.*, while, in the absence of frictions over space, a purely competitive market "could" result, and, if it did, there would be no profits because there would be no uncertainties.

It is *not* significant that the models used in this book were of the non-discriminatory f.o.b. mill price form. Generality exists because a spatially discriminatory pricing system *simply* changes price levels over space, outputs, profits, and market areas, where the word simply *is intended*.[1] It should

---

[1] The model used in this book was of the form (a) $p = p(q)$, (b) $p = m + x$, where x the freight rate per unit of goods per unit of distance is assumed to be numerically proportional (in

suffice for our purposes to observe in this connection that given the price structure over the space, the firm's output, its profits, and its market area, competitive entry and exit must have the effect described in this book. The fact that elsewhere this author expects to help establish the principle that competitive oligopolists will discriminate in their price schedules against buyers located nearer to them, just as would the spatial monopolist,[1] does not constitute collusion or a denial of any theory presented above.[2] For the purposes of a book designed to determine the equilibrium conditions of the firm in economic space, the more widely known (and understood) f.o.b. mill pricing technique offered advantages in this writer's opinion that would have been sacrificed in the confusion of describing discriminatory pricing over space and contending that it is the competitive form. Like Occams razor, we did without.

Our theory is, we contend, fully comprehensive. It encompasses situations

fact equal) to distance D, such that if we assume all other costs are zero, (c) $\dfrac{\partial}{\partial m}\left[m \int_0^D q(\mathrm{D})d\mathrm{D}\right]$

$= 0$ maximizes profits over the total space. We could, of course, treat D as an unknown by determining the profit maximizing distance via $(d/dD)(pq) = 0$.

The counterpart spatial discriminatory model then would involve (a') $p = p(q)$, (b') $qdp/dq + p = x$, and (c') $x = \mathrm{D}$, where we see in b' we are maximizing profits at each buying point in the market. By assuming tangency of concave, convex, and linear demand curves at the nonspatial profit maximizing price (namely $b/2$ under zero costs, as in Chapter 13), and taking the concave demand to be of the form $p = \sqrt{aq} + \beta$, the convex demand of the form $p = aq^2 + \delta$, and linear demand of the form $p = b - q$, we rule out the *irrelevant* cases of increasing, constant, or decreasing elasticity. These *irrelevant* elasticity types require the empirically unlikely situation of negative or excessive freight absorption by the seller over the economic space. Spatial irrelevance relates to discriminatory pricing under negative or excessive freight absorption (i.e. respectively where $dP/dD > 1$ and $dP/dD < 0$) for the following reasons: the former involves discrimination against distant buyers, and buyers located close to the seller would therefore be able to repackage the good and resell it at a profit to the distant buyers; the latter involves lower delivered prices to distant buyers, as if proximate buyers and the department of justice would ignore the practice.

It can be shown if the spatial discrimination model is properly defined, as indicated above, it yields a lower set of delivered prices over the space on the average than does the standard f.o.b. mill pricing system. Also, it yields greater outputs, profits, and distances. Consistency of properties can be shown with respect to concave, linear, and convex demands, depending on the full specifications of the constraints. Under those given in Chapter 13, and thinking for a moment in terms of a spatial monopolist, the convex demand would yield the greatest distance, the lowest schedule of prices, etc. then the linear, and finally the concave demand. Dropping the identical b intercept constraint of Chapter 13 would reverse the order of advantage. In any case, the relative positions remain unchanged with respect to the discriminatory and nondiscriminatory price systems. Finally, if spatial competition is introduced at a distance, the relative positions again remain unchanged. As is mentioned above in the text, though prices, structures, distances etc. are altered, the final equilibrium results are therefore fundamentally the same.

[1] See E. M. Hoover, "Spatial Price Discrimination," *Review of Economic Studies*, IV (1935–36), pp. 182–191.

[2] M. L Greenhut, *Plant Location in Theory and Practice* (Chapel Hill: University of North Carolina Press, 1956), pp. 156–161.

in which economic space is a factor and situations in which it does not constrain. We require a non-organized, non-monopoly, and non-monopolistically competitive world. Our first requirement is obtained by ruling out the organization of duopolists and oligopolists under our anti-trust law. The evils of monopoly are curbed by enlightened regulation when their existence has been identified. And we rule out the classical version of monopolistic competition as an inconsistent, illogical market system which contradicts the very postulates (such as opportunity costs) which seemed to give it validity. Most importantly, we suggest that a free enterprise system, as described in this book, is effective, efficient, want-satisfying, and perfectly viable.

Distances in the Triangle, Square, and Hexagon

Given: Equilateral triangle, square, and regular hexagon, all with equal areas.

I. $A_1 = 0.43301\,S_T^2$, where S_T = side of equilateral triangle and A_1 stands for area of the triangle.

Proof of I

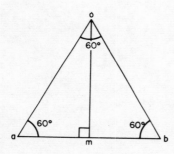

Figure A–1

1. equilateral triangle oab is equiangular.
2. $A_1 = 1/2\,(ab)\,(mo)$
3. $ab = S$
4. $(am)^2 + (mo)^2 = (ao)^2$ Pythagorean

4a. $\left(\dfrac{S_T}{2}\right)^2 + (mo)^2 = S_T^2$

   or $(mo)^2 = (3/4)\,S_T^2$

5. $mo = \dfrac{\sqrt{3}}{2}\,S_T$

6. $A_1 = 1/2\,(ab)\,(mo)$

   $= 1/2\,(S_T)\left(\dfrac{\sqrt{3}}{2}\,S_T\right) = \dfrac{\sqrt{3}}{4}\,S_T^2$

7. $\sqrt{3} \approx 1.732$, so $A_1 = \dfrac{1.732}{4}\,S_T^2 = .433\,S_T^2$ QED

II. $A_2 = S_S^2$ S_S = side of square

III. $A_3 = 2.598\,S_H^2$ S_H = side of hexagon

Proof of III

Hexagon (Regular $\Rightarrow$ equilateral and equiangular triangles)

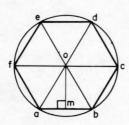

Figure A–2

1'. Any regular polygon can be inscribed in a a circle.

2'. Let o be the center of the circle, then $oa = ob = oc = od = oe = of$

3'. Then since $ab = bc = cd = de = ef = fa$ (reg. hexagon), we have $\triangle aob \simeq \triangle boc \simeq \triangle cod \simeq \triangle doe \simeq \triangle eof \simeq \triangle foa$ because of the Side Side Side Theorem of geometry. For example, $\triangle aob \simeq \triangle boc$ because $oa = oc$, $ob = ob$, and $ab = bc$.

374

$4'$. So, area of hexagon = 6 (area $\triangle$aob).

Now the area of $\triangle$aob = 1/2 (ab) (mo). Also note that $\angle$aob = $\angle$boc = , etc., and that 6 times the measure of $\angle$aob = 360° $\Rightarrow$ measure of $\angle$aob = 60°. Therefore $\triangle$aob is equilateral-equiangular. Then,

$5'$. mo = $\dfrac{\sqrt{3}}{2}$ S_H and area of $\triangle$aob = $\dfrac{\sqrt{3}}{4}$ S_H^2

$6'$. area of hexagon = 6 (area $\triangle$aob) = $\dfrac{3}{2}\sqrt{3}\,S_H^2$

$7'$. $\sqrt{3} \approx 1.732$, so $A_3 = 2.598\,S_H^2$

We may now compare the triangle, square, and hexagon directly. Continuing from 7 and $7'$:

(8). Let $A_1 = A_2 = A_3$ So $.433\,S_T^2 = S_S^2 = 2.598\,S_H^2$

Hence,

(9). $S_T = \dfrac{1}{\sqrt{.433}}\,S_S$ and $S_H = \dfrac{1}{\sqrt{2.598}}\,S_S$

(10). The perimeter of the triangle (P_1) $3S_T = 4.65_S$

(11). The perimeter of the square (P_2) is $4S_S$

So,

(12). The perimeter of the hexagon is (P_3) 3.7 S_S

So,

(13). $P_1 > P_2 > P_3 \Rightarrow$ greatest concentration in the hexagon

If we let the seller be located respectively at the market area center M_T, M_S, and M_H while N_A stands for the average distance to the consumers in the different market areas.

(14). $|M_H - N_A| < |M_S - N_A| < |M_T - N_A|$

The consumer in the hexagon is closest to the seller and, accordingly, it contains the greatest demand, *ceteris paribus*.

Personal Factors, Location, and Economic Development

A survey of plant location in Florida was conducted several years ago to determine the reasons for the industrial development of the state.[1] Among the major difficulties usually encountered in conducting this kind of survey are: (1) the frequent claims by company officials that they selected their location because of a personal preference to live in the area; (2) the often asserted view by officials that they expected smaller profits for a few years at the selected location but larger profits in the long run, because, for example, they anticipated a greater potential growth in that area than elsewhere; (3) the still more common argument that the locators were forced to choose between extremes—that is, one site appeared to offer the greatest profits or greatest possible losses, given alternative kinds of market area expansion, whereas another place seemed to offer less favorable profit potential but more favorable loss possibilities under equivalent development. In this case, which site is the maximum profit location—the one proffering the greatest possible gains (and possibly losses), or the one proffering a smaller range of possibilities?

The Florida survey uncovered a significant amount of indecision among company officials concerning this matter of profits. Most prevalent, it seemed, was the situation in which locators visualized different potential ranges of profits and losses at alternative locations and then selected their site because some range of returns appeared more appealing to them in the light of their financial resources, their desires for the future, some conjectured probabilities, and the individual's personality and hopes. We record below for interested readers the factors mentioned by plant locators as having had vital bearing on their decision to locate in Florida. Significantly, it will be seen that personal factors, as defined in the original study and repeated briefly in Chapter 2 of this book, are usually important only in the sense of merging with economic advantages which stem from acquaintanceships with bankers, suppliers, etc.

One final related aspect of the survey deserves brief mention in this book.

---

[1] See M. L. Greenhut and M. R. Colberg, *Factors in the Location of Florida Industry* (Tallahassee; Florida State Studies, No. 36, 1962).

We refer to the belief among economic planners that underdeveloped areas should not be permitted to remain underdeveloped and that instead "by artful movement of industry to such areas," the wealth of the nation could be maximized. A few remarks entered elsewhere by this writer appear applicable to this discussion.[1]

It has been said that the "introduction of industries does not necessarily bring employment for the unemployed", because only the type of labor which suits the subject industries may be employed and often this kind of labor must be brought in from elsewhere.[2] The author of this thought (Hisao Nishioka) goes on to observe that to match industries with the human and natural resources of the depressed areas involves bringing into the region precisely the same kind of industries already located there (which, in fact, are partly responsible for the regional decline). Either this results or else the planner must ignore the fundamental factors of industrial location. We might, indeed, add the proviso that these objections apply or else we must presume an inefficient, ineffective economic system such that private entrepreneurs are unable to identify the latent advantages of a depressed area. In turn, one would have to stipulate that only government officials are possessed of this expertise.[3]

It is, of course, true that many regions do possess advantages which have not yet been utilized, largely because agglomerating economies are required, and these advantages depend upon some substantial prior industrial development. In other words, the location theorist might visualize a region which possesses resource advantages which have not been tapped because, apart from resources, industrial location often requires agglomerating advantages.[4] This Weberian component of industrial location signifies that some industrial development of a region automatically produces further industrial development. So, in much the pattern of pump priming, it may be argued that when government induces a new location in an underdeveloped area, it will reap cumulative returns as auxiliary industry and other locations tend to be established in time. But would not the argument apply that the main task of government is to formulate a framework of authority and an institutional base within which industry and economic activity flourish? By providing a stable monetary and fiscal base, by helping to raise the cultural level of its people (and regions), by helping to enlighten its citizens as to the requirements

[1] See "Needed, a Return to the Classics in Regional Economic Development Theory," *Kyklos*, 1966, pp. 461–480.

[2] H. Nishioka, "On the Industrialization of Underdeveloped Regions," *Occasional Papers No. 3, The Economic Institute of the Aoyama Gakuin University* (July, 1965), esp. p. 12.

[3] Before World War II, the depressed area policy of Great Britain stressed the relocation of labor; after the war, the government bureaucrat became an agent behind industrial location.

[4] Walter Isard is a leading exponent of this view. See his *Location and Space Economy* (New York: Wiley and Sons, 1956), pp. 173–188, 256–285.

Factors Mentioned as Inducing Location in the State of Florida*

	Cited as Primary Factor	As Second Factor	As Third Factor
Demand Factors:			
Access to markets	391	64	13
Anticipation of growth of markets	97	100	59
Cost Factors:			
Amicable labor relations	13	34	9
Lower wages	20	48	53
Higher productivity	1	10	0
Florida labor laws	0	4	1
Availability of labor already in Florida	7	52	47
Ease of attracting out-of-state skilled labor (including research personnel)	36	14	21
Low seller's mill price on raw materials	3	6	1
Low freight cost on raw materials	58	33	21
Availability of raw material	5	66	14
Low cost of fuel	0	0	15
Adequate supply of required water	0	1	0
Availability of capital	0	6	10
Low freight cost on final product	81	48	104
Adequate waste disposal facilities	0	0	17
Climate (as it affects operations)	14	108	46
Community facilities (educational, medical, police, and fire)	1	6	35
Community attitudes and aids	0	0	2
State and/or municipal tax structure	1	11	29
Climate (as an attraction to top management)	22	16	89
Personal (with economic advantages, e.g., friendship with customers, suppliers, or bankers)†	2	17	42
The Purely Personal Factor:			
Personal (without economic advantage)	0	36	28
	752	680	656

* Table reprinted from the writer's paper in the *Review of Economics and Statistics* (1959). For a brief explanation of terms and information of related kind, see "An Empirical Model and a Survey: New Plant Locations in Florida," pp. 433–438.

† We include the personal factor with economic advantages under the Cost Factor list since generally it involves savings of cost.

of and gains from industrial development, the basis for growth can be established and in the process a growth will be witnessed which is attributable to comparative advantages.[1] Whatever mistakes arise would then be natural to free enterprise rather than extra to this particular system of economic relations.

We aver, accordingly, that the true role of the state is to eliminate cultural barriers, to simplify and improve the tax base, to help develop the skills of its people, to establish institutions and generate information conducive to new activity or entrepreneurship, and even to adjust saving/income proportions. The proper distribution of savings among investments projects, we believe, will follow the lines most appropriate and natural to the country (or region) at hand and the burden of proof should rest on those who advocate interference with consumer preferences.[2] Manifestly, our Theory of the Firm in Economic Space is based on the premise that the free enterprise system will move inexorably *towards* optimal results if the proper cultural base, including interpersonal relations, proper tax policy, anti-trust laws, *etc.*, as noted previously in this book and in this appendix, are established for it by its government.

[1] See M. L. Greenhut, "Industrial Development of Underdeveloped Areas in the United States," *Land Economics*, XXXVI (November, 1960), pp. 371–379; and B. Chinitz, "Transportation and Regional Economic Growth," *Traffic Quarterly*, 14 (1960), pp. 129–142.

[2] The two sides of economic development first presented in the P. Rosenstein-Rodan paper, "Problems of Industrialization of Eastern and Southeastern Europe," *The Economic Journal*, Vol. 53 (June, 1943), pp. 205–216, might be recalled here by the reader.

Author Index

Stein, J., 152
Stevens, B., 351, 352
Stigler, G., 347, 355
Stocking, G. W., 347, 366
Stolper, W., 52, 244
Sweezy, P., 52
Sykes, J., 53

Thompson, M. K., 350
Thompson, W. R., 252, 259, 314
Triffin, R., 203, 332
Turner, D. F., 364

Ullman, E. L., 218, 255

Vernon, R., 252

von Thünen, J., 5, 47, 215, 232, 262–267, 351

Wald, V., 7, 34
Warntz, W., 259–260
Watkins, M. W., 347, 366
Weber, A., 5, 224, 262, 264–267, 281, 346
Wheeler, J. T., 356
White, L. D., 215
Whitman, W. T., 253
Willcox, C., 356, 359, 361
Wingo, L., Jr., 259
Woglom, W. H., 52

Yntema, T. O., 33

Subject Index

385